WELCOME TO THE BALLROOM

no. 8 | TOMO TAKEUCH

Contents

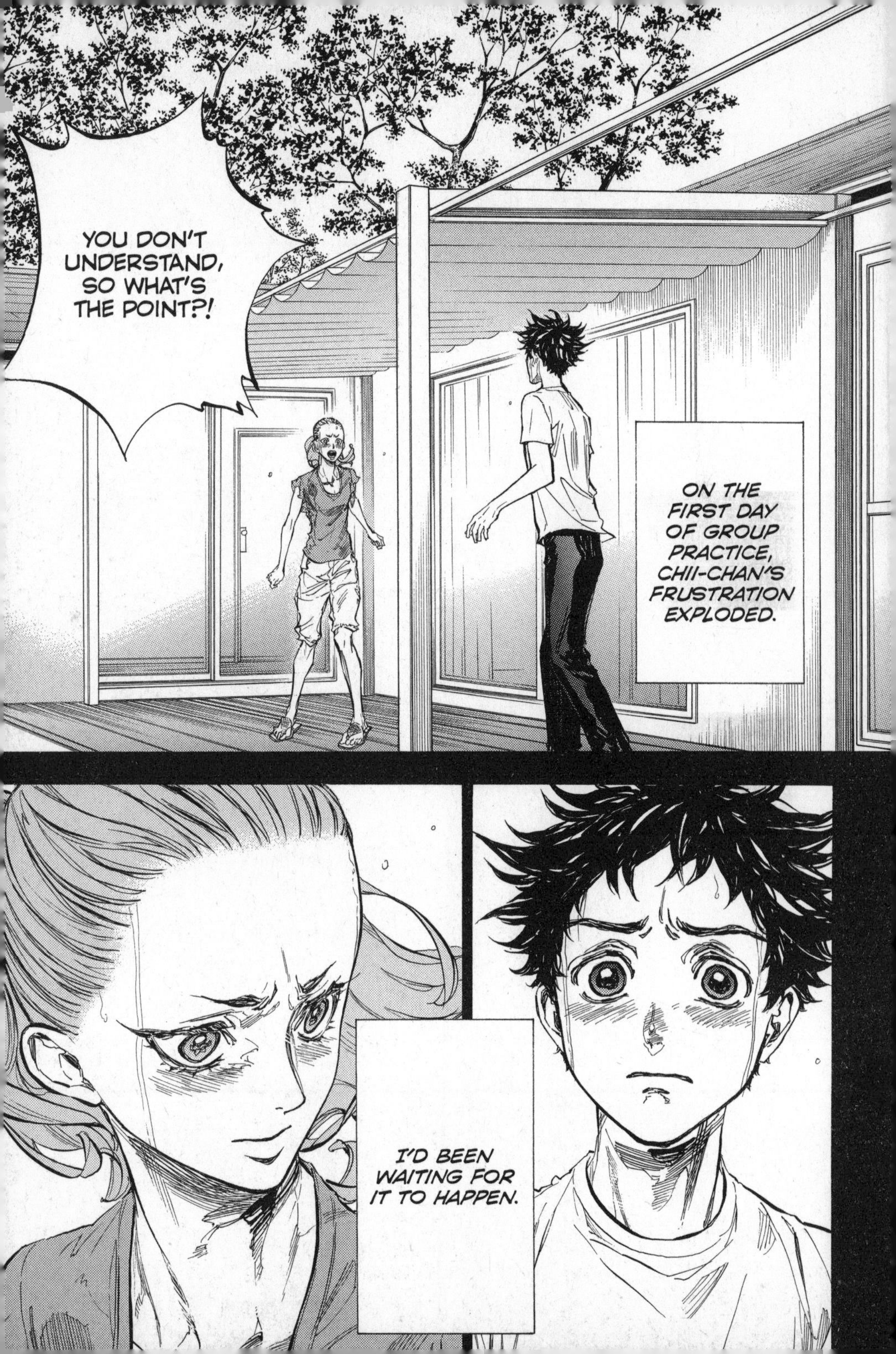
YOU DON'T UNDERSTAND, SO WHAT'S THE POINT?!
ON THE FIRST DAY OF GROUP PRACTICE, CHII-CHAN'S FRUSTRATION EXPLODED.
I'D BEEN WAITING FOR IT TO HAPPEN.

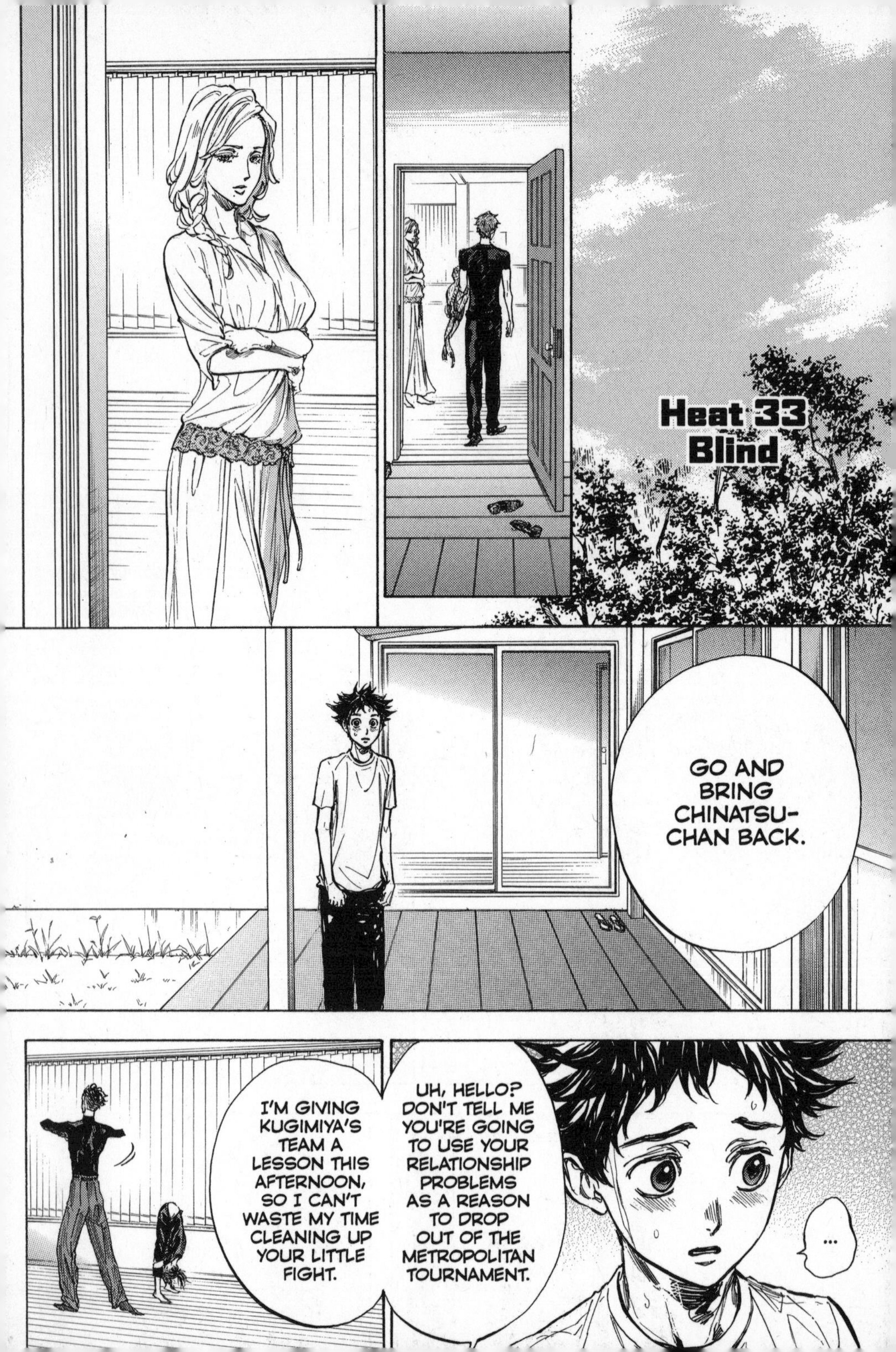
Heat 33
Blind
GO AND BRING CHINATSU-CHAN BACK.
...
UH, HELLO? DON'T TELL ME YOU'RE GOING TO USE YOUR RELATIONSHIP PROBLEMS AS A REASON TO DROP OUT OF THE METROPOLITAN TOURNAMENT.
I'M GIVING KUGIMIYA'S TEAM A LESSON THIS AFTERNOON, SO I CAN'T WASTE MY TIME CLEANING UP YOUR LITTLE FIGHT.

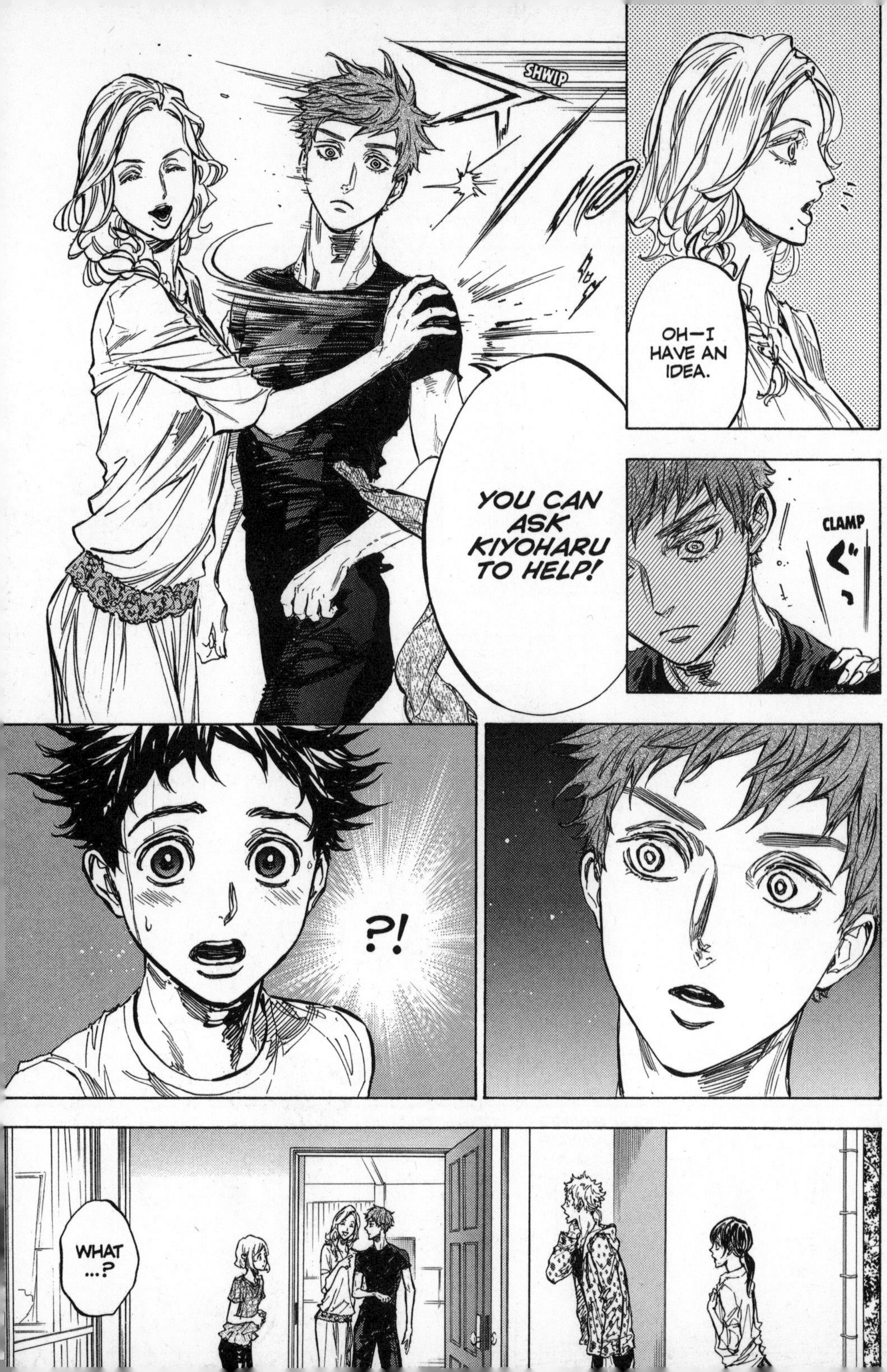
OH—I HAVE AN IDEA.
CLAMP
SHWIP
YOU CAN ASK KIYOHARU TO HELP!
?!
WHAT ...?

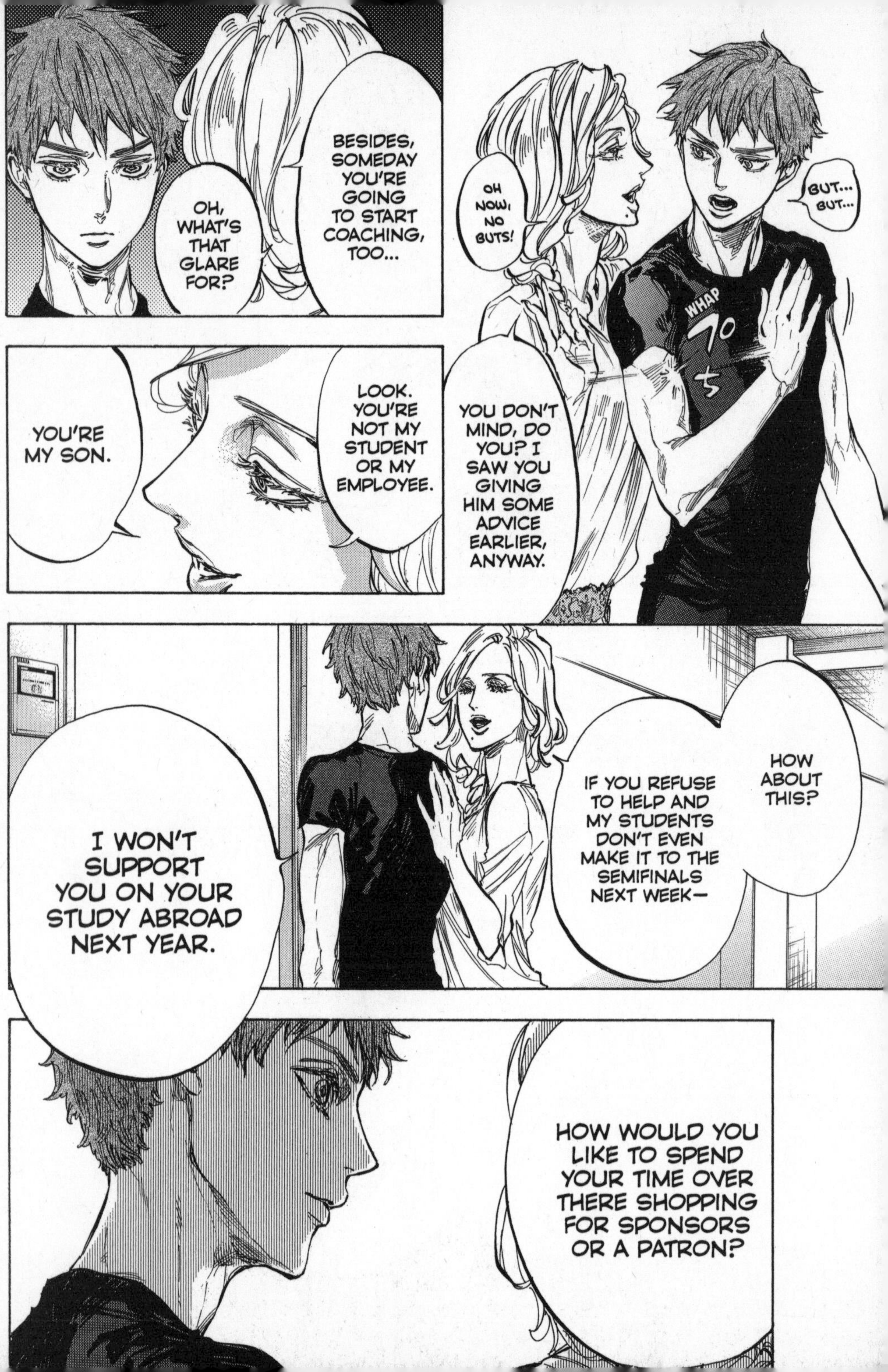
BUT... BUT...
OH NOW, NO BUTS!
WHAP
YOU DON'T MIND, DO YOU? I SAW YOU GIVING HIM SOME ADVICE EARLIER, ANYWAY.
BESIDES, SOMEDAY YOU'RE GOING TO START COACHING, TOO...
OH, WHAT'S THAT GLARE FOR?
LOOK. YOU'RE NOT MY STUDENT OR MY EMPLOYEE.
YOU'RE MY SON.
HOW ABOUT THIS?
IF YOU REFUSE TO HELP AND MY STUDENTS DON'T EVEN MAKE IT TO THE SEMIFINALS NEXT WEEK—
I WON'T SUPPORT YOU ON YOUR STUDY ABROAD NEXT YEAR.
HOW WOULD YOU LIKE TO SPEND YOUR TIME OVER THERE SHOPPING FOR SPONSORS OR A PATRON?

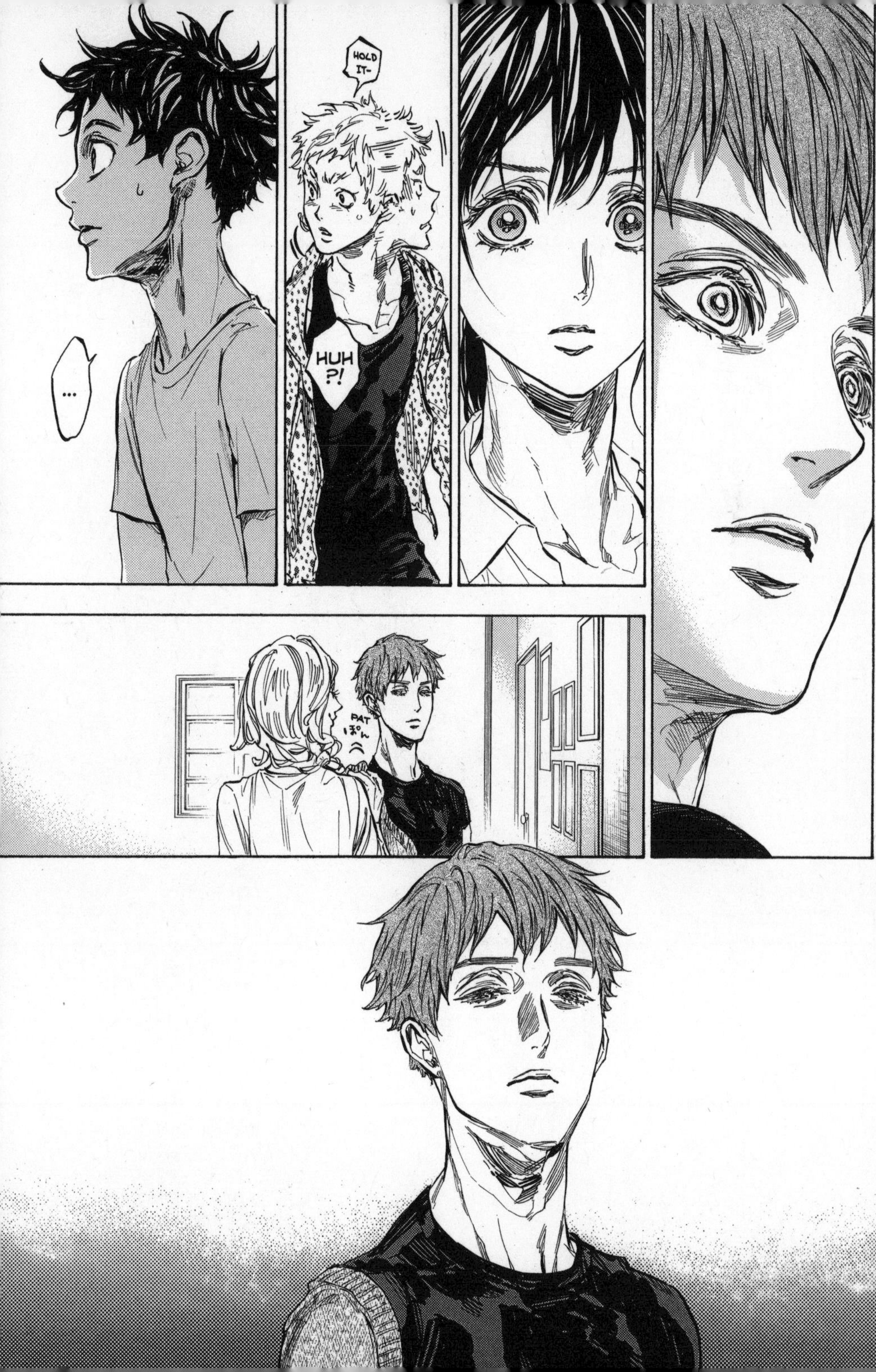
HOLD IT-
HUH ?!
...
PAT ぽん

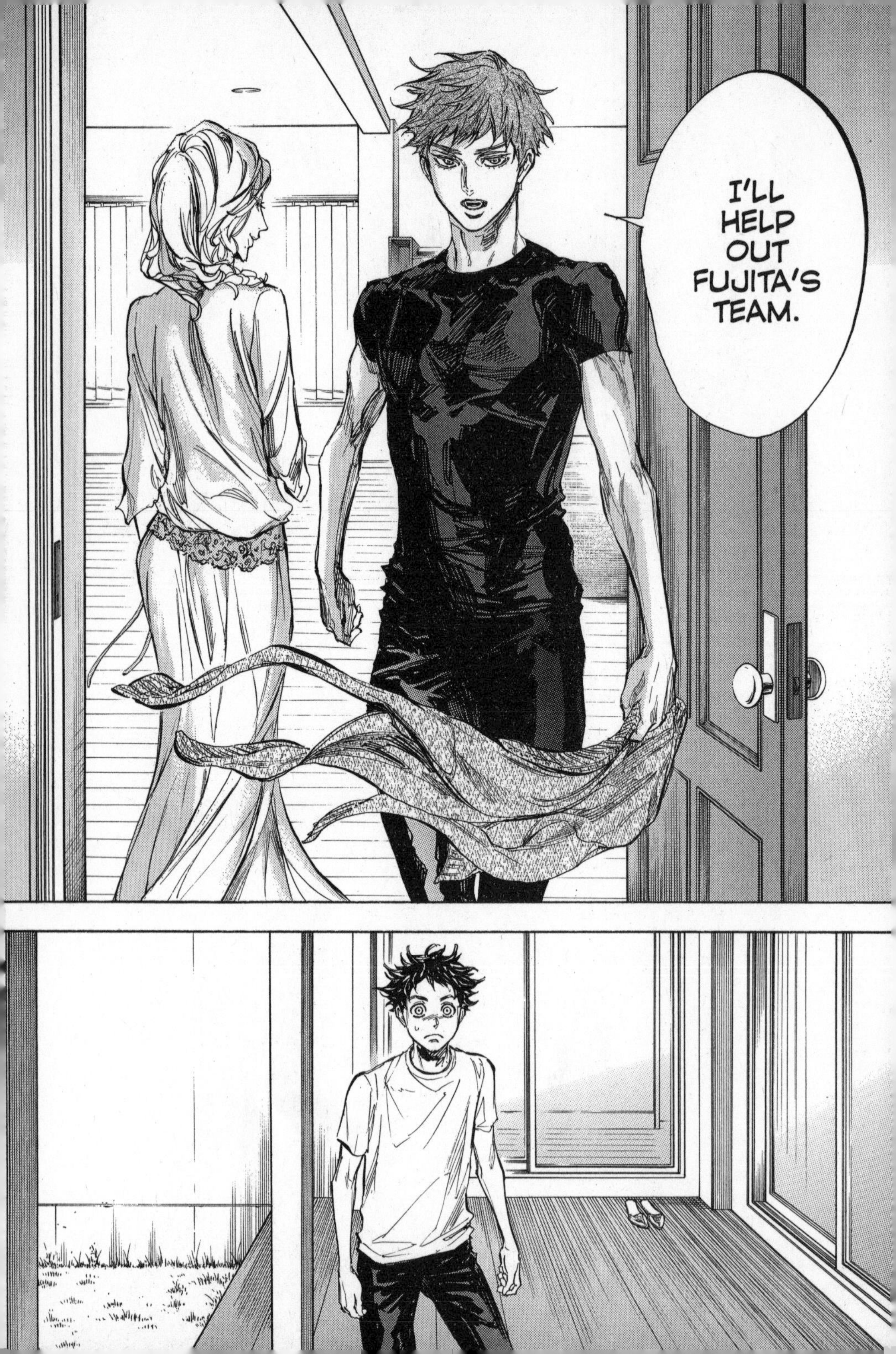
I'LL HELP OUT FUJITA'S TEAM.

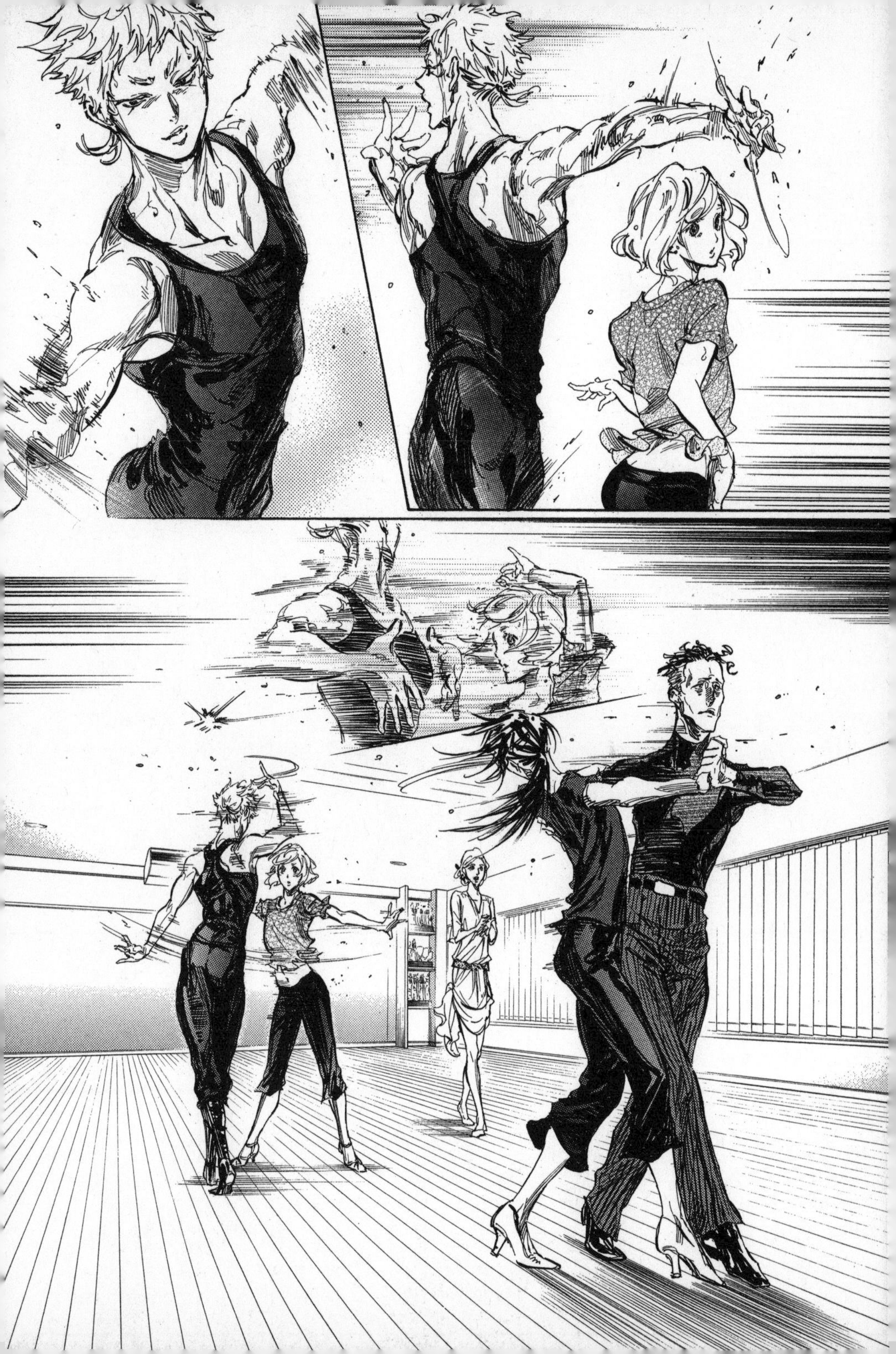

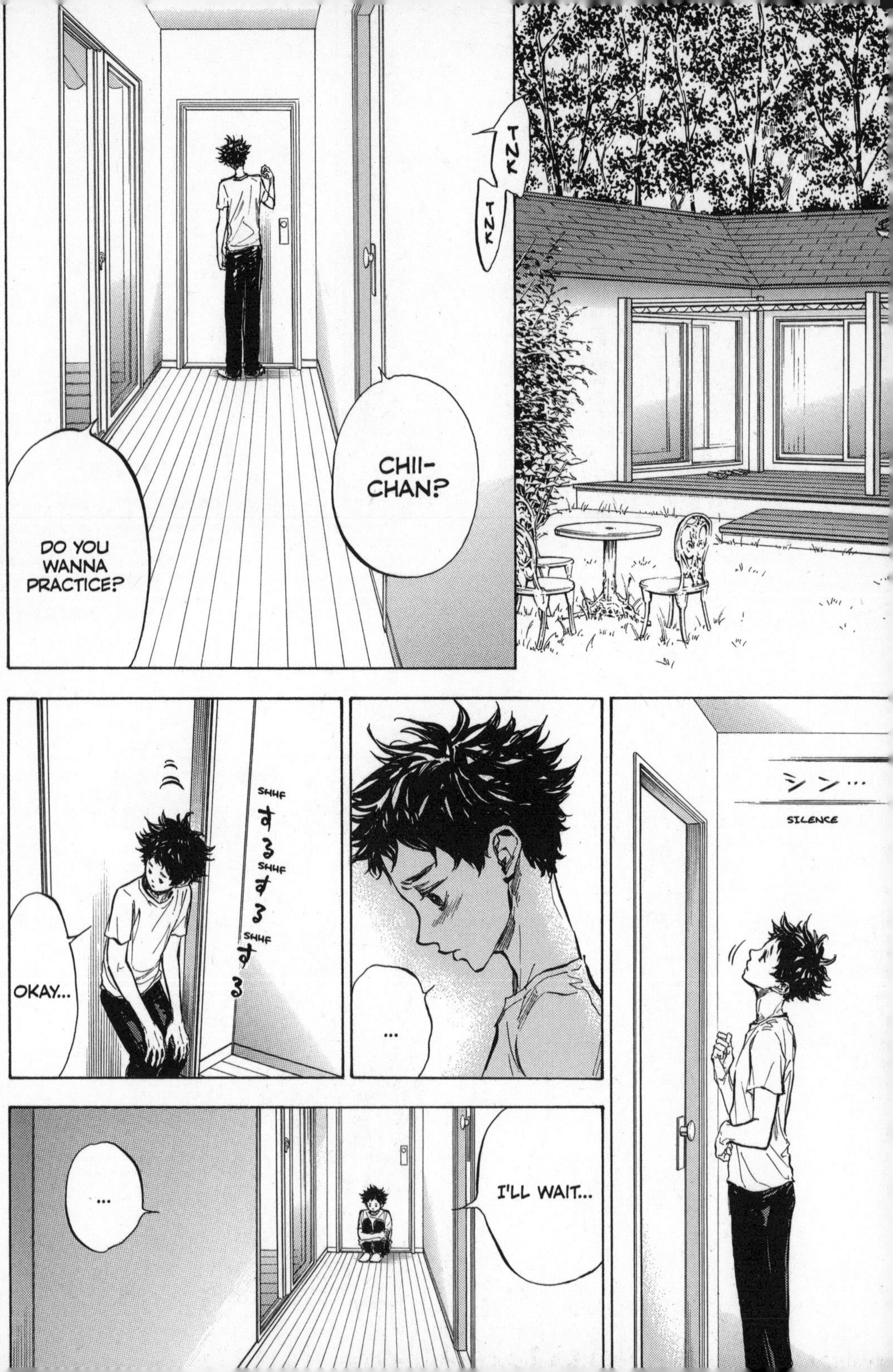
TNK
TNK
CHII-CHAN?
DO YOU WANNA PRACTICE?
シン…
SILENCE
…
SHHF する SHHF する SHHF する
OKAY...
I'LL WAIT...
...

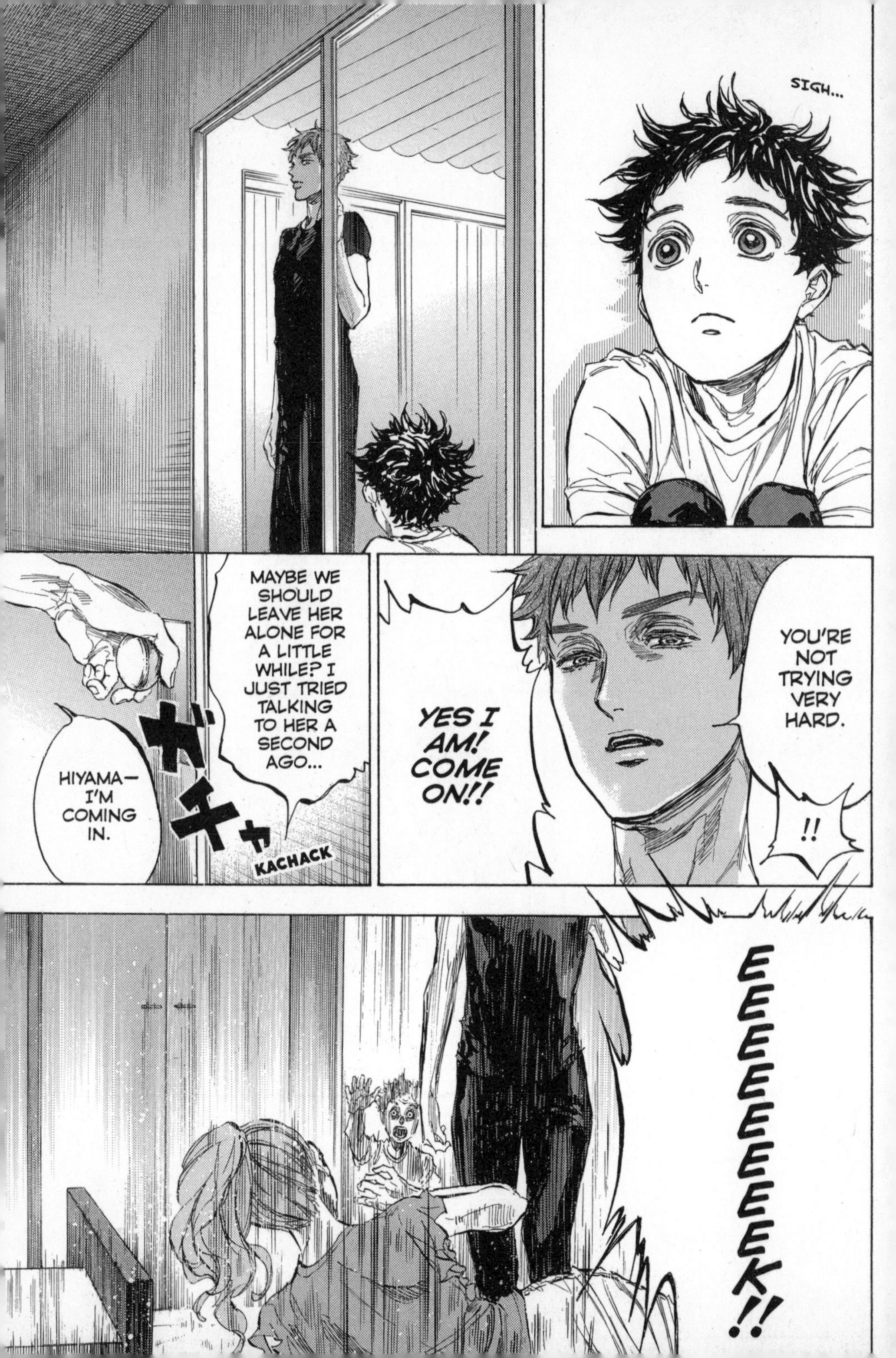
SIGH...
YOU'RE NOT TRYING VERY HARD.
!!
YES I AM! COME ON!!
MAYBE WE SHOULD LEAVE HER ALONE FOR A LITTLE WHILE? I JUST TRIED TALKING TO HER A SECOND AGO...
ガチャ
KACHACK
HIYAMA— I'M COMING IN.
EEEEEEEEEK!!

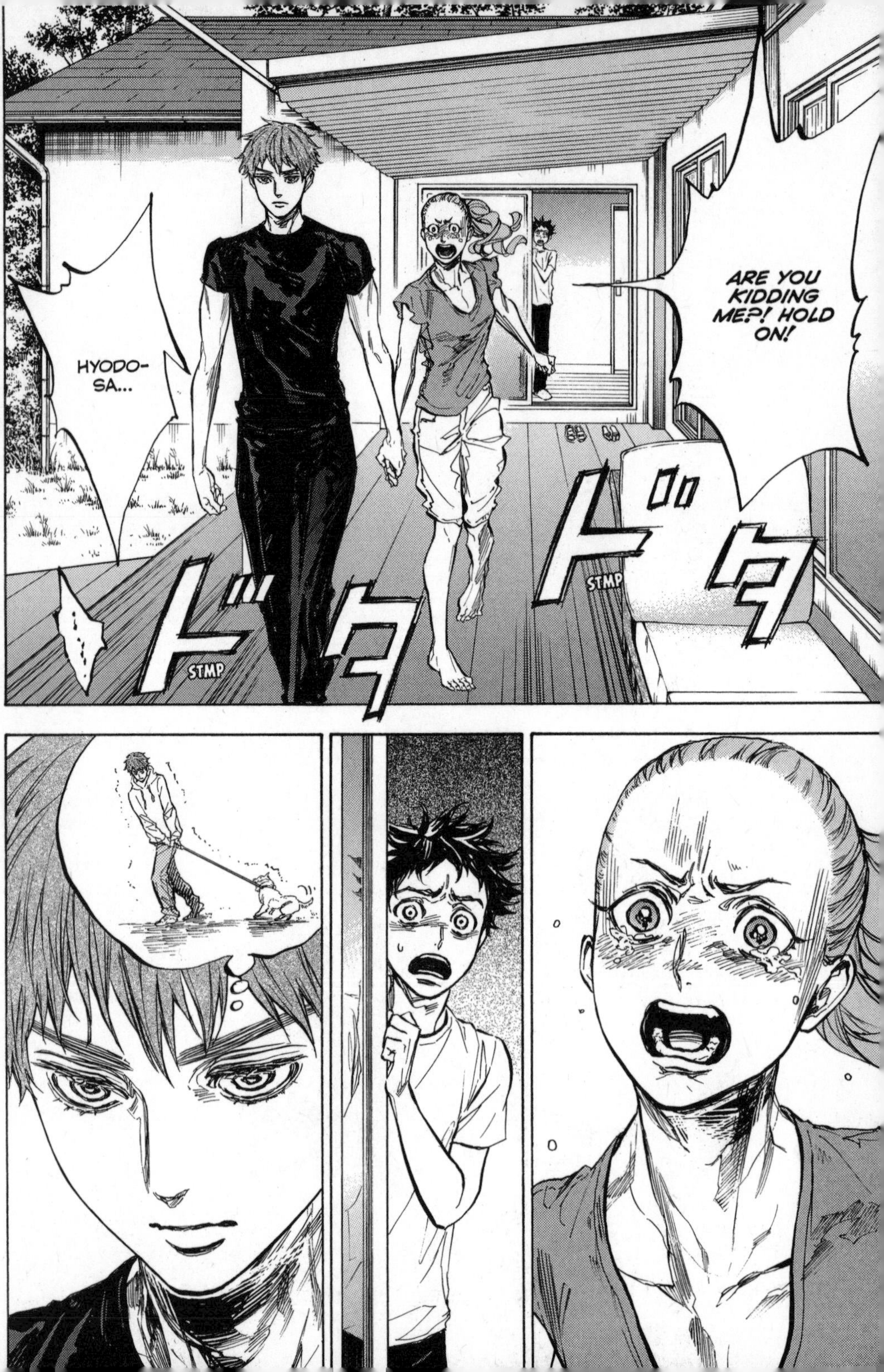
ARE YOU KIDDING ME?! HOLD ON!
HYODO-SA...
ドタ
STMP
ドタ
STMP

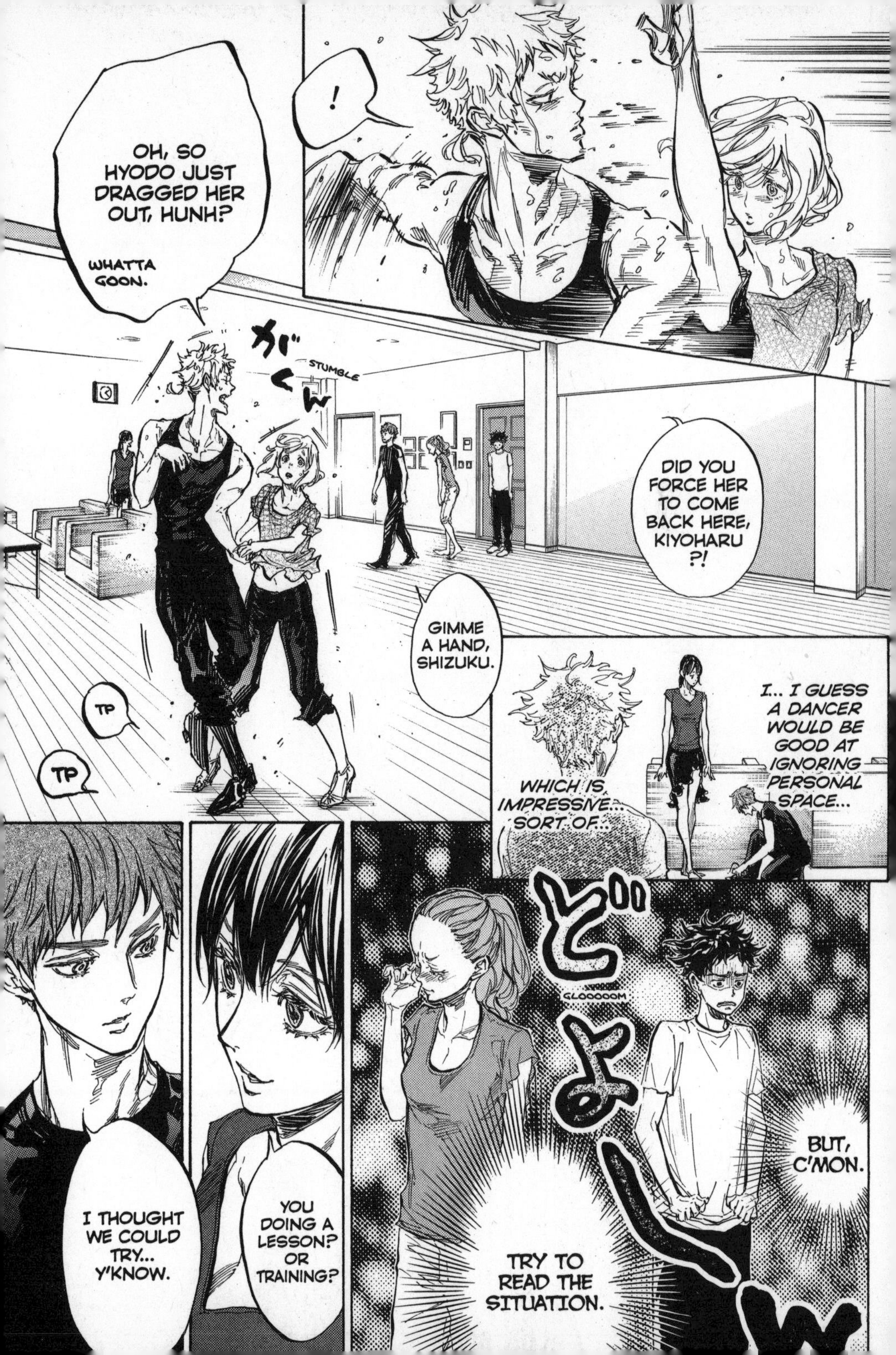
!
OH, SO HYODO JUST DRAGGED HER OUT, HUNH?
WHATTA GOON.
DID YOU FORCE HER TO COME BACK HERE, KIYOHARU ?!
ガくん
STUMBLE
GIMME A HAND, SHIZUKU.
TP
TP
I... I GUESS A DANCER WOULD BE GOOD AT IGNORING PERSONAL SPACE...
WHICH IS IMPRESSIVE... SORT OF...
どよーん
GLOOOOOM
BUT, C'MON.
TRY TO READ THE SITUATION.
YOU DOING A LESSON? OR TRAINING?
I THOUGHT WE COULD TRY... Y'KNOW.

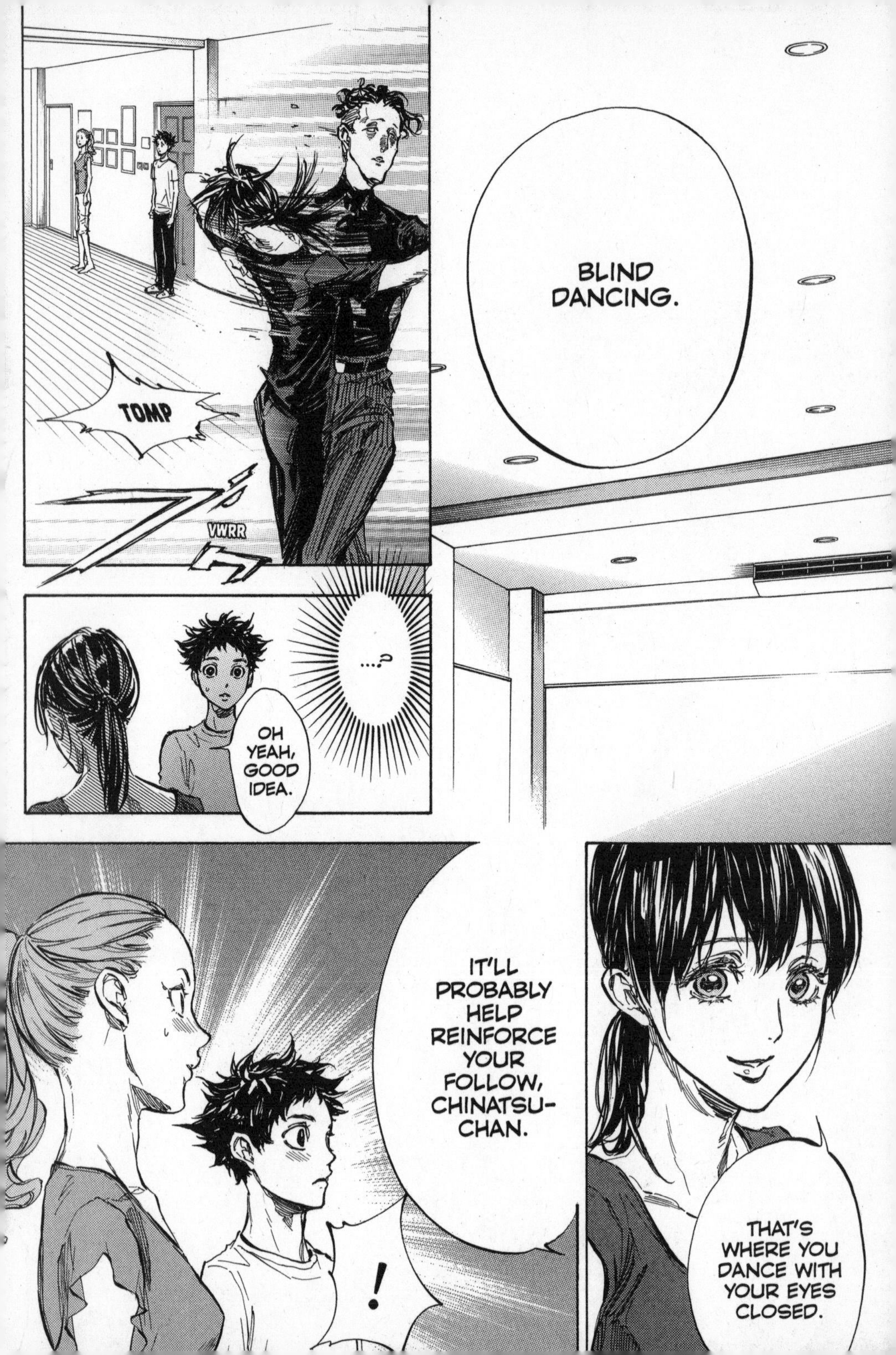
BLIND DANCING.
TOMP
VWRR
...?
OH YEAH, GOOD IDEA.
THAT'S WHERE YOU DANCE WITH YOUR EYES CLOSED.
IT'LL PROBABLY HELP REINFORCE YOUR FOLLOW, CHINATSU-CHAN.
!

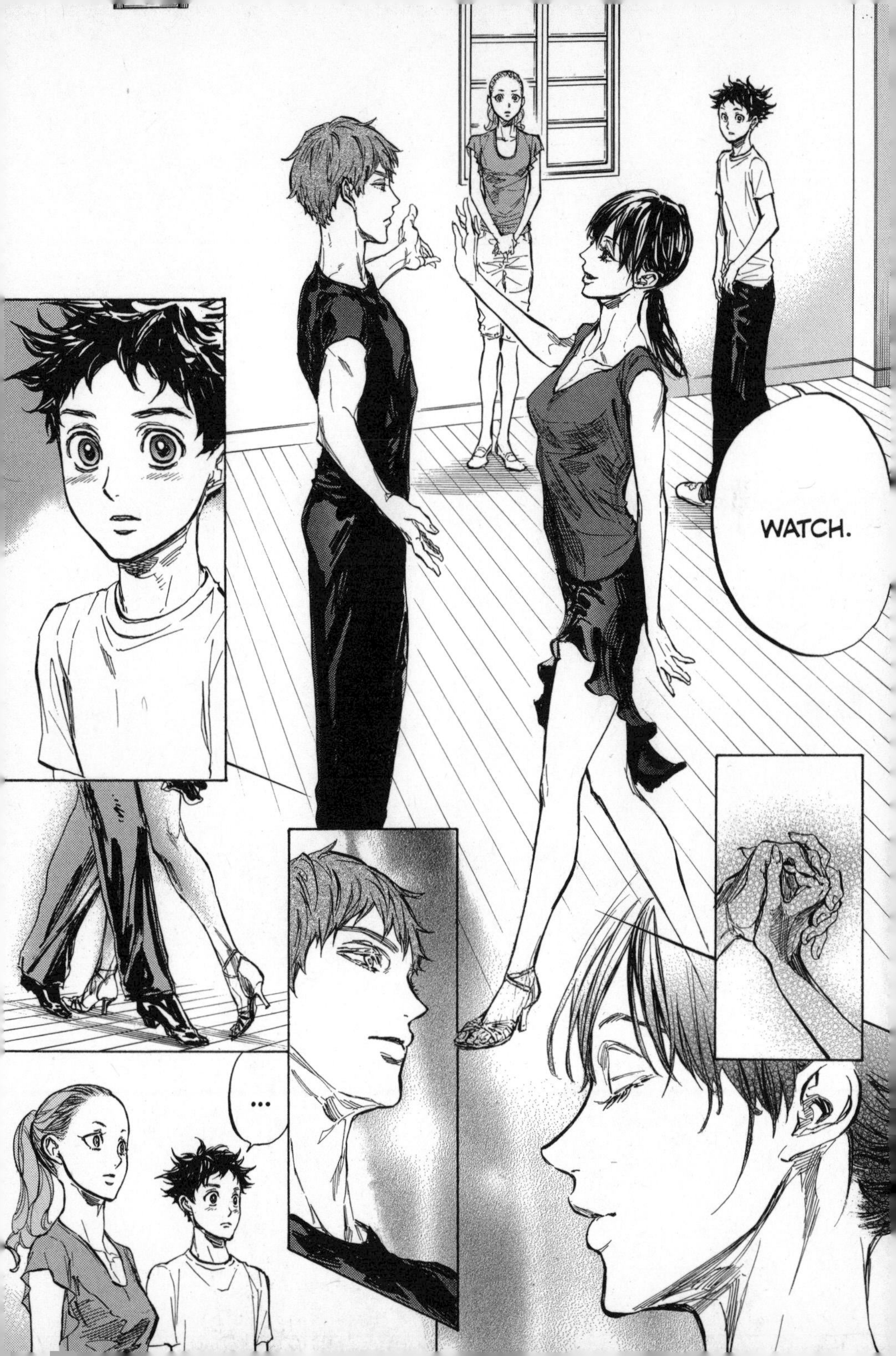
WATCH.
...

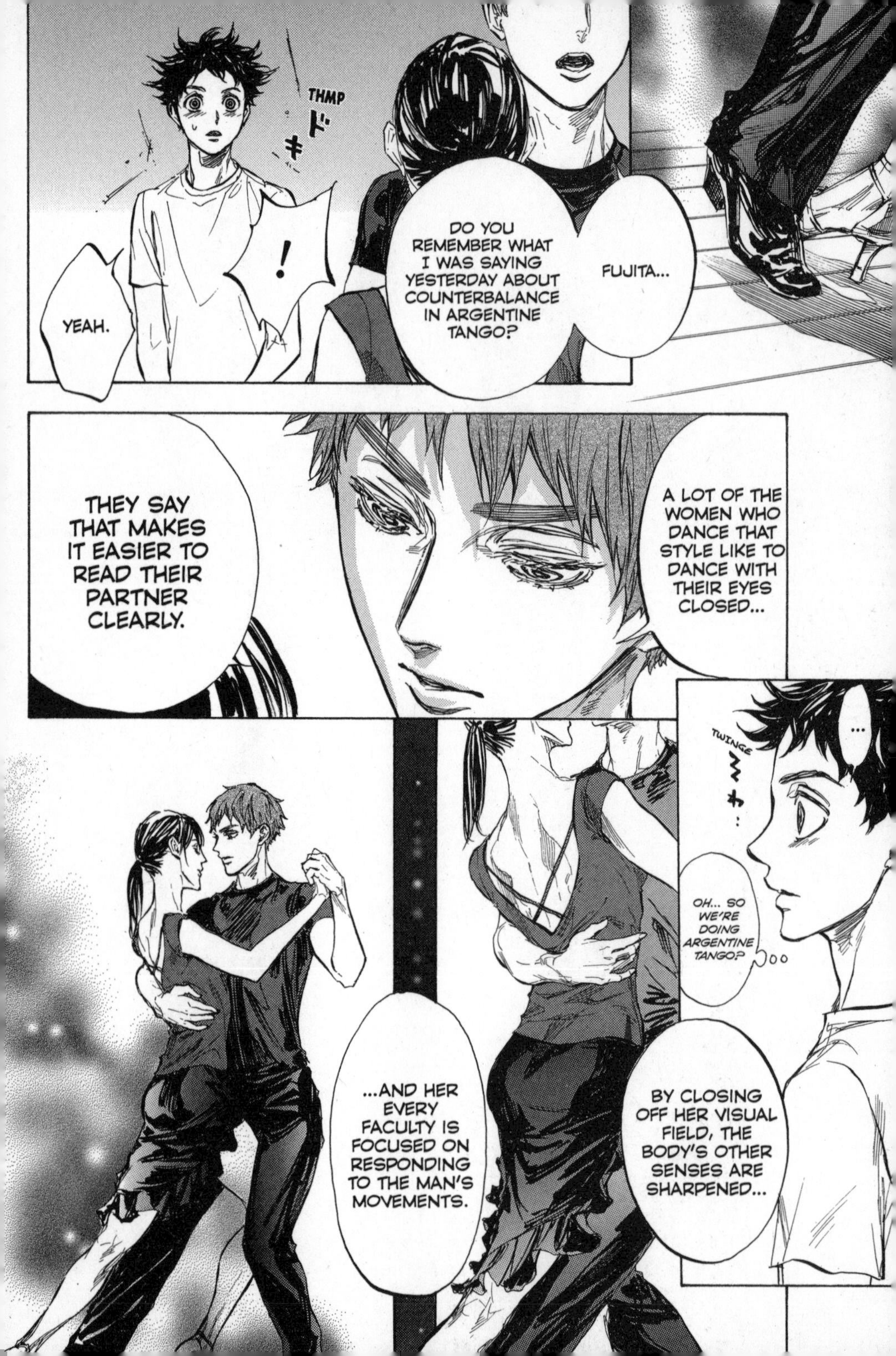
FUJITA...
DO YOU REMEMBER WHAT I WAS SAYING YESTERDAY ABOUT COUNTERBALANCE IN ARGENTINE TANGO?
THMP
ドキ
!
YEAH.
A LOT OF THE WOMEN WHO DANCE THAT STYLE LIKE TO DANCE WITH THEIR EYES CLOSED...
THEY SAY THAT MAKES IT EASIER TO READ THEIR PARTNER CLEARLY.
...
TWINGE
ズキ..
OH... SO WE'RE DOING ARGENTINE TANGO?
BY CLOSING OFF HER VISUAL FIELD, THE BODY'S OTHER SENSES ARE SHARPENED...
...AND HER EVERY FACULTY IS FOCUSED ON RESPONDING TO THE MAN'S MOVEMENTS.

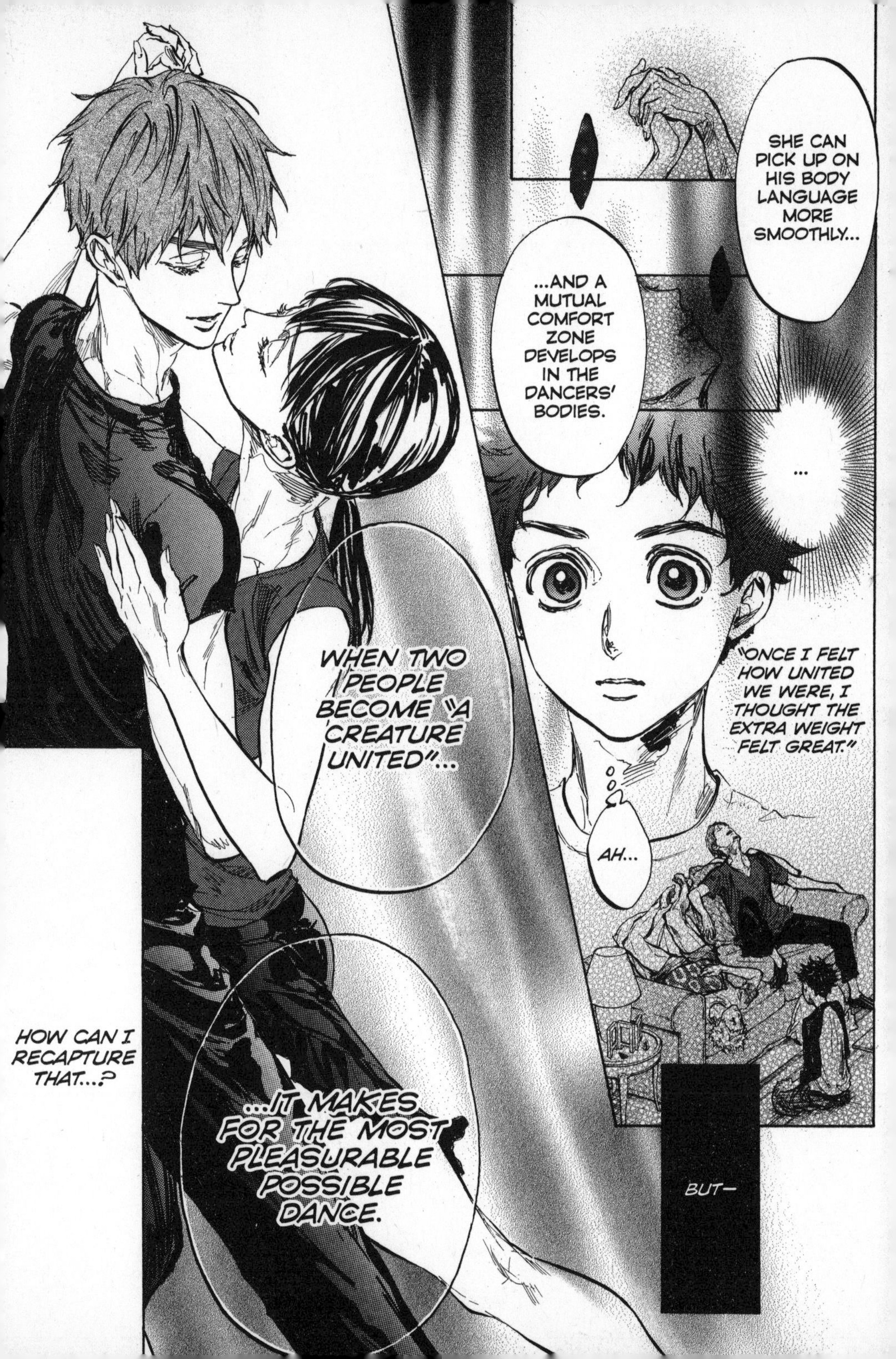
SHE CAN PICK UP ON HIS BODY LANGUAGE MORE SMOOTHLY...
...AND A MUTUAL COMFORT ZONE DEVELOPS IN THE DANCERS' BODIES.
...
"ONCE I FELT HOW UNITED WE WERE, I THOUGHT THE EXTRA WEIGHT FELT GREAT."
AH...
BUT—
WHEN TWO PEOPLE BECOME "A CREATURE UNITED"...
...IT MAKES FOR THE MOST PLEASURABLE POSSIBLE DANCE.
HOW CAN I RECAPTURE THAT...?

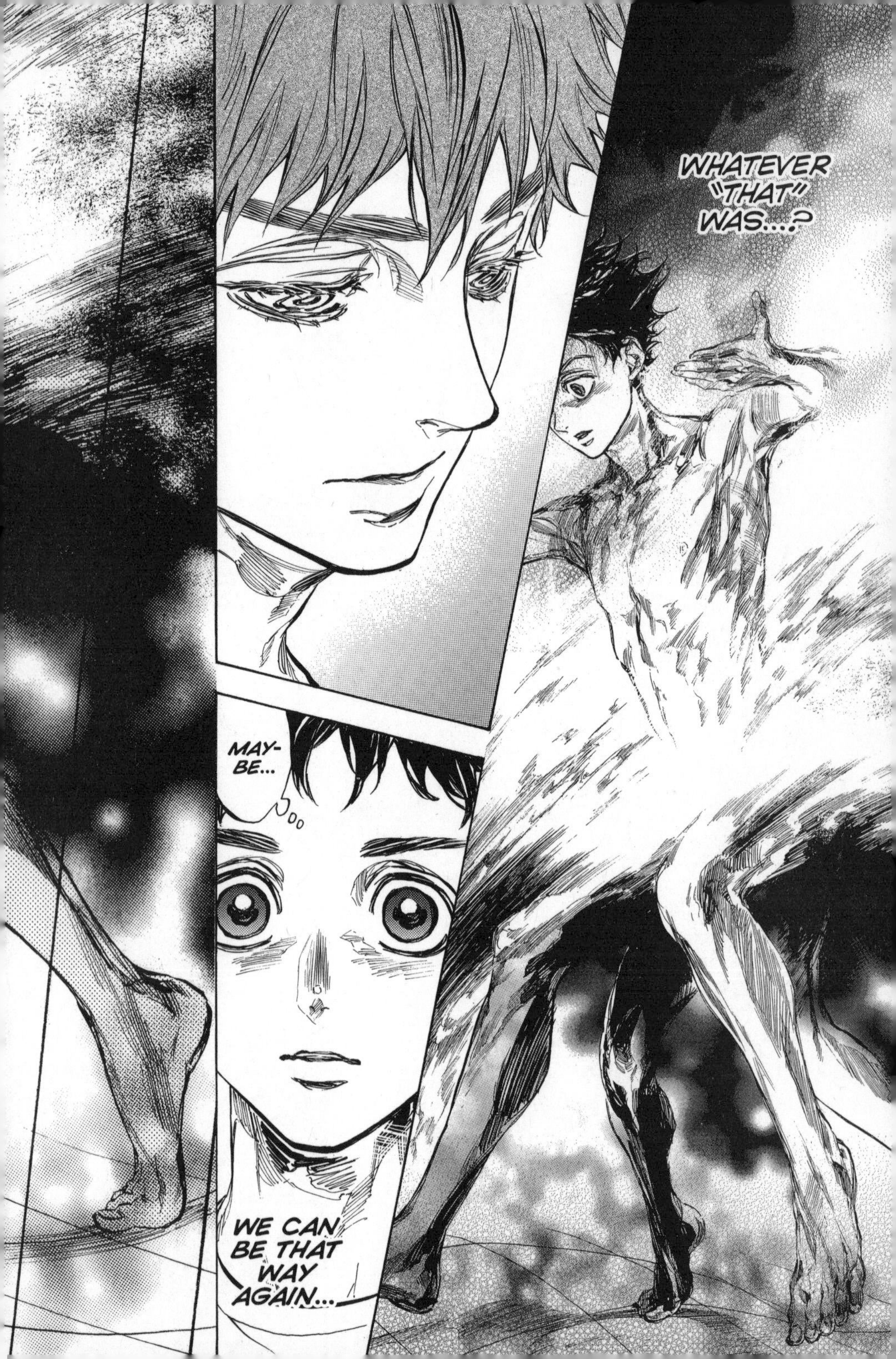
WHATEVER "THAT" WAS...?
MAY-BE...
WE CAN BE THAT WAY AGAIN...

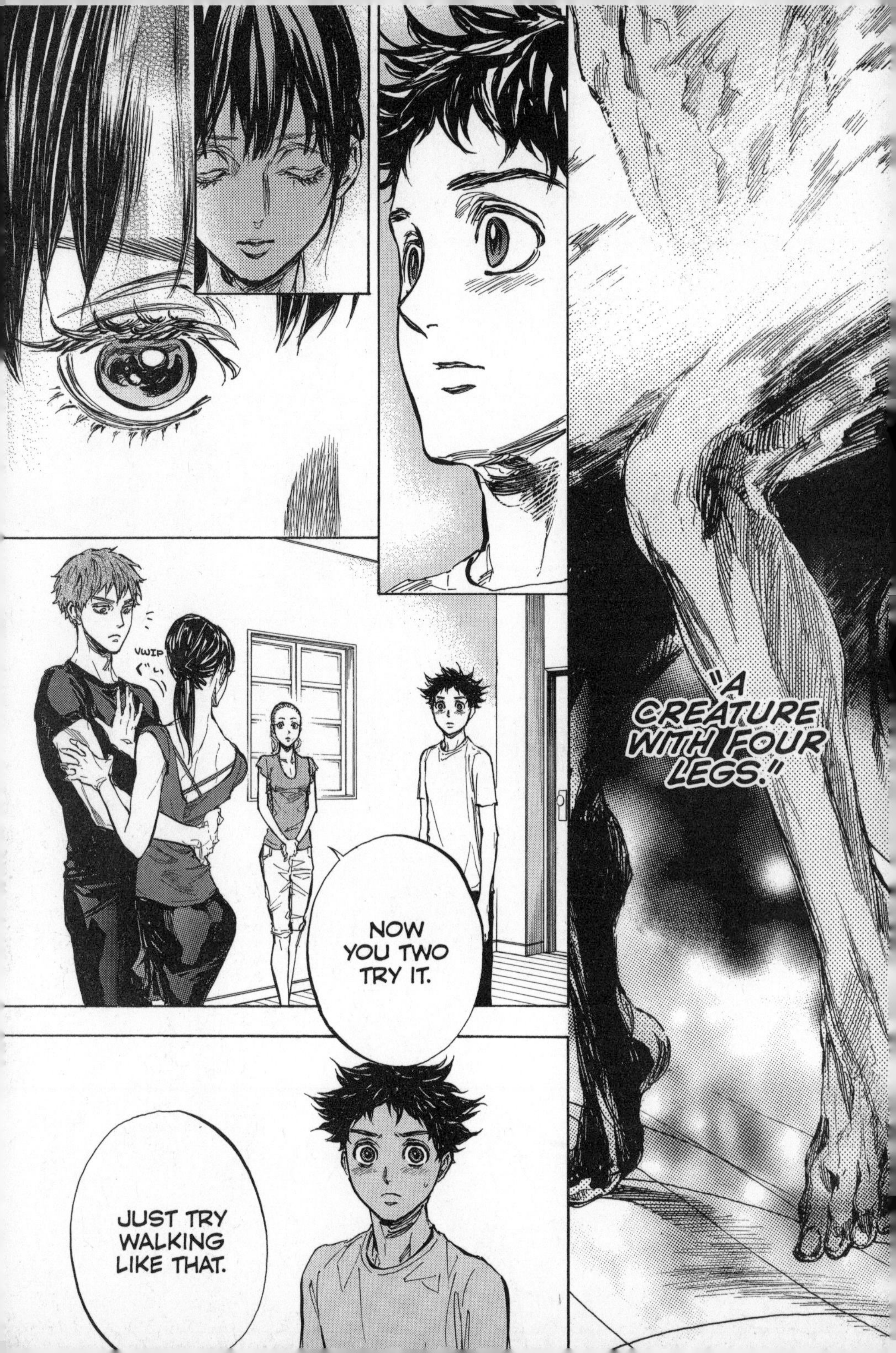
"A CREATURE WITH FOUR LEGS."
VWIP
NOW YOU TWO TRY IT.
JUST TRY WALKING LIKE THAT.

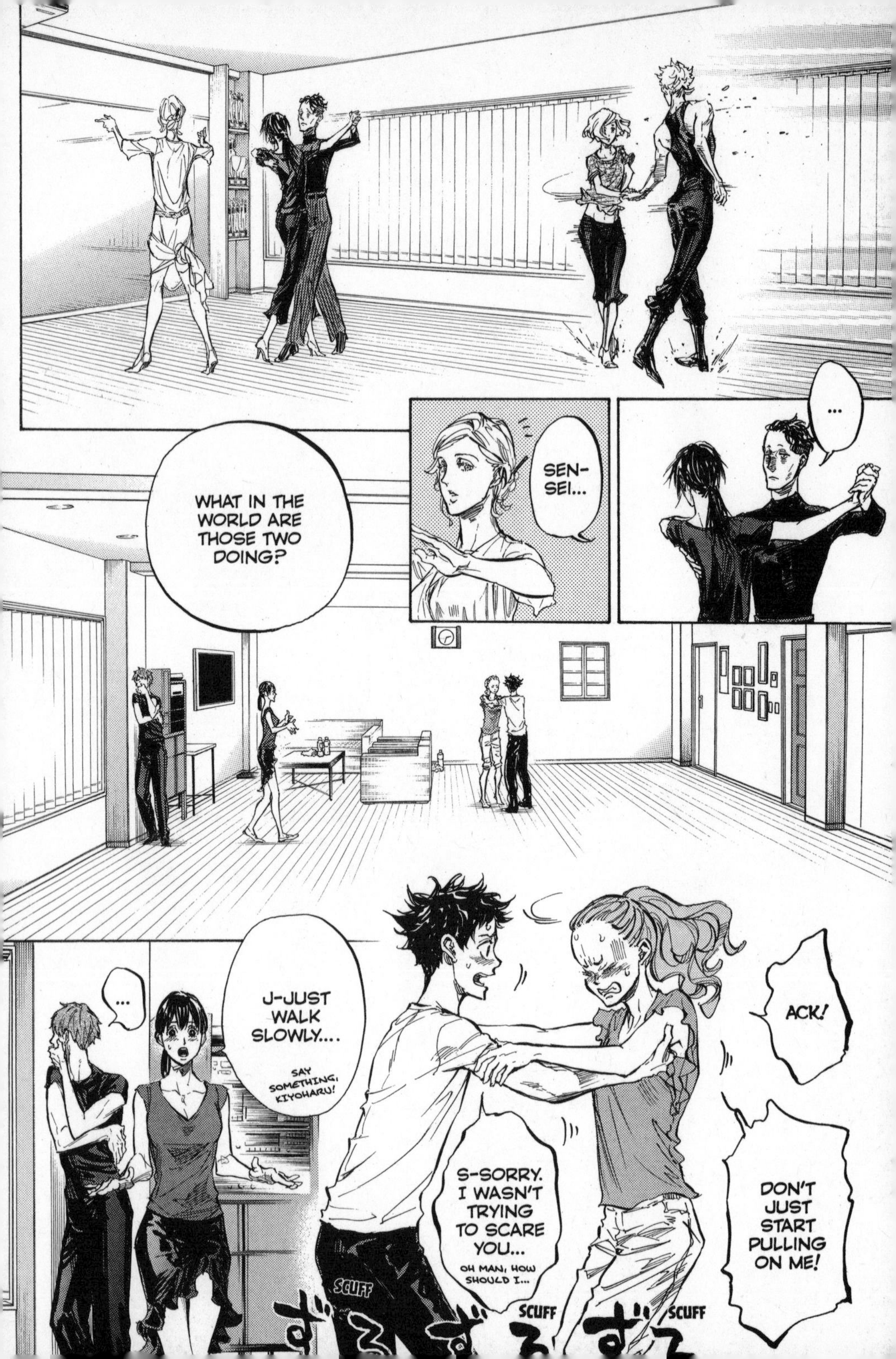
...
SEN-SEI...
WHAT IN THE WORLD ARE THOSE TWO DOING?
ACK!
DON'T JUST START PULLING ON ME!
S-SORRY. I WASN'T TRYING TO SCARE YOU...
OH MAN, HOW SHOULD I...
J-JUST WALK SLOWLY....
SAY SOMETHING, KIYOHARU!
...
SCUFF
SCUFF
SCUFF

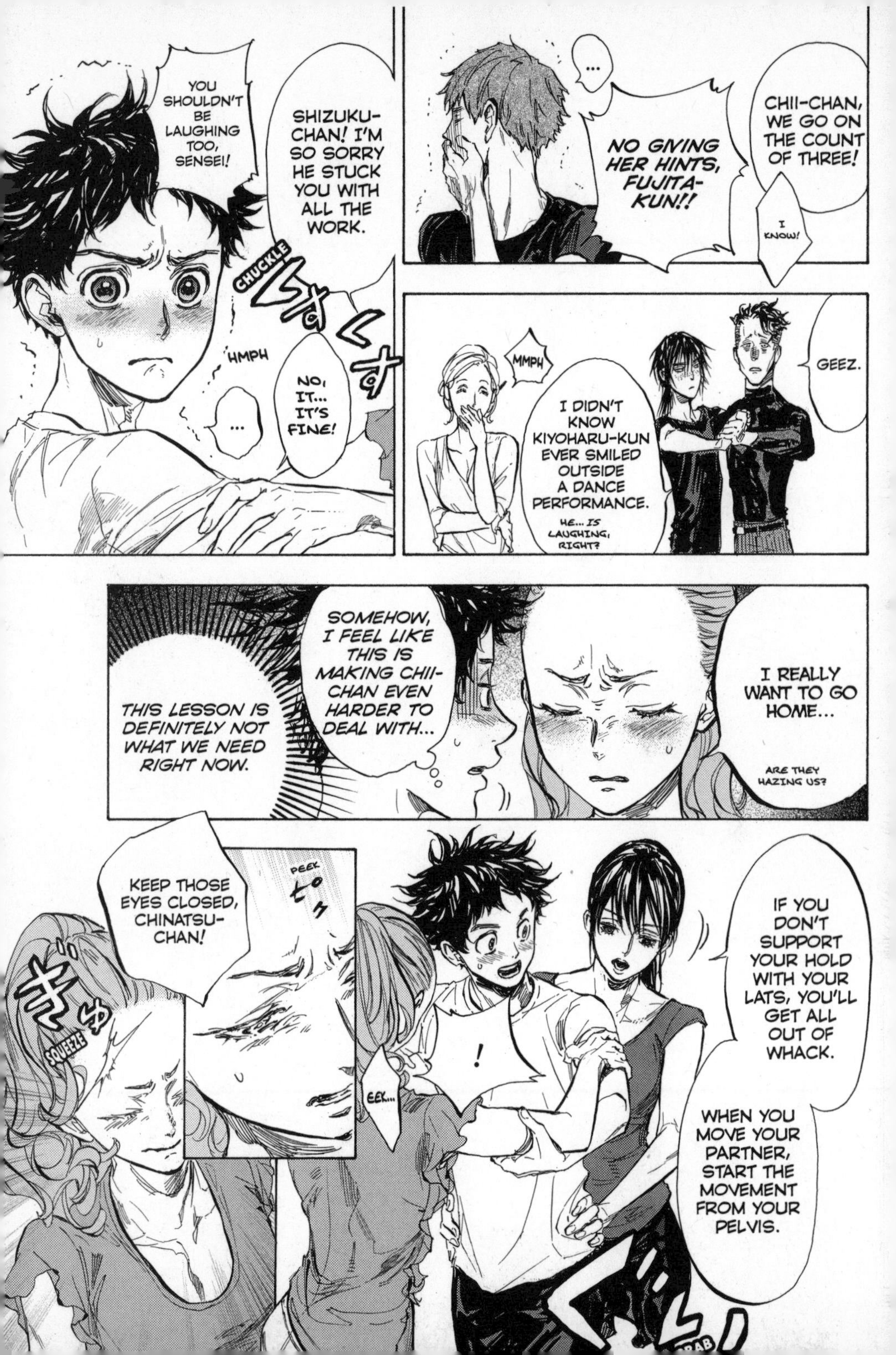

CHII-CHAN, WE GO ON THE COUNT OF THREE!
I KNOW!
NO GIVING HER HINTS, FUJITA-KUN!!
...
GEEZ.
MMPH
I DIDN'T KNOW KIYOHARU-KUN EVER SMILED OUTSIDE A DANCE PERFORMANCE.
HE... IS LAUGHING, RIGHT?
SHIZUKU-CHAN! I'M SO SORRY HE STUCK YOU WITH ALL THE WORK.
YOU SHOULDN'T BE LAUGHING TOO, SENSEI!
CHUCKLE
NO, IT... IT'S FINE!
HMPH
...
I REALLY WANT TO GO HOME...
ARE THEY HAZING US?
SOMEHOW, I FEEL LIKE THIS IS MAKING CHII-CHAN EVEN HARDER TO DEAL WITH...
THIS LESSON IS DEFINITELY NOT WHAT WE NEED RIGHT NOW.
IF YOU DON'T SUPPORT YOUR HOLD WITH YOUR LATS, YOU'LL GET ALL OUT OF WHACK.
WHEN YOU MOVE YOUR PARTNER, START THE MOVEMENT FROM YOUR PELVIS.
GRAB
!
EEK...
PEEK
KEEP THOSE EYES CLOSED, CHINATSU-CHAN!
SQUEEZE

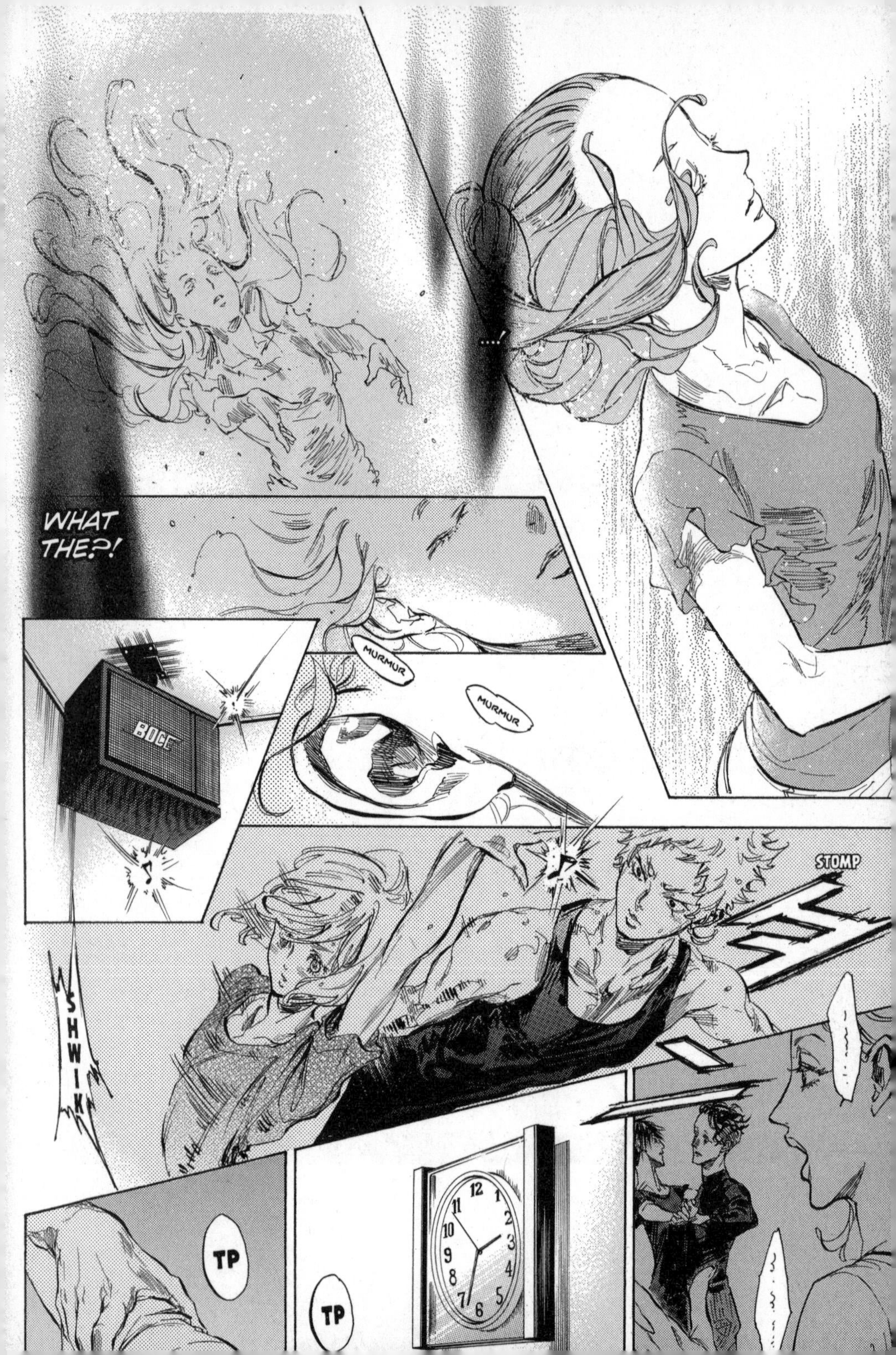

...!
WHAT THE?!
MURMUR
MURMUR
STOMP
SHWIK
TP
TP

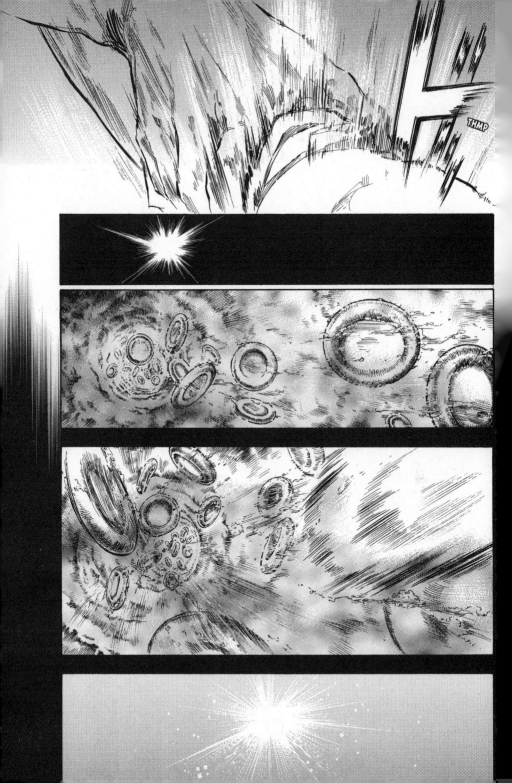

THMP

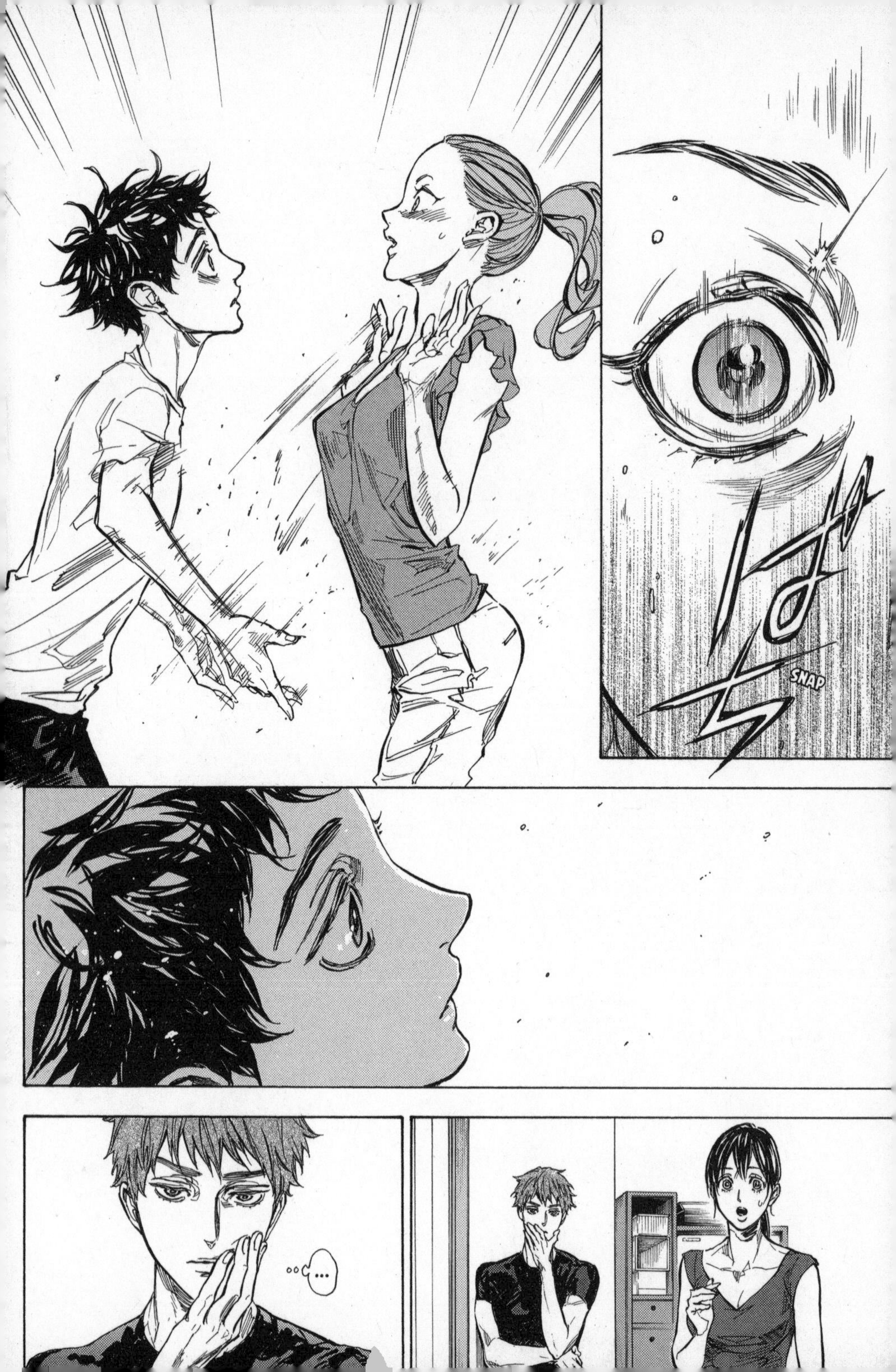
はっ
SNAP
....

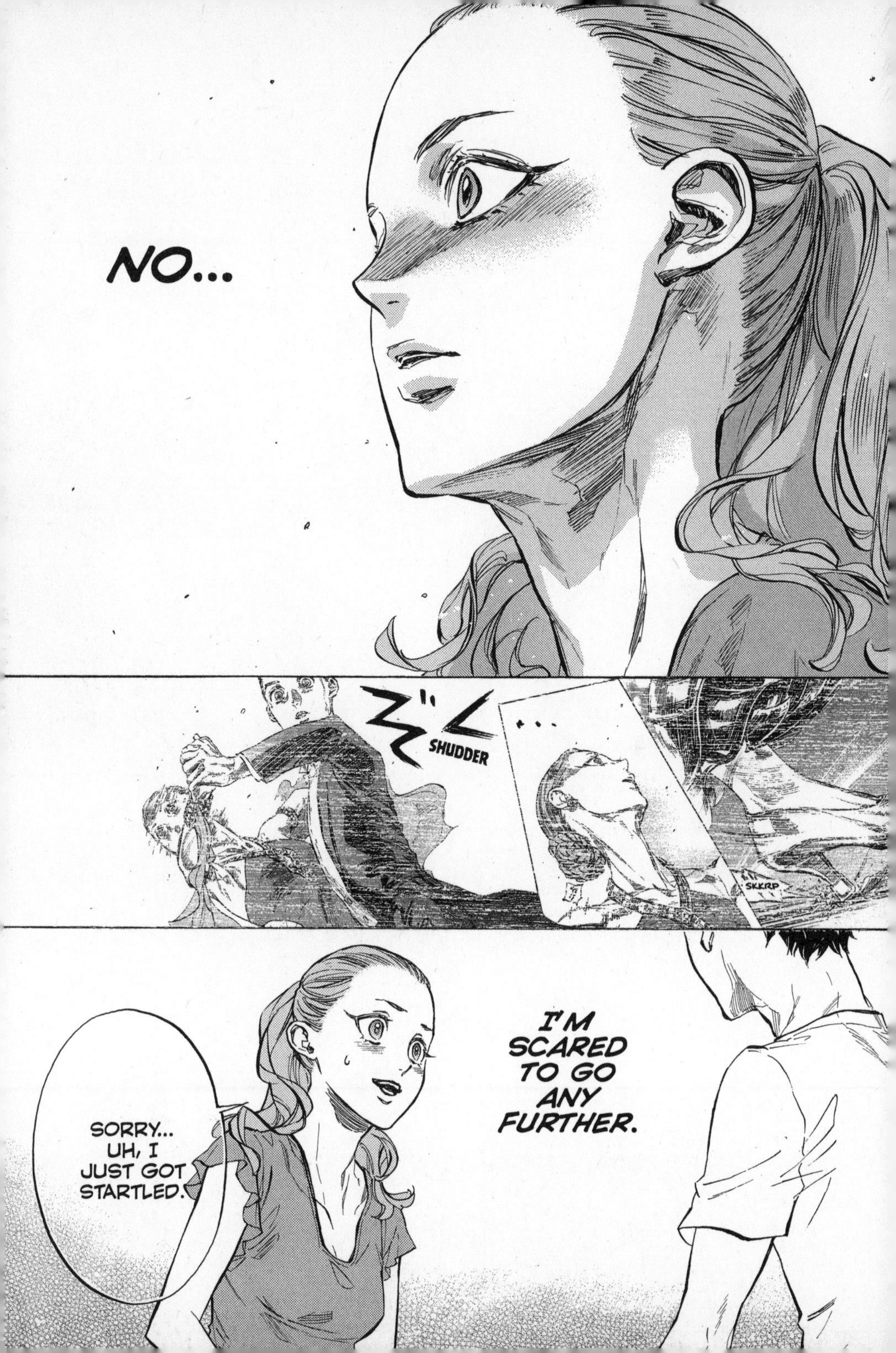
NO...
...
SKKRP
SHUDDER
I'M SCARED TO GO ANY FURTHER.
SORRY... UH, I JUST GOT STARTLED.

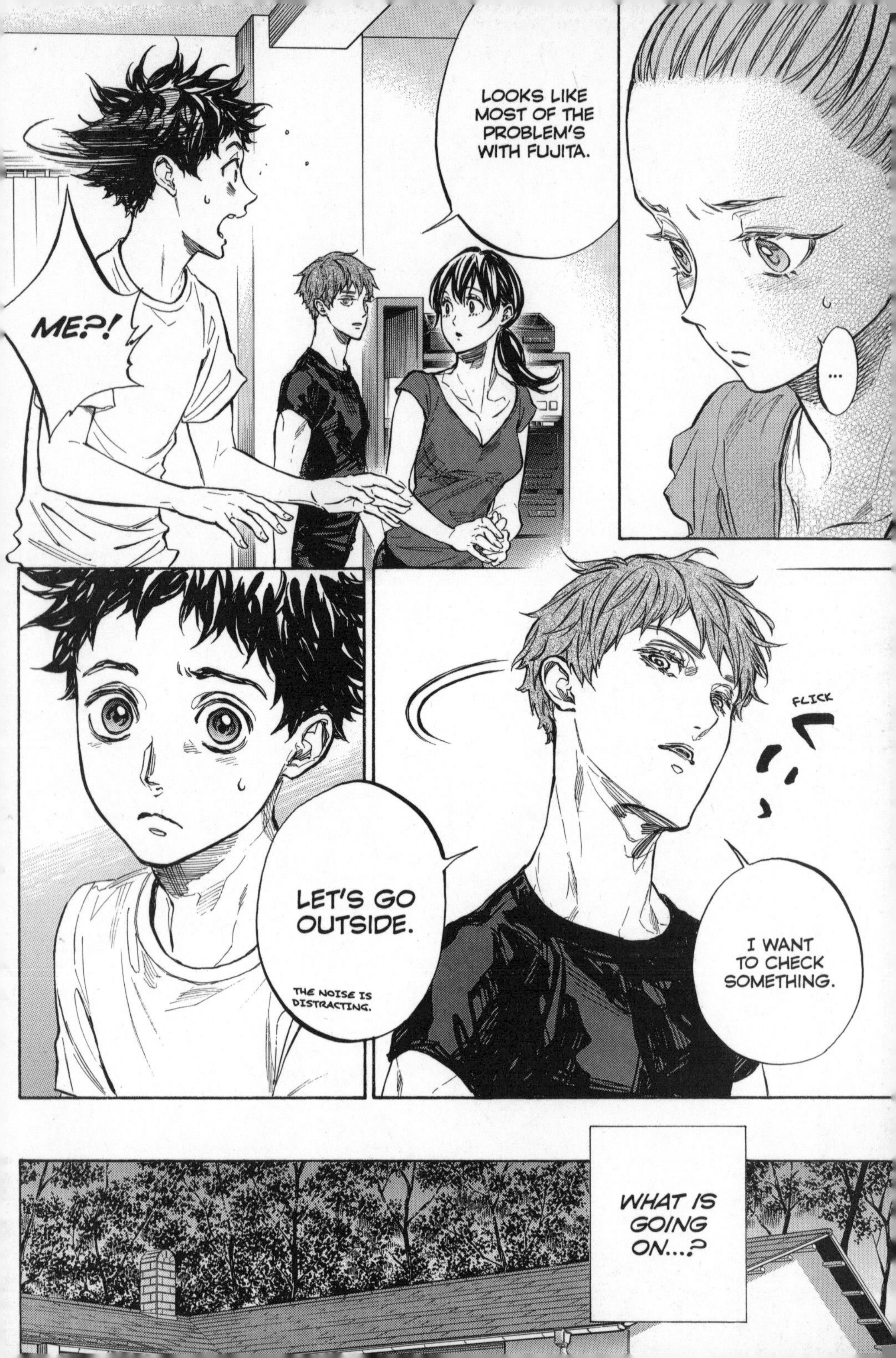
...
LOOKS LIKE MOST OF THE PROBLEM'S WITH FUJITA.
ME?!
FLICK
I WANT TO CHECK SOMETHING.
LET'S GO OUTSIDE.
THE NOISE IS DISTRACTING.
WHAT IS GOING ON...?

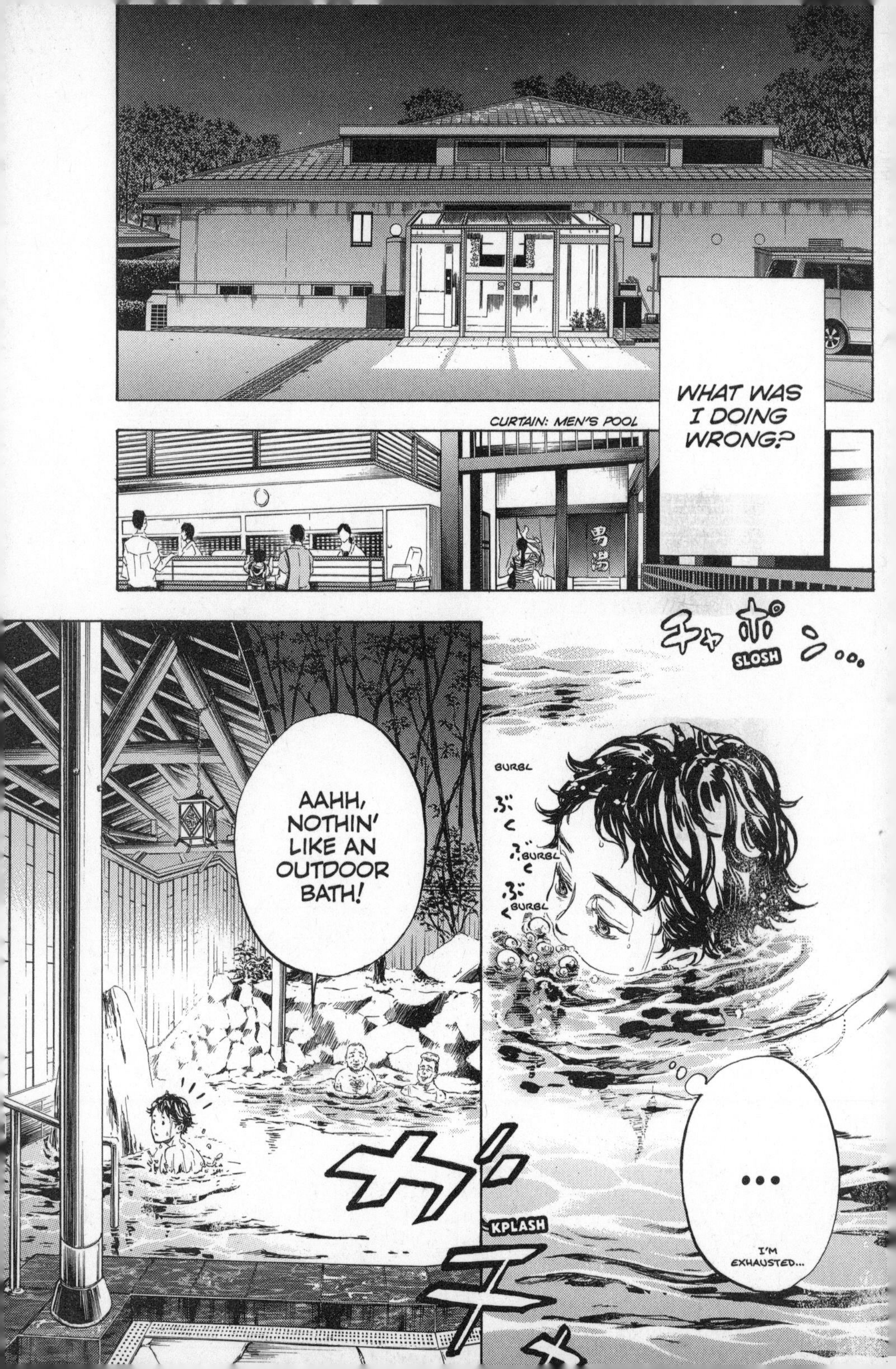
WHAT WAS I DOING WRONG?
CURTAIN: MEN'S POOL
SLOSH
BURBL
BURBL
BURBL
...
I'M EXHAUSTED...
AAHH, NOTHIN' LIKE AN OUTDOOR BATH!
KPLASH

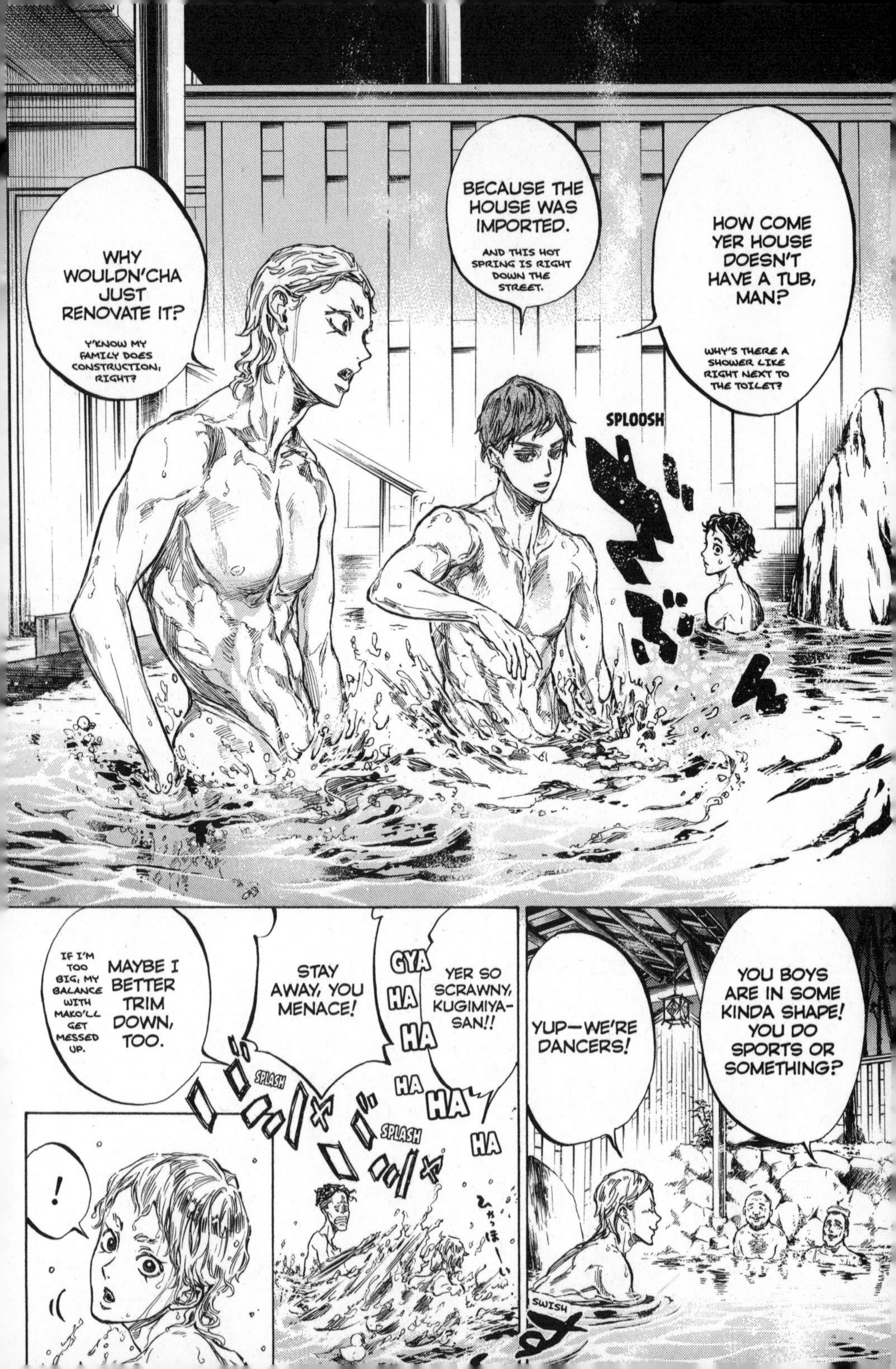
HOW COME YER HOUSE DOESN'T HAVE A TUB, MAN?
WHY'S THERE A SHOWER LIKE RIGHT NEXT TO THE TOILET?
BECAUSE THE HOUSE WAS IMPORTED.
AND THIS HOT SPRING IS RIGHT DOWN THE STREET.
SPLOOSH
WHY WOULDN'CHA JUST RENOVATE IT?
Y'KNOW MY FAMILY DOES CONSTRUCTION, RIGHT?
YOU BOYS ARE IN SOME KINDA SHAPE! YOU DO SPORTS OR SOMETHING?
YUP—WE'RE DANCERS!
SWISH
YER SO SCRAWNY, KUGIMIYA-SAN!!
GYA HA HA HA HA HA
ひゃっほーい
STAY AWAY, YOU MENACE!
SPLASH
SPLASH
MAYBE I BETTER TRIM DOWN, TOO.
IF I'M TOO BIG, MY BALANCE WITH MAKO'LL GET MESSED UP.
!

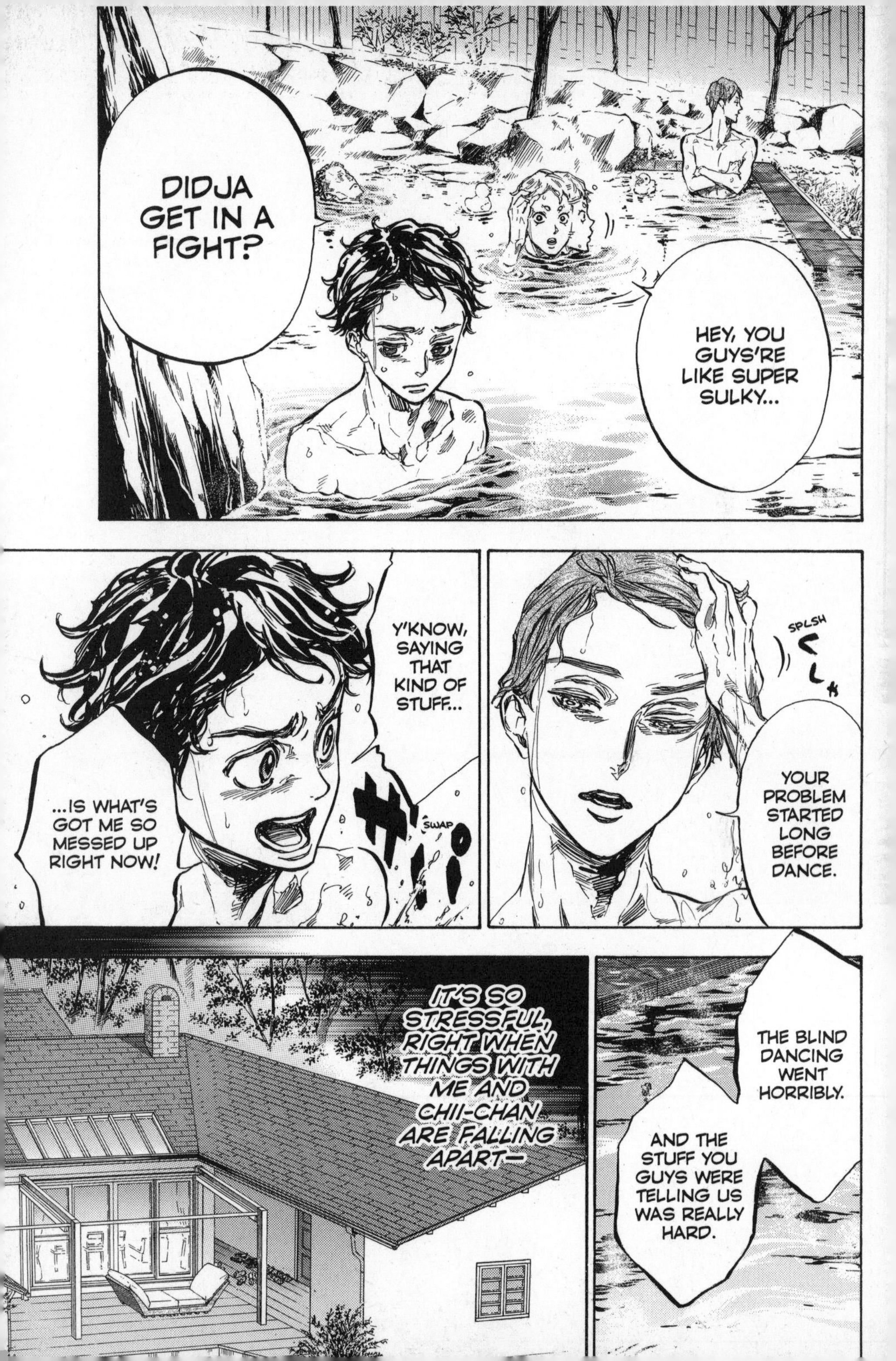
HEY, YOU GUYS'RE LIKE SUPER SULKY...
DIDJA GET IN A FIGHT?
SPLSH
YOUR PROBLEM STARTED LONG BEFORE DANCE.
Y'KNOW, SAYING THAT KIND OF STUFF...
SWAP
...IS WHAT'S GOT ME SO MESSED UP RIGHT NOW!
THE BLIND DANCING WENT HORRIBLY.
AND THE STUFF YOU GUYS WERE TELLING US WAS REALLY HARD.
IT'S SO STRESSFUL, RIGHT WHEN THINGS WITH ME AND CHII-CHAN ARE FALLING APART—

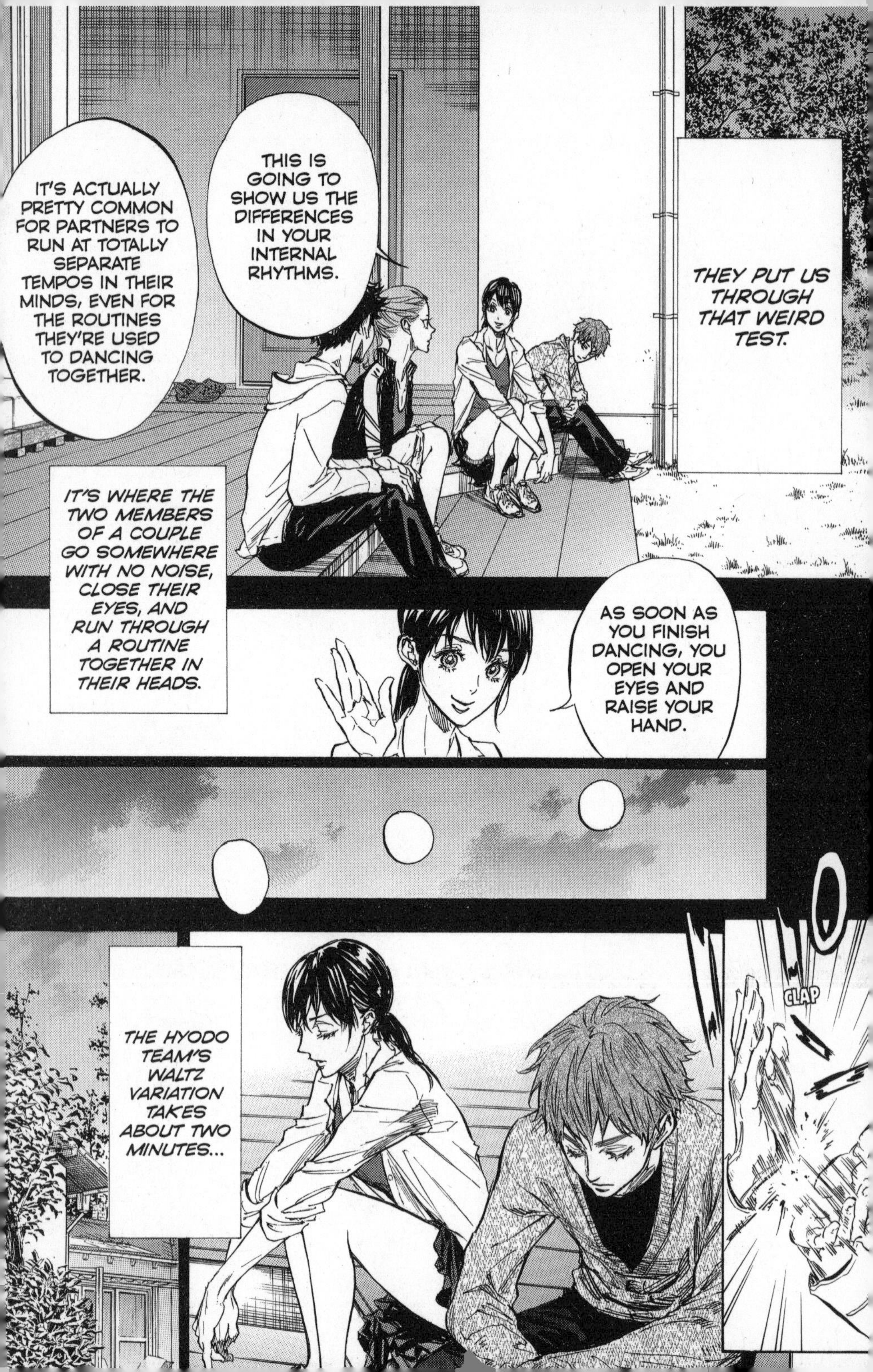
THEY PUT US THROUGH THAT WEIRD TEST.
THIS IS GOING TO SHOW US THE DIFFERENCES IN YOUR INTERNAL RHYTHMS.
IT'S ACTUALLY PRETTY COMMON FOR PARTNERS TO RUN AT TOTALLY SEPARATE TEMPOS IN THEIR MINDS, EVEN FOR THE ROUTINES THEY'RE USED TO DANCING TOGETHER.
IT'S WHERE THE TWO MEMBERS OF A COUPLE GO SOMEWHERE WITH NO NOISE, CLOSE THEIR EYES, AND RUN THROUGH A ROUTINE TOGETHER IN THEIR HEADS.
AS SOON AS YOU FINISH DANCING, YOU OPEN YOUR EYES AND RAISE YOUR HAND.
CLAP
THE HYODO TEAM'S WALTZ VARIATION TAKES ABOUT TWO MINUTES...

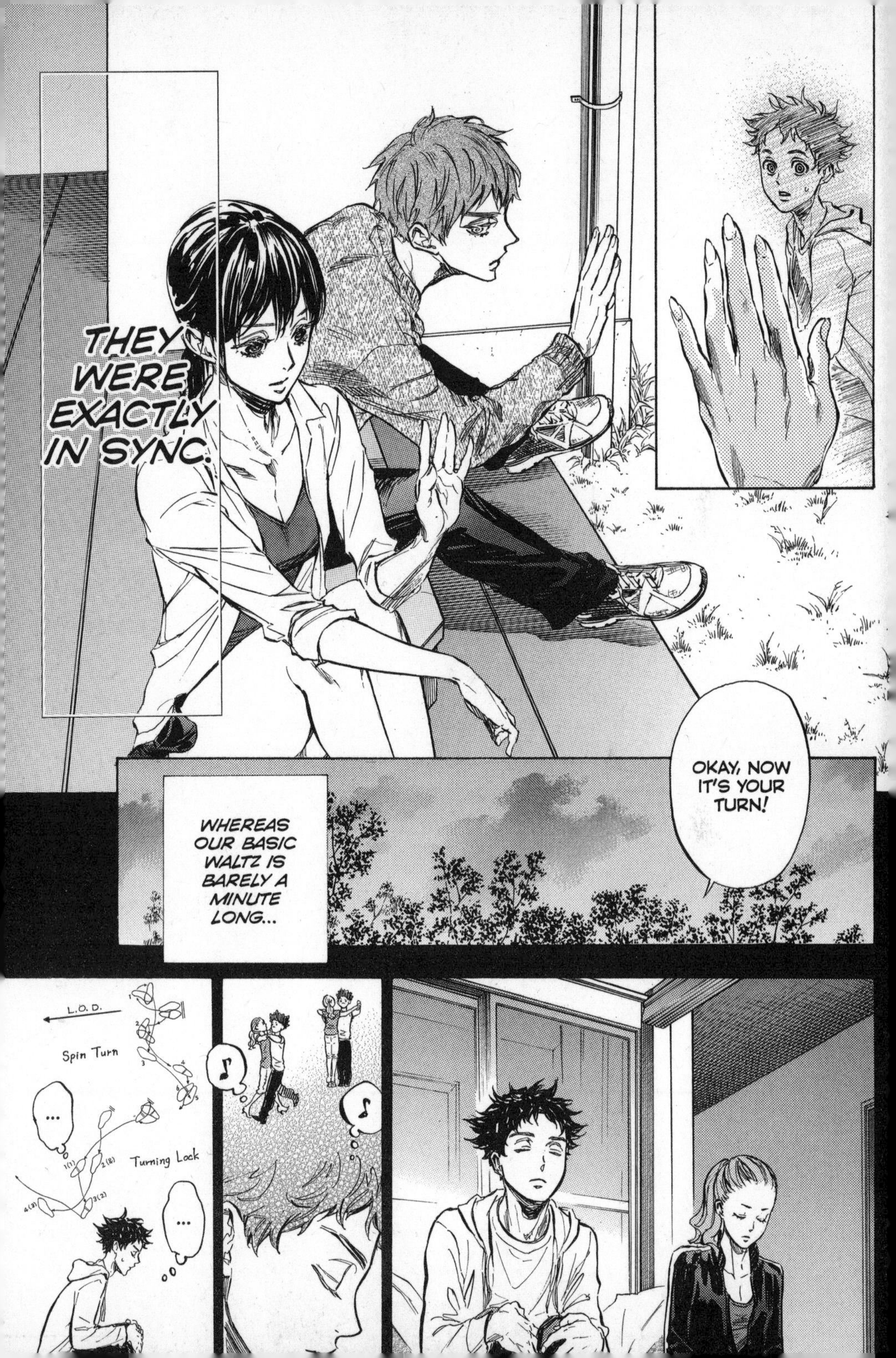
THEY WERE EXACTLY IN SYNC.
OKAY, NOW IT'S YOUR TURN!
WHEREAS OUR BASIC WALTZ IS BARELY A MINUTE LONG...
L.O.D.
Spin Turn
...
Turning Lock
...

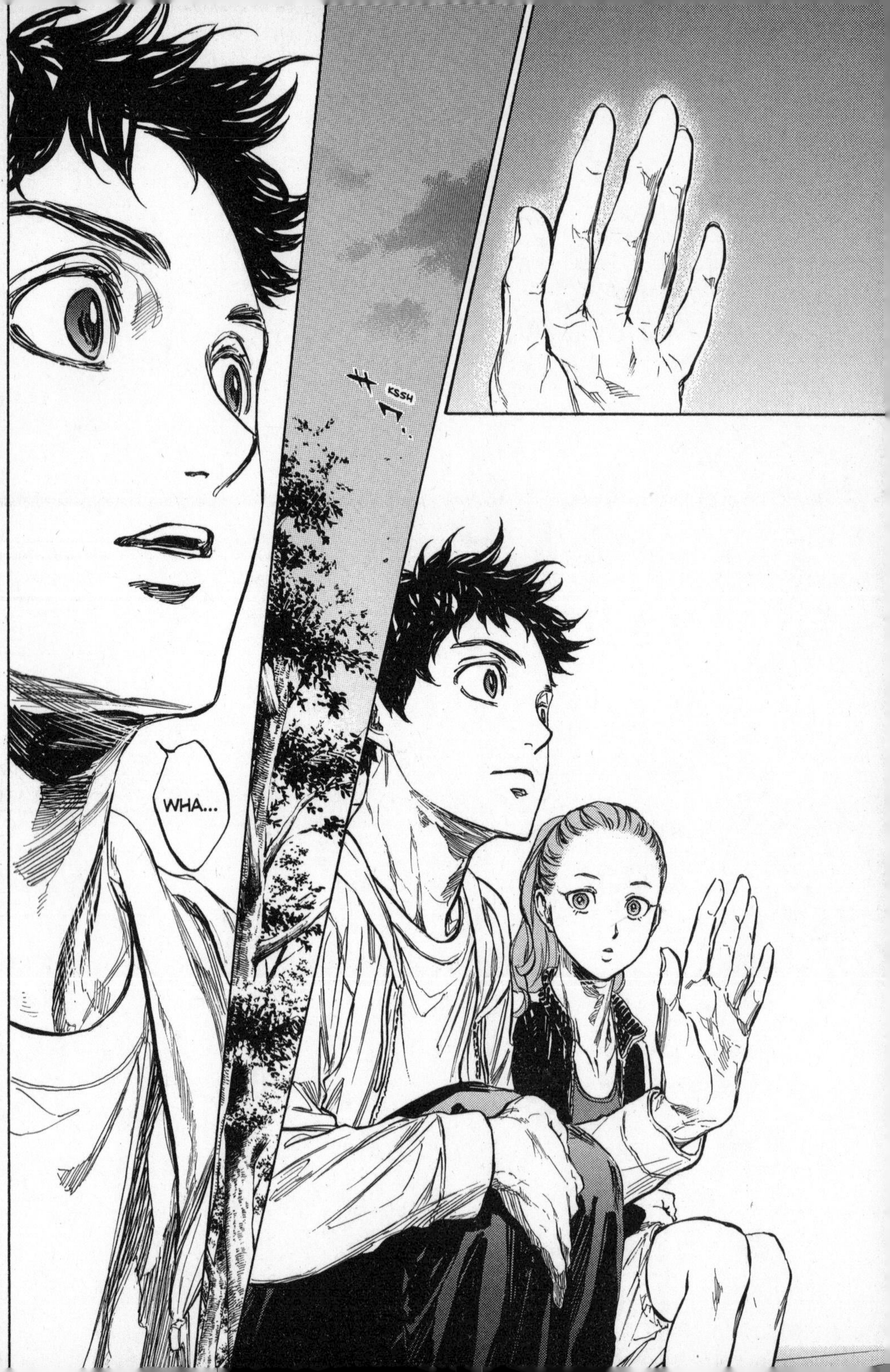
KSSH
WHA...

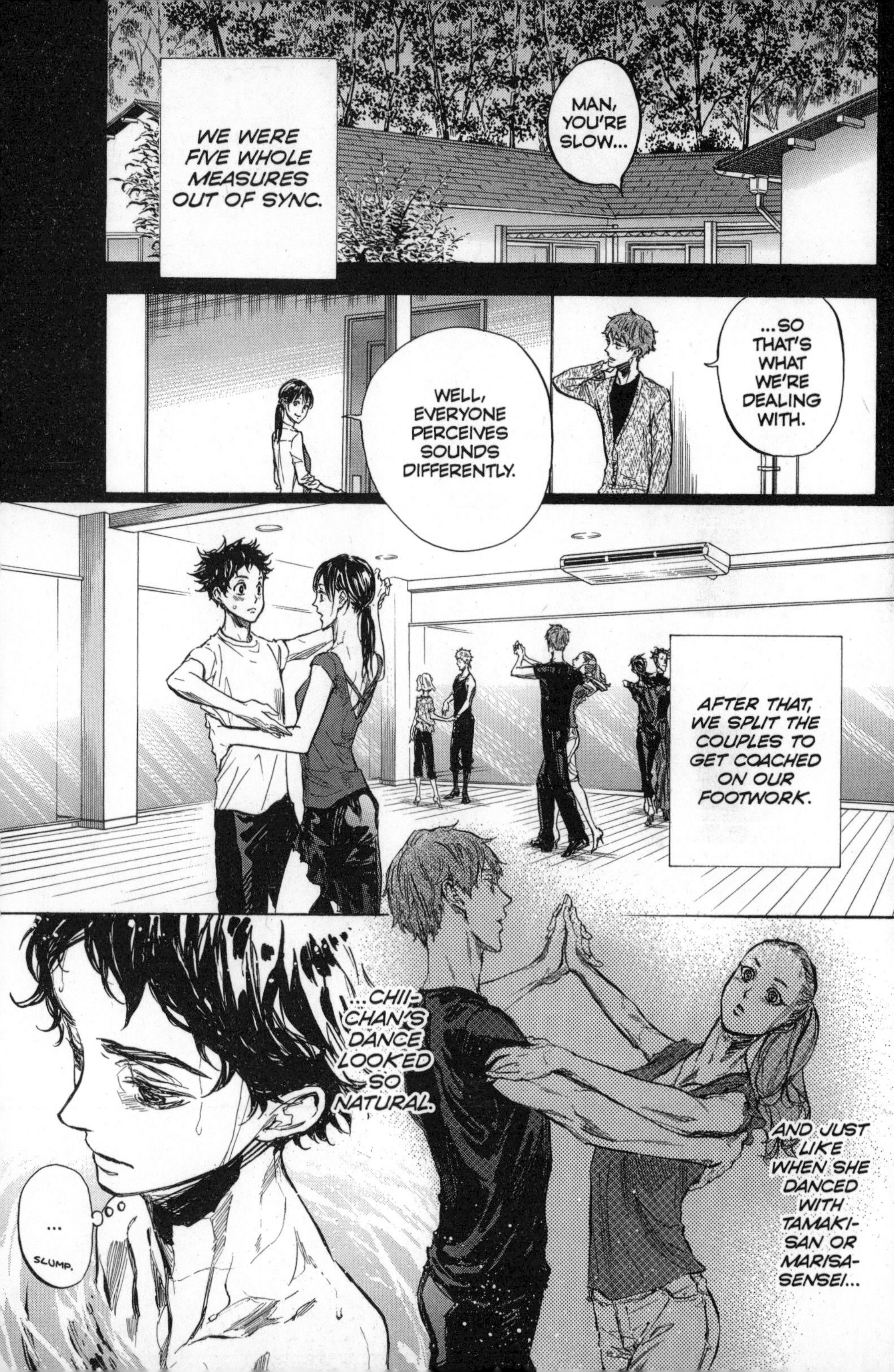
WE WERE FIVE WHOLE MEASURES OUT OF SYNC.
MAN, YOU'RE SLOW...
...SO THAT'S WHAT WE'RE DEALING WITH.
WELL, EVERYONE PERCEIVES SOUNDS DIFFERENTLY.
AFTER THAT, WE SPLIT THE COUPLES TO GET COACHED ON OUR FOOTWORK.
AND JUST LIKE WHEN SHE DANCED WITH TAMAKI-SAN OR MARISA-SENSEI...
...CHII-CHAN'S DANCE LOOKED SO NATURAL.
...
SLUMP.

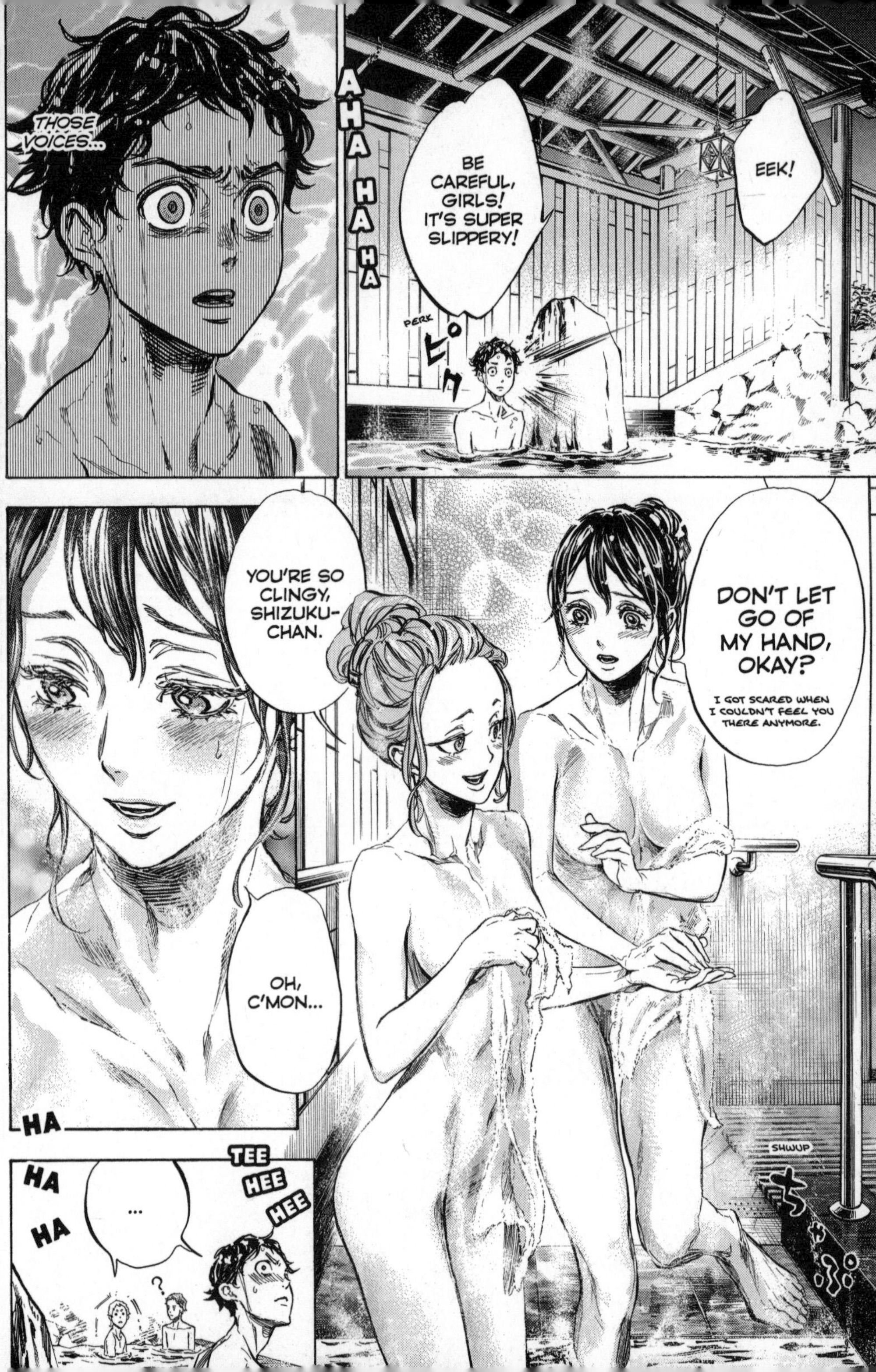
EEK!
BE CAREFUL, GIRLS! IT'S SUPER SLIPPERY!
AHA HA HA HA
PERK
THOSE VOICES...
DON'T LET GO OF MY HAND, OKAY?
I GOT SCARED WHEN I COULDN'T FEEL YOU THERE ANYMORE.
YOU'RE SO CLINGY, SHIZUKU-CHAN.
OH, C'MON...
SHWUP
HA
TEE HEE HEE
HA HA
...

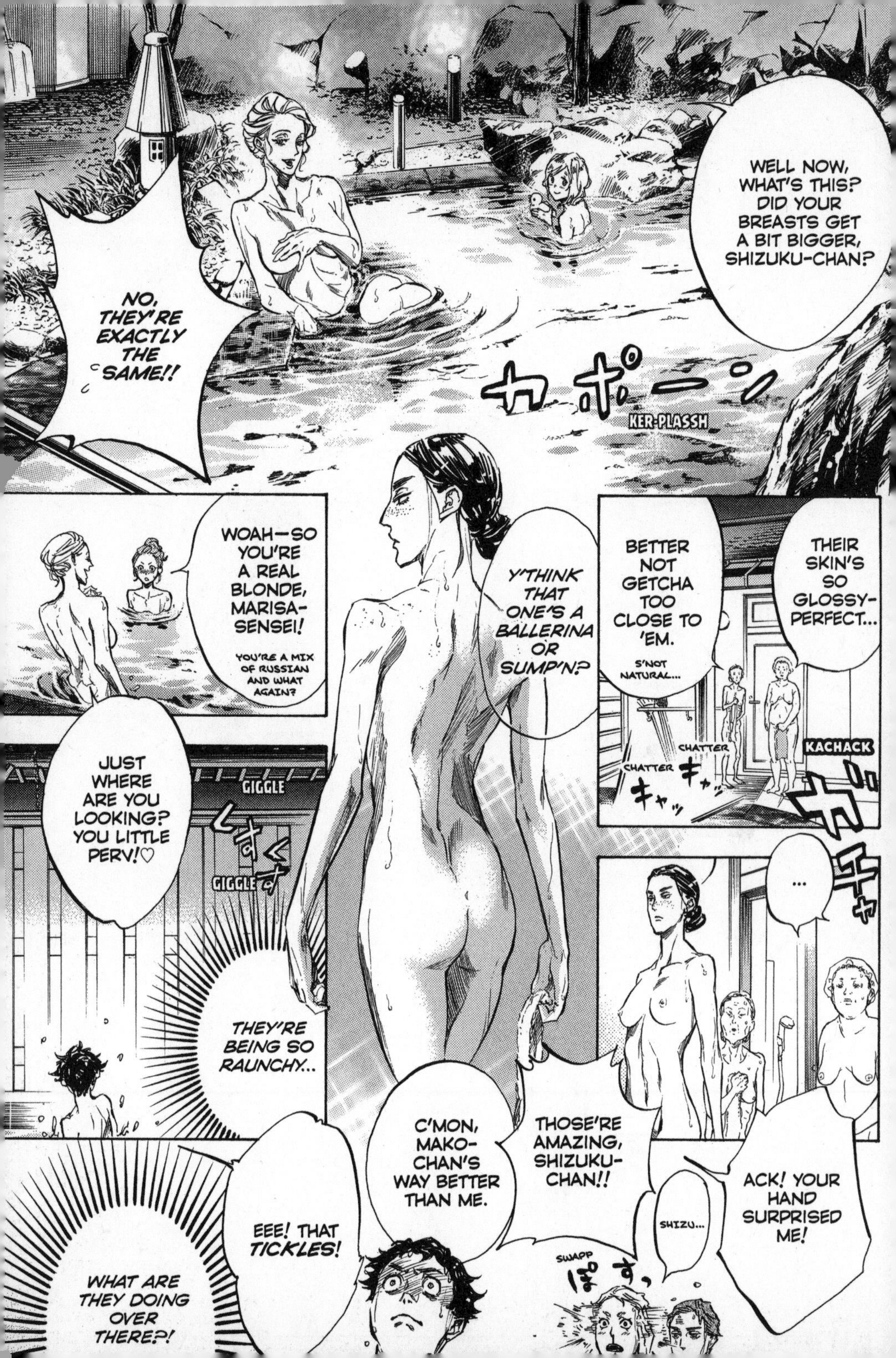
WELL NOW, WHAT'S THIS? DID YOUR BREASTS GET A BIT BIGGER, SHIZUKU-CHAN?
NO, THEY'RE EXACTLY THE SAME!!
KER-PLASSH
THEIR SKIN'S SO GLOSSY-PERFECT...
BETTER NOT GETCHA TOO CLOSE TO 'EM.
S'NOT NATURAL...
CHATTER
CHATTER
KACHACK
...
Y'THINK THAT ONE'S A BALLERINA OR SUMP'N?
WOAH—SO YOU'RE A REAL BLONDE, MARISA-SENSEI!
YOU'RE A MIX OF RUSSIAN AND WHAT AGAIN?
JUST WHERE ARE YOU LOOKING? YOU LITTLE PERV!♡
GIGGLE
GIGGLE
THEY'RE BEING SO RAUNCHY...
ACK! YOUR HAND SURPRISED ME!
SHIZU...
THOSE'RE AMAZING, SHIZUKU-CHAN!!
C'MON, MAKO-CHAN'S WAY BETTER THAN ME.
SWAPP
EEE! THAT TICKLES!
WHAT ARE THEY DOING OVER THERE?!

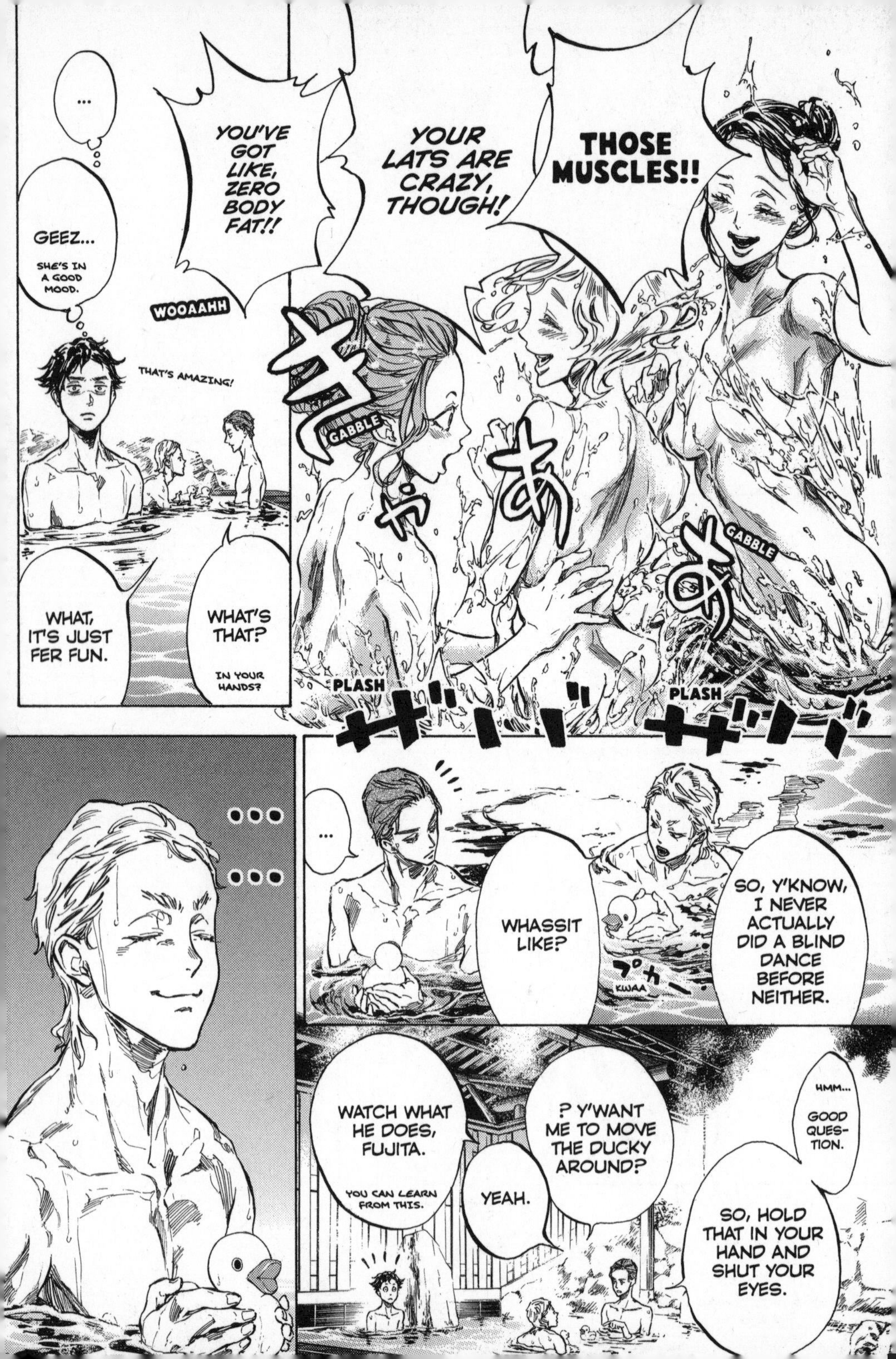
THOSE MUSCLES!!
YOUR LATS ARE CRAZY, THOUGH!
YOU'VE GOT LIKE, ZERO BODY FAT!!
GABBLE
GABBLE
PLASH
PLASH
...
GEEZ... SHE'S IN A GOOD MOOD.
WOOAAHH
THAT'S AMAZING!
WHAT'S THAT? IN YOUR HANDS?
WHAT, IT'S JUST FER FUN.
SO, Y'KNOW, I NEVER ACTUALLY DID A BLIND DANCE BEFORE NEITHER.
WHASSIT LIKE?
KWAA
...
HMM... GOOD QUESTION.
SO, HOLD THAT IN YOUR HAND AND SHUT YOUR EYES.
? Y'WANT ME TO MOVE THE DUCKY AROUND?
YEAH.
WATCH WHAT HE DOES, FUJITA. YOU CAN LEARN FROM THIS.

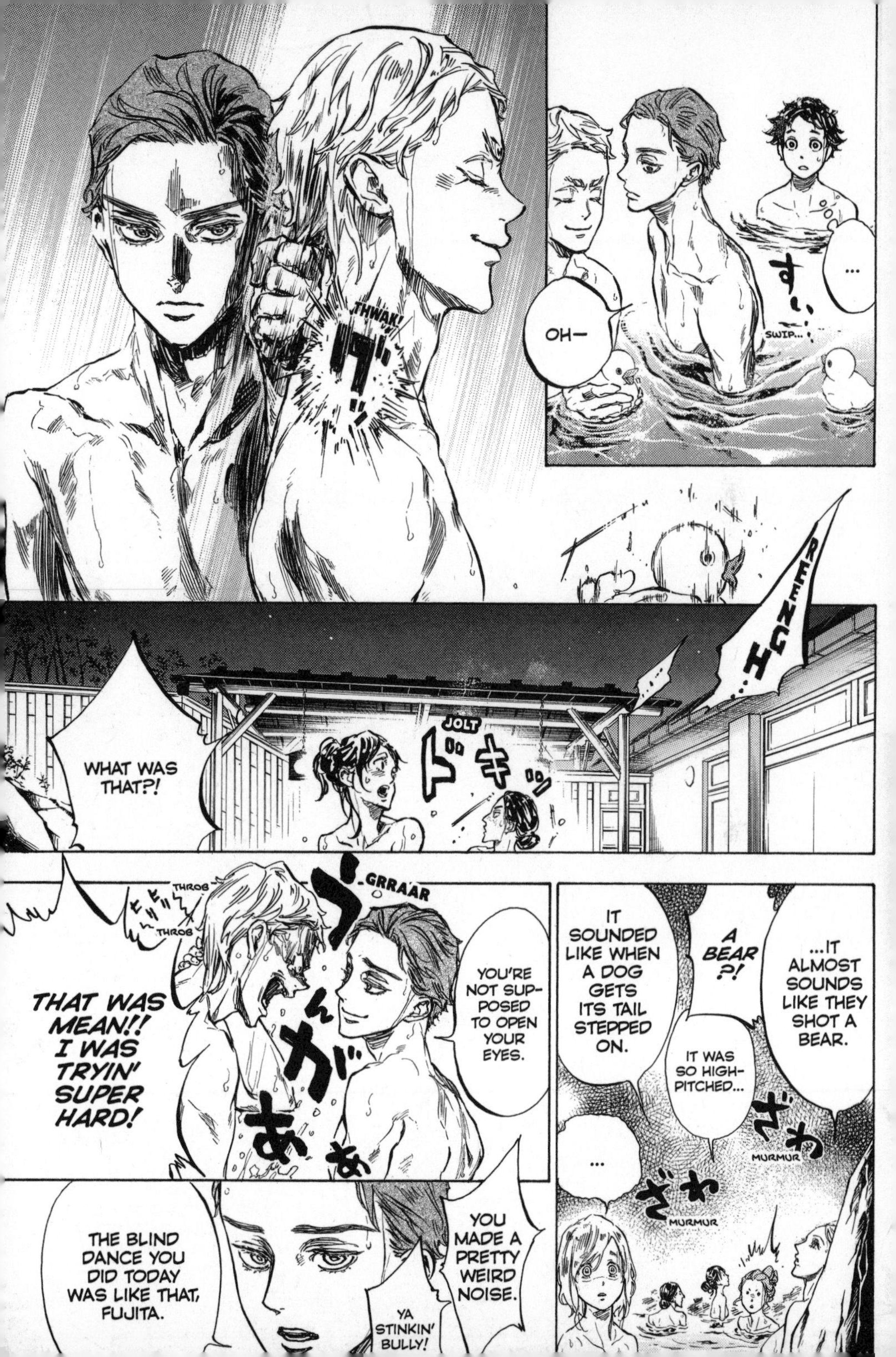
...
す
SWIP...
OH—
THWAK!
ガッ
REENGH
WHAT WAS THAT?!
ドキッ
JOLT
...IT ALMOST SOUNDS LIKE THEY SHOT A BEAR.
A BEAR?!
IT SOUNDED LIKE WHEN A DOG GETS ITS TAIL STEPPED ON.
IT WAS SO HIGH-PITCHED...
ざわ
MURMUR
...
ざわ
MURMUR
YOU'RE NOT SUP-POSED TO OPEN YOUR EYES.
GRRAAR
THROB
THROB
THAT WAS MEAN!! I WAS TRYIN' SUPER HARD!
YOU MADE A PRETTY WEIRD NOISE.
YA STINKIN' BULLY!
THE BLIND DANCE YOU DID TODAY WAS LIKE THAT, FUJITA.

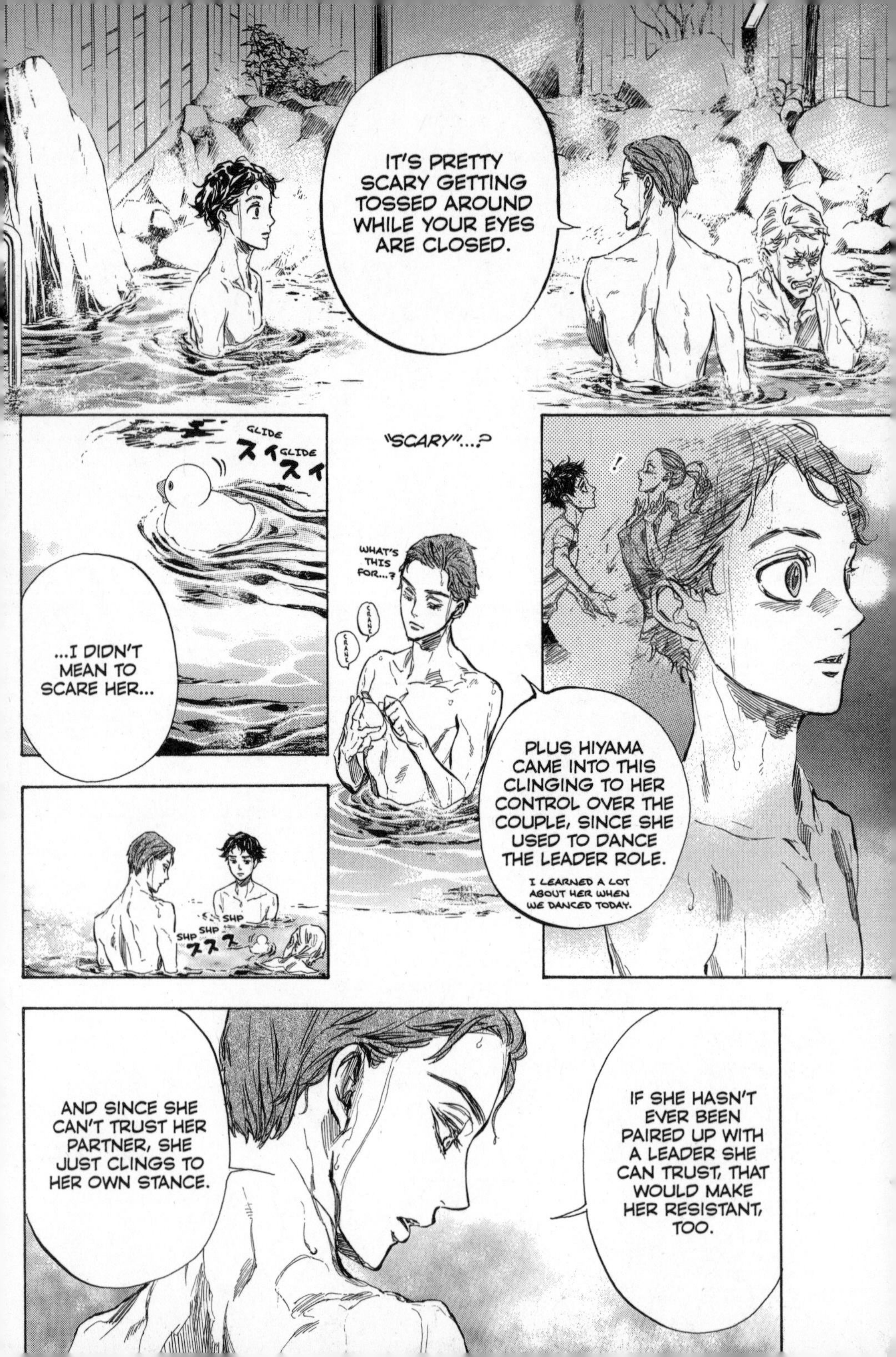
IT'S PRETTY SCARY GETTING TOSSED AROUND WHILE YOUR EYES ARE CLOSED.
!
"SCARY"...?
WHAT'S THIS FOR...?
CRANK
CRANK
PLUS HIYAMA CAME INTO THIS CLINGING TO HER CONTROL OVER THE COUPLE, SINCE SHE USED TO DANCE THE LEADER ROLE.
I LEARNED A LOT ABOUT HER WHEN WE DANCED TODAY.
GLIDE GLIDE
スイスイ
...I DIDN'T MEAN TO SCARE HER...
SHP SHP SHP
ススス
IF SHE HASN'T EVER BEEN PAIRED UP WITH A LEADER SHE CAN TRUST, THAT WOULD MAKE HER RESISTANT, TOO.
AND SINCE SHE CAN'T TRUST HER PARTNER, SHE JUST CLINGS TO HER OWN STANCE.

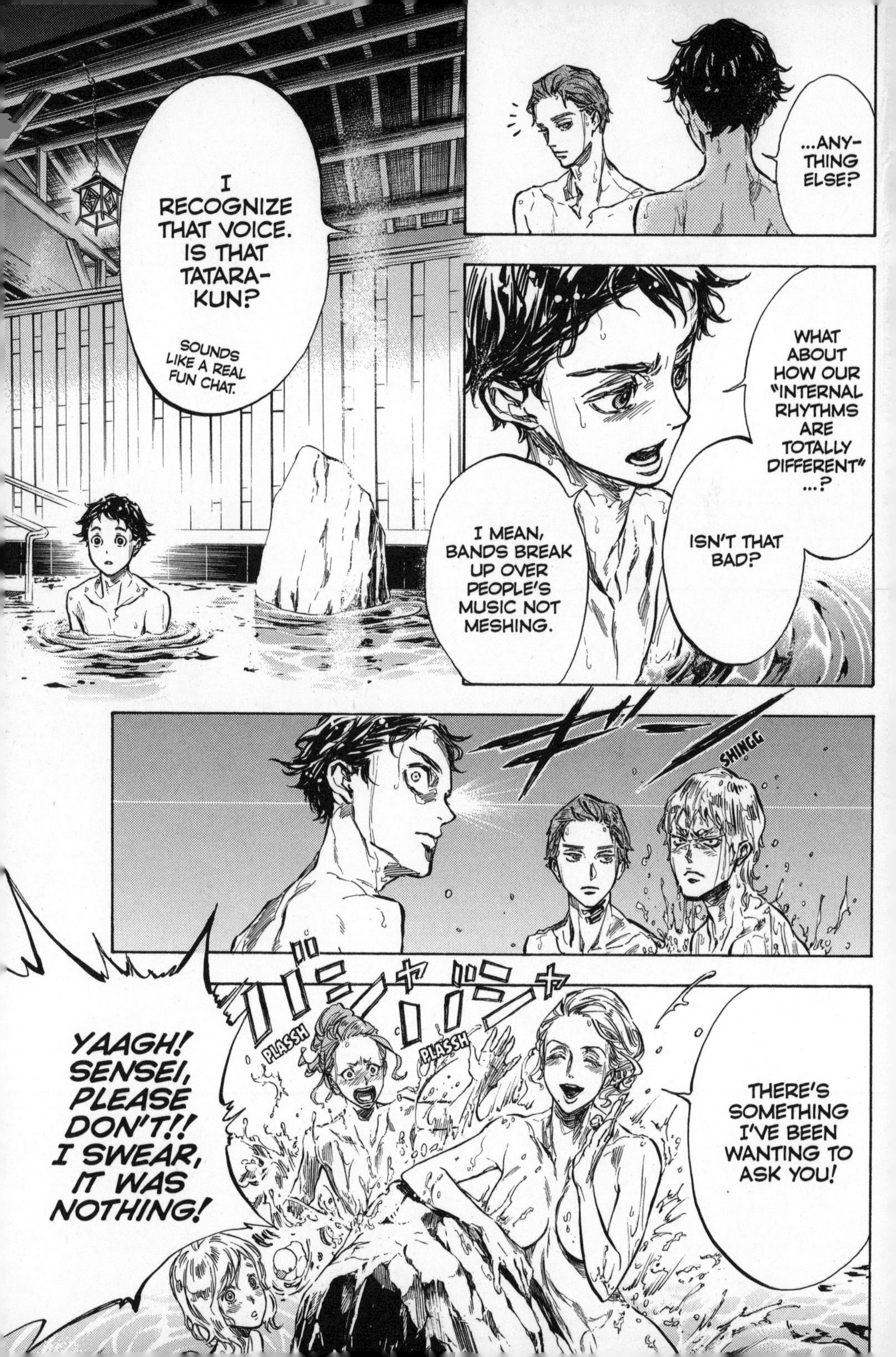

...ANY-THING ELSE?
WHAT ABOUT HOW OUR "INTERNAL RHYTHMS ARE TOTALLY DIFFERENT" ...?
ISN'T THAT BAD?
I MEAN, BANDS BREAK UP OVER PEOPLE'S MUSIC NOT MESHING.
I RECOGNIZE THAT VOICE. IS THAT TATARA-KUN?
SOUNDS LIKE A REAL FUN CHAT.
SHINGG
THERE'S SOMETHING I'VE BEEN WANTING TO ASK YOU!
PLASSH
PLASSH
YAAGH! SENSEI, PLEASE DON'T!! I SWEAR, IT WAS NOTHING!

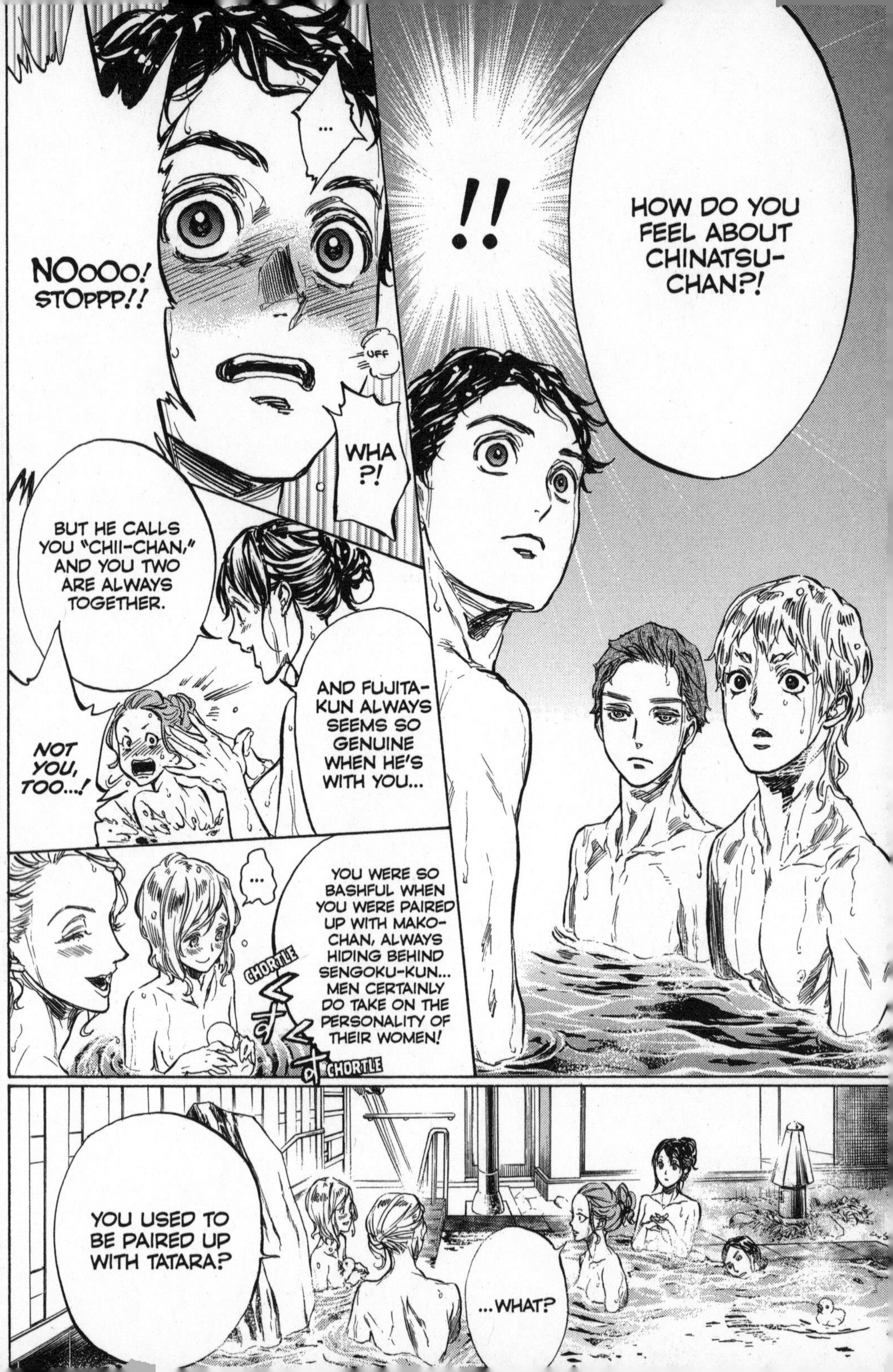
HOW DO YOU FEEL ABOUT CHINATSU-CHAN?!
!!
...
UFF
WHA ?!
NOoOO! STOPPP!!
BUT HE CALLS YOU "CHII-CHAN," AND YOU TWO ARE ALWAYS TOGETHER.
AND FUJITA-KUN ALWAYS SEEMS SO GENUINE WHEN HE'S WITH YOU...
NOT YOU, TOO...!
...
YOU WERE SO BASHFUL WHEN YOU WERE PAIRED UP WITH MAKO-CHAN, ALWAYS HIDING BEHIND SENGOKU-KUN... MEN CERTAINLY DO TAKE ON THE PERSONALITY OF THEIR WOMEN!
CHORTLE
CHORTLE
YOU USED TO BE PAIRED UP WITH TATARA?
...WHAT?

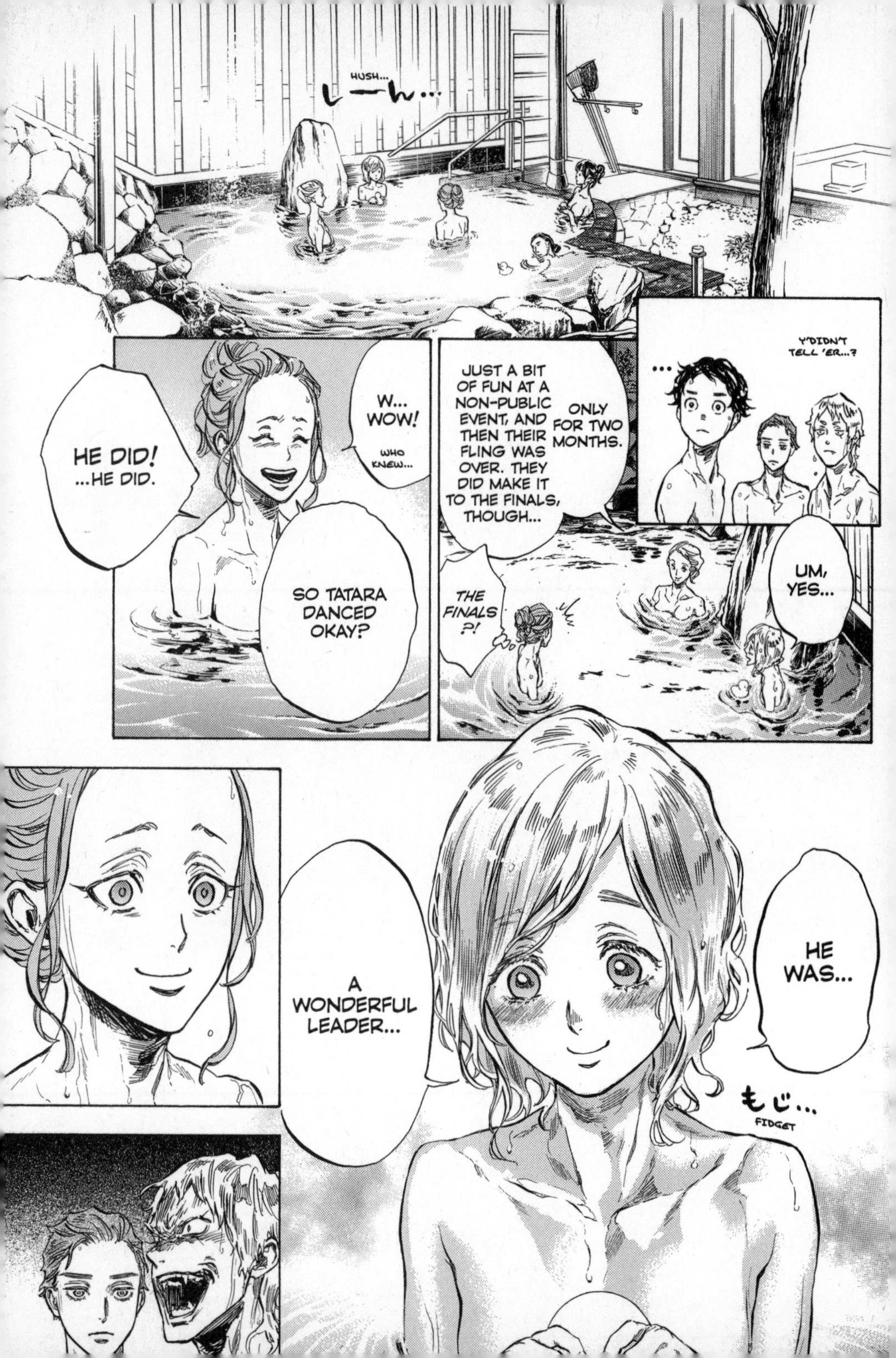

HUSH...
しーん...
...
Y'DIDN'T TELL 'ER...?
ONLY FOR TWO MONTHS.
JUST A BIT OF FUN AT A NON-PUBLIC EVENT, AND THEN THEIR FLING WAS OVER. THEY DID MAKE IT TO THE FINALS, THOUGH...
UM, YES...
THE FINALS?!
W... WOW!
WHO KNEW...
SO TATARA DANCED OKAY?
HE DID! ...HE DID.
HE WAS...
もじ...
FIDGET
A WONDERFUL LEADER...

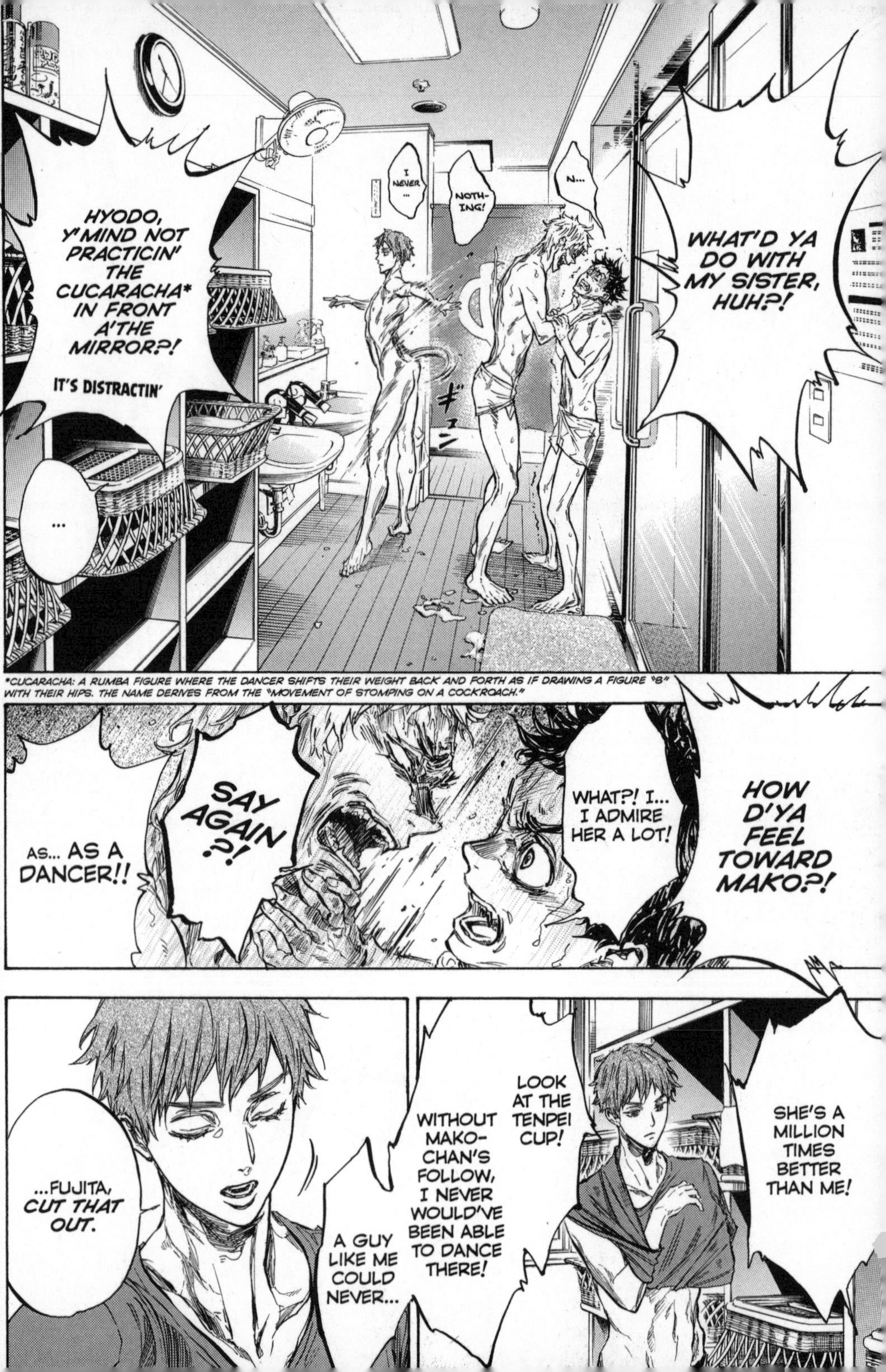
WHAT'D YA DO WITH MY SISTER, HUH?!
N...
NOTHING!
I NEVER...
HYODO, Y'MIND NOT PRACTICIN' THE CUCARACHA* IN FRONT A'THE MIRROR?!
IT'S DISTRACTIN'
...
ギュン
HOW D'YA FEEL TOWARD MAKO?!
WHAT?! I... I ADMIRE HER A LOT!
SAY AGAIN?!
AS... AS A DANCER!!
SHE'S A MILLION TIMES BETTER THAN ME!
LOOK AT THE TENPEI CUP!
WITHOUT MAKO-CHAN'S FOLLOW, I NEVER WOULD'VE BEEN ABLE TO DANCE THERE!
A GUY LIKE ME COULD NEVER...
...FUJITA, CUT THAT OUT.

*CUCARACHA: A RUMBA FIGURE WHERE THE DANCER SHIFTS THEIR WEIGHT BACK AND FORTH AS IF DRAWING A FIGURE "8" WITH THEIR HIPS. THE NAME DERIVES FROM THE "MOVEMENT OF STOMPING ON A COCKROACH."

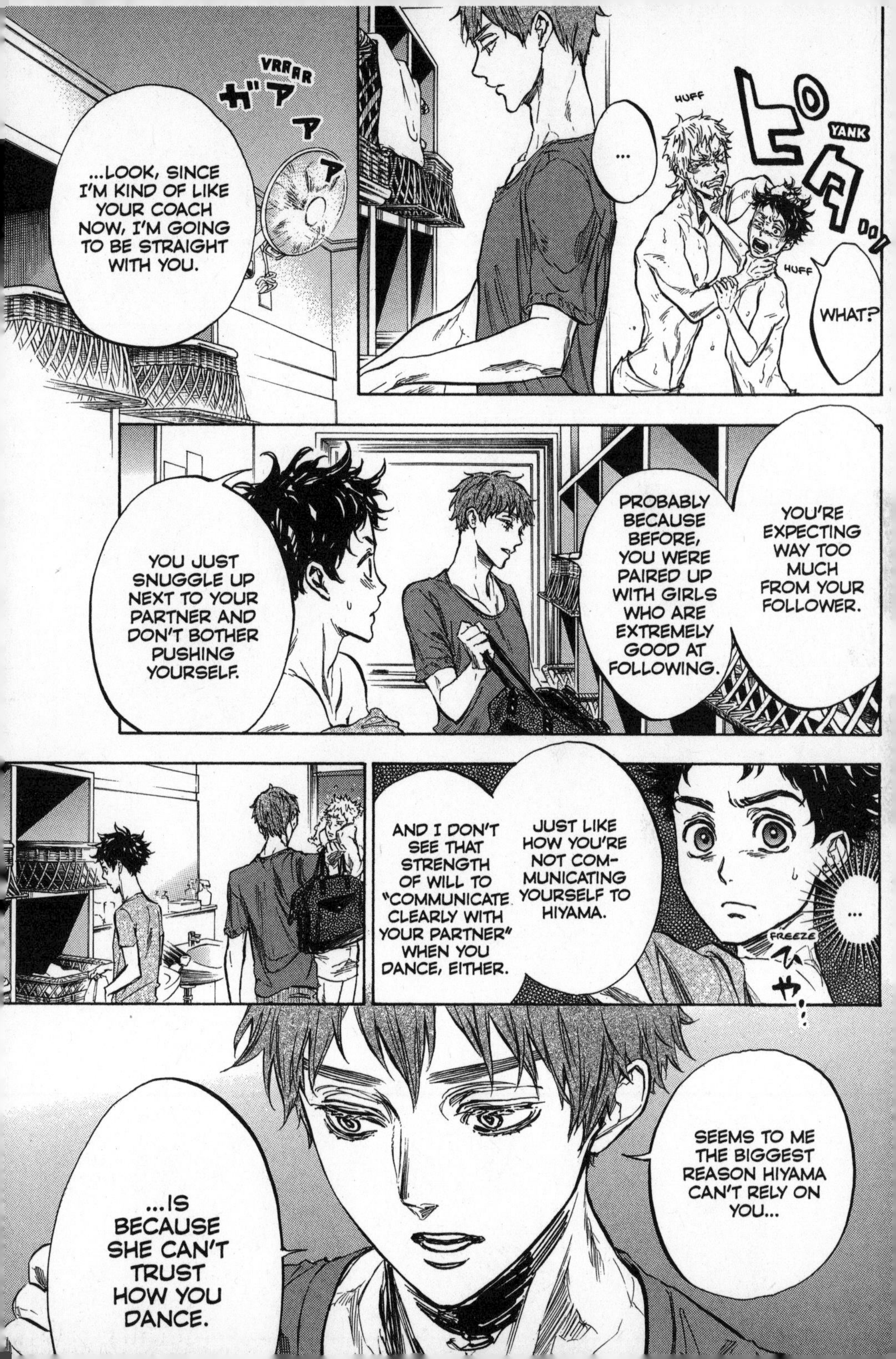
YANK
HUFF
...
HUFF
WHAT?
VRRRR
...LOOK, SINCE I'M KIND OF LIKE YOUR COACH NOW, I'M GOING TO BE STRAIGHT WITH YOU.
YOU'RE EXPECTING WAY TOO MUCH FROM YOUR FOLLOWER.
PROBABLY BECAUSE BEFORE, YOU WERE PAIRED UP WITH GIRLS WHO ARE EXTREMELY GOOD AT FOLLOWING.
YOU JUST SNUGGLE UP NEXT TO YOUR PARTNER AND DON'T BOTHER PUSHING YOURSELF.
...
FREEZE
JUST LIKE HOW YOU'RE NOT COM- MUNICATING YOURSELF TO HIYAMA.
AND I DON'T SEE THAT STRENGTH OF WILL TO "COMMUNICATE CLEARLY WITH YOUR PARTNER" WHEN YOU DANCE, EITHER.
SEEMS TO ME THE BIGGEST REASON HIYAMA CAN'T RELY ON YOU...
...IS BECAUSE SHE CAN'T TRUST HOW YOU DANCE.

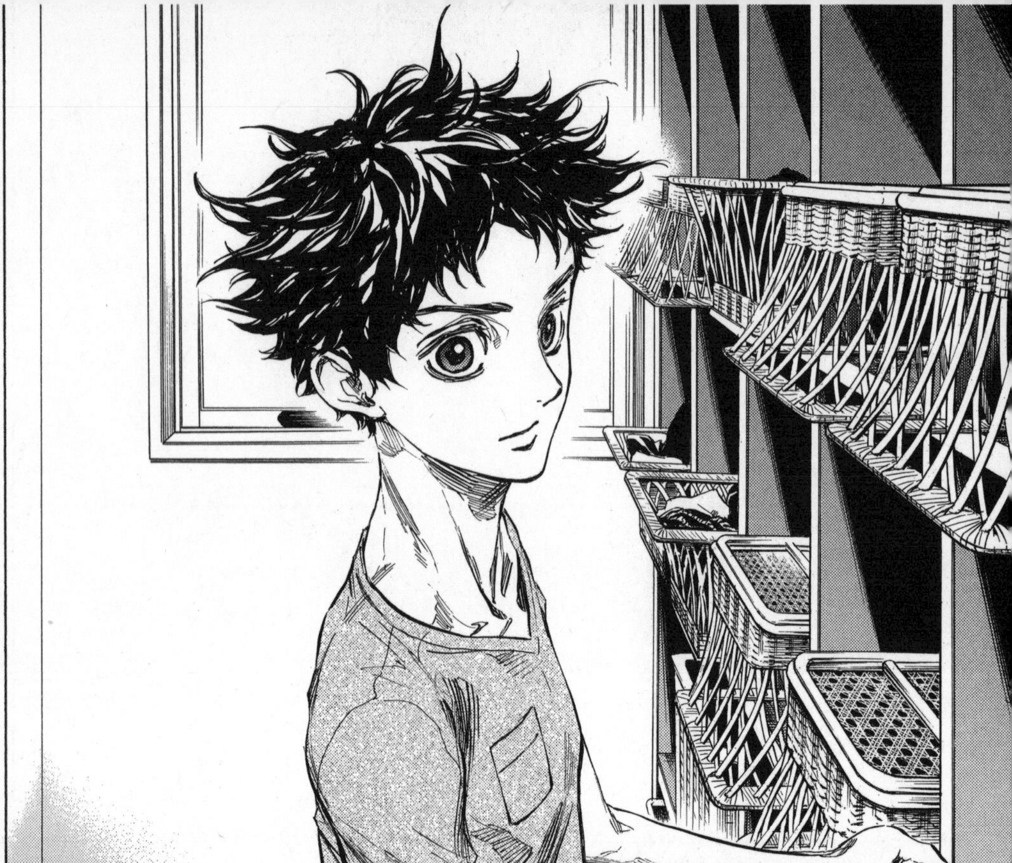
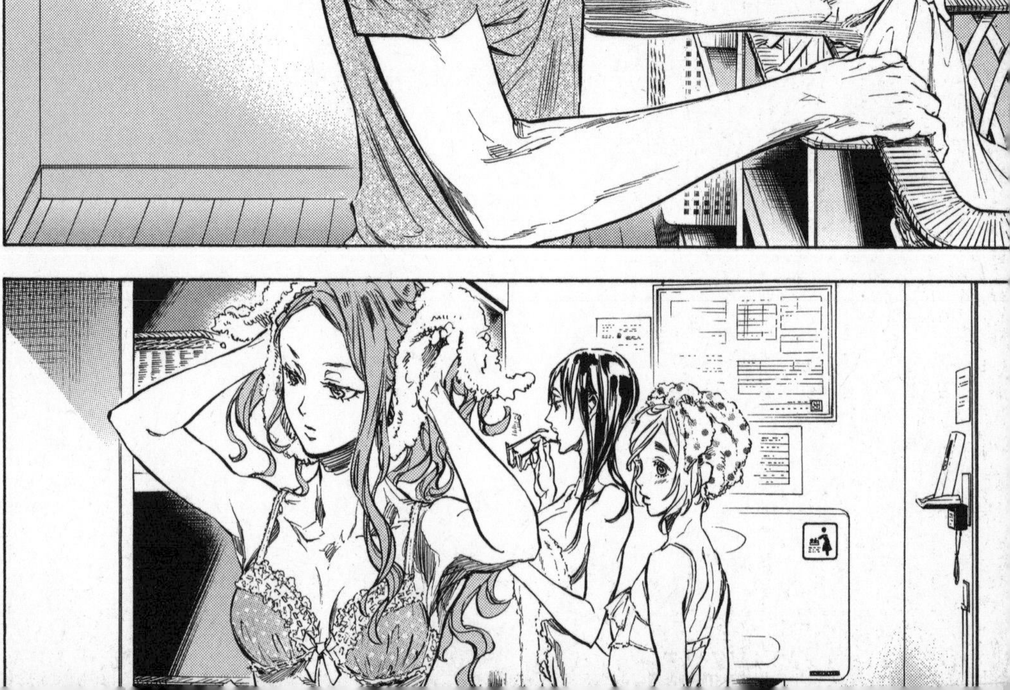

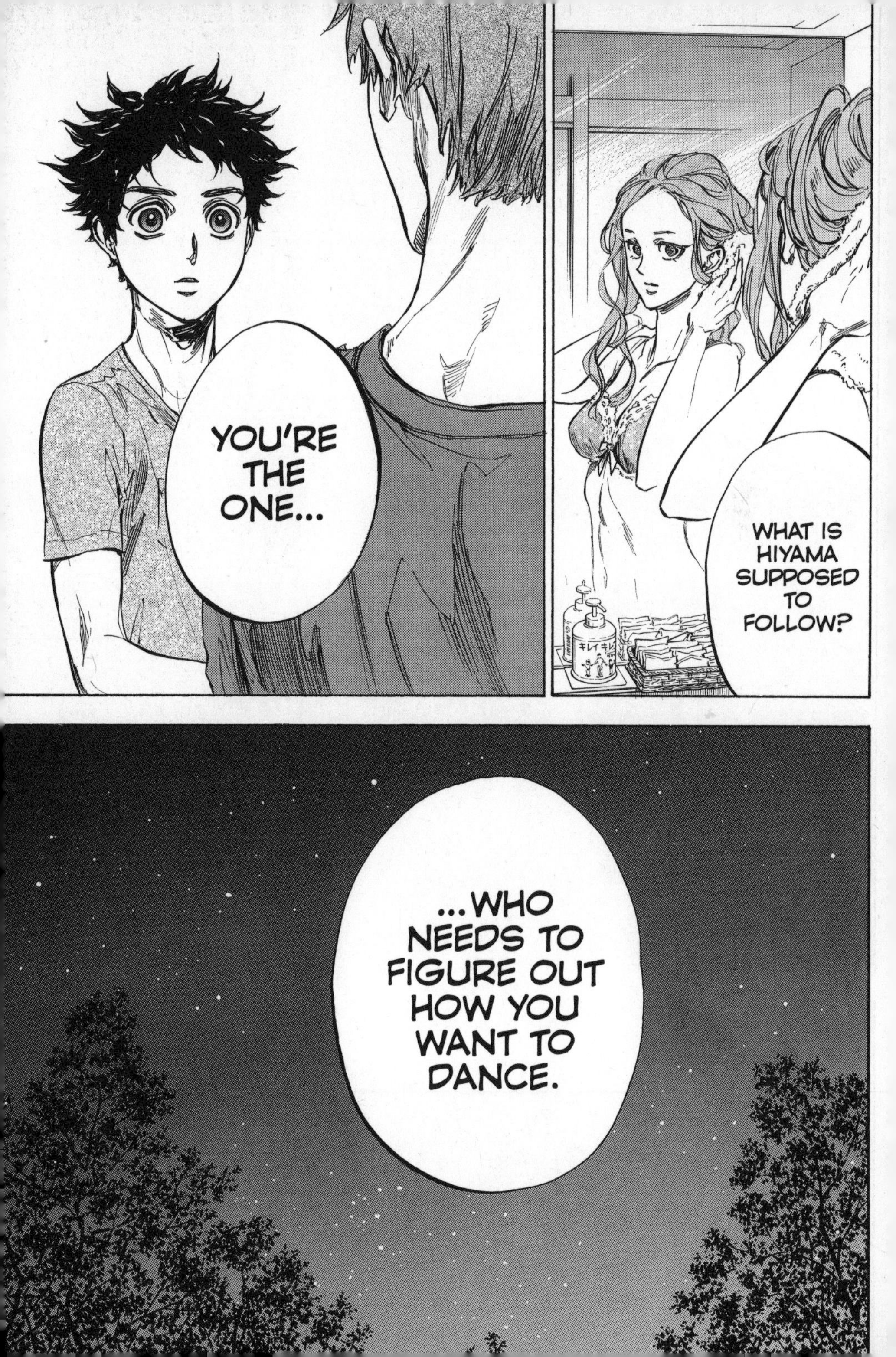
WHAT IS HIYAMA SUPPOSED TO FOLLOW?
YOU'RE THE ONE...
...WHO NEEDS TO FIGURE OUT HOW YOU WANT TO DANCE.

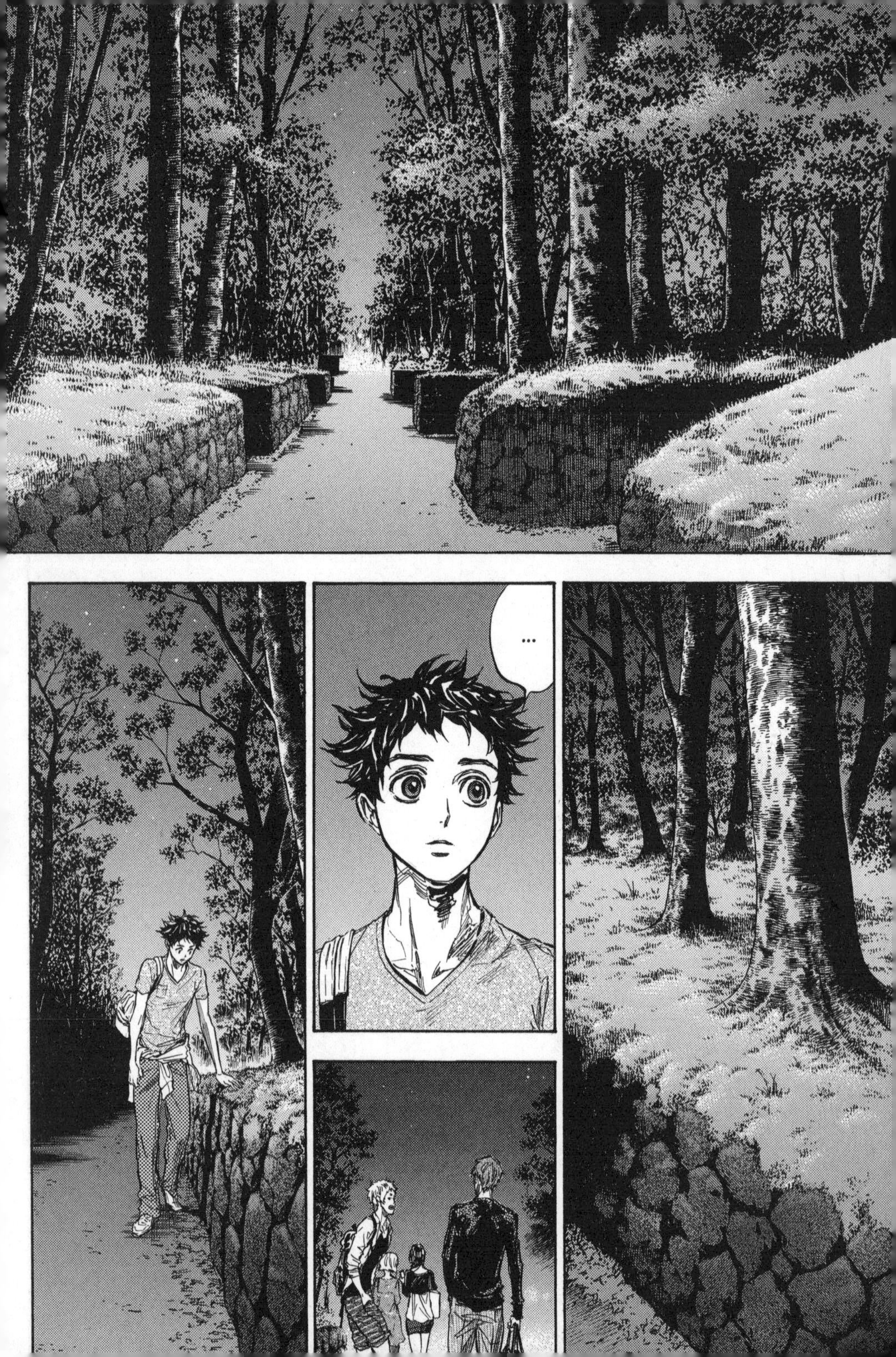
...

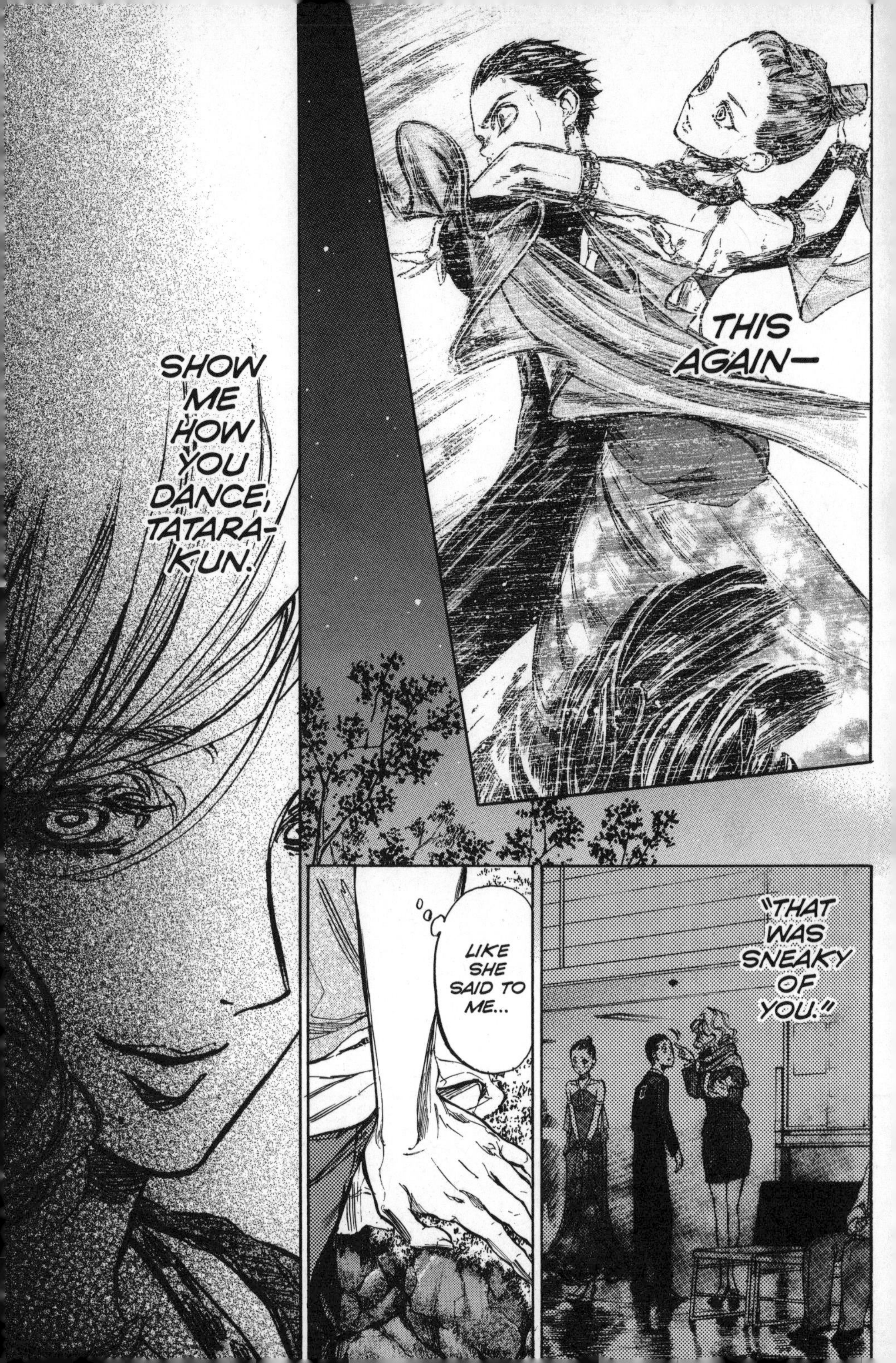
THIS AGAIN—
"THAT WAS SNEAKY OF YOU."
LIKE SHE SAID TO ME...
SHOW ME HOW YOU DANCE, TATARA-KUN.

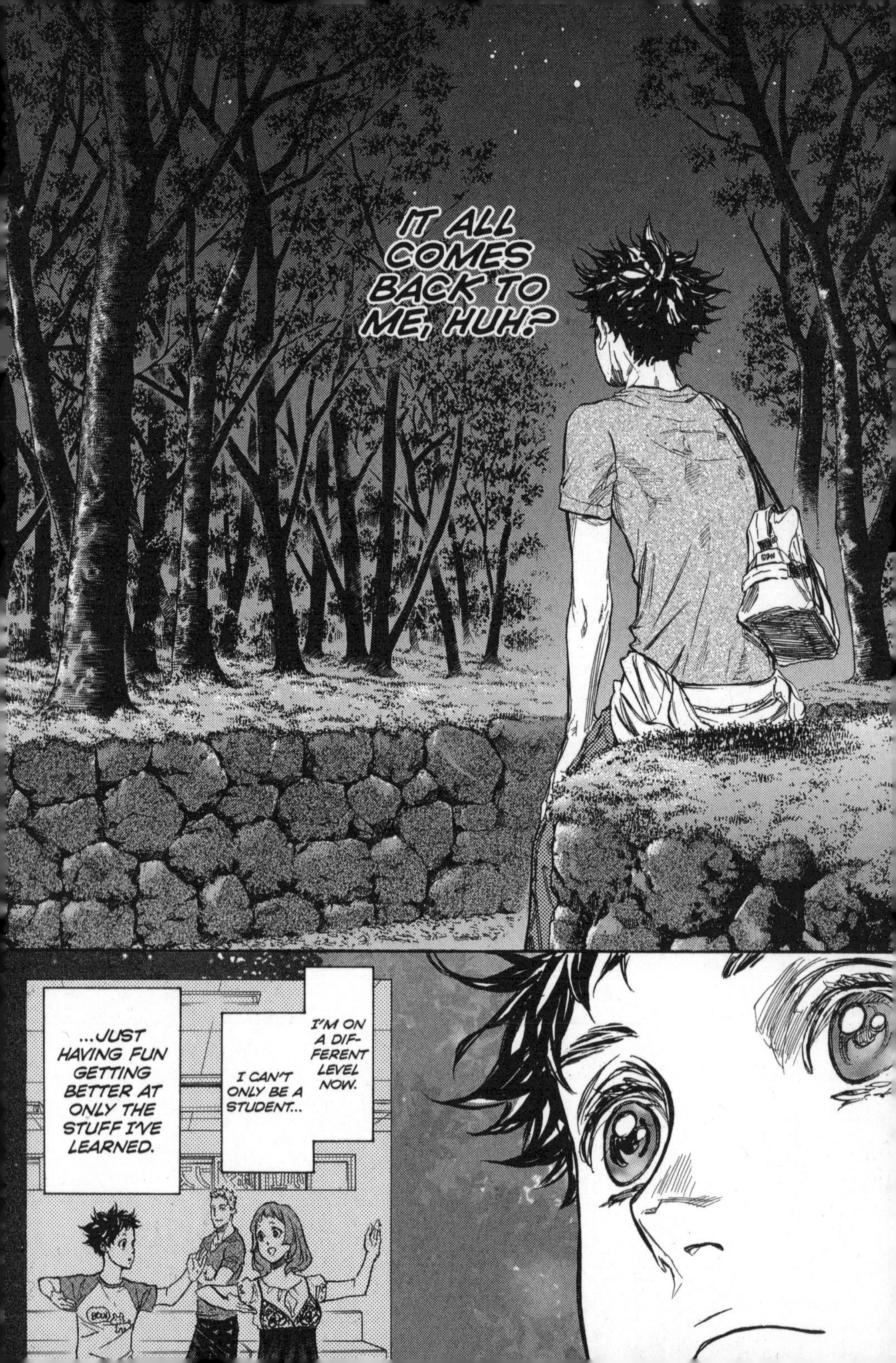
IT ALL COMES BACK TO ME, HUH?
I'M ON A DIF-FERENT LEVEL NOW.
I CAN'T ONLY BE A STUDENT...
...JUST HAVING FUN GETTING BETTER AT ONLY THE STUFF I'VE LEARNED.

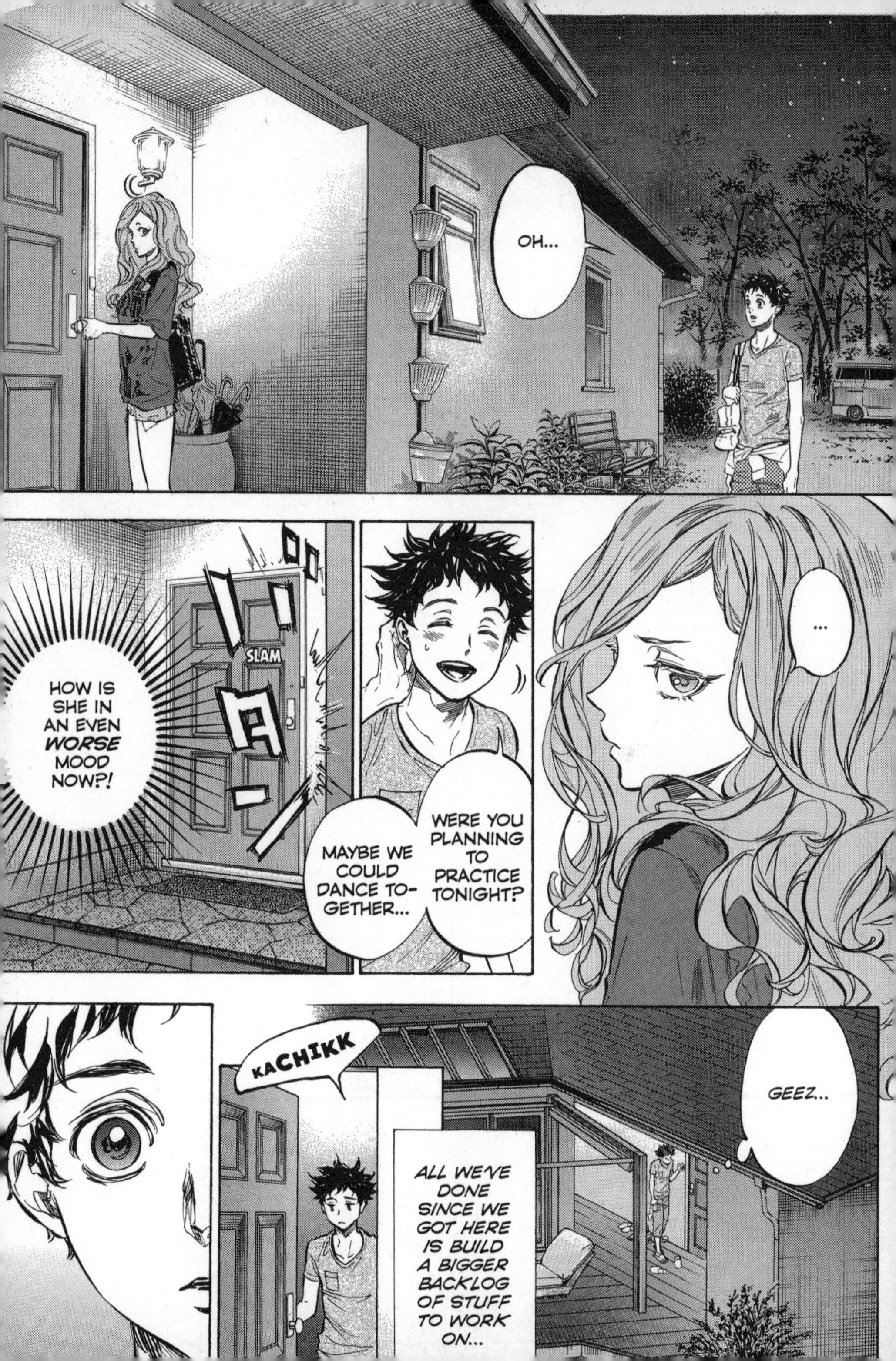
OH...
...
WERE YOU PLANNING TO PRACTICE TONIGHT?
MAYBE WE COULD DANCE TO-GETHER...
SLAM
HOW IS SHE IN AN EVEN WORSE MOOD NOW?!
GEEZ...
ALL WE'VE DONE SINCE WE GOT HERE IS BUILD A BIGGER BACKLOG OF STUFF TO WORK ON...
KACHIKK

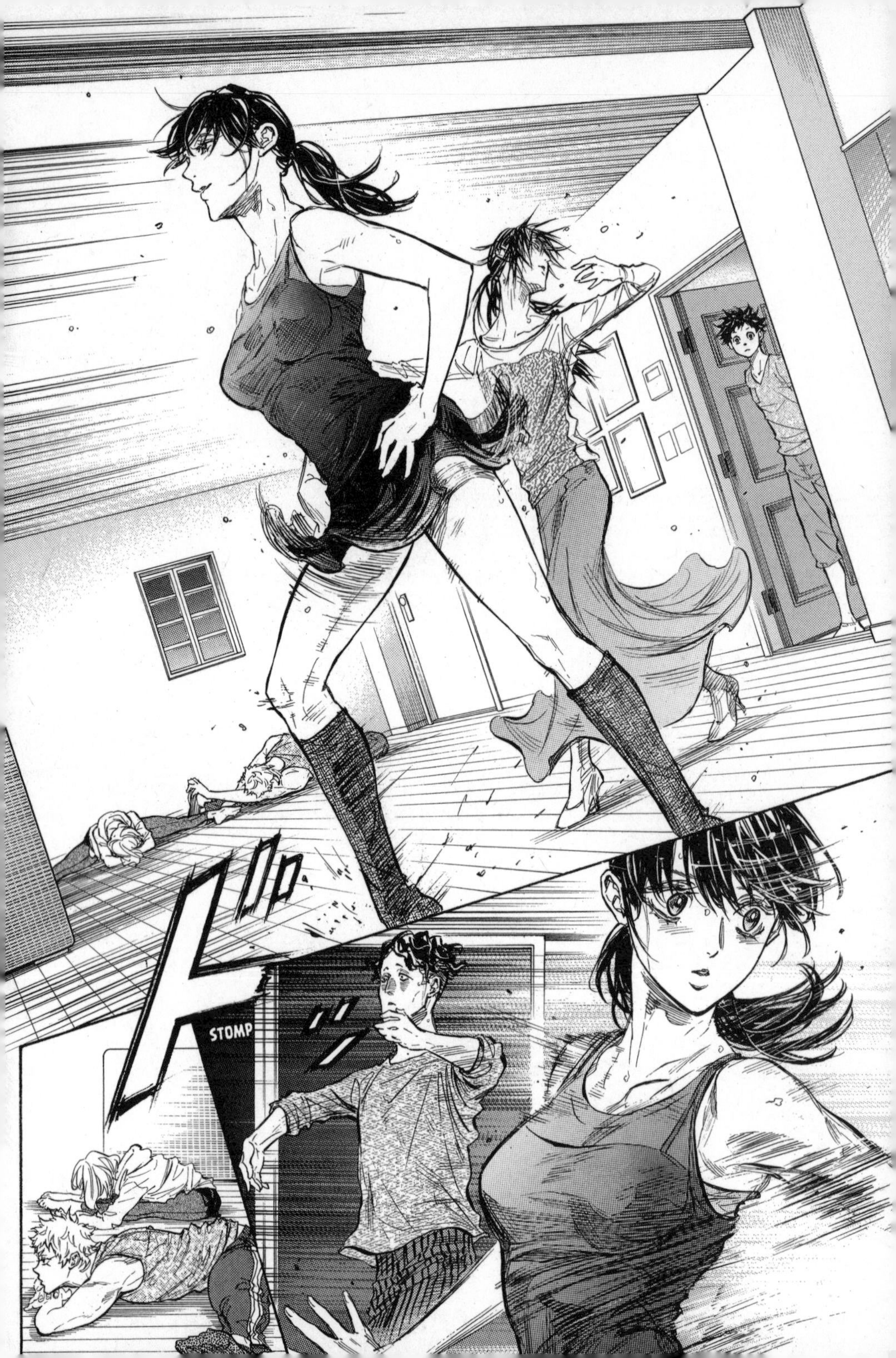
STOMP

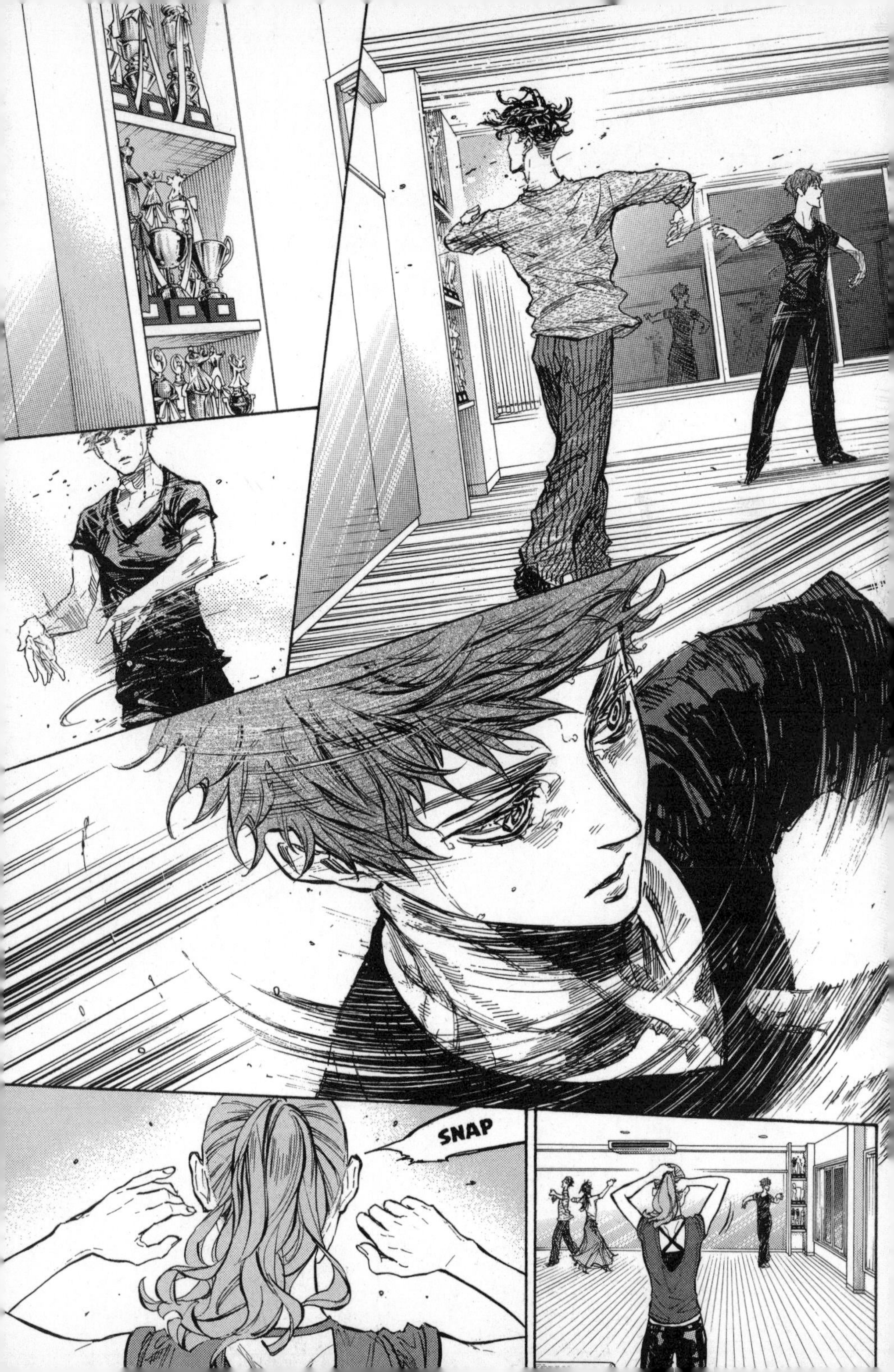
SNAP

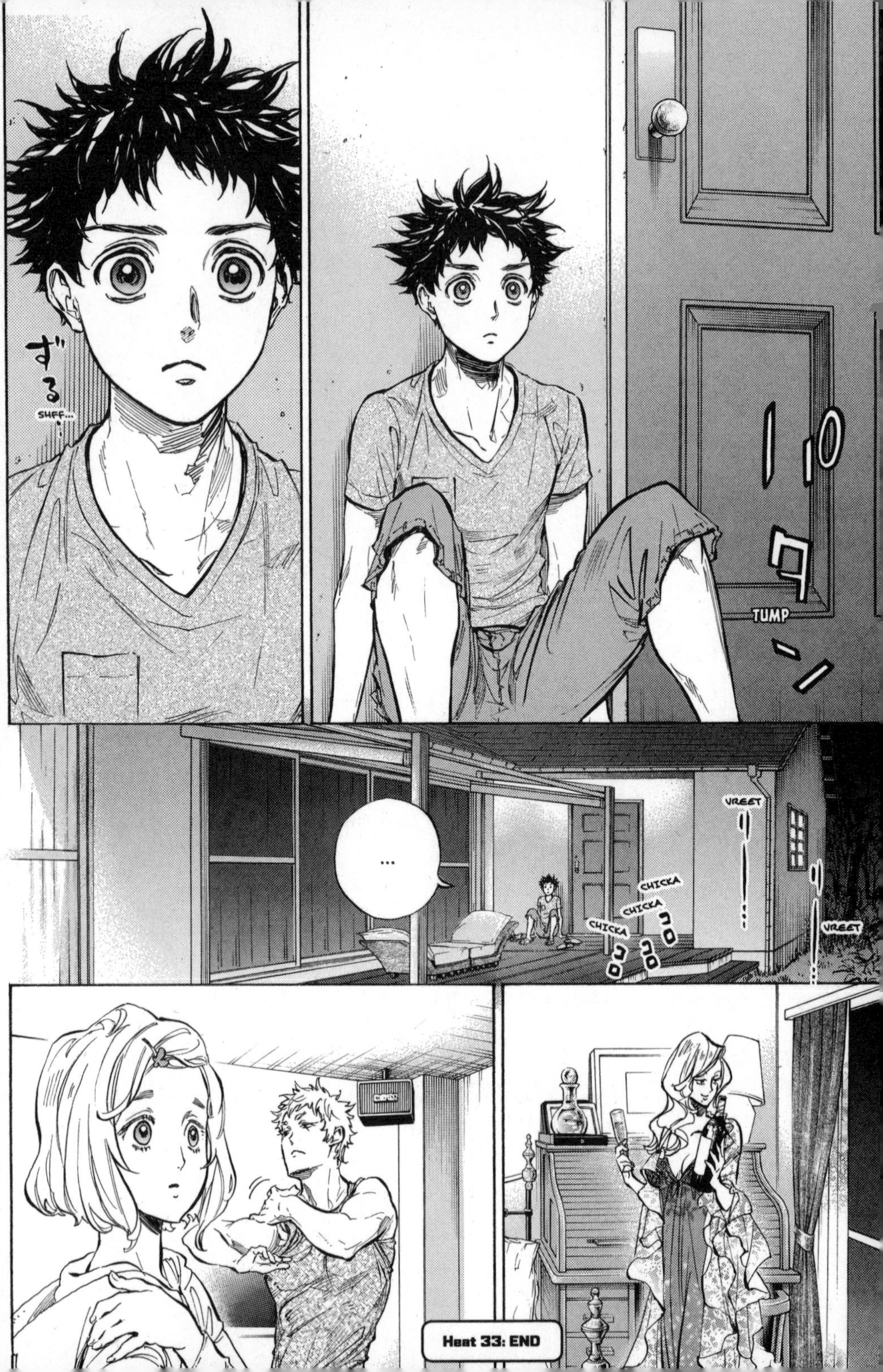
パタン
TUMP
ずる
SHFF...
VREET
VREET
CHICKA
CHICKA
CHICKA
コロ
コロ
コロ
...
Heat 33: END

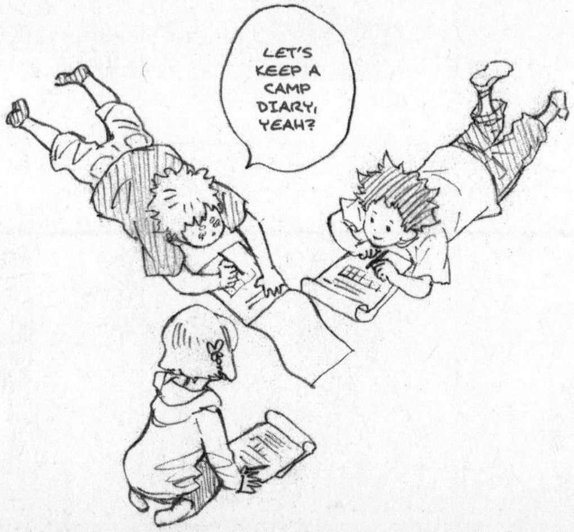
LET'S KEEP A CAMP DIARY, YEAH?

CAMP LOG

	DAY 1	DAY 2	DAY 3	DAY 4	DAY 5	DAY 6
8AM	GET UP					
	AM PRACTICE, JOGGING, STRETCHING					
	BREAKFAST					
	CLEAN					
10	WEEDING					
	LESSON W/ MARISA-SENSEI					
12PM	COUPLES PRACTICE					
2						
	LESSON W/ TEAM HYODO					
4						
	SHADOW					
6	PREP					
	DINNER					
	TIDY					
8	BREAK					
	BATH					
10	PM PRACTICE (SHADOW)					
	STRETCH W/ MUSIC					
12	ASLEEP					
IMPRESSIONS	THE BARBEQUE I HAD FOR LUNCH WAS REALLY GOOD. CAN'T COMMUNICATE WITH MY PARTNER. HYODO-KUN & HANAOKA-SAN TAUGHT US LOTS OF VERY DIFFICULT THINGS.					

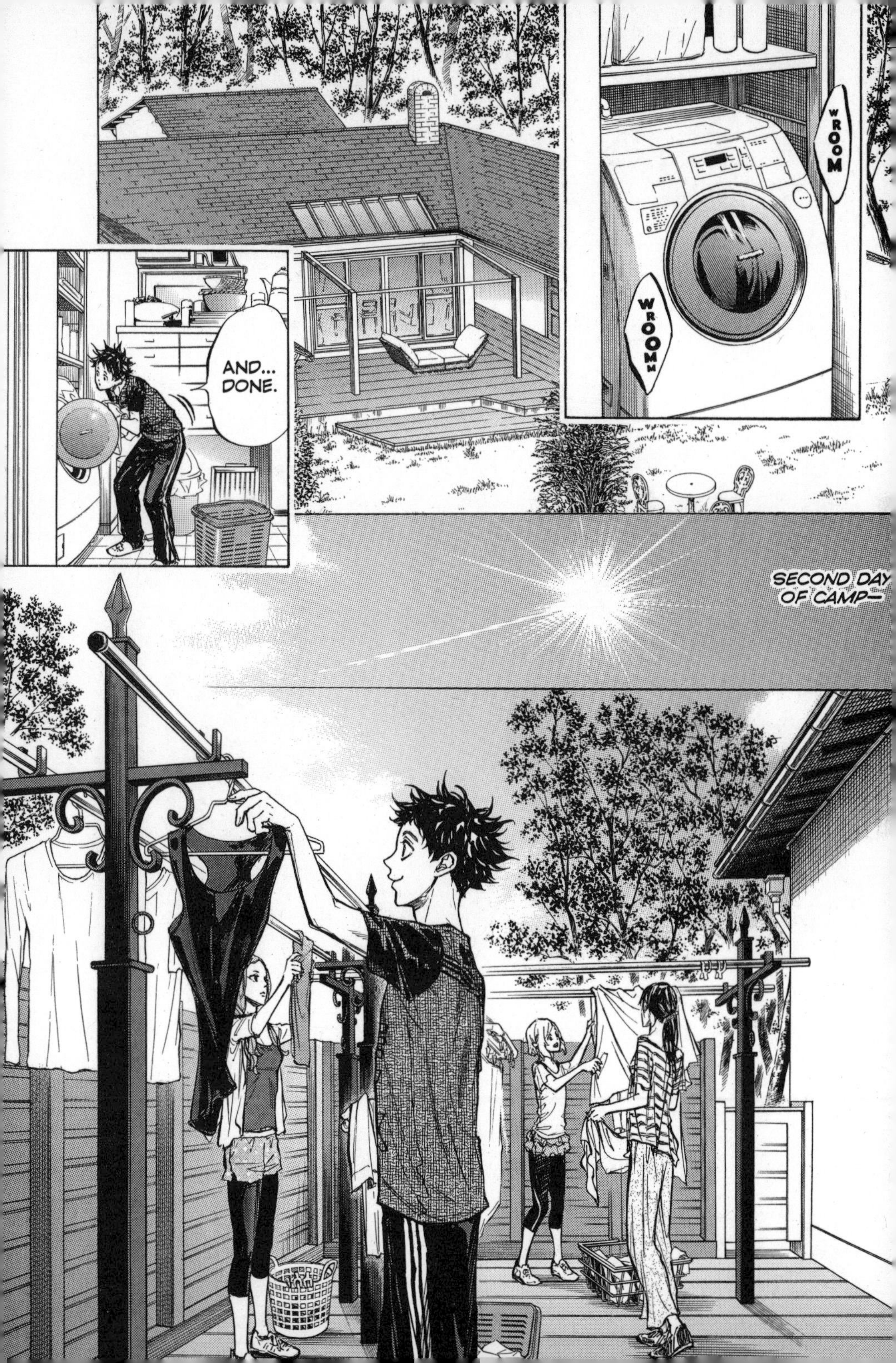
WROOM
WROOMM
AND... DONE.
SECOND DAY OF CAMP—

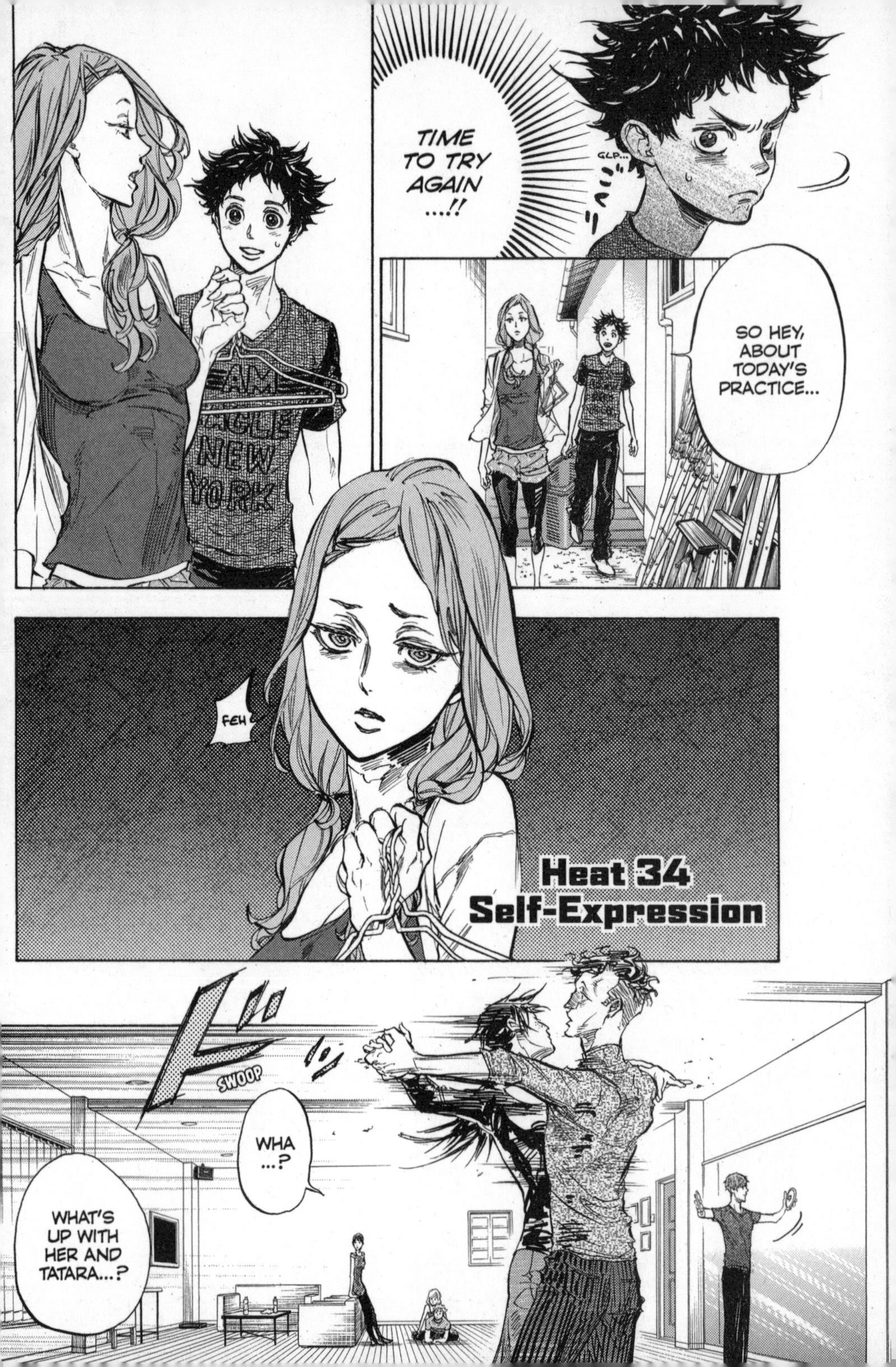
GLP...
TIME TO TRY AGAIN ...!!
SO HEY, ABOUT TODAY'S PRACTICE...
FEH
Heat 34
Self-Expression
SWOOP
WHA ...?
WHAT'S UP WITH HER AND TATARA...?

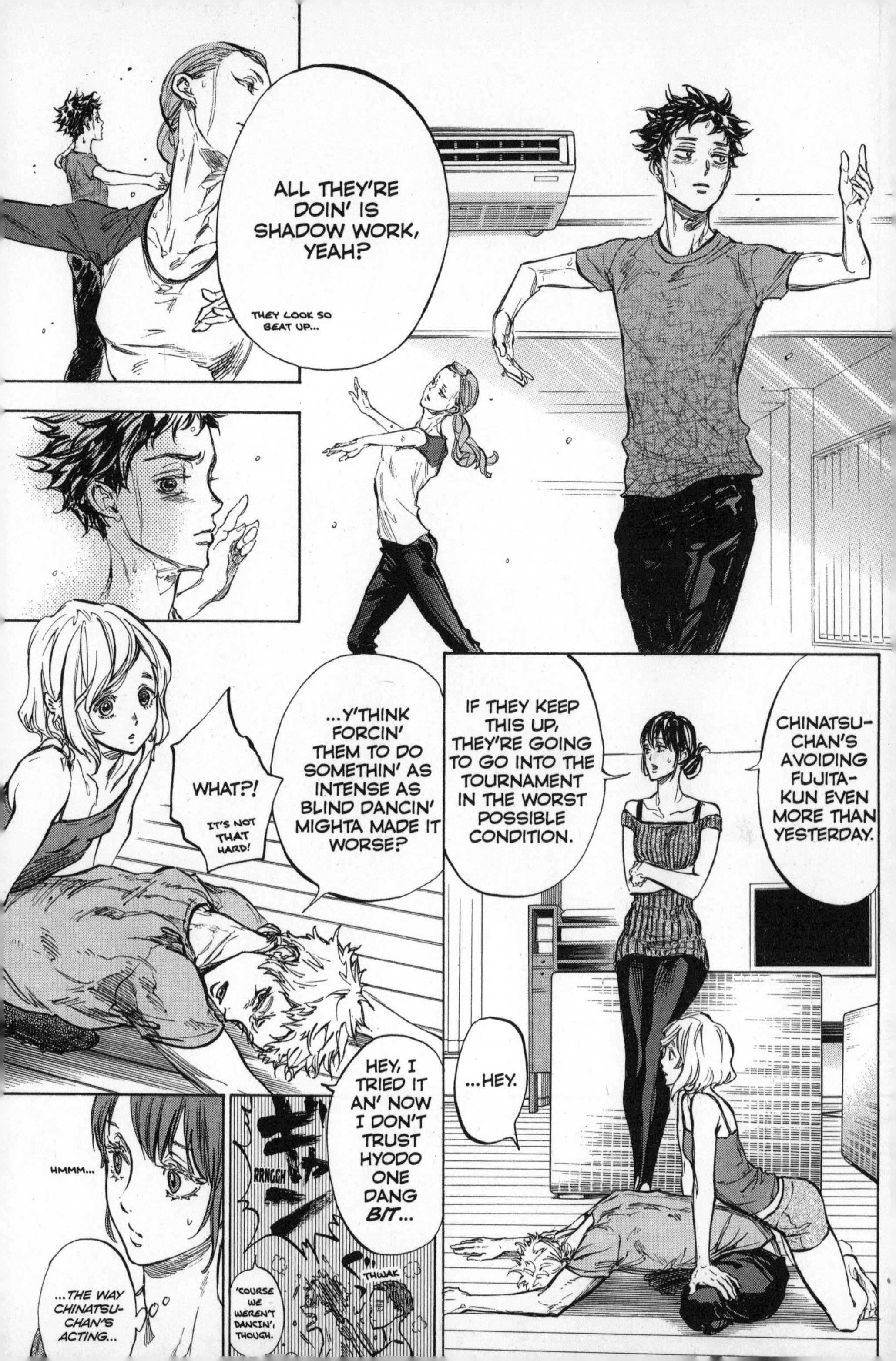
ALL THEY'RE DOIN' IS SHADOW WORK, YEAH?
THEY LOOK SO BEAT UP...
CHINATSU-CHAN'S AVOIDING FUJITA-KUN EVEN MORE THAN YESTERDAY.
IF THEY KEEP THIS UP, THEY'RE GOING TO GO INTO THE TOURNAMENT IN THE WORST POSSIBLE CONDITION.
...HEY.
...Y'THINK FORCIN' THEM TO DO SOMETHIN' AS INTENSE AS BLIND DANCIN' MIGHTA MADE IT WORSE?
WHAT?!
IT'S NOT THAT HARD!
HEY, I TRIED IT AN' NOW I DON'T TRUST HYODO ONE DANG *BIT*...
RRNGGH
THWAK
'COURSE WE WEREN'T DANCIN', THOUGH.
HMMM...
...THE WAY CHINATSU-CHAN'S ACTING...

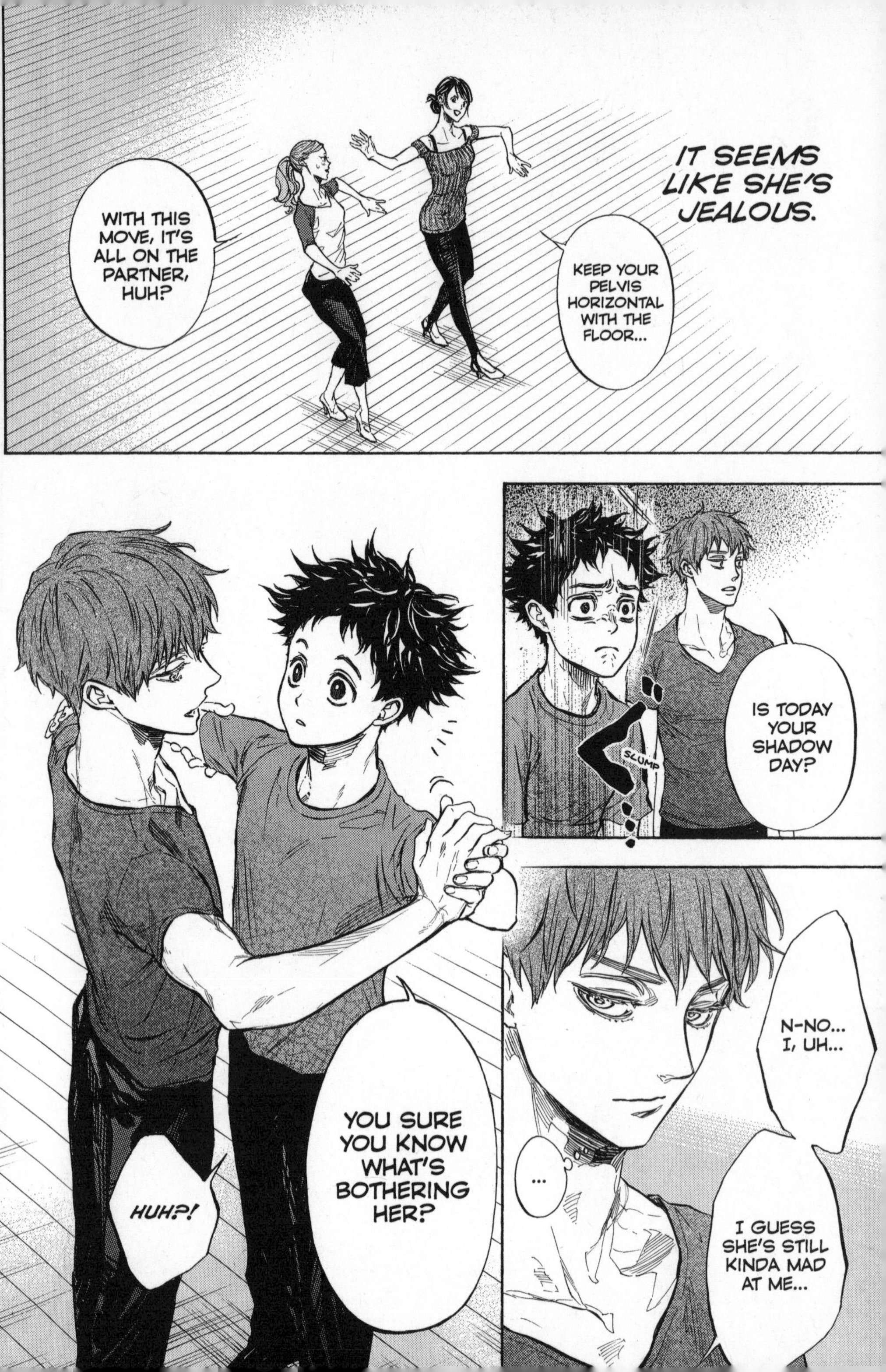
IT SEEMS LIKE SHE'S JEALOUS.
KEEP YOUR PELVIS HORIZONTAL WITH THE FLOOR...
WITH THIS MOVE, IT'S ALL ON THE PARTNER, HUH?
IS TODAY YOUR SHADOW DAY?
SLUMP
N-NO... I, UH...
I GUESS SHE'S STILL KINDA MAD AT ME...
...
YOU SURE YOU KNOW WHAT'S BOTHERING HER?
HUH?!

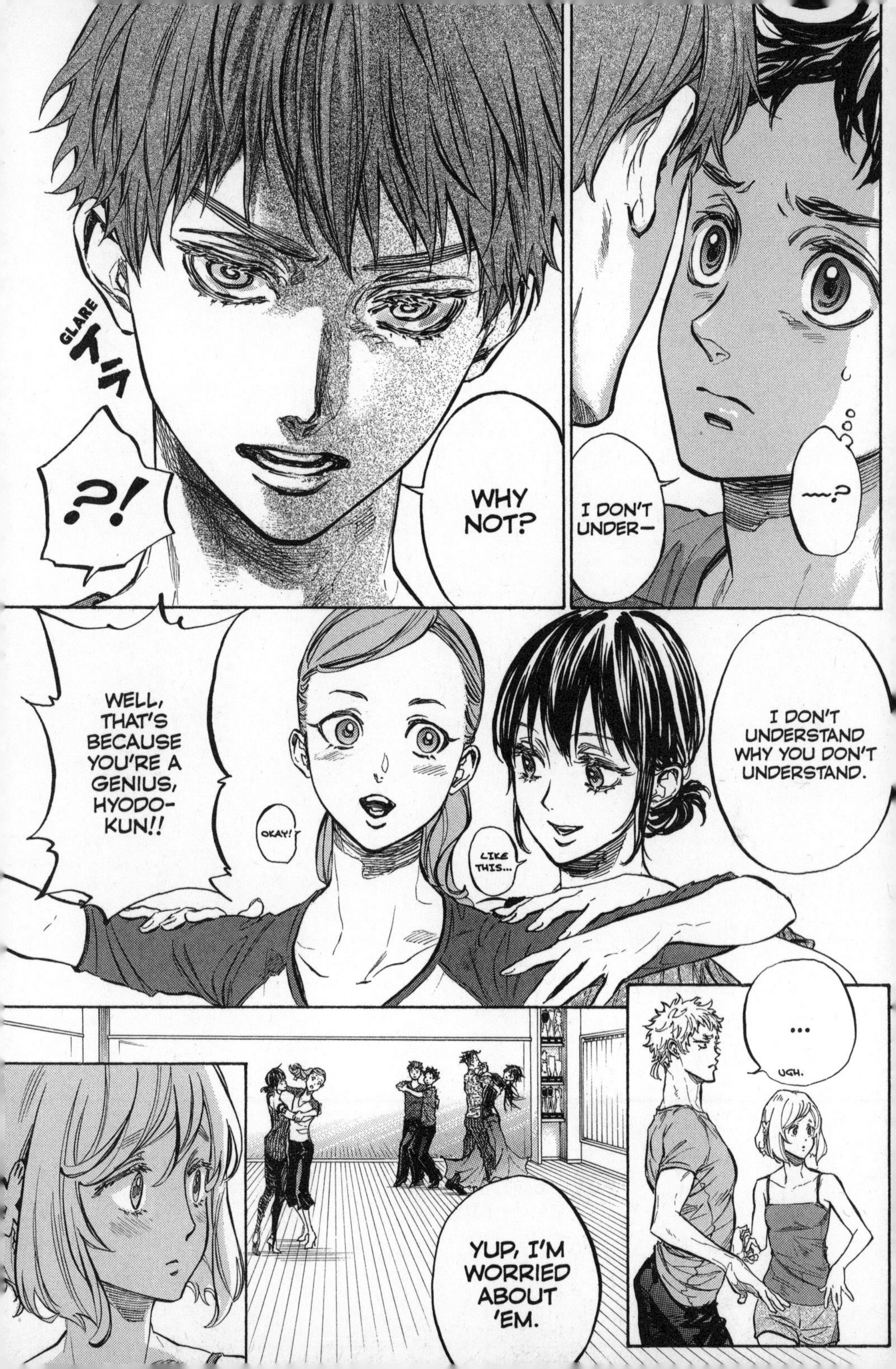
—?
I DON'T UNDER—
WHY NOT?
?!
GLARE イラ
I DON'T UNDERSTAND WHY YOU DON'T UNDERSTAND.
LIKE THIS...
OKAY!
WELL, THAT'S BECAUSE YOU'RE A GENIUS, HYODO-KUN!!
...
UGH.
YUP, I'M WORRIED ABOUT 'EM.

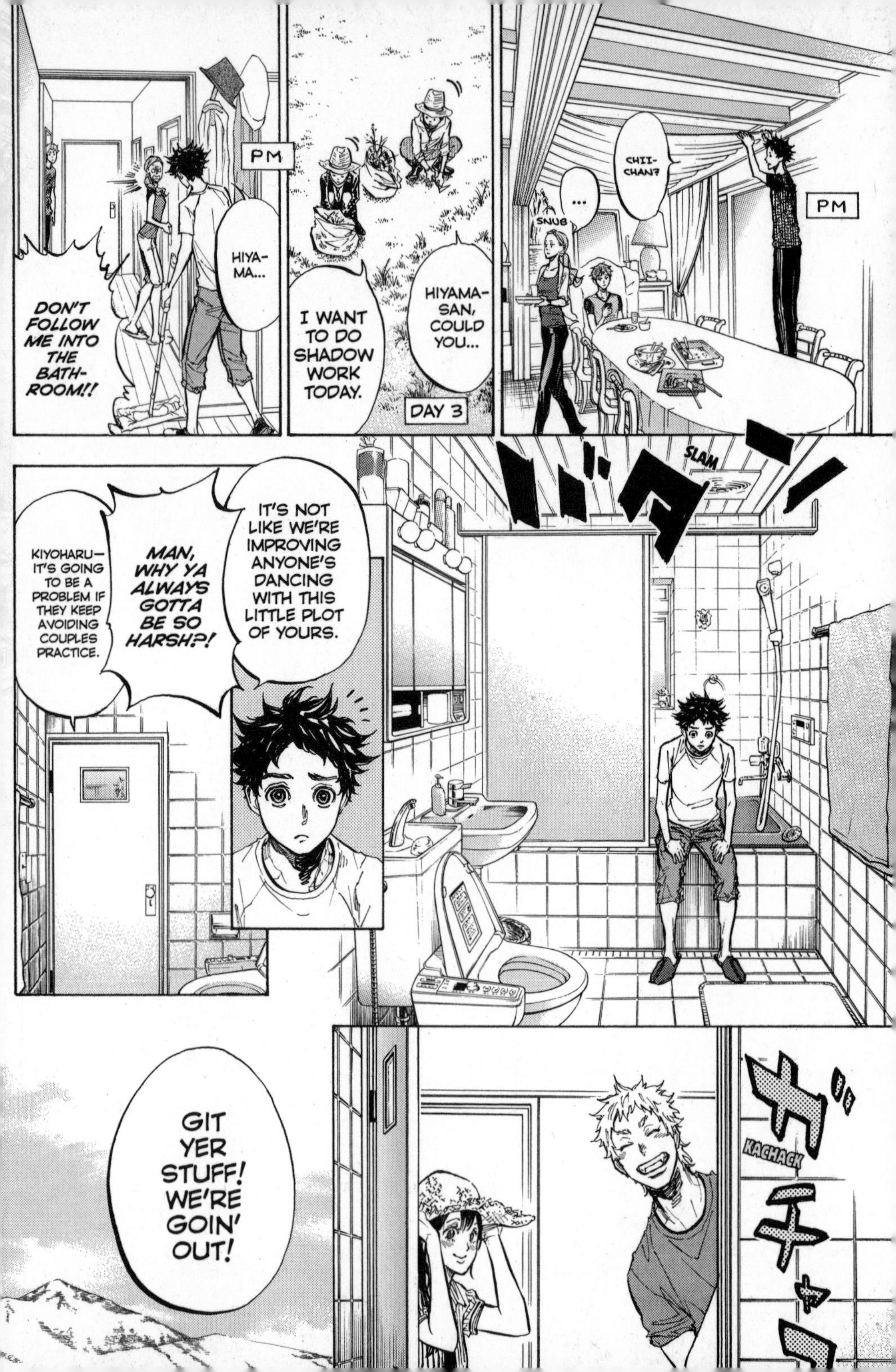
CHII-CHAN?
PM
...
SNUB
HIYAMA-SAN, COULD YOU...
I WANT TO DO SHADOW WORK TODAY.
DAY 3
PM
HIYAMA...
DON'T FOLLOW ME INTO THE BATH-ROOM!!
SLAM
IT'S NOT LIKE WE'RE IMPROVING ANYONE'S DANCING WITH THIS LITTLE PLOT OF YOURS.
MAN, WHY YA ALWAYS GOTTA BE SO HARSH?!
KIYOHARU— IT'S GOING TO BE A PROBLEM IF THEY KEEP AVOIDING COUPLES PRACTICE.
KACHACK
GIT YER STUFF! WE'RE GOIN' OUT!

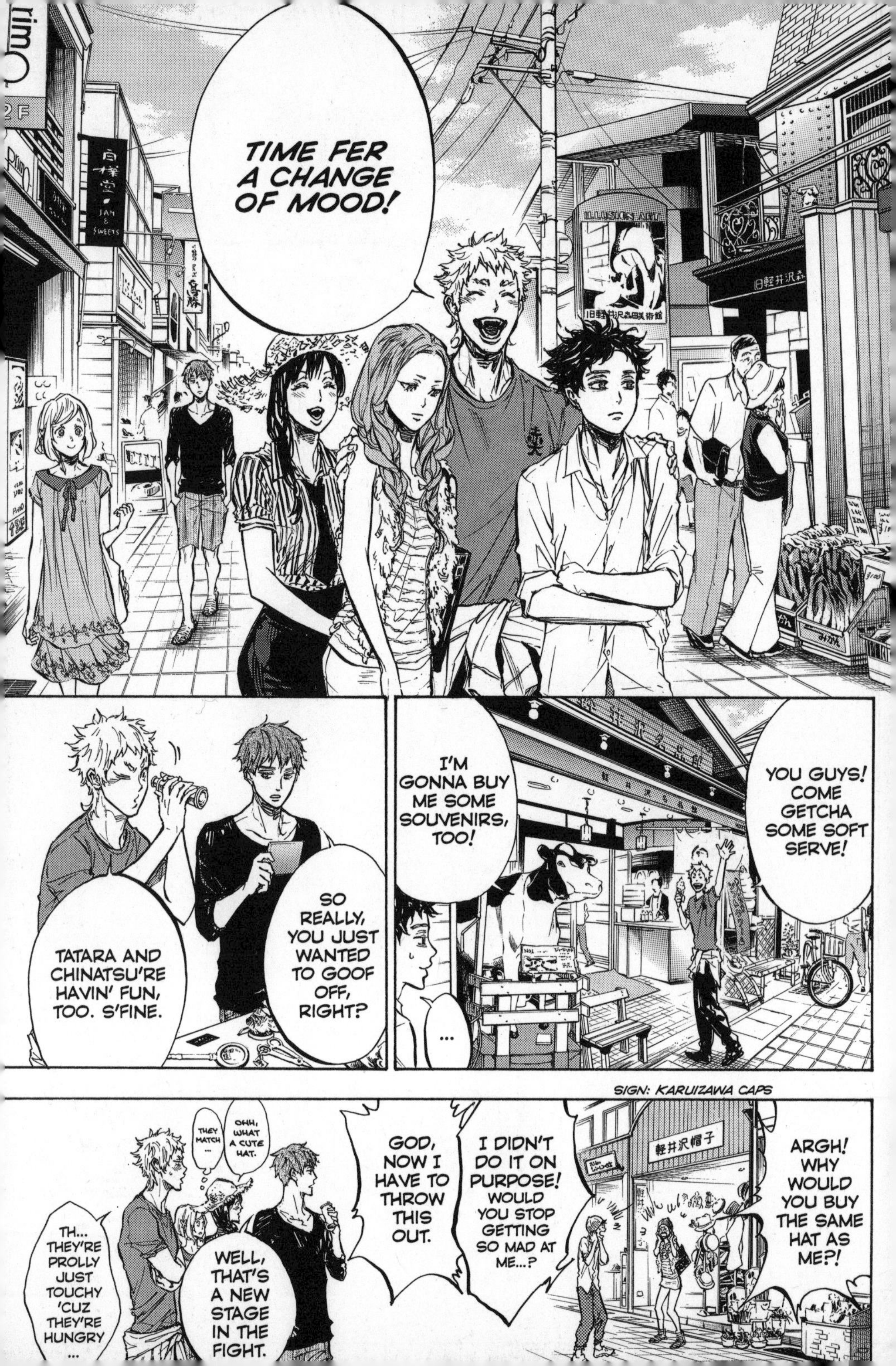
TIME FER A CHANGE OF MOOD!
YOU GUYS! COME GETCHA SOME SOFT SERVE!
I'M GONNA BUY ME SOME SOUVENIRS, TOO!
...
SO REALLY, YOU JUST WANTED TO GOOF OFF, RIGHT?
TATARA AND CHINATSU'RE HAVIN' FUN, TOO. S'FINE.
SIGN: KARUIZAWA CAPS
軽井沢帽子
ARGH! WHY WOULD YOU BUY THE SAME HAT AS ME?!
I DIDN'T DO IT ON PURPOSE! WOULD YOU STOP GETTING SO MAD AT ME...?
GOD, NOW I HAVE TO THROW THIS OUT.
OHH, WHAT A CUTE HAT.
THEY MATCH ...
WELL, THAT'S A NEW STAGE IN THE FIGHT.
TH... THEY'RE PROLLY JUST TOUCHY 'CUZ THEY'RE HUNGRY ...

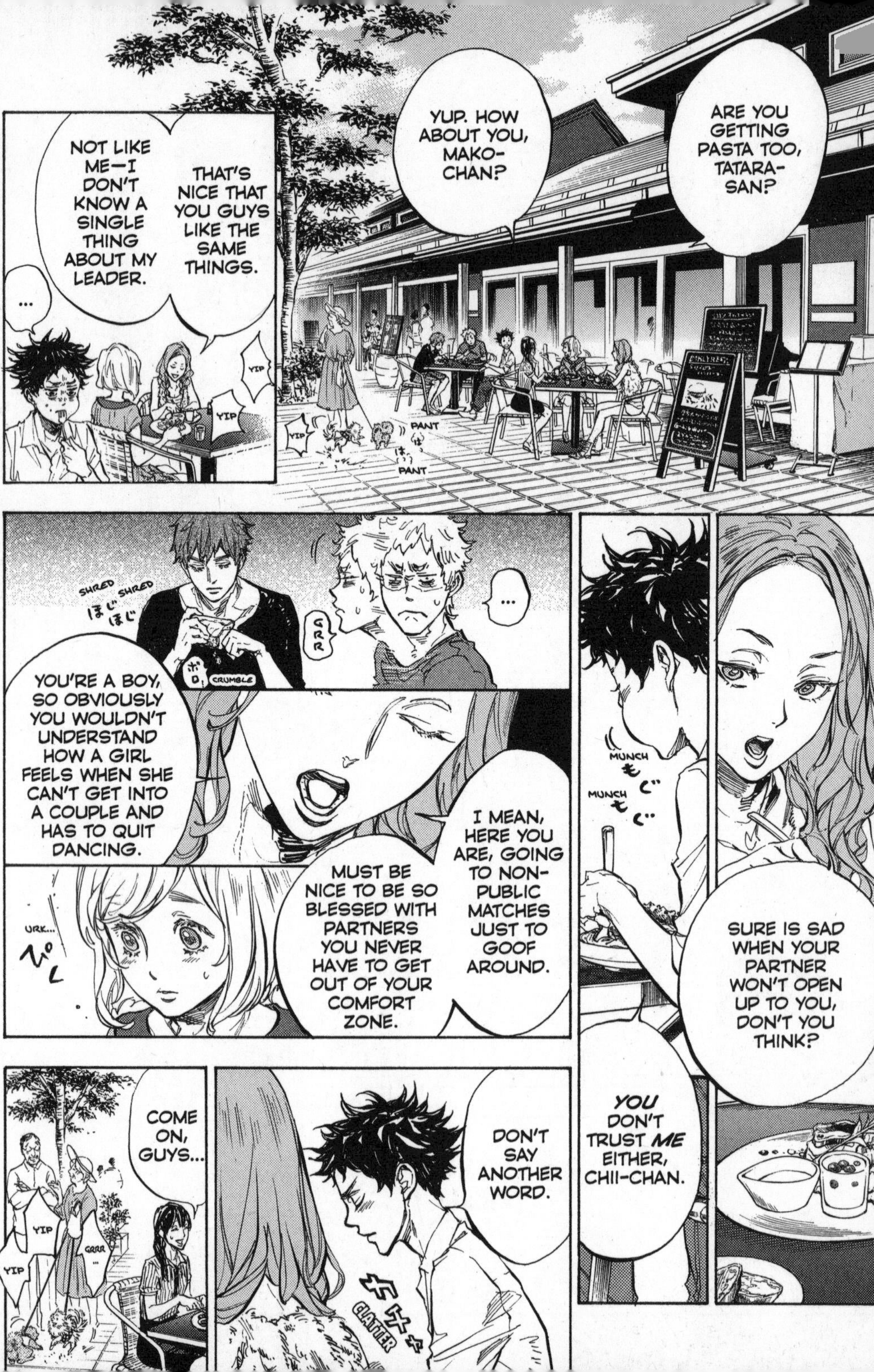
ARE YOU GETTING PASTA TOO, TATARA-SAN?
YUP. HOW ABOUT YOU, MAKO-CHAN?
YIP
YIP
PANT
PANT
THAT'S NICE THAT YOU GUYS LIKE THE SAME THINGS.
NOT LIKE ME—I DON'T KNOW A SINGLE THING ABOUT MY LEADER.
...
YIP
YIP
SURE IS SAD WHEN YOUR PARTNER WON'T OPEN UP TO YOU, DON'T YOU THINK?
MUNCH
MUNCH
YOU DON'T TRUST ME EITHER, CHII-CHAN.
...
GRR
SHRED SHRED
CRUMBLE
YOU'RE A BOY, SO OBVIOUSLY YOU WOULDN'T UNDERSTAND HOW A GIRL FEELS WHEN SHE CAN'T GET INTO A COUPLE AND HAS TO QUIT DANCING.
I MEAN, HERE YOU ARE, GOING TO NON-PUBLIC MATCHES JUST TO GOOF AROUND.
MUST BE NICE TO BE SO BLESSED WITH PARTNERS YOU NEVER HAVE TO GET OUT OF YOUR COMFORT ZONE.
URK...
DON'T SAY ANOTHER WORD.
CLATTER
COME ON, GUYS...
GRRR...
YIP
YIP

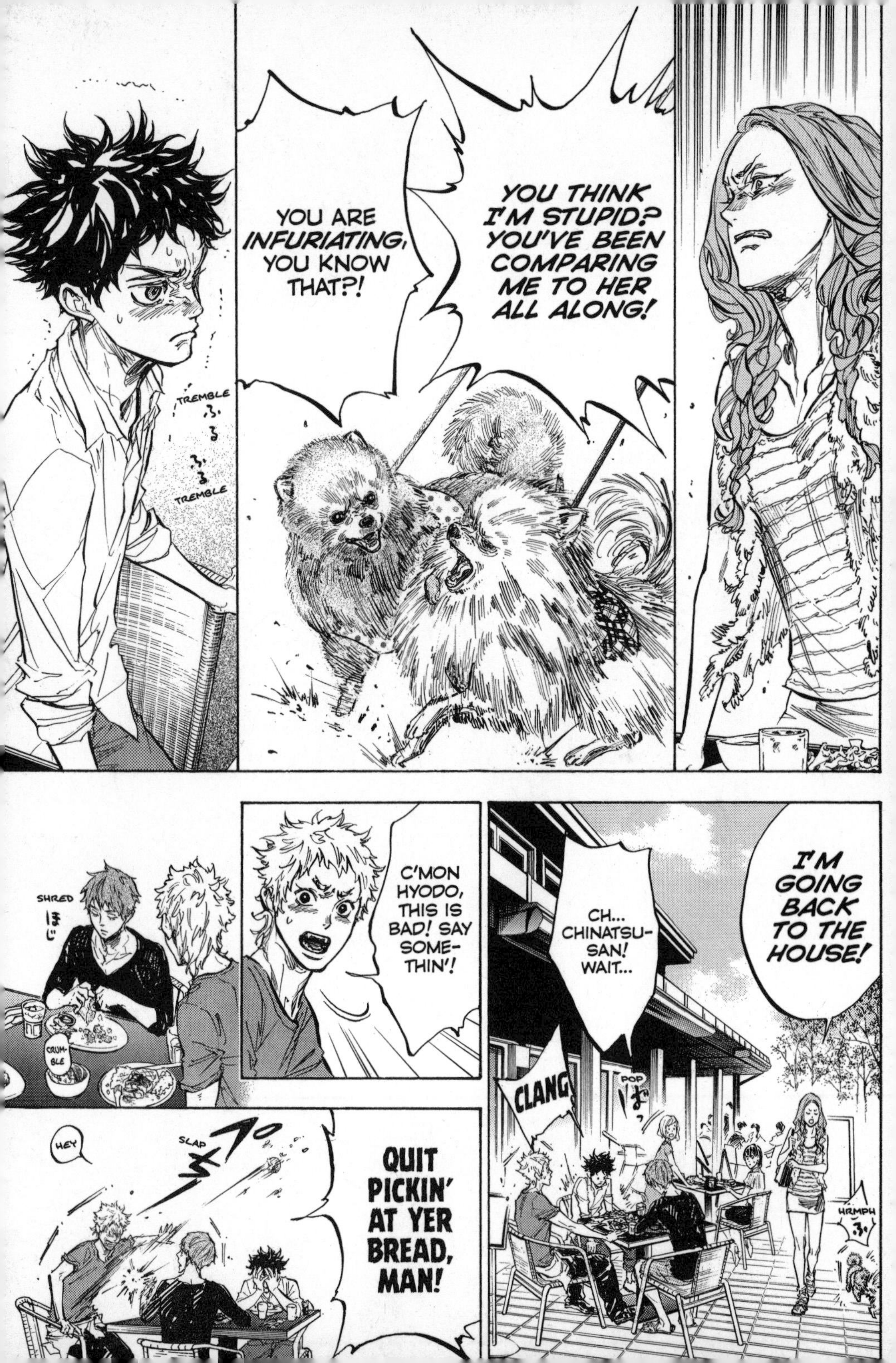
YOU THINK I'M STUPID? YOU'VE BEEN COMPARING ME TO HER ALL ALONG!
YOU ARE INFURIATING, YOU KNOW THAT?!
TREMBLE
TREMBLE
I'M GOING BACK TO THE HOUSE!
CH... CHINATSU-SAN! WAIT...
CLANG
POP
HRMPH
C'MON HYODO, THIS IS BAD! SAY SOME-THIN'!
SHRED
CRUM-BLE
QUIT PICKIN' AT YER BREAD, MAN!
SLAP
HEY

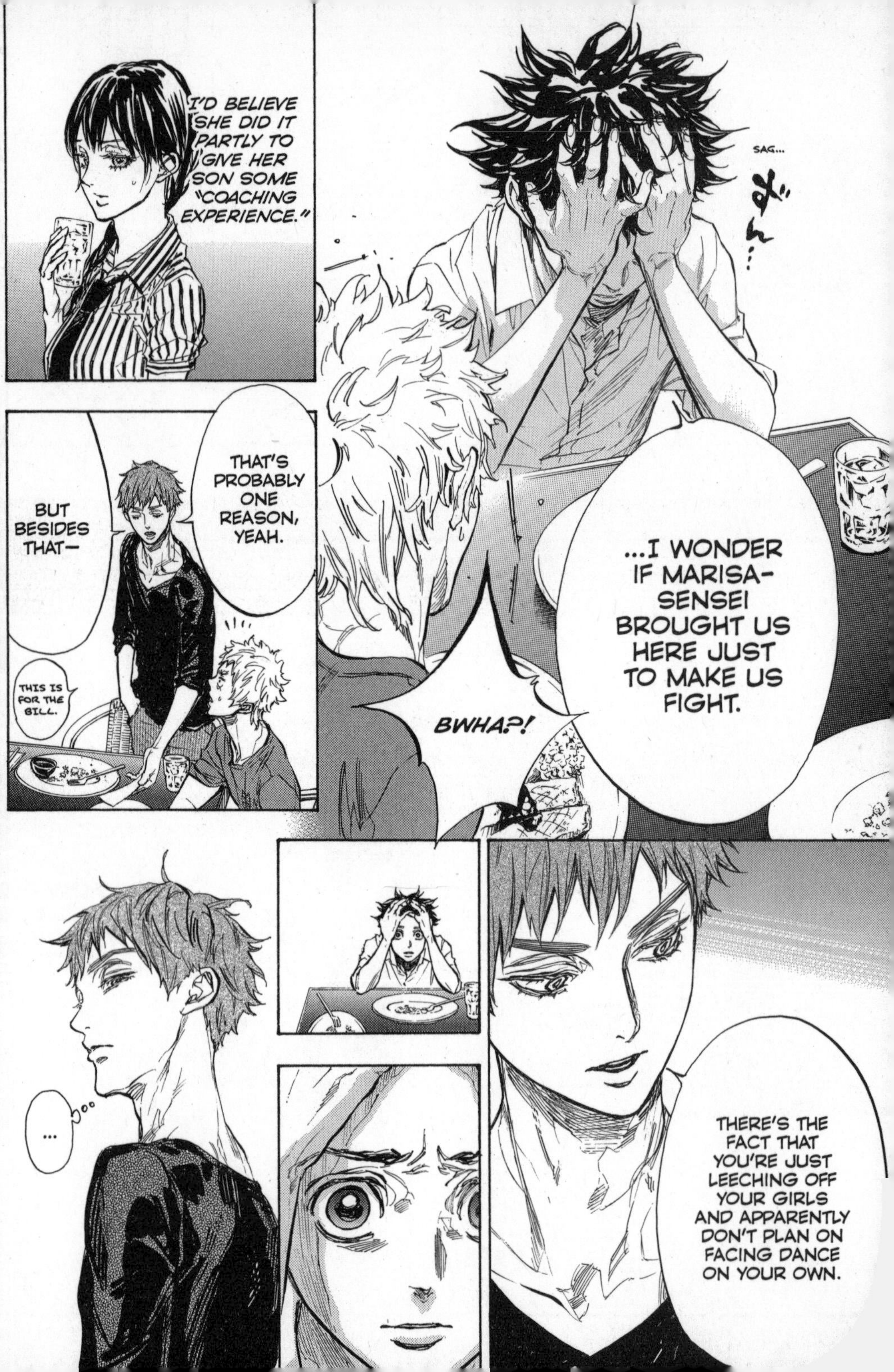
SAG...
ずん…
...I WONDER IF MARISA-SENSEI BROUGHT US HERE JUST TO MAKE US FIGHT.
BWHA?!
I'D BELIEVE SHE DID IT PARTLY TO GIVE HER SON SOME "COACHING EXPERIENCE."
THAT'S PROBABLY ONE REASON, YEAH.
BUT BESIDES THAT—
THIS IS FOR THE BILL.
THERE'S THE FACT THAT YOU'RE JUST LEECHING OFF YOUR GIRLS AND APPARENTLY DON'T PLAN ON FACING DANCE ON YOUR OWN.
...

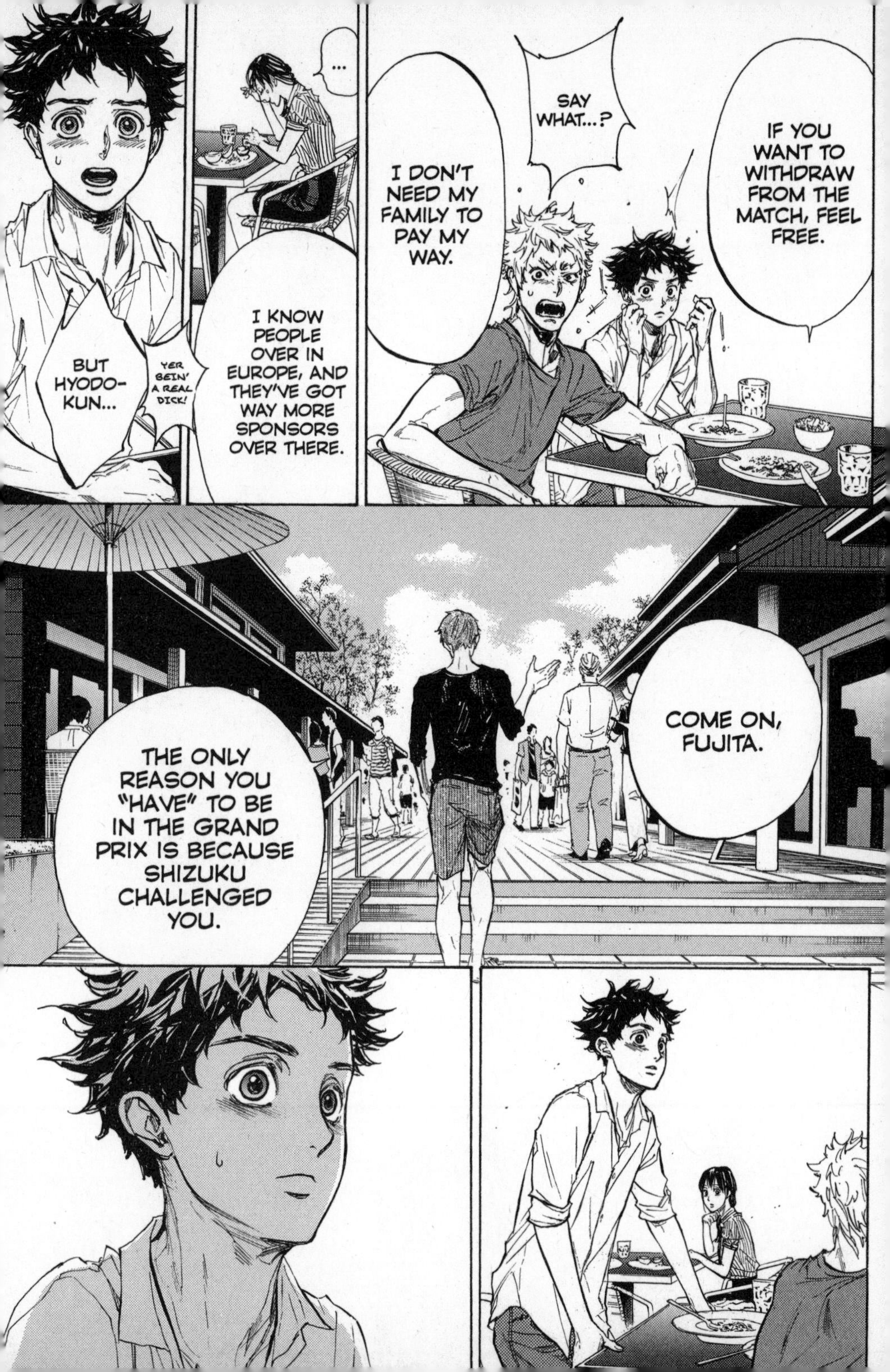
IF YOU WANT TO WITHDRAW FROM THE MATCH, FEEL FREE.
SAY WHAT...?
I DON'T NEED MY FAMILY TO PAY MY WAY.
...
I KNOW PEOPLE OVER IN EUROPE, AND THEY'VE GOT WAY MORE SPONSORS OVER THERE.
YER BEIN' A REAL DICK!
BUT HYODO-KUN...
COME ON, FUJITA.
THE ONLY REASON YOU "HAVE" TO BE IN THE GRAND PRIX IS BECAUSE SHIZUKU CHALLENGED YOU.

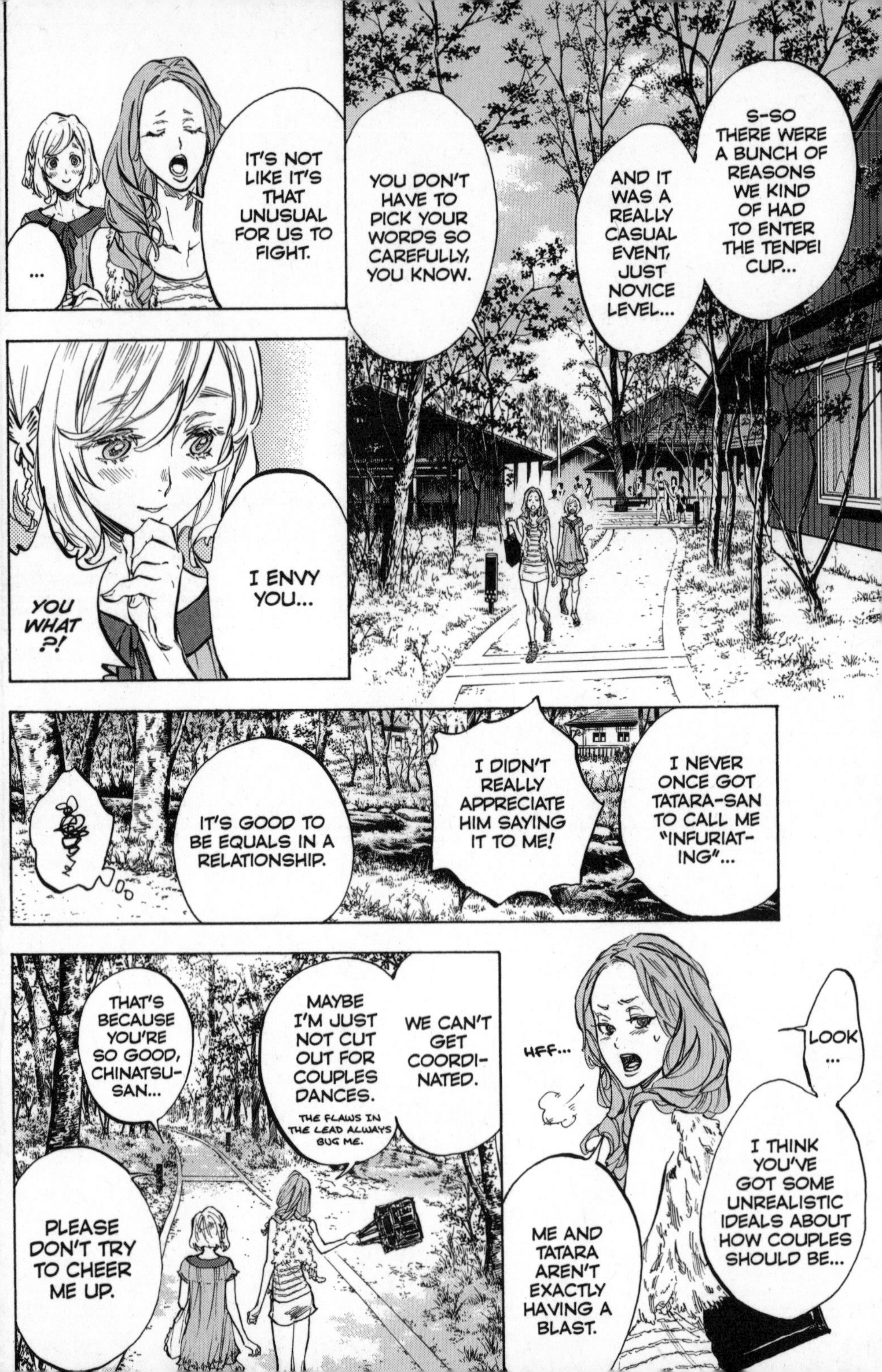
S-SO THERE WERE A BUNCH OF REASONS WE KIND OF HAD TO ENTER THE TENPEI CUP...
AND IT WAS A REALLY CASUAL EVENT, JUST NOVICE LEVEL...
YOU DON'T HAVE TO PICK YOUR WORDS SO CAREFULLY, YOU KNOW.
IT'S NOT LIKE IT'S THAT UNUSUAL FOR US TO FIGHT.
...
I ENVY YOU...
YOU WHAT ?!
I NEVER ONCE GOT TATARA-SAN TO CALL ME "INFURIAT-ING"...
I DIDN'T REALLY APPRECIATE HIM SAYING IT TO ME!
IT'S GOOD TO BE EQUALS IN A RELATIONSHIP.
LOOK...
I THINK YOU'VE GOT SOME UNREALISTIC IDEALS ABOUT HOW COUPLES SHOULD BE...
HFF...
ME AND TATARA AREN'T EXACTLY HAVING A BLAST.
WE CAN'T GET COORDI-NATED.
MAYBE I'M JUST NOT CUT OUT FOR COUPLES DANCES.
THE FLAWS IN THE LEAD ALWAYS BUG ME.
THAT'S BECAUSE YOU'RE SO GOOD, CHINATSU-SAN...
PLEASE DON'T TRY TO CHEER ME UP.

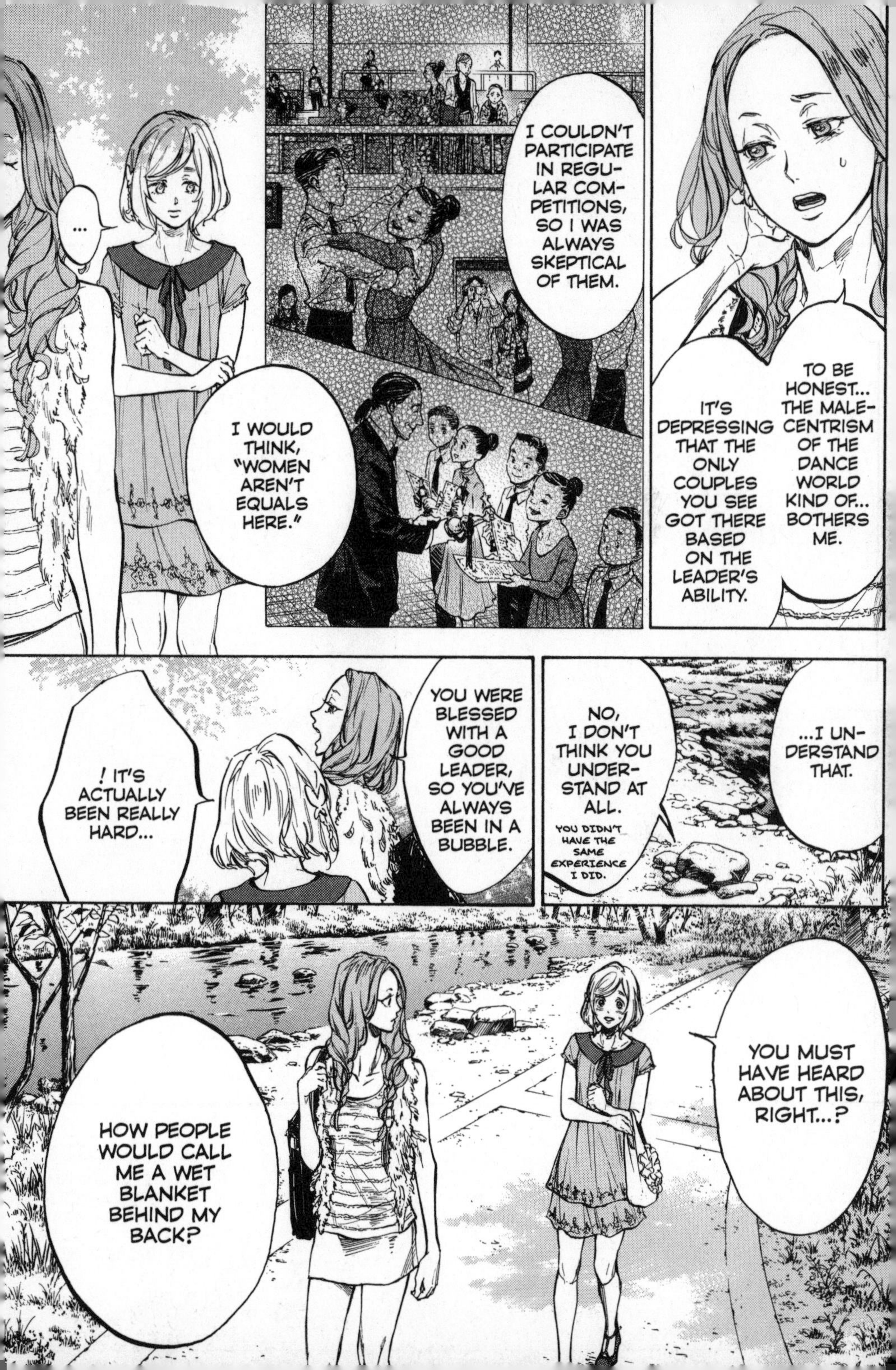
TO BE HONEST... THE MALE-CENTRISM OF THE DANCE WORLD KIND OF... BOTHERS ME.
IT'S DEPRESSING THAT THE ONLY COUPLES YOU SEE GOT THERE BASED ON THE LEADER'S ABILITY.
I COULDN'T PARTICIPATE IN REGULAR COMPETITIONS, SO I WAS ALWAYS SKEPTICAL OF THEM.
I WOULD THINK, "WOMEN AREN'T EQUALS HERE."
...
...I UNDERSTAND THAT.
NO, I DON'T THINK YOU UNDERSTAND AT ALL.
YOU DIDN'T HAVE THE SAME EXPERIENCE I DID.
YOU WERE BLESSED WITH A GOOD LEADER, SO YOU'VE ALWAYS BEEN IN A BUBBLE.
! IT'S ACTUALLY BEEN REALLY HARD...
YOU MUST HAVE HEARD ABOUT THIS, RIGHT...?
HOW PEOPLE WOULD CALL ME A WET BLANKET BEHIND MY BACK?

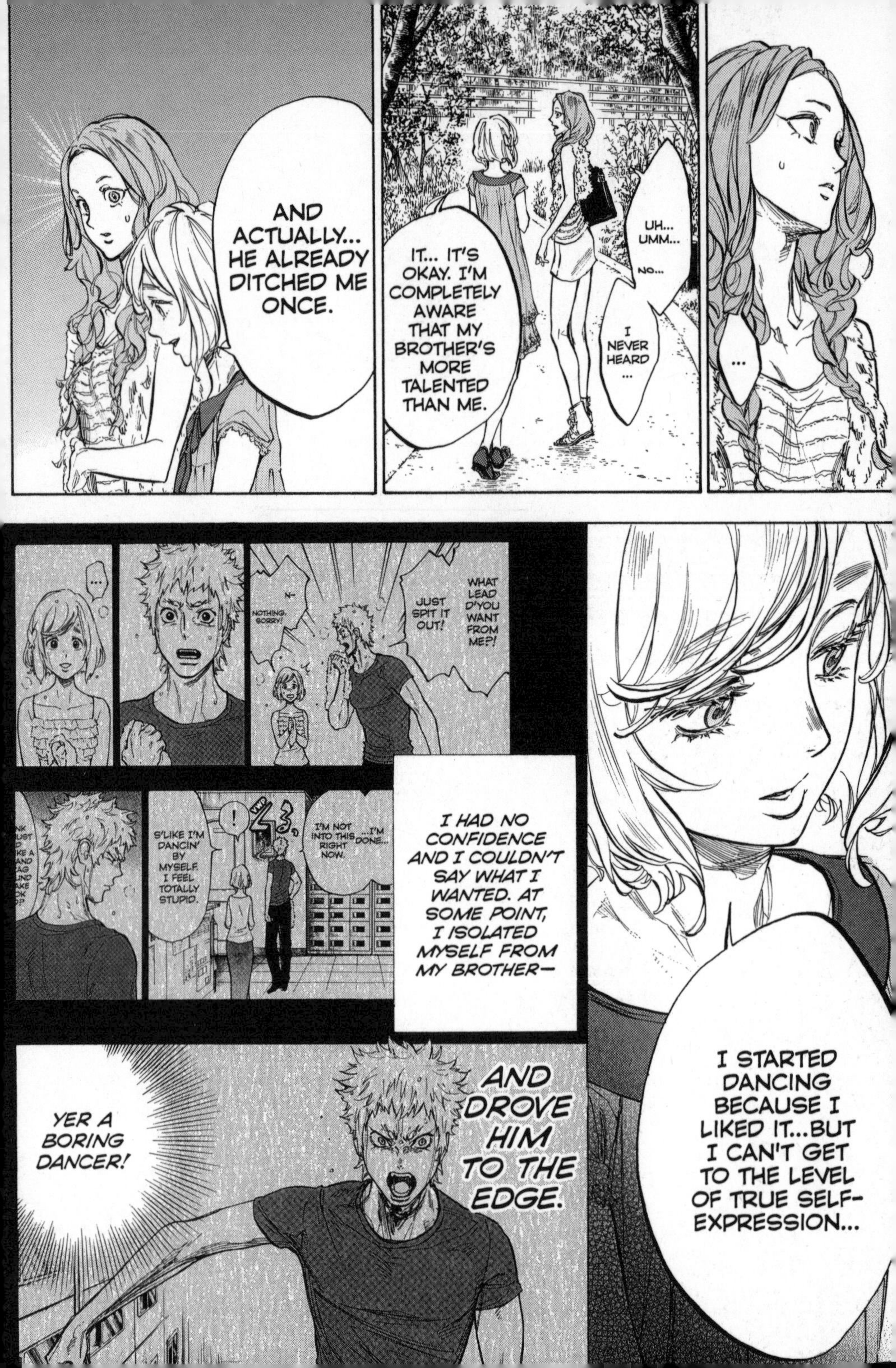
...
UH... UMM... NO... I NEVER HEARD...
IT... IT'S OKAY. I'M COMPLETELY AWARE THAT MY BROTHER'S MORE TALENTED THAN ME.
AND ACTUALLY... HE ALREADY DITCHED ME ONCE.
I STARTED DANCING BECAUSE I LIKED IT...BUT I CAN'T GET TO THE LEVEL OF TRUE SELF-EXPRESSION...
WHAT LEAD D'YOU WANT FROM ME?!
JUST SPIT IT OUT!
N- NOTHING, SORRY!
...
I HAD NO CONFIDENCE AND I COULDN'T SAY WHAT I WANTED. AT SOME POINT, I ISOLATED MYSELF FROM MY BROTHER—
...I'M DONE...
I'M NOT INTO THIS RIGHT NOW.
!
S'LIKE I'M DANCIN' BY MYSELF. I FEEL TOTALLY STUPID.
AND DROVE HIM TO THE EDGE.
YER A BORING DANCER!

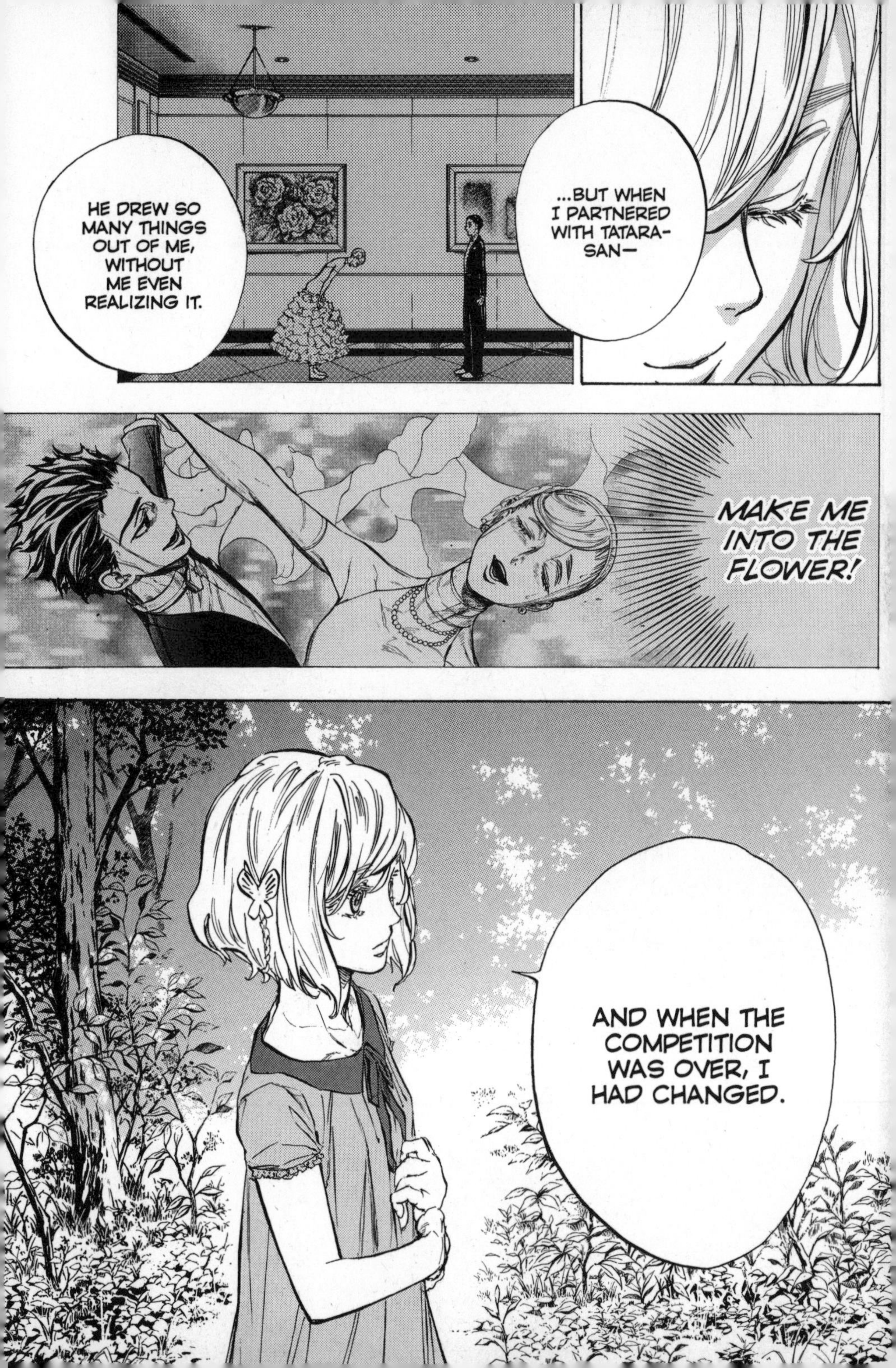
...BUT WHEN I PARTNERED WITH TATARA-SAN—
HE DREW SO MANY THINGS OUT OF ME, WITHOUT ME EVEN REALIZING IT.
MAKE ME INTO THE FLOWER!
AND WHEN THE COMPETITION WAS OVER, I HAD CHANGED.

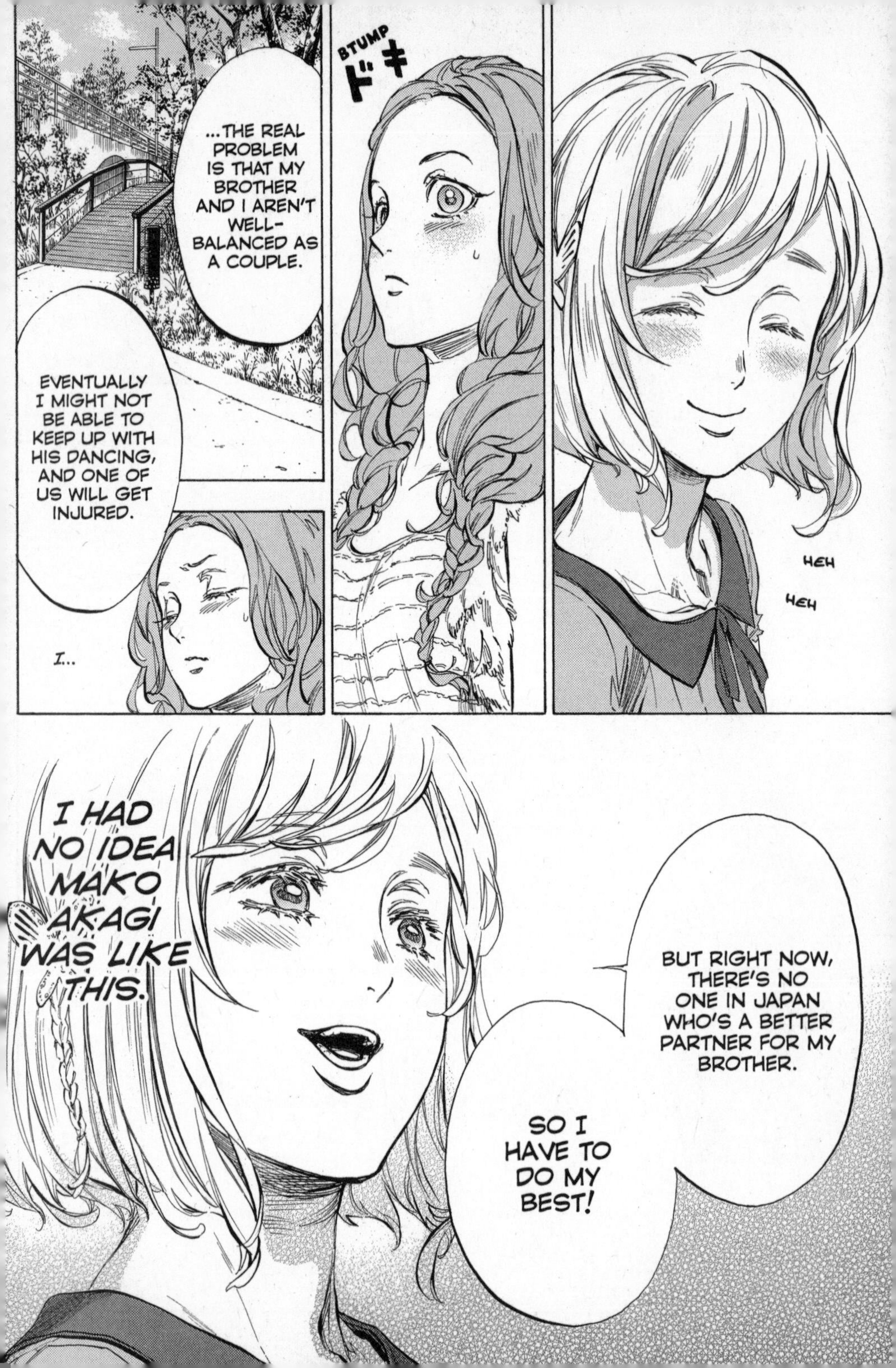
HEH
HEH
BTUMP
ドキ
...THE REAL PROBLEM IS THAT MY BROTHER AND I AREN'T WELL-BALANCED AS A COUPLE.
EVENTUALLY I MIGHT NOT BE ABLE TO KEEP UP WITH HIS DANCING, AND ONE OF US WILL GET INJURED.
I...
BUT RIGHT NOW, THERE'S NO ONE IN JAPAN WHO'S A BETTER PARTNER FOR MY BROTHER.
SO I HAVE TO DO MY BEST!
I HAD NO IDEA MAKO AKAGI WAS LIKE THIS.

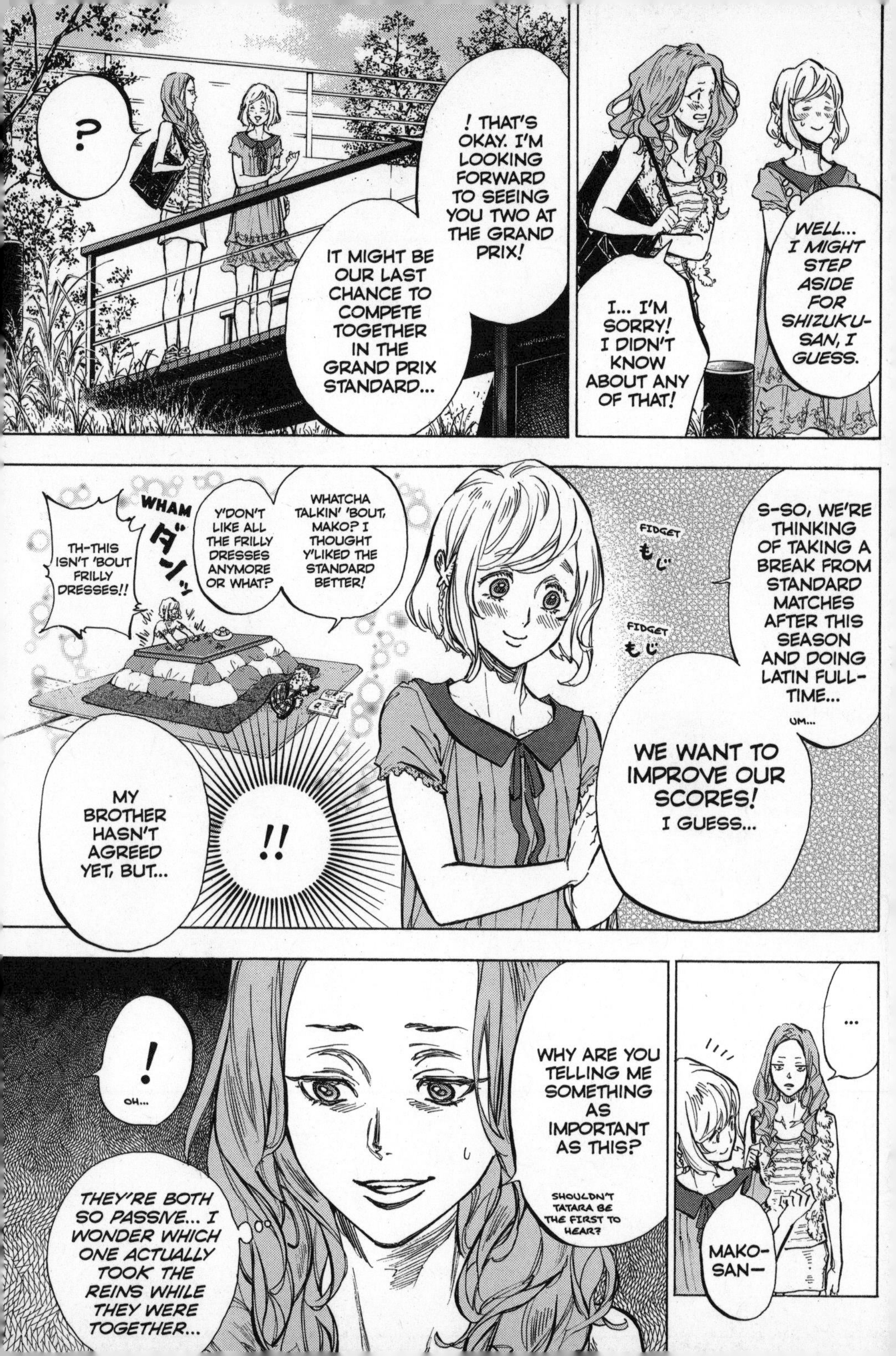
WELL... I MIGHT STEP ASIDE FOR SHIZUKU-SAN, I GUESS.
I... I'M SORRY! I DIDN'T KNOW ABOUT ANY OF THAT!
! THAT'S OKAY. I'M LOOKING FORWARD TO SEEING YOU TWO AT THE GRAND PRIX!
IT MIGHT BE OUR LAST CHANCE TO COMPETE TOGETHER IN THE GRAND PRIX STANDARD...
?
S-SO, WE'RE THINKING OF TAKING A BREAK FROM STANDARD MATCHES AFTER THIS SEASON AND DOING LATIN FULL-TIME...
UM...
FIDGET もじ
FIDGET もじ
WE WANT TO IMPROVE OUR SCORES! I GUESS...
!!
WHATCHA TALKIN' 'BOUT, MAKO? I THOUGHT Y'LIKED THE STANDARD BETTER!
Y'DON'T LIKE ALL THE FRILLY DRESSES ANYMORE OR WHAT?
WHAM ダーンッ
TH-THIS ISN'T 'BOUT FRILLY DRESSES!!
MY BROTHER HASN'T AGREED YET, BUT...
...
MAKO-SAN—
WHY ARE YOU TELLING ME SOMETHING AS IMPORTANT AS THIS?
SHOULDN'T TATARA BE THE FIRST TO HEAR?
!
OH...
THEY'RE BOTH SO PASSIVE... I WONDER WHICH ONE ACTUALLY TOOK THE REINS WHILE THEY WERE TOGETHER...

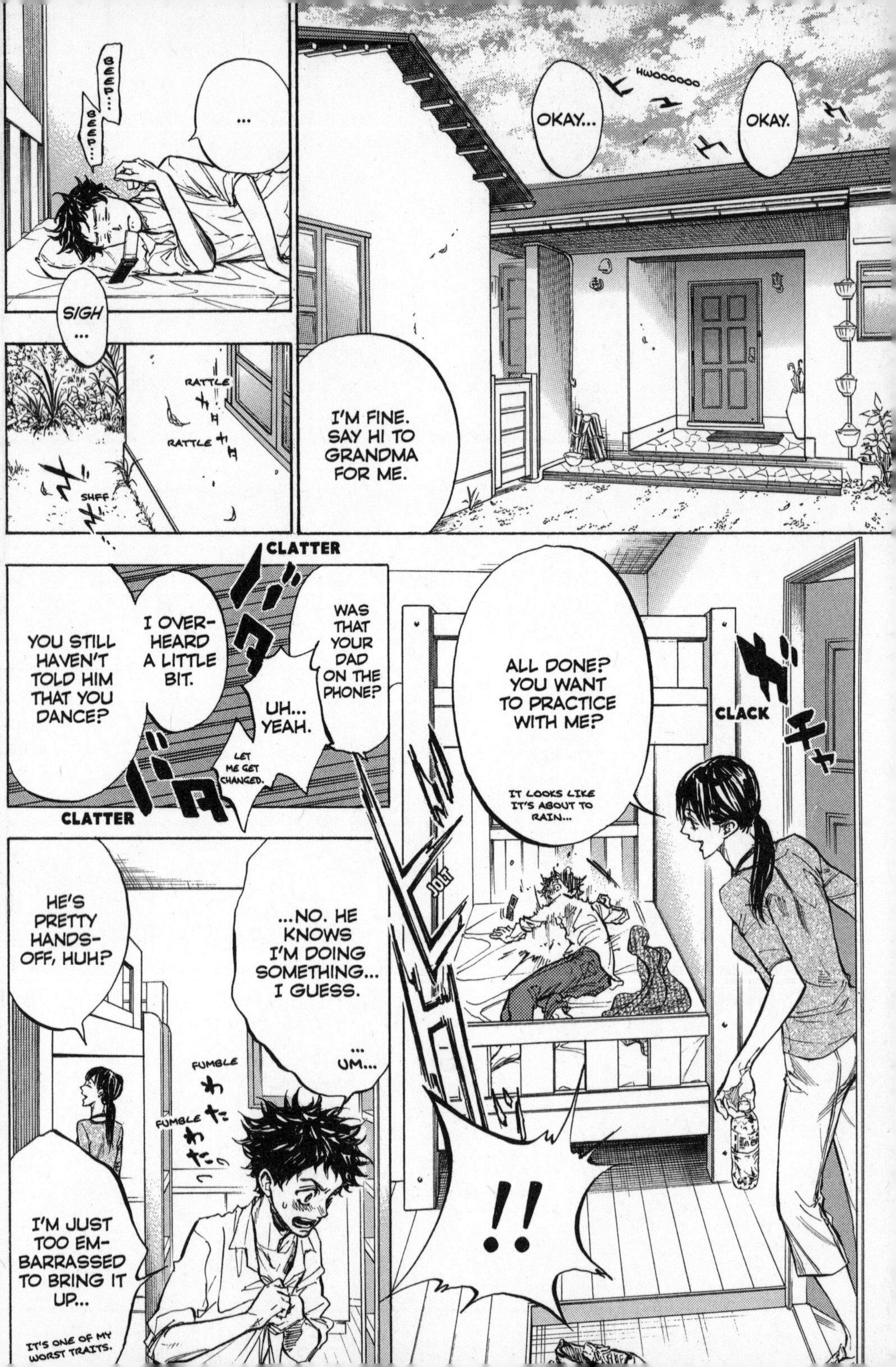
OKAY.
HWOOOOOO
OKAY...
I'M FINE. SAY HI TO GRANDMA FOR ME.
BEEP... BEEP...
...
SIGH ...
RATTLE
RATTLE
SHFF
CLACK
ALL DONE? YOU WANT TO PRACTICE WITH ME?
IT LOOKS LIKE IT'S ABOUT TO RAIN...
JOLT
!!
CLATTER
WAS THAT YOUR DAD ON THE PHONE?
UH... YEAH.
LET ME GET CHANGED.
I OVER-HEARD A LITTLE BIT.
YOU STILL HAVEN'T TOLD HIM THAT YOU DANCE?
CLATTER
...NO. HE KNOWS I'M DOING SOMETHING... I GUESS.
... UM...
HE'S PRETTY HANDS-OFF, HUH?
FUMBLE
FUMBLE
I'M JUST TOO EM-BARRASSED TO BRING IT UP...
IT'S ONE OF MY WORST TRAITS.

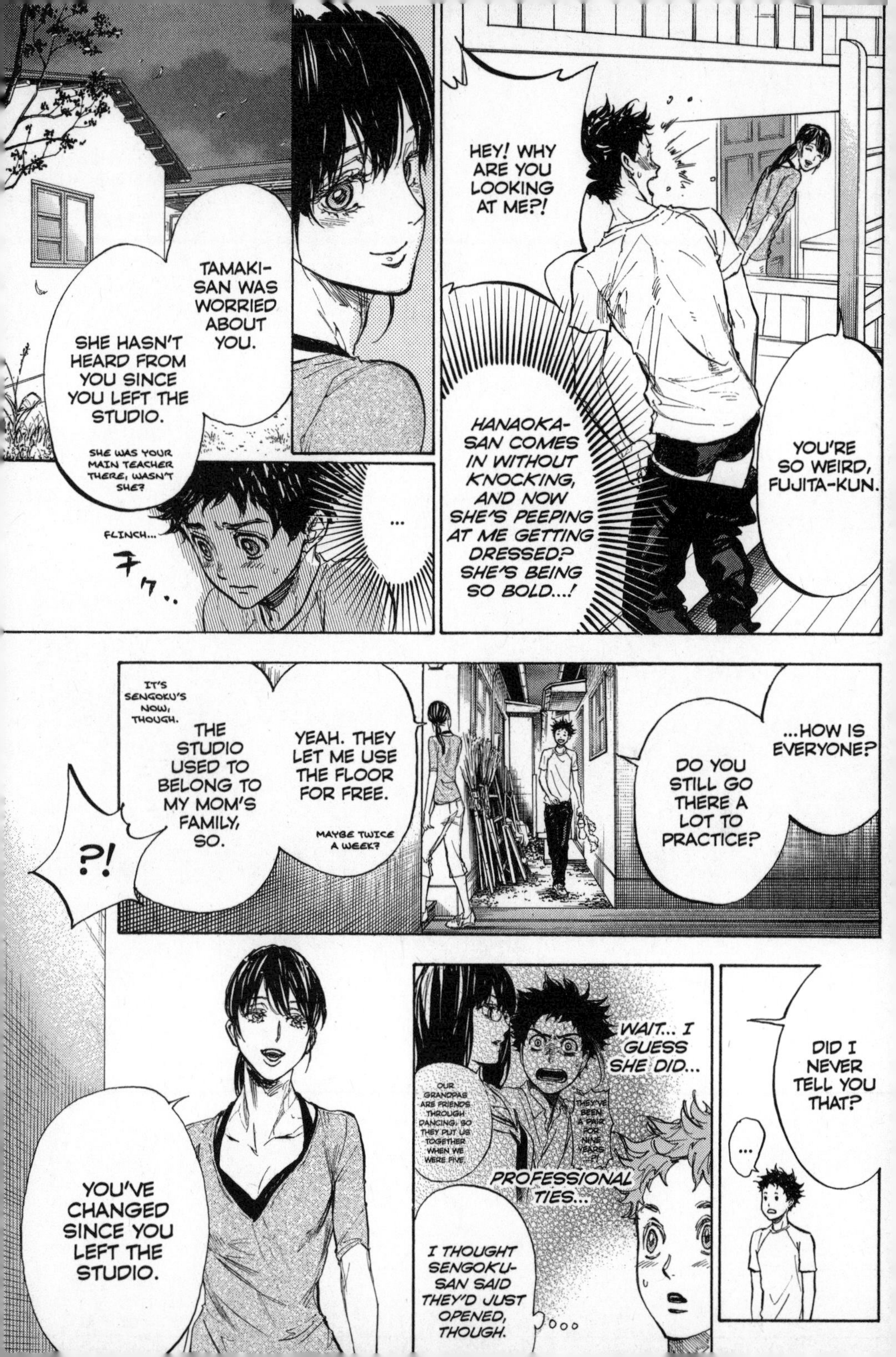
HEY! WHY ARE YOU LOOKING AT ME?!
YOU'RE SO WEIRD, FUJITA-KUN.
HANAOKA-SAN COMES IN WITHOUT KNOCKING, AND NOW SHE'S PEEPING AT ME GETTING DRESSED? SHE'S BEING SO BOLD...!
TAMAKI-SAN WAS WORRIED ABOUT YOU.
SHE HASN'T HEARD FROM YOU SINCE YOU LEFT THE STUDIO.
SHE WAS YOUR MAIN TEACHER THERE, WASN'T SHE?
...
FLINCH...
ギク..
...HOW IS EVERYONE?
DO YOU STILL GO THERE A LOT TO PRACTICE?
YEAH. THEY LET ME USE THE FLOOR FOR FREE.
MAYBE TWICE A WEEK?
THE STUDIO USED TO BELONG TO MY MOM'S FAMILY, SO.
IT'S SENGOKU'S NOW, THOUGH.
?!
DID I NEVER TELL YOU THAT?
...
WAIT... I GUESS SHE DID...
THEY'VE BEEN A PAIR FOR NINE YEARS...?!
OUR GRANDPAS ARE FRIENDS THROUGH DANCING, SO THEY PUT US TOGETHER WHEN WE WERE FIVE.
PROFESSIONAL TIES...
I THOUGHT SENGOKU-SAN SAID THEY'D JUST OPENED, THOUGH.
YOU'VE CHANGED SINCE YOU LEFT THE STUDIO.

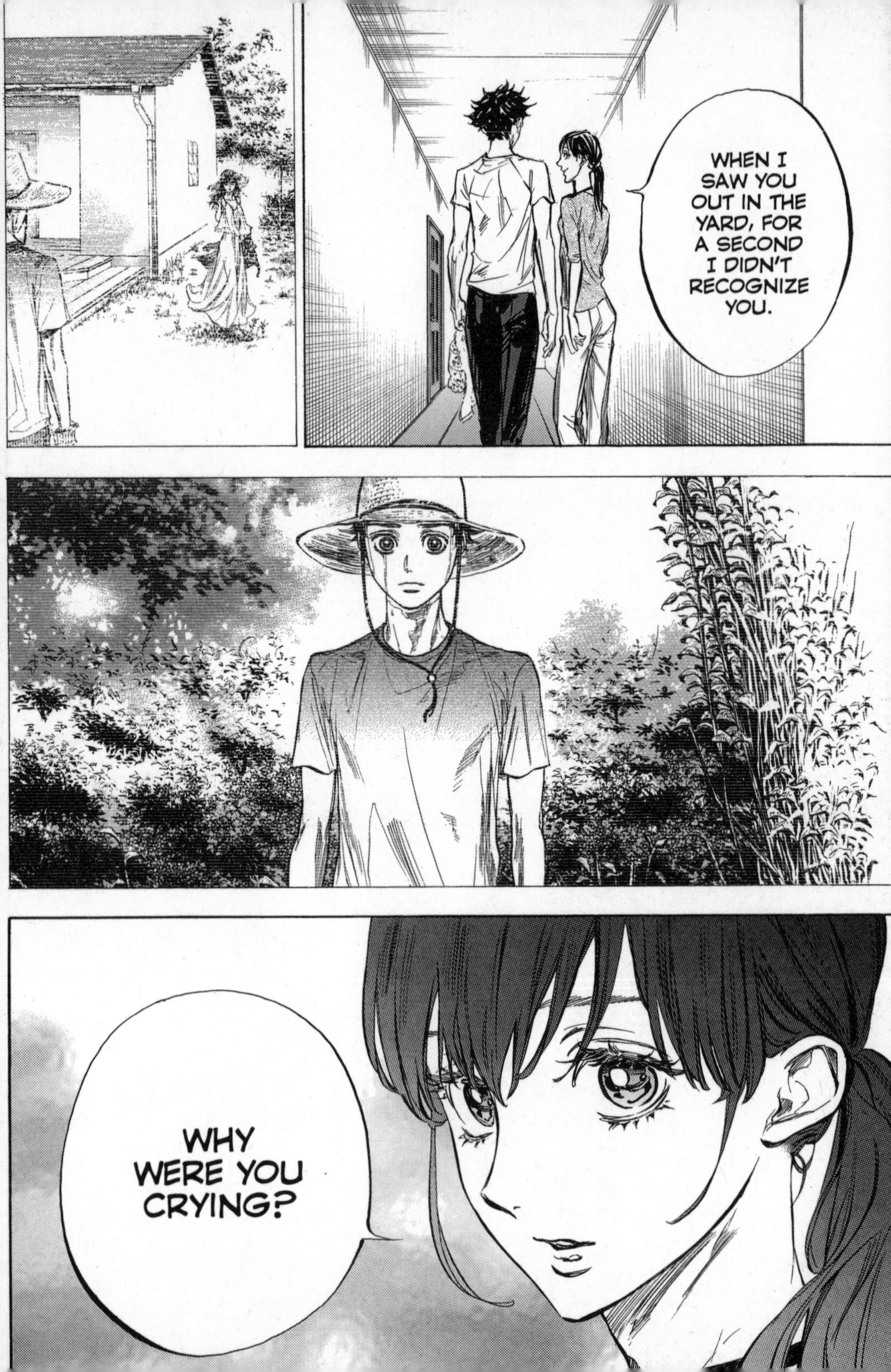
WHEN I SAW YOU OUT IN THE YARD, FOR A SECOND I DIDN'T RECOGNIZE YOU.
WHY WERE YOU CRYING?

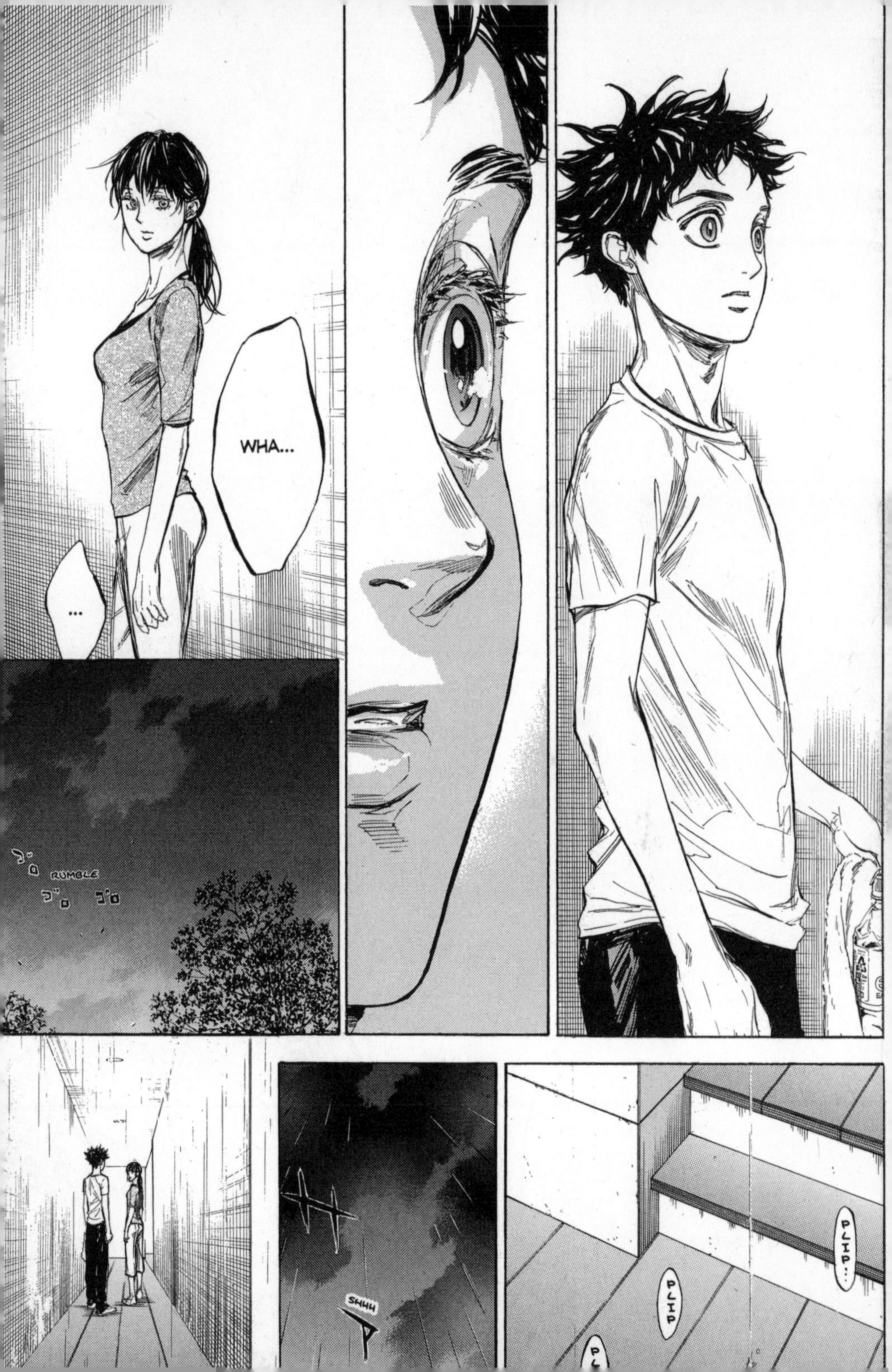
WHA...
...
RUMBLE
PLIP...
PLIP
SHHH

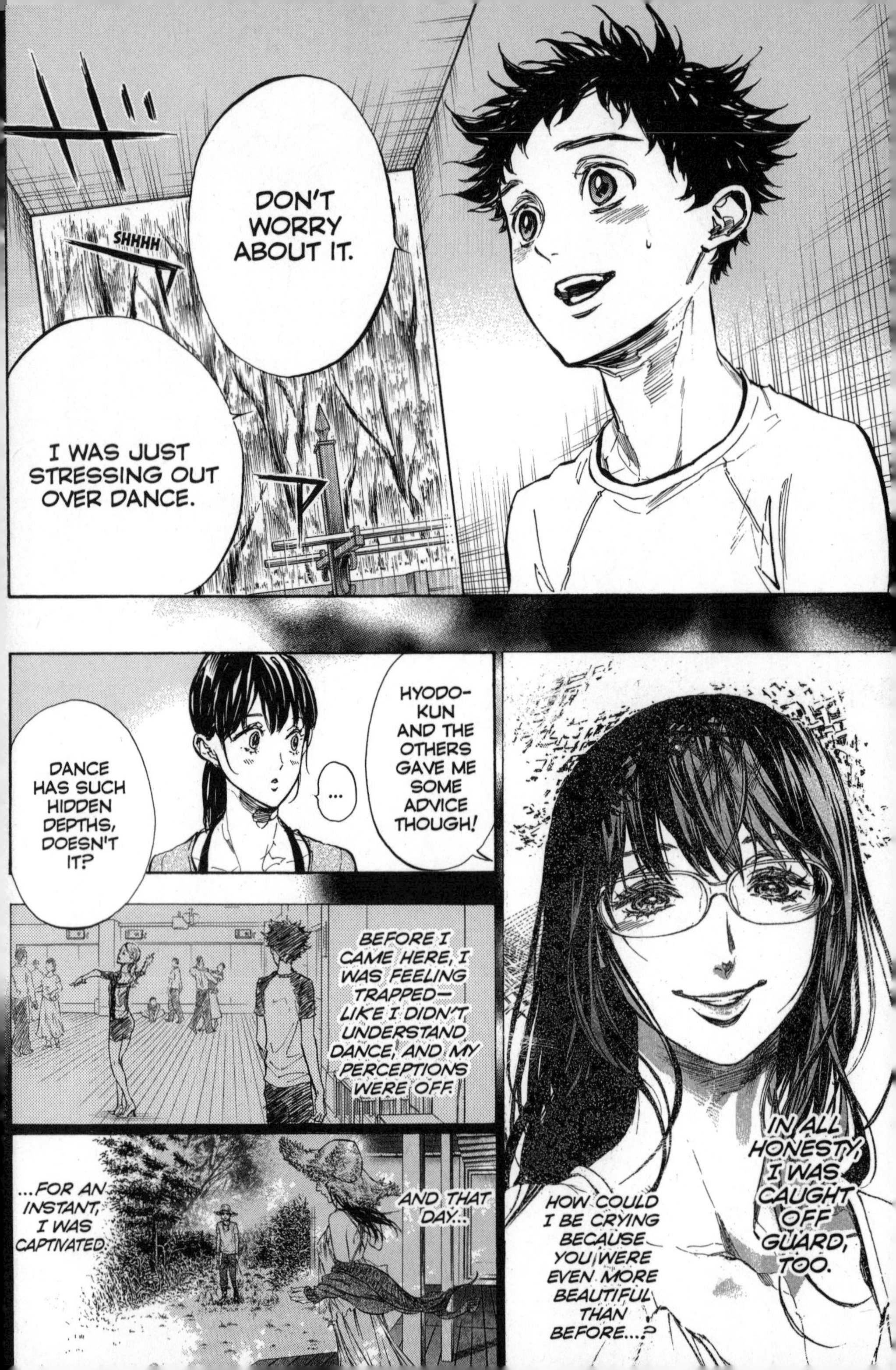

SHHHH
DON'T WORRY ABOUT IT.
I WAS JUST STRESSING OUT OVER DANCE.
IN ALL HONESTY, I WAS CAUGHT OFF GUARD, TOO.
HOW COULD I BE CRYING BECAUSE YOU WERE EVEN MORE BEAUTIFUL THAN BEFORE...?
HYODO-KUN AND THE OTHERS GAVE ME SOME ADVICE THOUGH!
...
DANCE HAS SUCH HIDDEN DEPTHS, DOESN'T IT?
BEFORE I CAME HERE, I WAS FEELING TRAPPED—LIKE I DIDN'T UNDERSTAND DANCE, AND MY PERCEPTIONS WERE OFF.
AND THAT DAY...
...FOR AN INSTANT, I WAS CAPTIVATED.

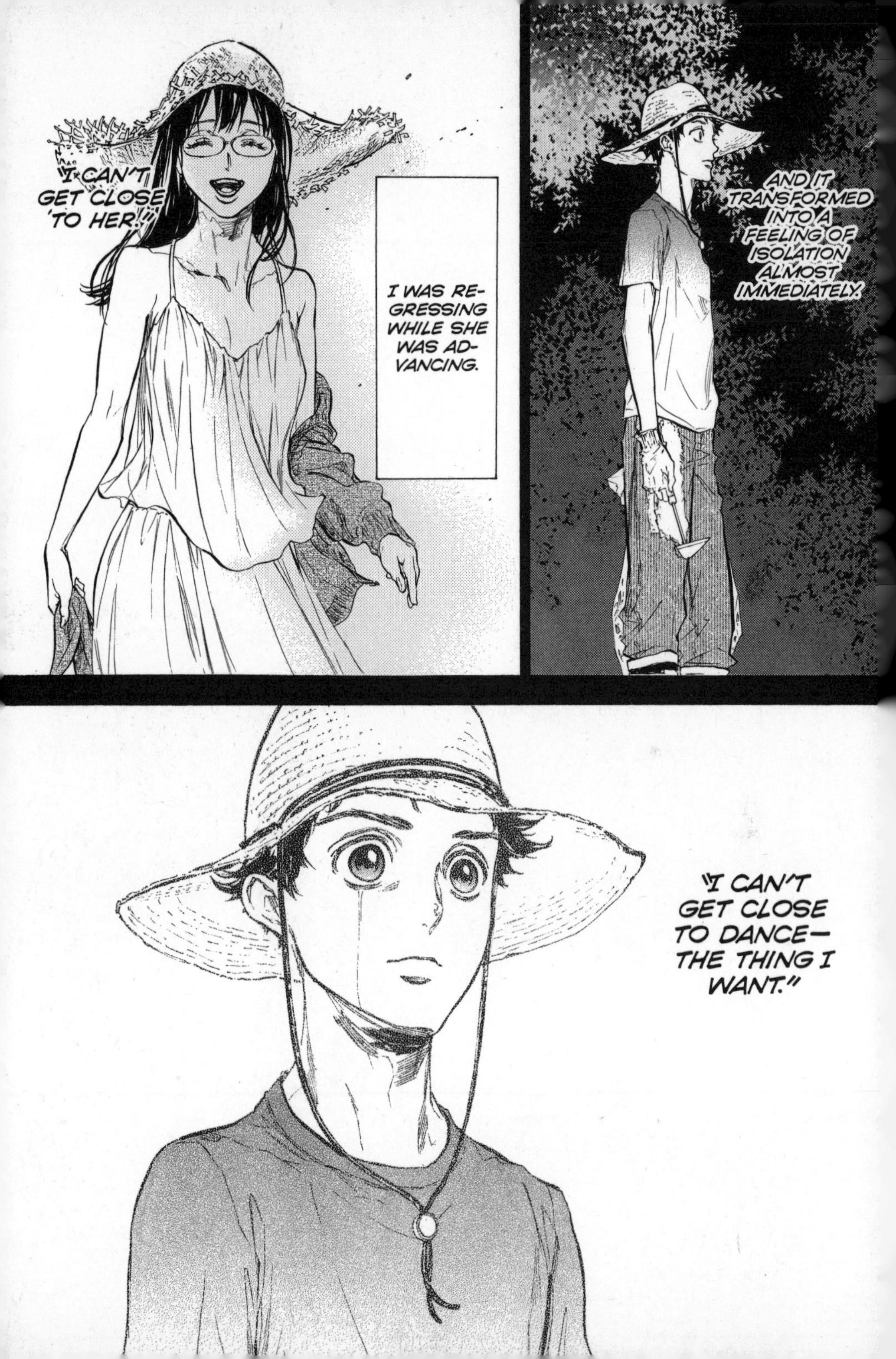
AND IT TRANSFORMED INTO A FEELING OF ISOLATION ALMOST IMMEDIATELY.
I WAS RE-GRESSING WHILE SHE WAS AD-VANCING.
"I CAN'T GET CLOSE TO HER!"
"I CAN'T GET CLOSE TO DANCE— THE THING I WANT."

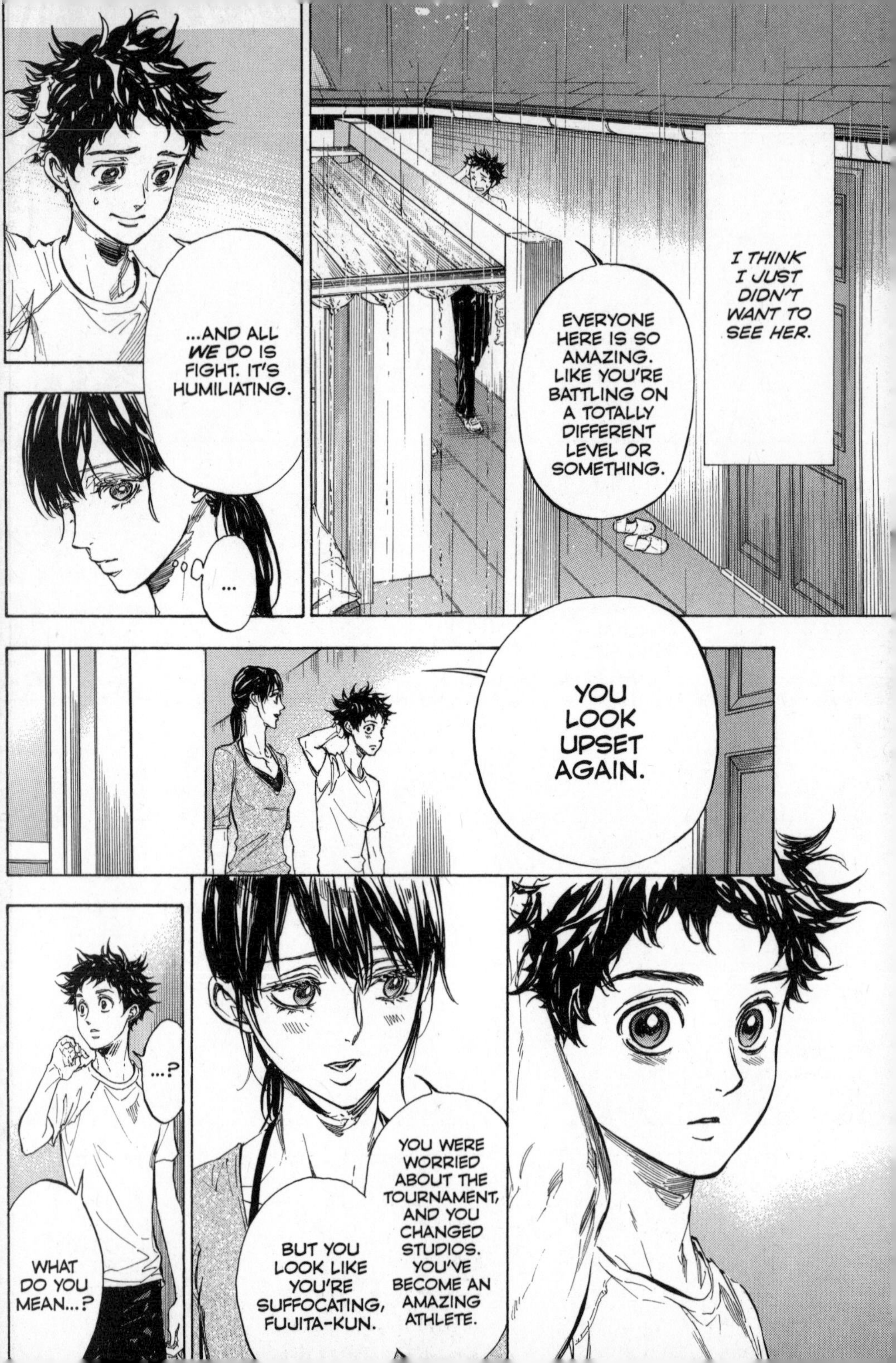
I THINK I JUST DIDN'T WANT TO SEE HER.
EVERYONE HERE IS SO AMAZING. LIKE YOU'RE BATTLING ON A TOTALLY DIFFERENT LEVEL OR SOMETHING.
...AND ALL *WE* DO IS FIGHT. IT'S HUMILIATING.
...
YOU LOOK UPSET AGAIN.
YOU WERE WORRIED ABOUT THE TOURNAMENT, AND YOU CHANGED STUDIOS. YOU'VE BECOME AN AMAZING ATHLETE.
BUT YOU LOOK LIKE YOU'RE SUFFOCATING, FUJITA-KUN.
...?
WHAT DO YOU MEAN...?

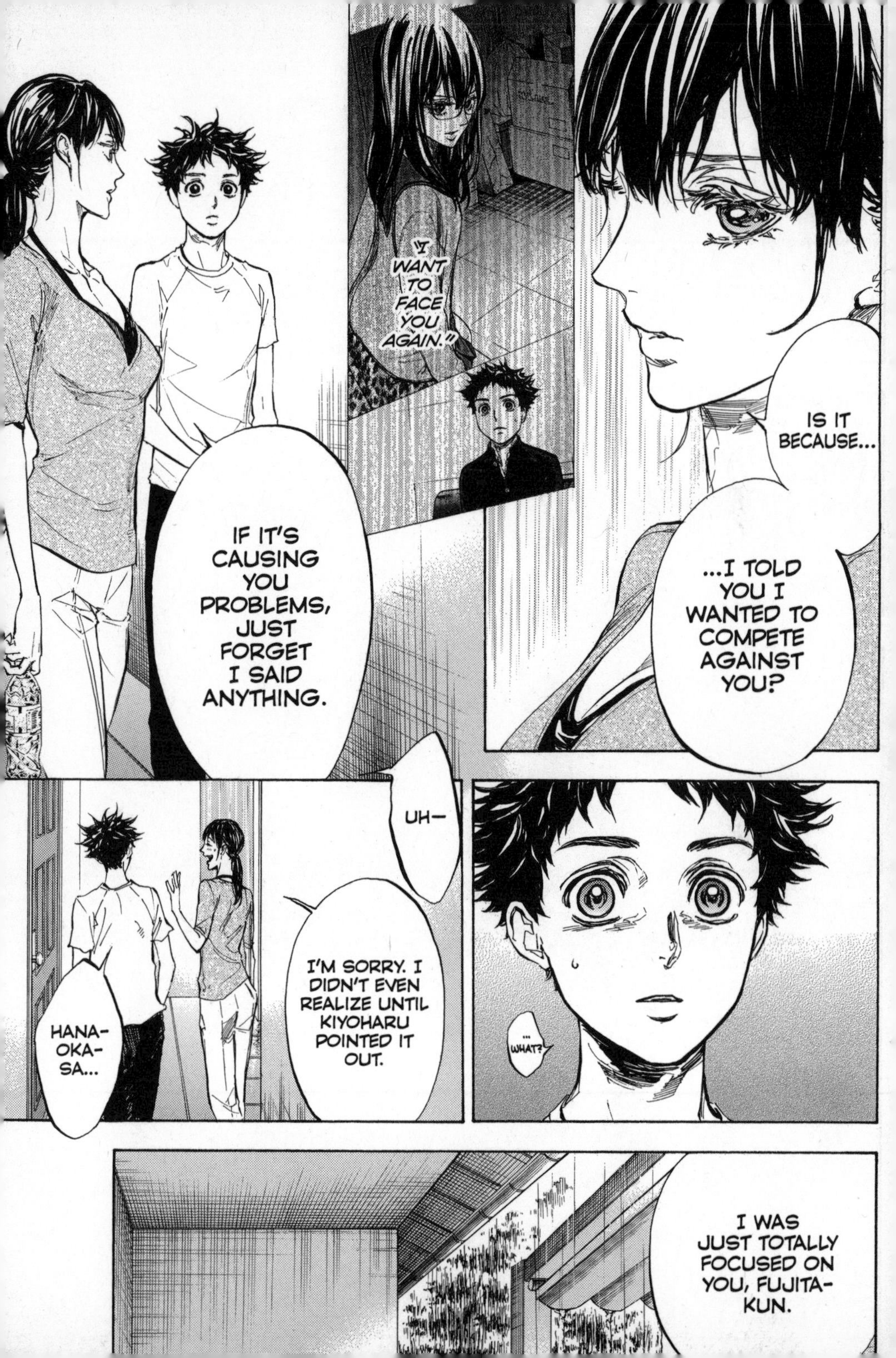
IS IT BECAUSE...
...I TOLD YOU I WANTED TO COMPETE AGAINST YOU?
"I WANT TO FACE YOU AGAIN."
IF IT'S CAUSING YOU PROBLEMS, JUST FORGET I SAID ANYTHING.
...WHAT?
UH—
I'M SORRY. I DIDN'T EVEN REALIZE UNTIL KIYOHARU POINTED IT OUT.
HANA-OKA-SA...
I WAS JUST TOTALLY FOCUSED ON YOU, FUJITA-KUN.

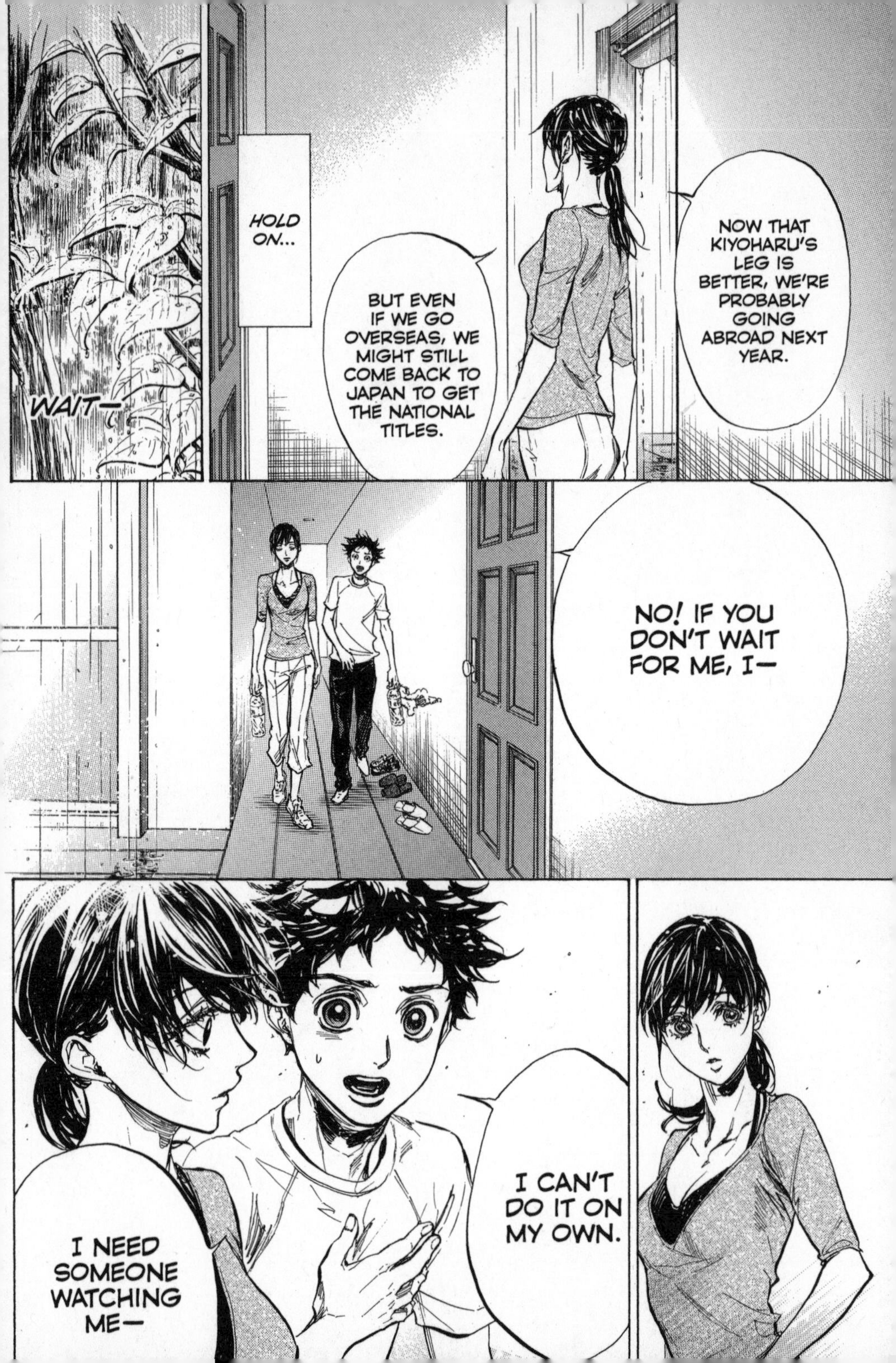
NOW THAT KIYOHARU'S LEG IS BETTER, WE'RE PROBABLY GOING ABROAD NEXT YEAR.
BUT EVEN IF WE GO OVERSEAS, WE MIGHT STILL COME BACK TO JAPAN TO GET THE NATIONAL TITLES.
HOLD ON...
WAIT—
NO! IF YOU DON'T WAIT FOR ME, I—
I CAN'T DO IT ON MY OWN.
I NEED SOMEONE WATCHING ME—

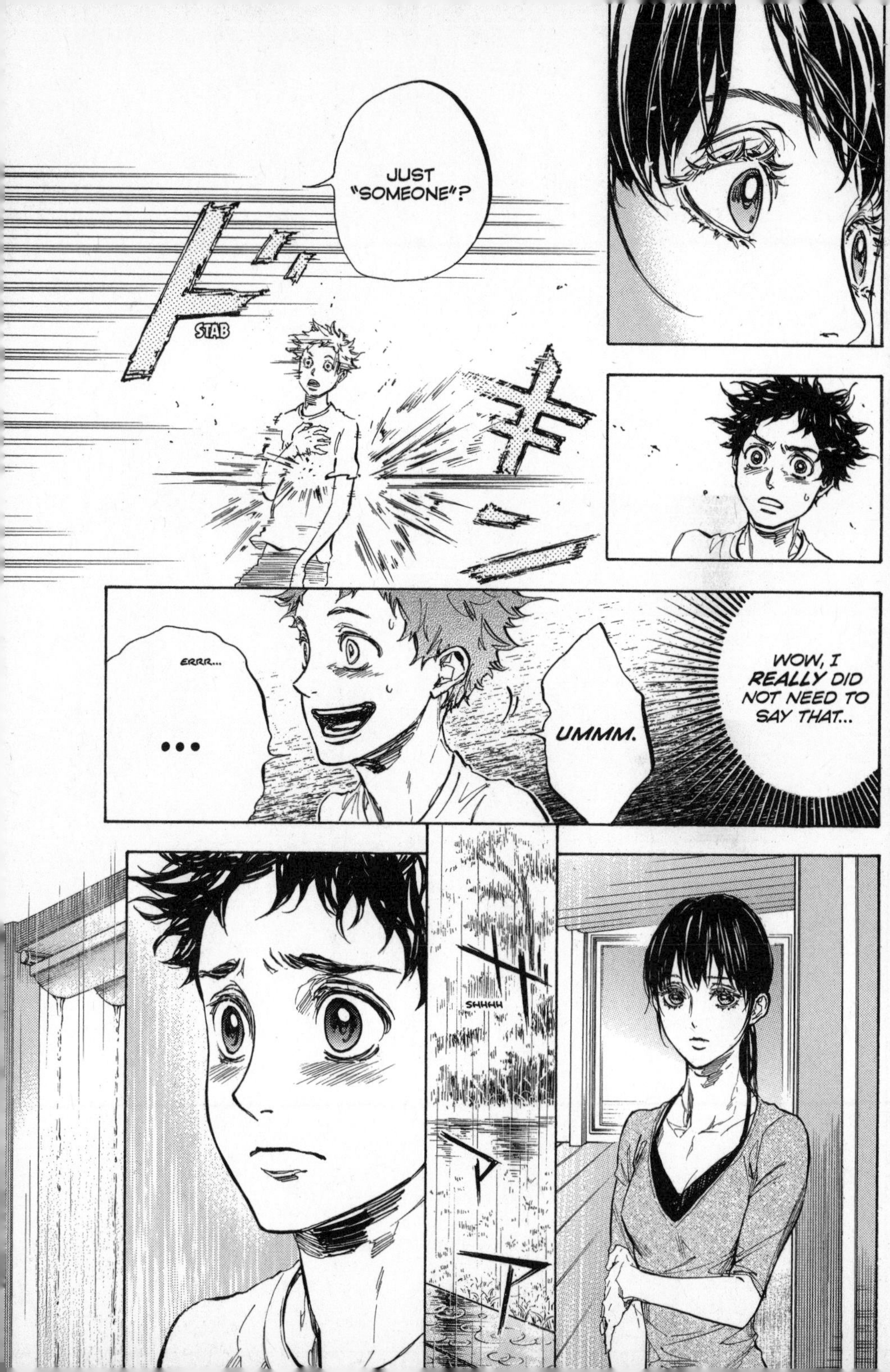
JUST "SOMEONE"?
STAB
WOW, I REALLY DID NOT NEED TO SAY THAT...
UMMM.
ERRR...
...
SHHHH

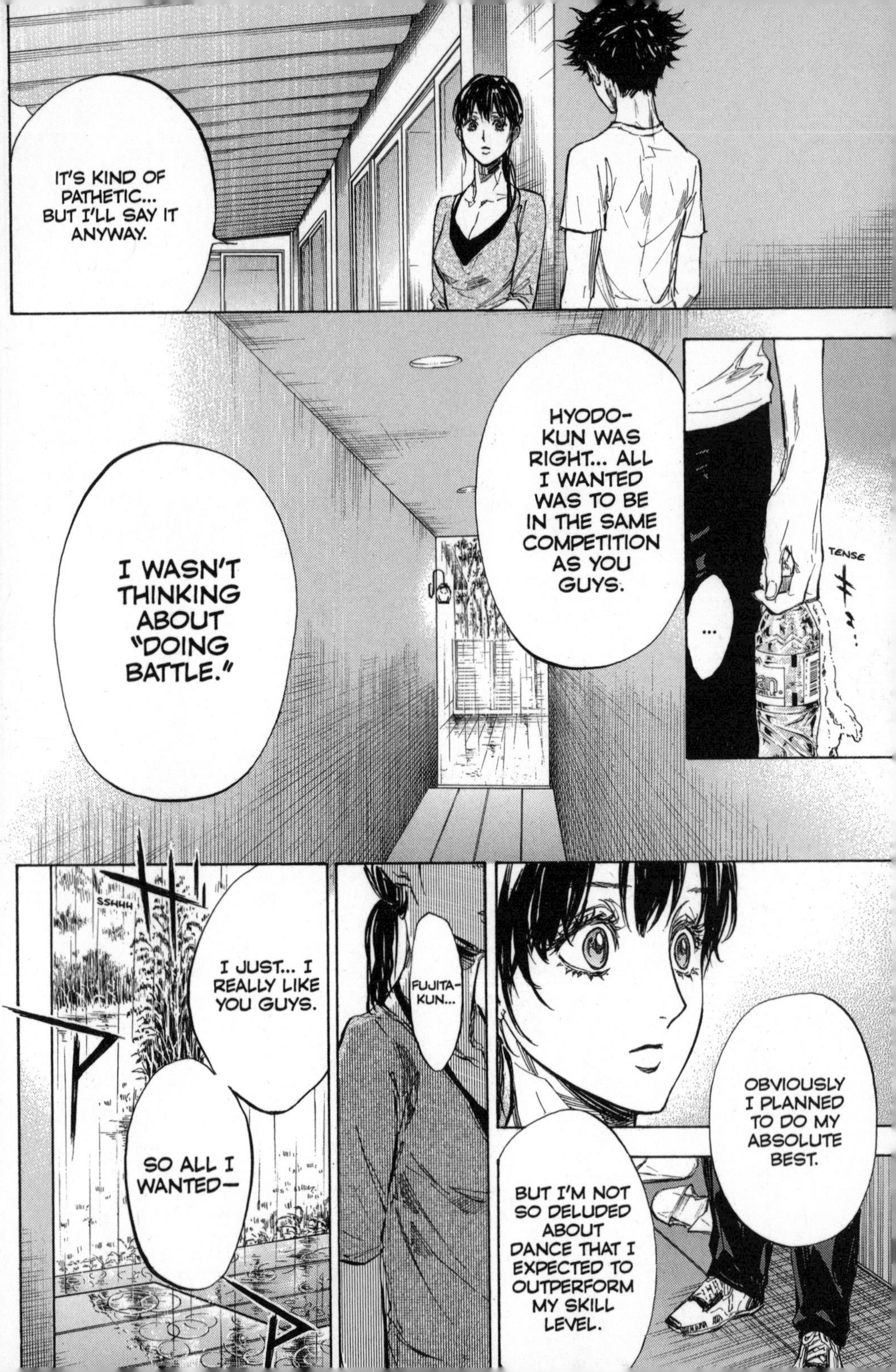
IT'S KIND OF PATHETIC... BUT I'LL SAY IT ANYWAY.
TENSE
...
HYODO-KUN WAS RIGHT... ALL I WANTED WAS TO BE IN THE SAME COMPETITION AS YOU GUYS.
I WASN'T THINKING ABOUT "DOING BATTLE."
OBVIOUSLY I PLANNED TO DO MY ABSOLUTE BEST.
BUT I'M NOT SO DELUDED ABOUT DANCE THAT I EXPECTED TO OUTPERFORM MY SKILL LEVEL.
FUJITA-KUN...
SSHHH
I JUST... I REALLY LIKE YOU GUYS.
SO ALL I WANTED—

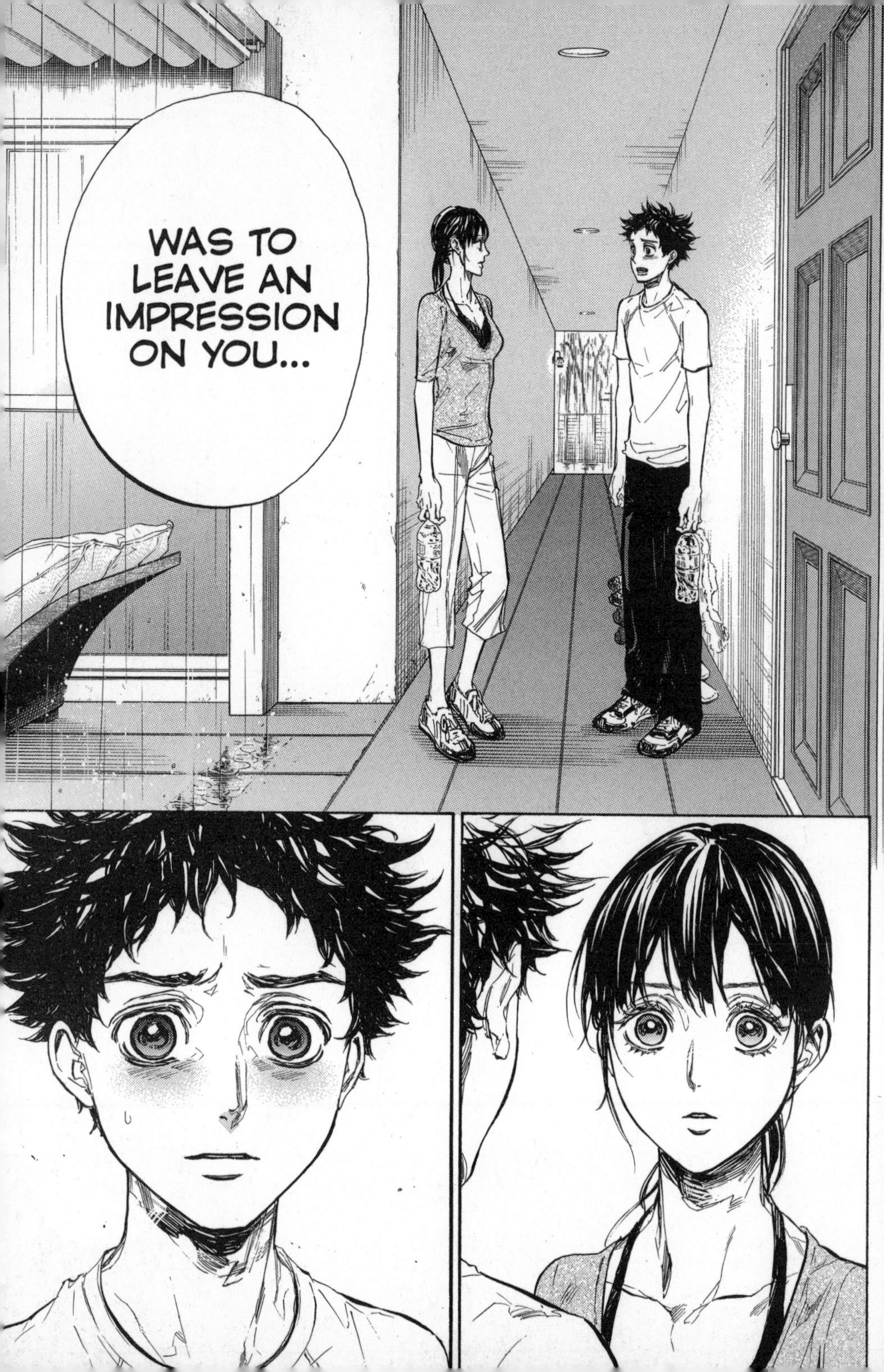
WAS TO LEAVE AN IMPRESSION ON YOU...

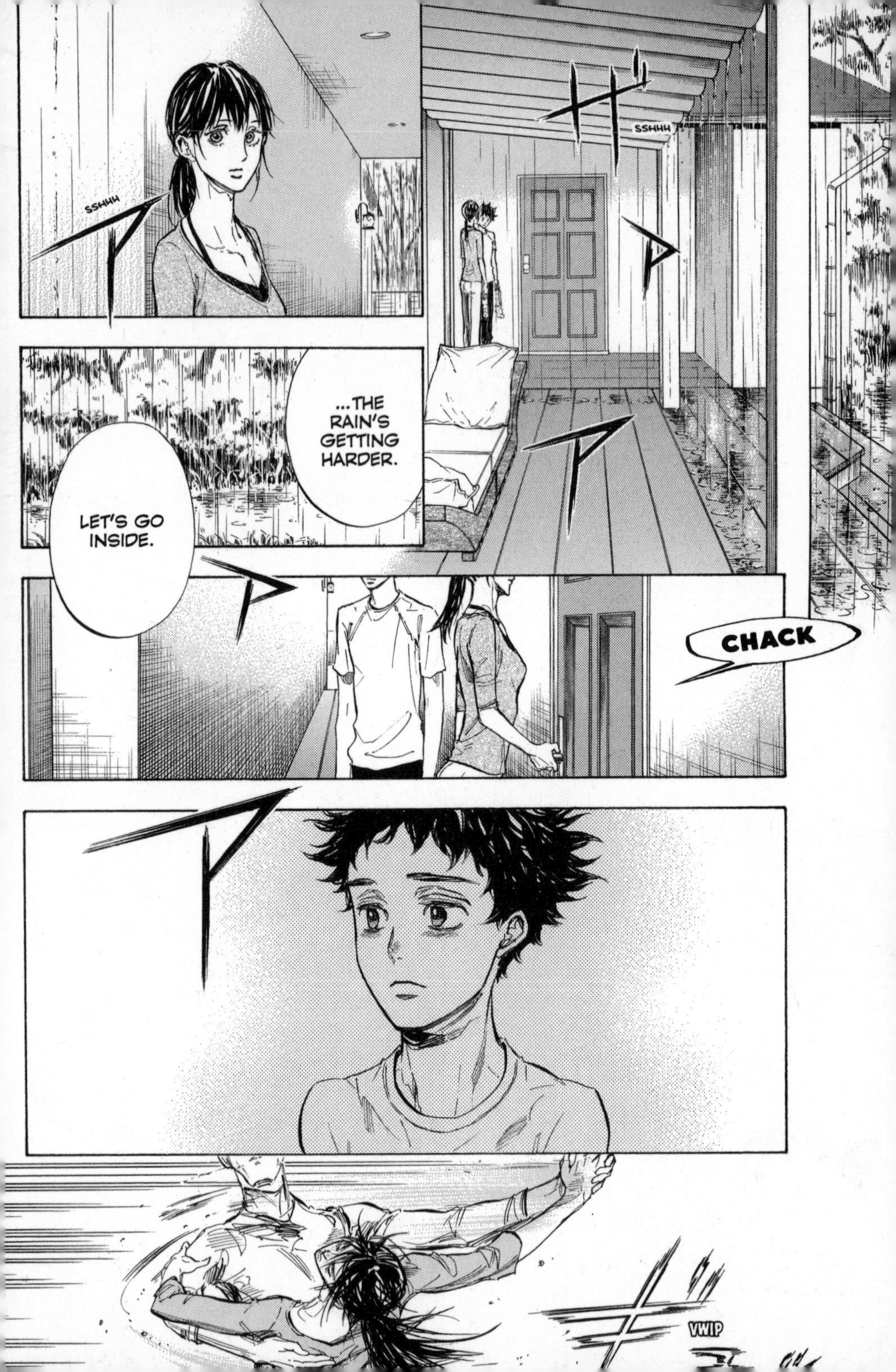
SSHHH
SSHHH
...THE RAIN'S GETTING HARDER.
LET'S GO INSIDE.
CHACK
VWIP

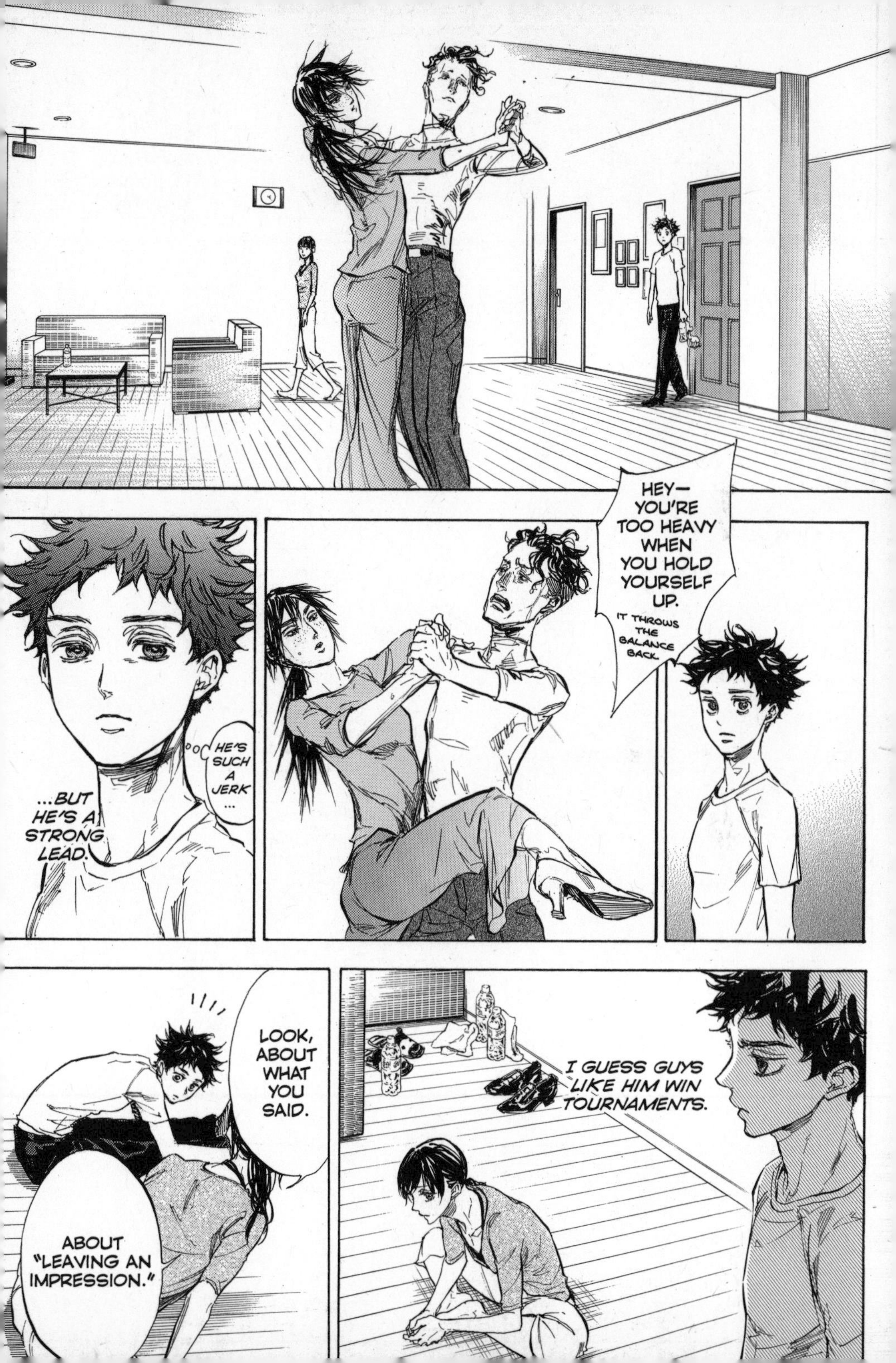
HEY— YOU'RE TOO HEAVY WHEN YOU HOLD YOURSELF UP.
IT THROWS THE BALANCE BACK.
HE'S SUCH A JERK ...
...BUT HE'S A STRONG LEAD.
I GUESS GUYS LIKE HIM WIN TOURNAMENTS.
LOOK, ABOUT WHAT YOU SAID.
ABOUT "LEAVING AN IMPRESSION."

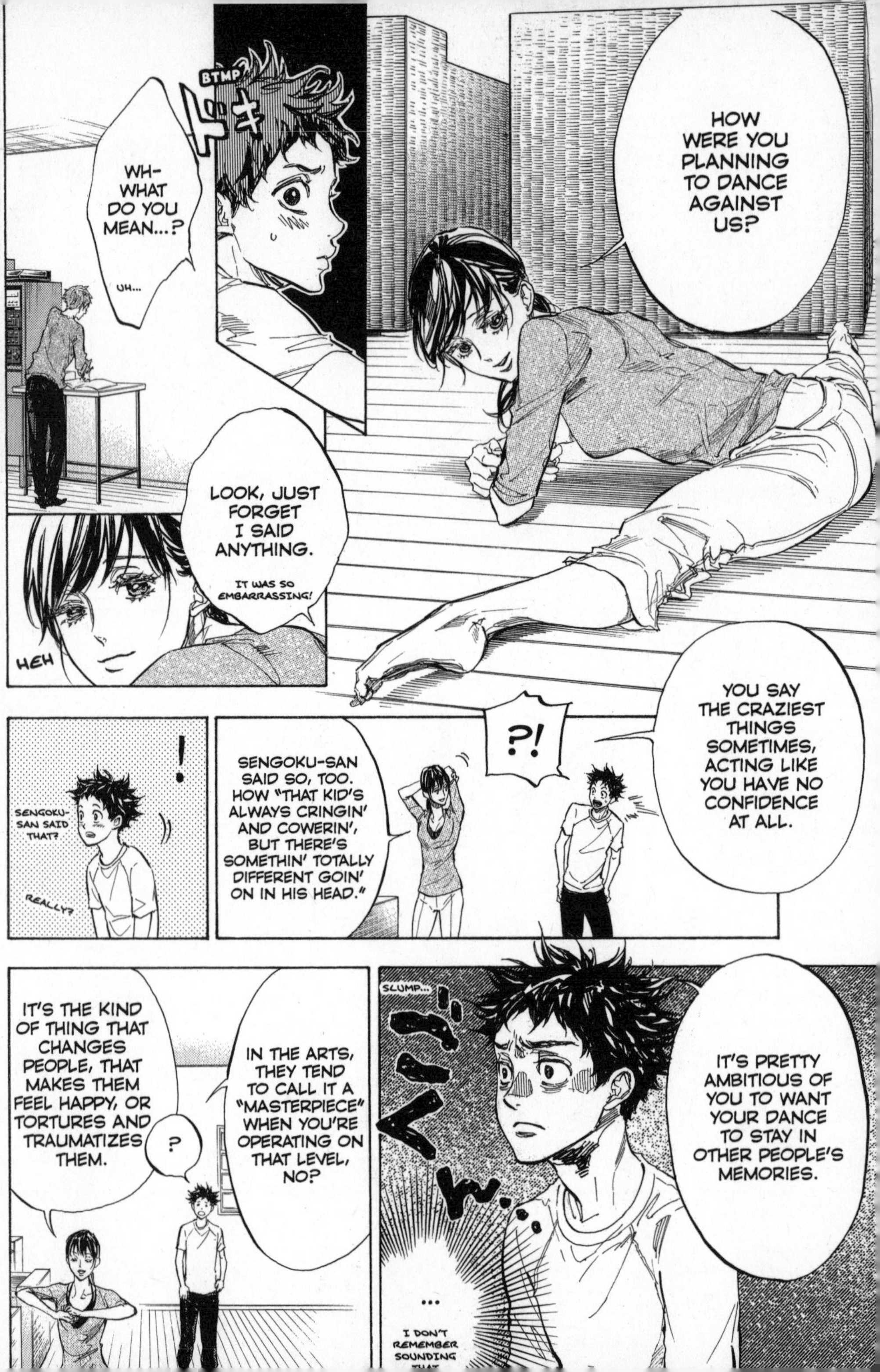
HOW WERE YOU PLANNING TO DANCE AGAINST US?
BTMP
WH- WHAT DO YOU MEAN...?
UH...
LOOK, JUST FORGET I SAID ANYTHING.
IT WAS SO EMBARRASSING!
HEH
YOU SAY THE CRAZIEST THINGS SOMETIMES, ACTING LIKE YOU HAVE NO CONFIDENCE AT ALL.
?!
SENGOKU-SAN SAID SO, TOO. HOW "THAT KID'S ALWAYS CRINGIN' AND COWERIN', BUT THERE'S SOMETHIN' TOTALLY DIFFERENT GOIN' ON IN HIS HEAD."
!
SENGOKU-SAN SAID THAT?
REALLY?
IT'S PRETTY AMBITIOUS OF YOU TO WANT YOUR DANCE TO STAY IN OTHER PEOPLE'S MEMORIES.
SLUMP...
...
I DON'T REMEMBER SOUNDING
IN THE ARTS, THEY TEND TO CALL IT A "MASTERPIECE" WHEN YOU'RE OPERATING ON THAT LEVEL, NO?
IT'S THE KIND OF THING THAT CHANGES PEOPLE, THAT MAKES THEM FEEL HAPPY, OR TORTURES AND TRAUMATIZES THEM.
?

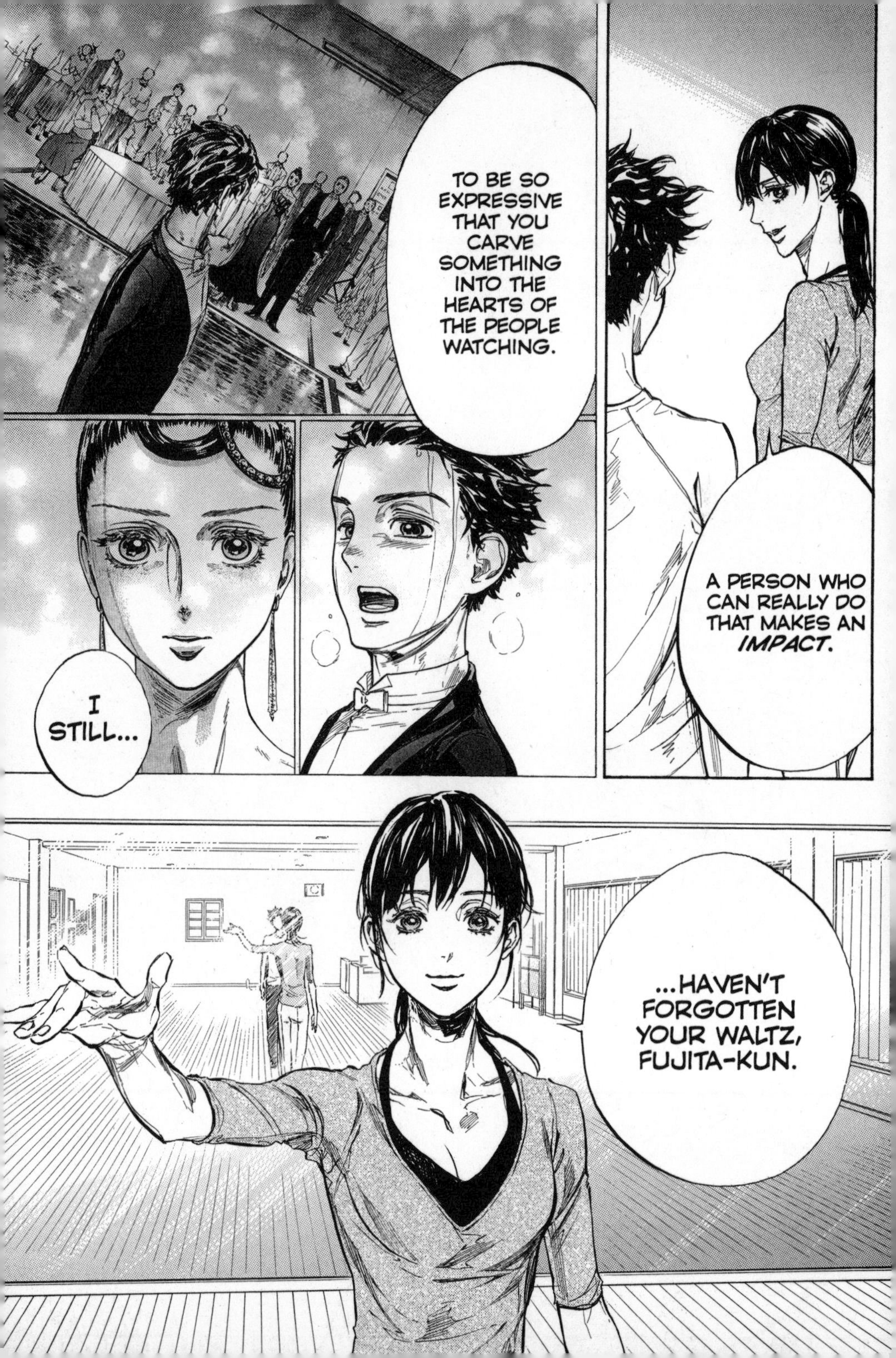

TO BE SO EXPRESSIVE THAT YOU CARVE SOMETHING INTO THE HEARTS OF THE PEOPLE WATCHING.
A PERSON WHO CAN REALLY DO THAT MAKES AN *IMPACT*.
I STILL...
...HAVEN'T FORGOTTEN YOUR WALTZ, FUJITA-KUN.

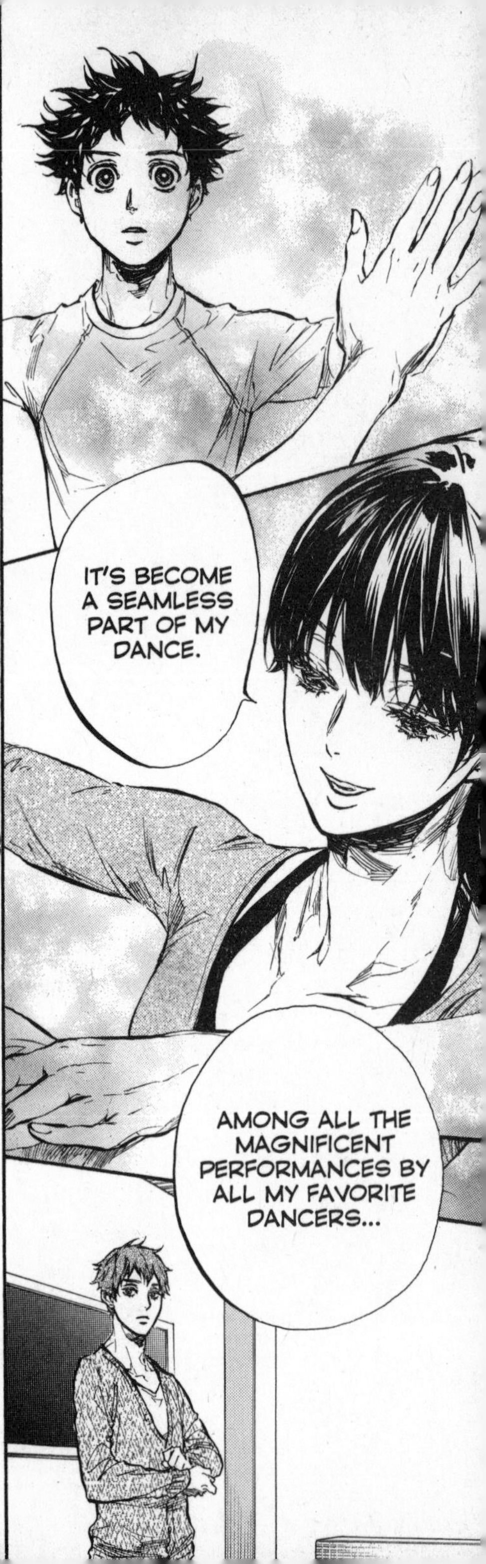
IT'S BECOME A SEAMLESS PART OF MY DANCE.
AMONG ALL THE MAGNIFICENT PERFORMANCES BY ALL MY FAVORITE DANCERS...
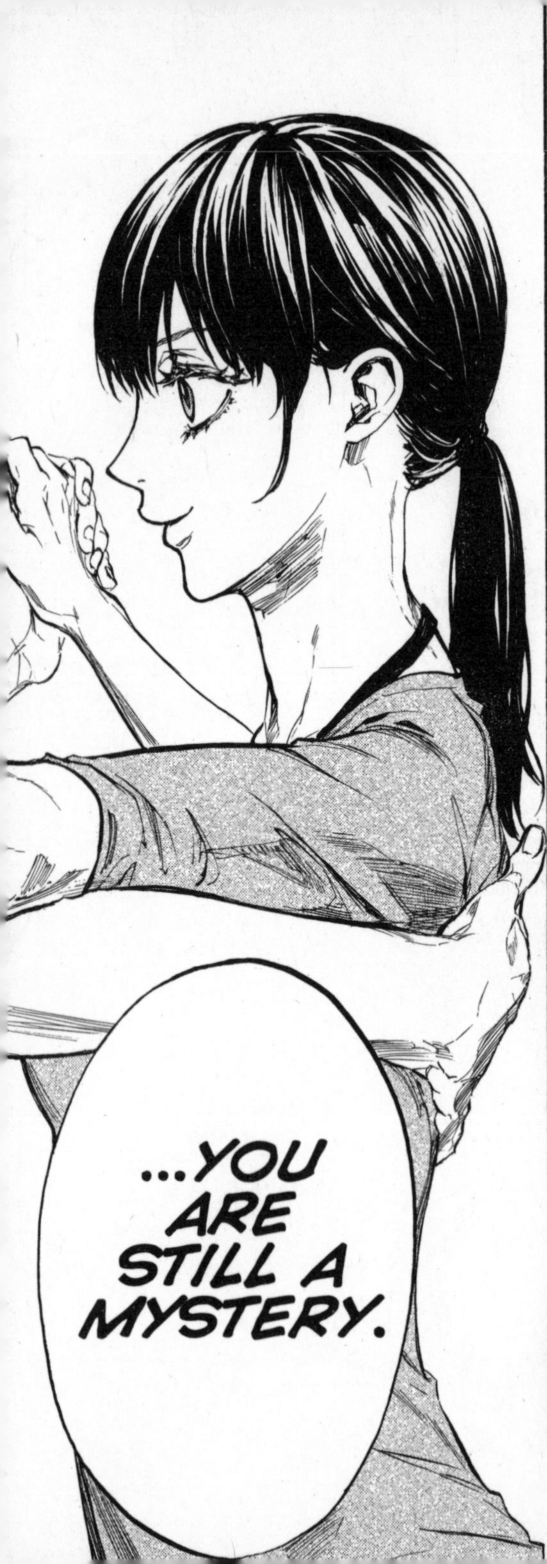
...YOU ARE STILL A MYSTERY.

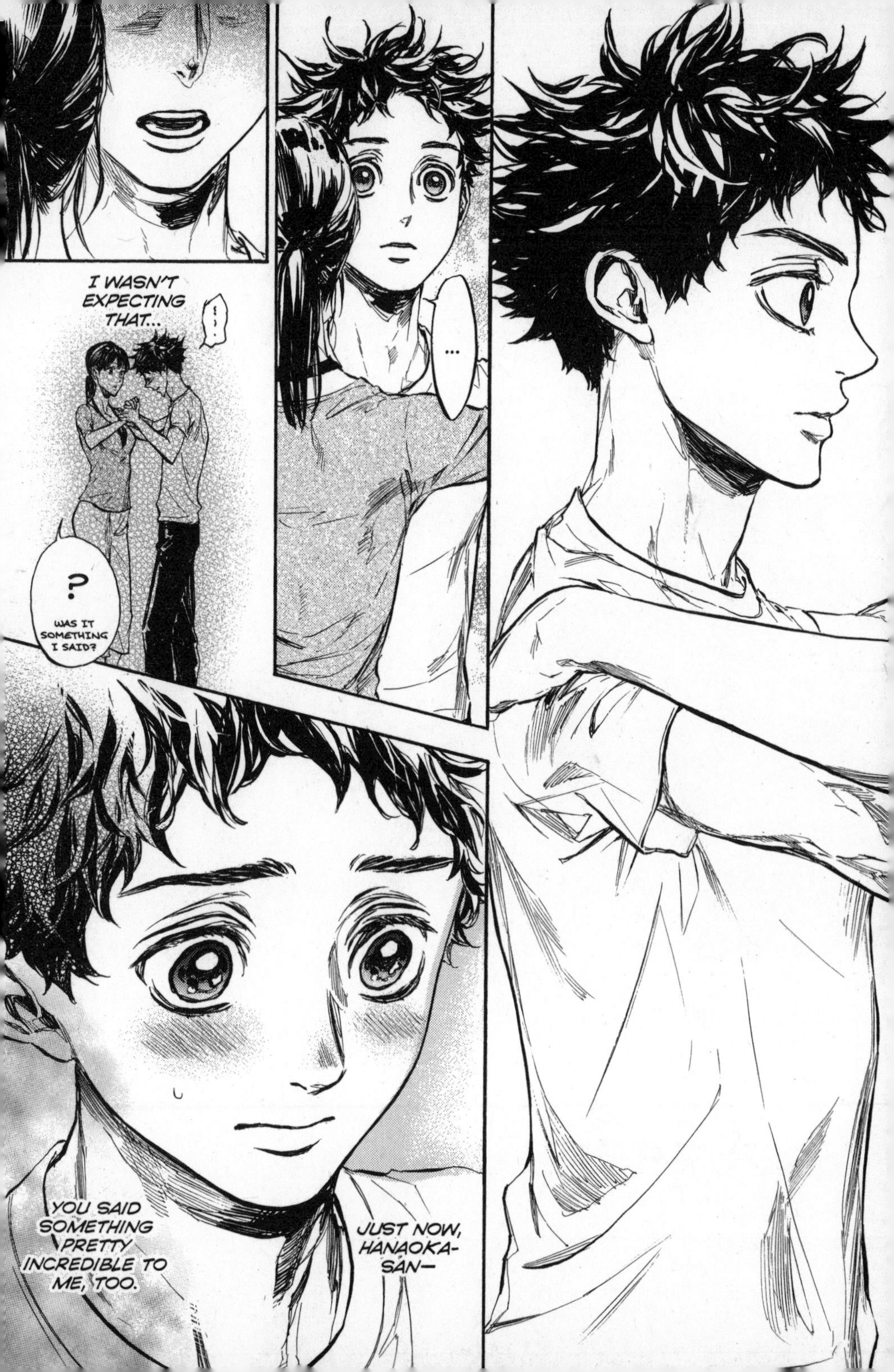

...
I WASN'T EXPECTING THAT...
?
WAS IT SOMETHING I SAID?
JUST NOW, HANAOKA-SAN—
YOU SAID SOMETHING PRETTY INCREDIBLE TO ME, TOO.

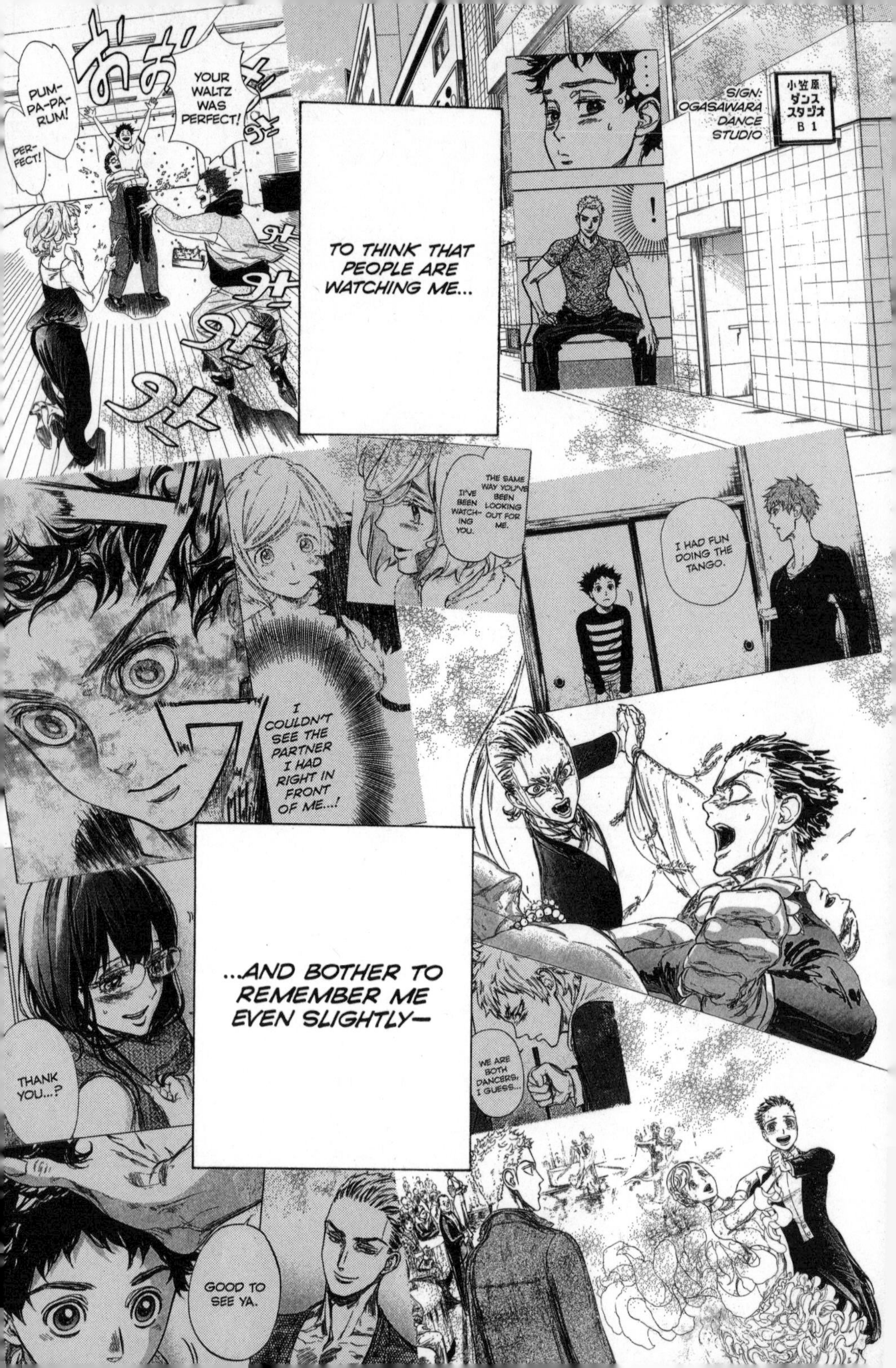

小笠原
ダンス
スタジオ
B 1
SIGN: OGASAWARA DANCE STUDIO
...
!
TO THINK THAT PEOPLE ARE WATCHING ME...
YOUR WALTZ WAS PERFECT!
PUM-PA-PA-RUM!
PERFECT!
I HAD FUN DOING THE TANGO.
THE SAME WAY YOU'VE BEEN LOOKING OUT FOR ME.
I'VE BEEN WATCHING YOU.
I COULDN'T SEE THE PARTNER I HAD RIGHT IN FRONT OF ME...!
WE ARE BOTH DANCERS, I GUESS...
...AND BOTHER TO REMEMBER ME EVEN SLIGHTLY—
THANK YOU...?
GOOD TO SEE YA.

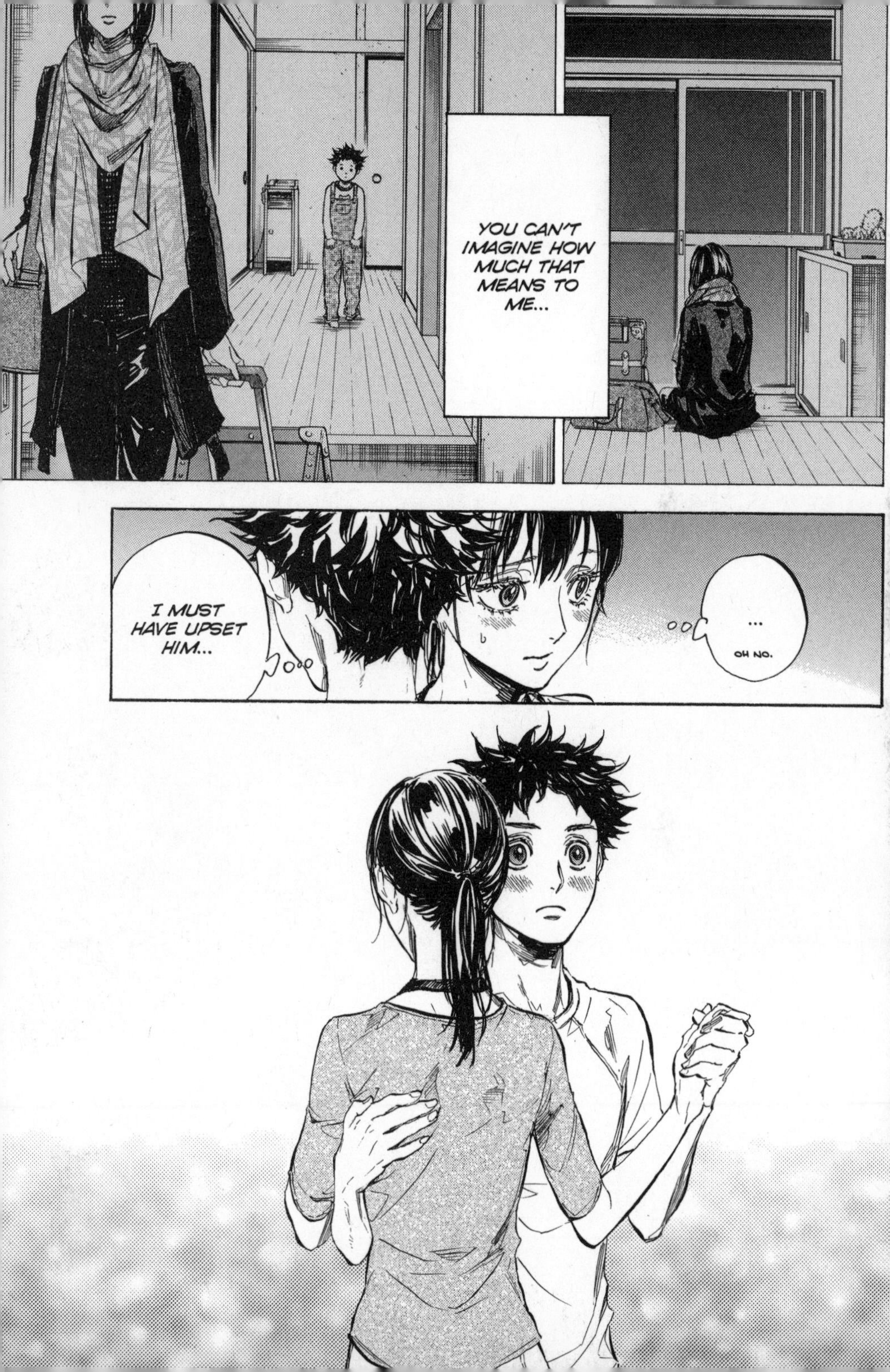

YOU CAN'T IMAGINE HOW MUCH THAT MEANS TO ME...
...
OH NO.
I MUST HAVE UPSET HIM...

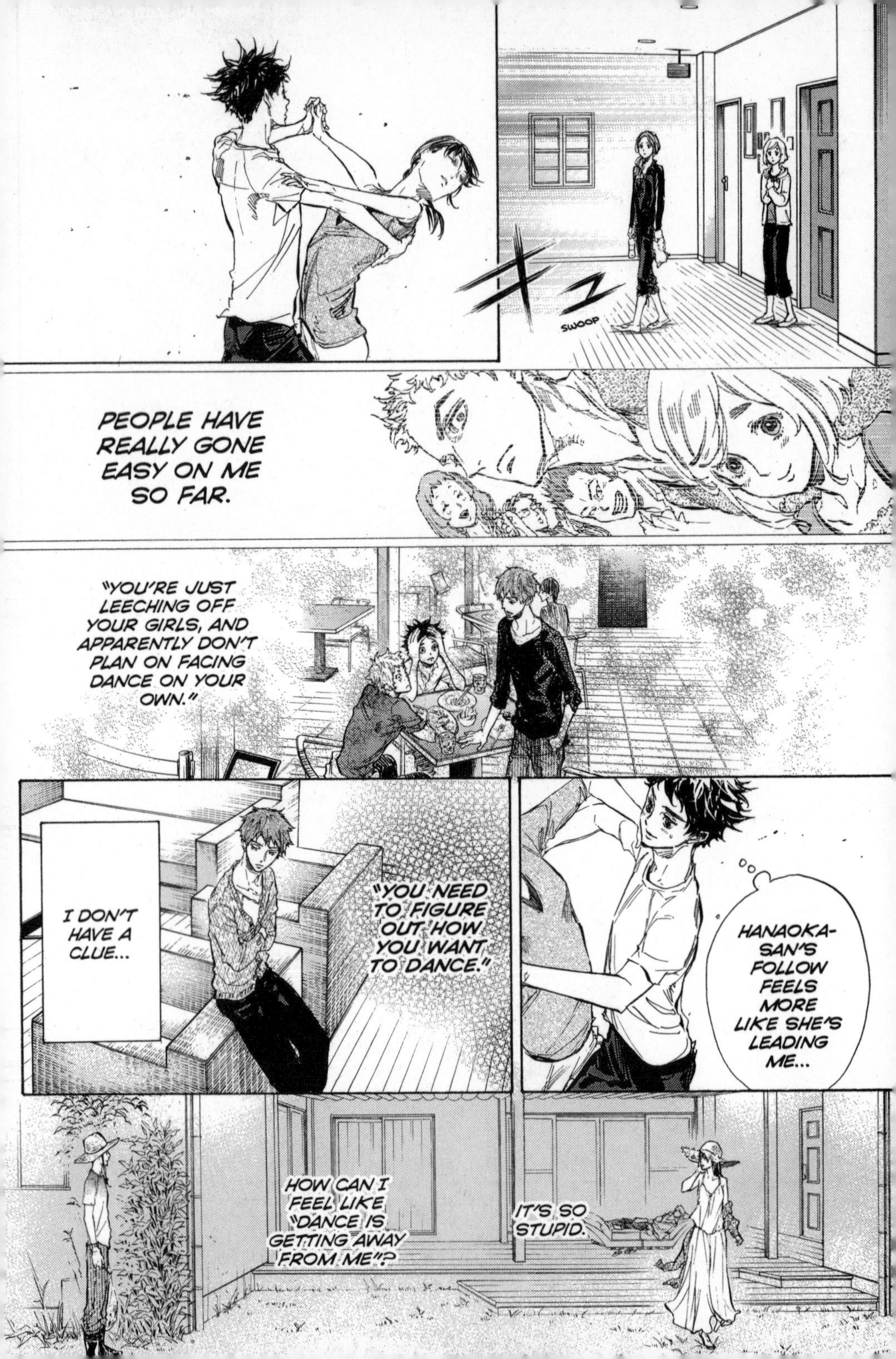
SWOOP
PEOPLE HAVE REALLY GONE EASY ON ME SO FAR.
"YOU'RE JUST LEECHING OFF YOUR GIRLS, AND APPARENTLY DON'T PLAN ON FACING DANCE ON YOUR OWN."
HANAOKA-SAN'S FOLLOW FEELS MORE LIKE SHE'S LEADING ME...
"YOU NEED TO FIGURE OUT HOW YOU WANT TO DANCE."
I DON'T HAVE A CLUE...
IT'S SO STUPID.
HOW CAN I FEEL LIKE "DANCE IS GETTING AWAY FROM ME"?

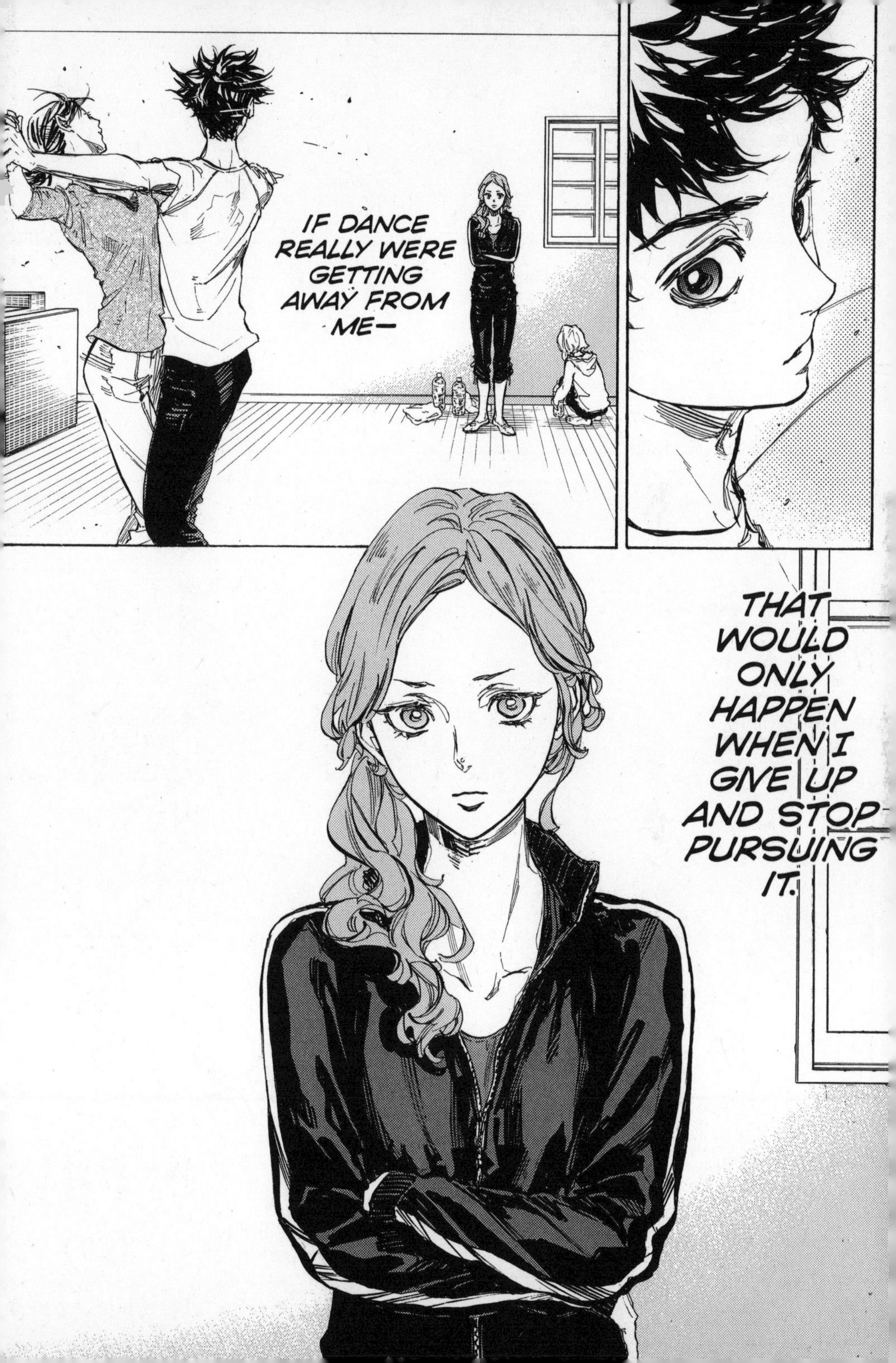
IF DANCE REALLY WERE GETTING AWAY FROM ME—
THAT WOULD ONLY HAPPEN WHEN I GIVE UP AND STOP PURSUING IT.

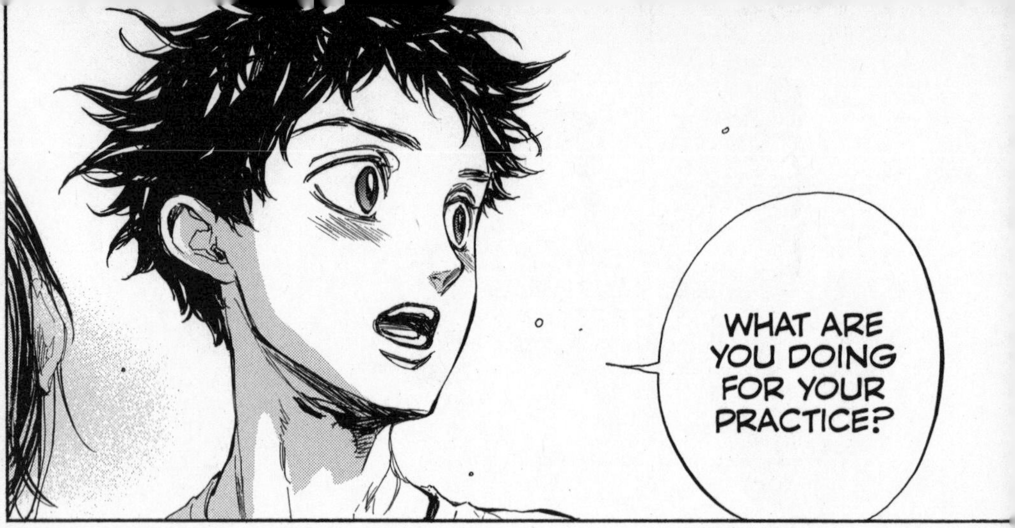
WHAT ARE YOU DOING FOR YOUR PRACTICE?
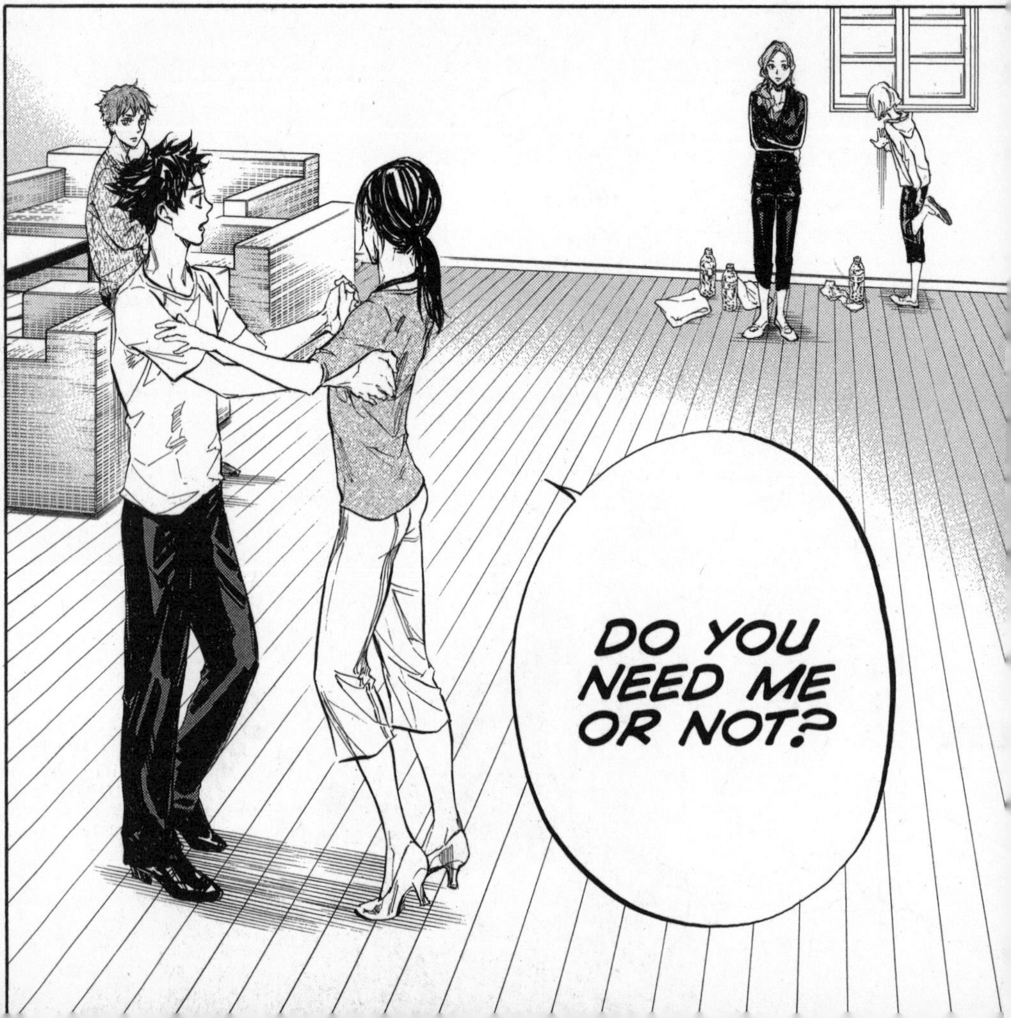
DO YOU NEED ME OR NOT?

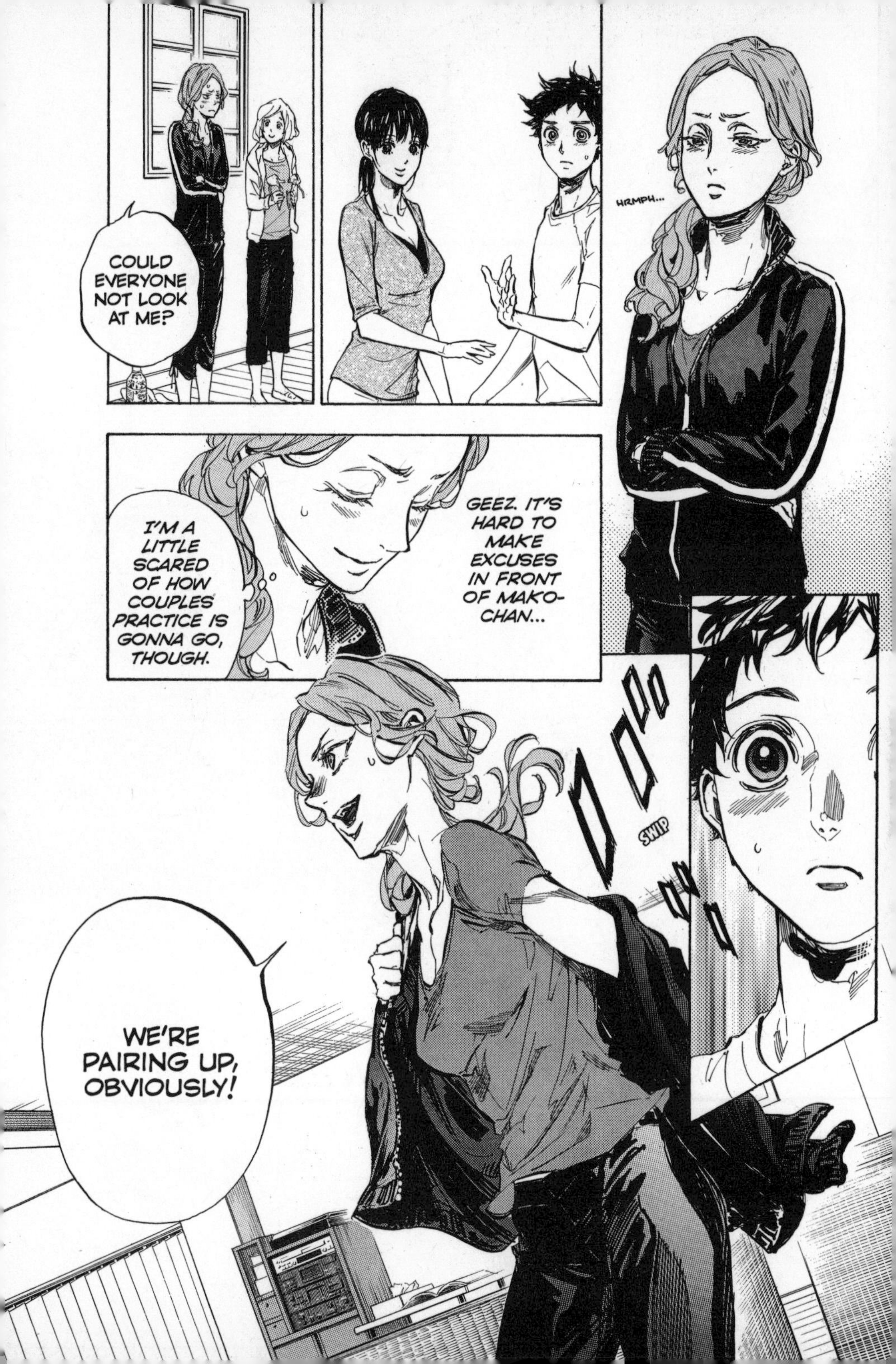
HRMPH...
COULD EVERYONE NOT LOOK AT ME?
GEEZ. IT'S HARD TO MAKE EXCUSES IN FRONT OF MAKO-CHAN...
I'M A LITTLE SCARED OF HOW COUPLES PRACTICE IS GONNA GO, THOUGH.
SWIP
WE'RE PAIRING UP, OBVIOUSLY!

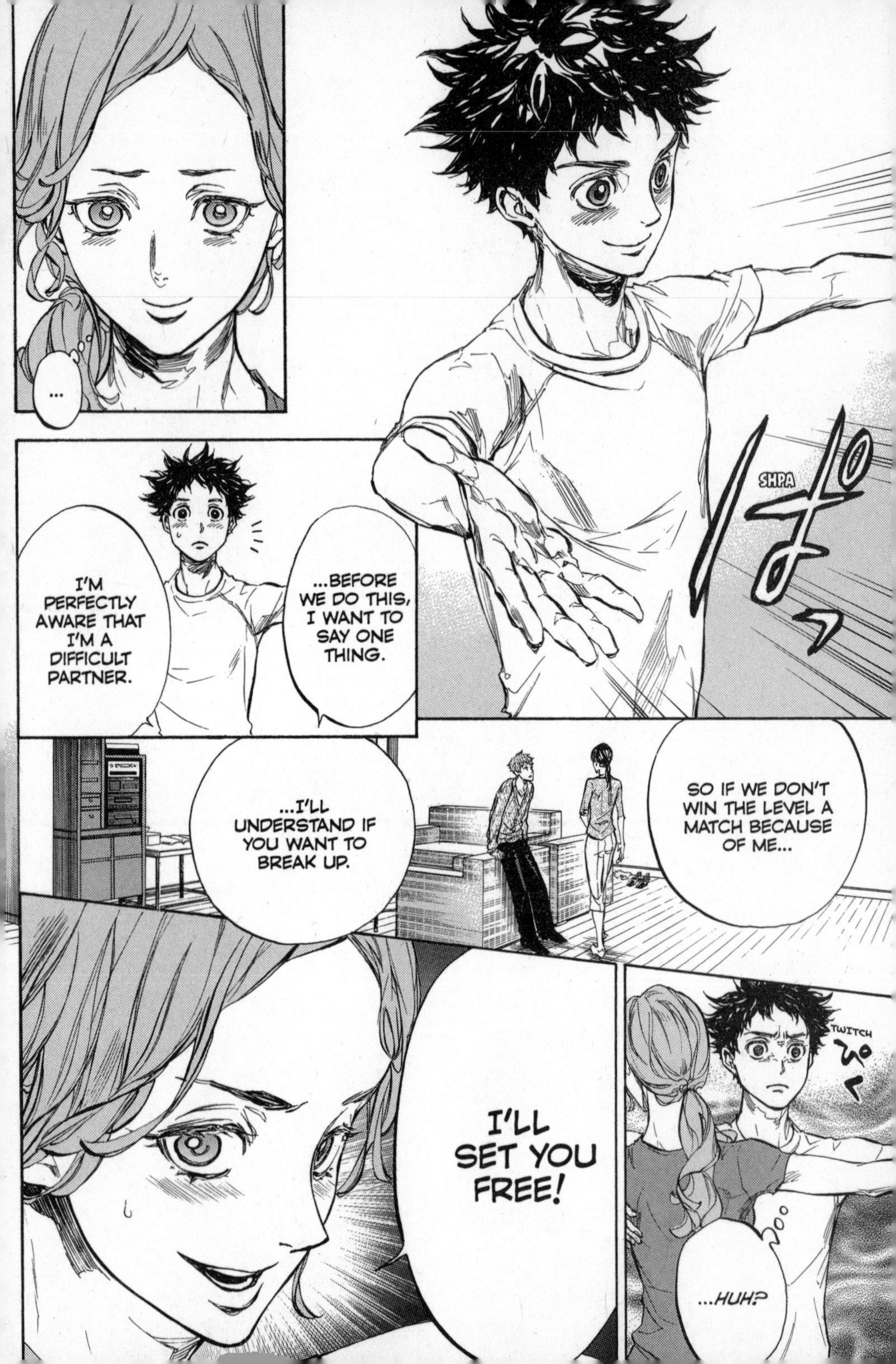
SHPA
...
...BEFORE WE DO THIS, I WANT TO SAY ONE THING.
I'M PERFECTLY AWARE THAT I'M A DIFFICULT PARTNER.
SO IF WE DON'T WIN THE LEVEL A MATCH BECAUSE OF ME...
...I'LL UNDERSTAND IF YOU WANT TO BREAK UP.
I'LL SET YOU FREE!
TWITCH
...HUH?

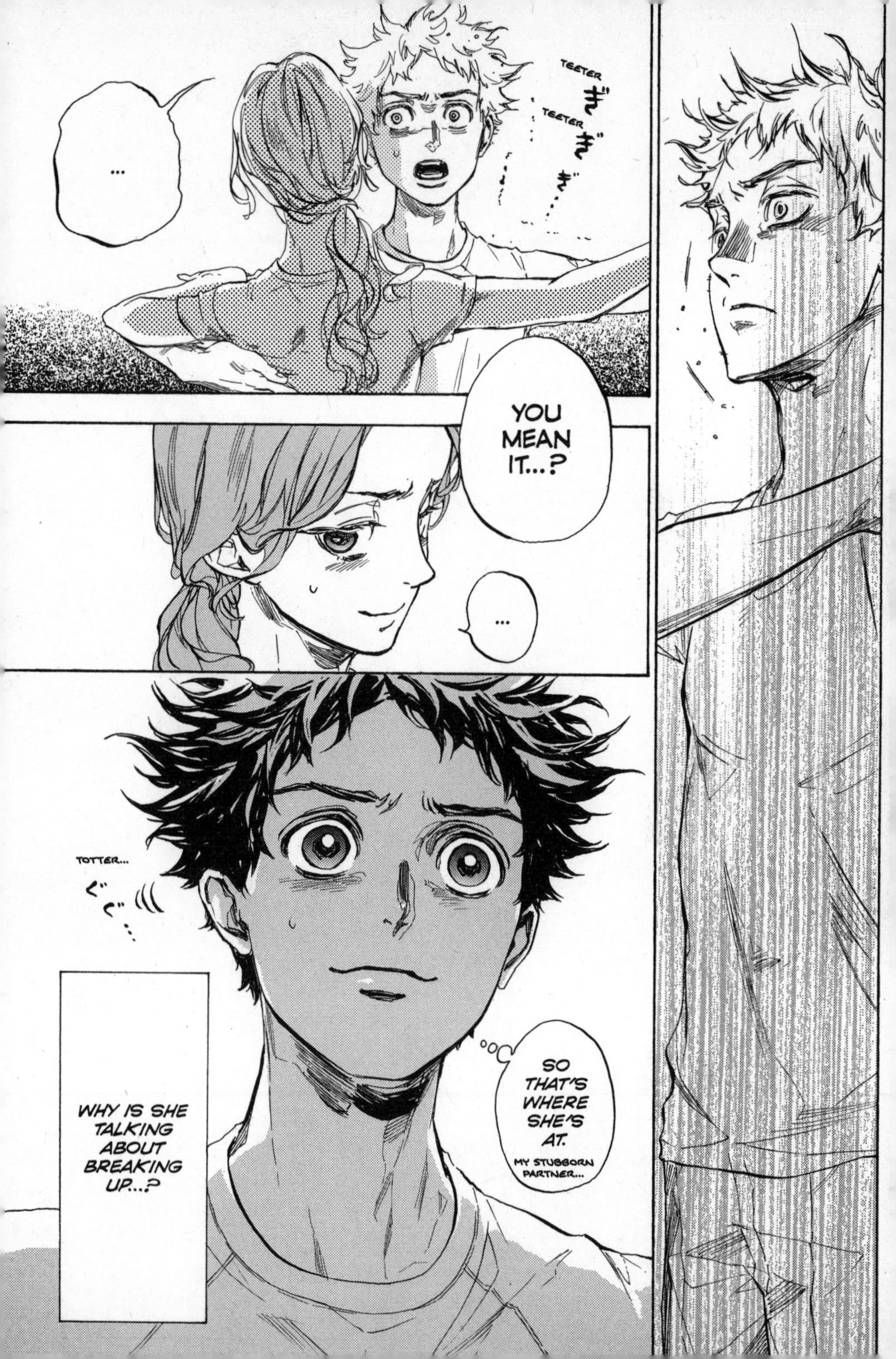
TEETER
TEETER
...
YOU MEAN IT...?
...
SO THAT'S WHERE SHE'S AT.
MY STUBBORN PARTNER...
TOTTER...
WHY IS SHE TALKING ABOUT BREAKING UP...?

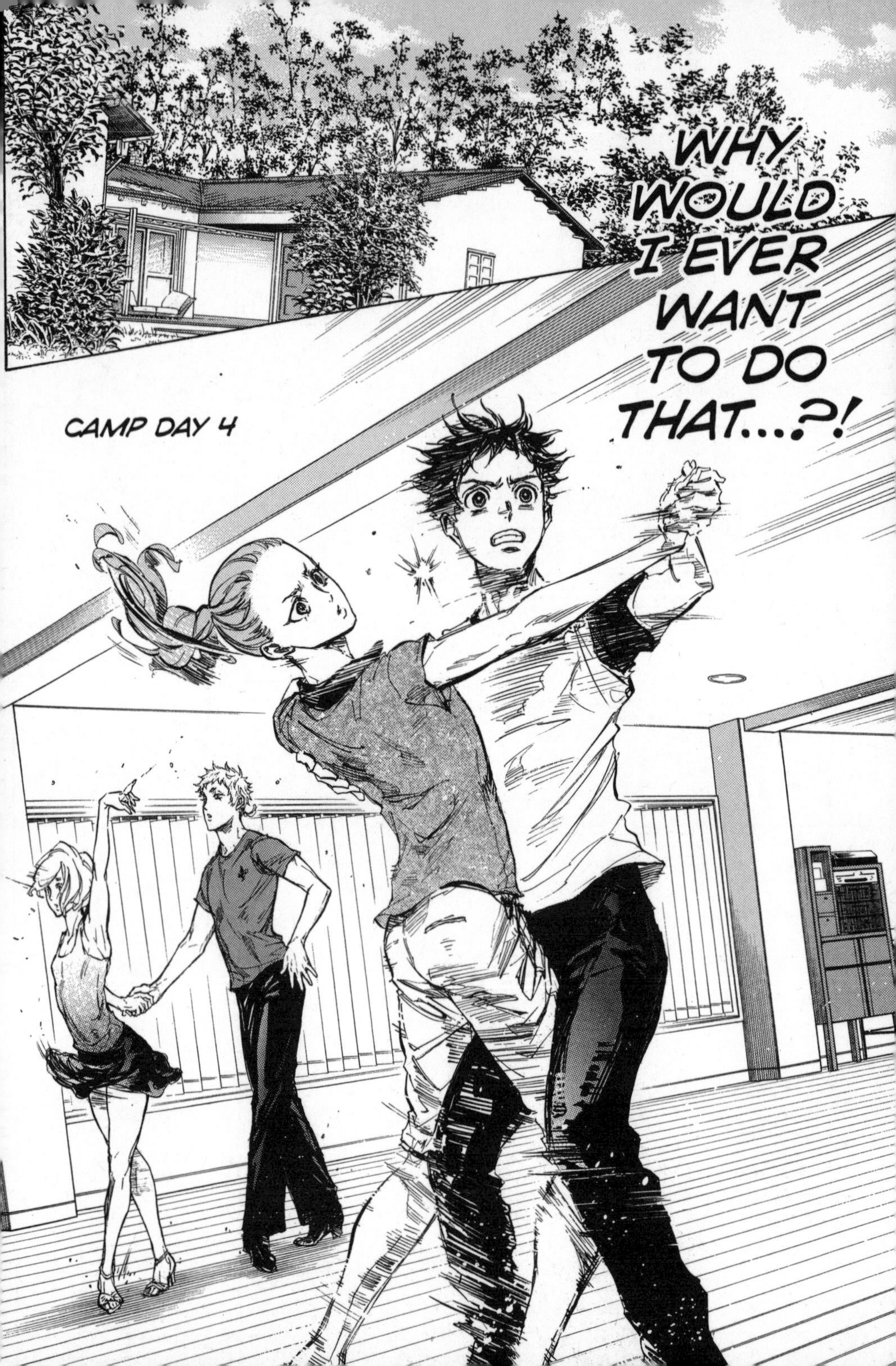
WHY WOULD I EVER WANT TO DO THAT...?!
CAMP DAY 4

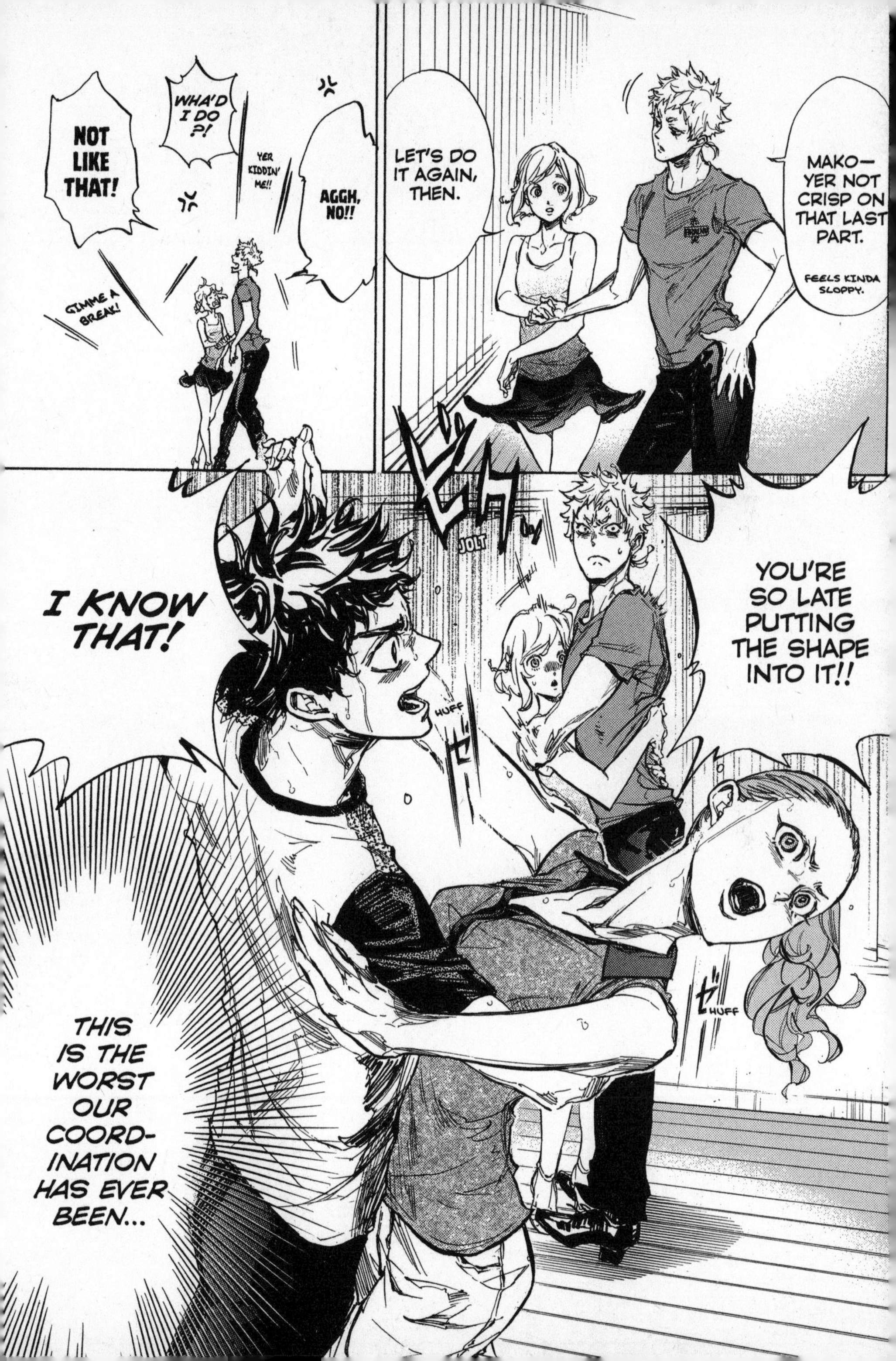
MAKO— YER NOT CRISP ON THAT LAST PART.
FEELS KINDA SLOPPY.
LET'S DO IT AGAIN, THEN.
AGGH, NO!!
YER KIDDIN' ME!!
WHA'D I DO ?!
NOT LIKE THAT!
GIMME A BREAK!
JOLT
YOU'RE SO LATE PUTTING THE SHAPE INTO IT!!
I KNOW THAT!
HUFF
HUFF
THIS IS THE WORST OUR COORD-INATION HAS EVER BEEN...

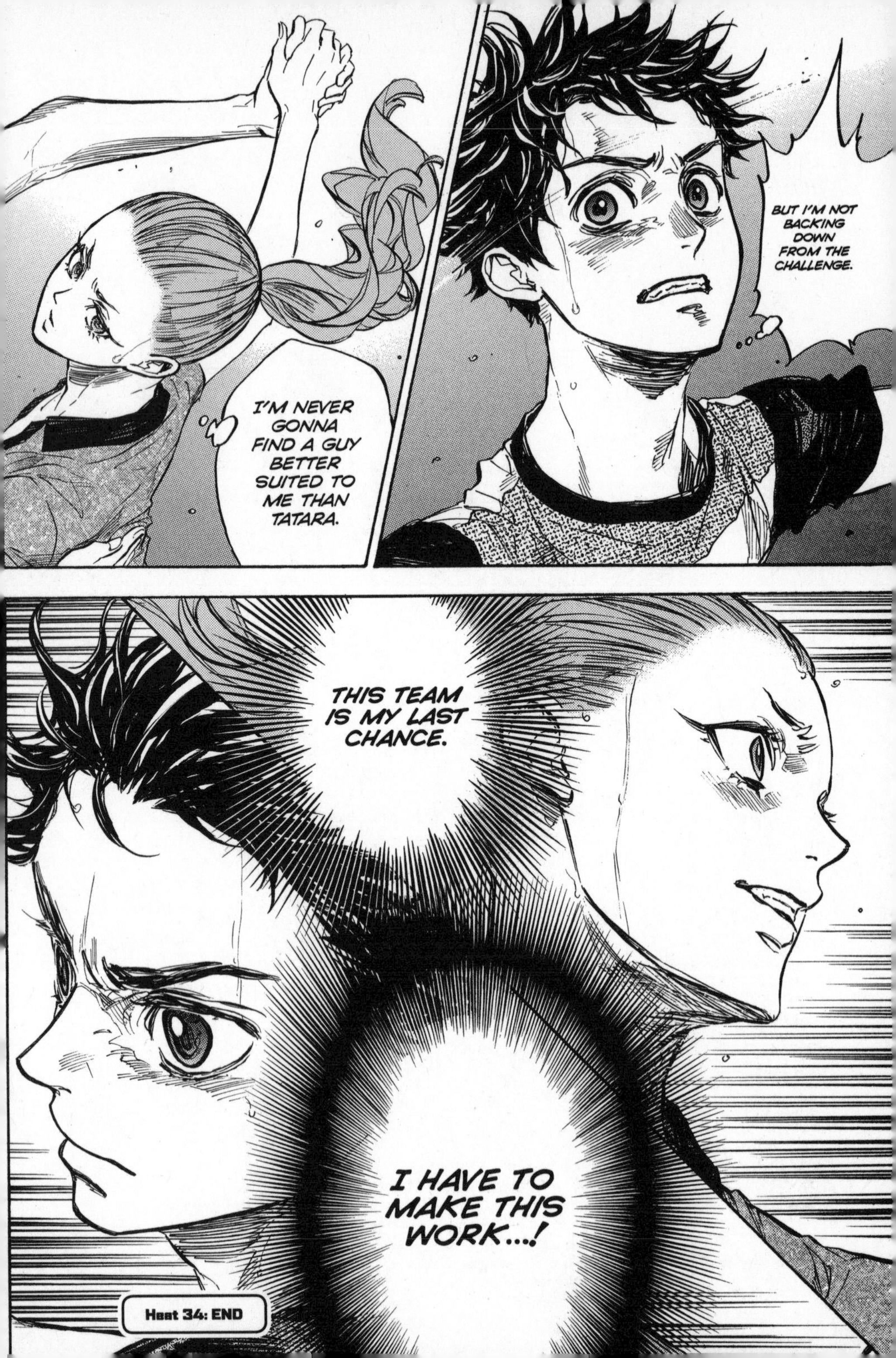
BUT I'M NOT BACKING DOWN FROM THE CHALLENGE.
I'M NEVER GONNA FIND A GUY BETTER SUITED TO ME THAN TATARA.
THIS TEAM IS MY LAST CHANCE.
I HAVE TO MAKE THIS WORK...!
Heat 34: END

ザァ
HSSHHH
ガチャッ
KACHAK
OH, SORRY.
...
KIYO-HARU!!

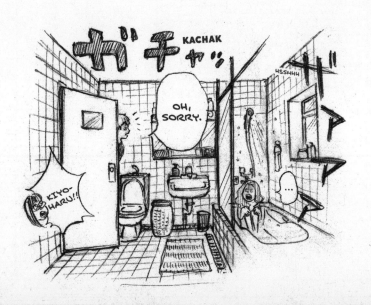

CAMP LOG

	DAY 1	DAY 2	DAY 3	DAY 4	DAY 5	DAY 6
8AM	GET UP					
	AM PRACTICE, JOGGING, STRETCHING	AM PRACTICE	AM PRACTICE	AM PRACTICE		
	BREAKFAST	BREAKFAST	BREAKFAST	BREAKFAST		
	CLEAN	WEEDING		WEEDING		
10	WEEDING	SHADOW	WEEDING			
	LESSON W/ MARISA-SENSEI	HYODO-KUN		COUPLES PRACTICE		
12PM	COUPLES PRACTICE	SHADOW	SHADOW			
			MUSCLE TRAINING			
		LUNCH	SHADOW	SHADOW		
		JOGGING		LUNCH		
2		VIDEO		LESSON W/ MARISA-SENSEI		
	LESSON W/ TEAM HYODO	PHYSICAL TRAINING	EXCURSION	COUPLES PRACTICE		
4				STRETCHING		
		VIDEO (GRAND PRIX IN OSAKA)		PHYSICAL & MUSCLE TRAINING		
	SHADOW		LESSON W/ HANAOKA-SAN			
6	PREP	SHOPPING (W/ IDOGAWA-SAN)	COUPLES PRACTICE	COUPLES PRACTICE		
	DINNER	PREP				
	TIDY	DINNER		PREP		
8	BREAK	TIDY	DINNER	DINNER		
	BATH	BREAK		VIDEO		
		SHADOW	COUPLES PRACTICE	SHADOW		
10	PM PRACTICE (SHADOW)	MUSCLE TRAINING				
		SHOWER		BATH		
	STRETCH W/ MUSIC	STRETCHING	SHOWER	STRETCHING		
		ASLEEP	STRETCHING			
12	ASLEEP		ASLEEP	ASLEEP		
IMPRESSIONS	THE BARBEQUE I HAD FOR LUNCH WAS REALLY GOOD. CAN'T COMMUNICATE WITH MY PARTNER. HYODO-KUN & HANAOKA-SAN TAUGHT US LOTS OF VERY DIFFICULT THINGS.	GOT GUIDANCE ON SHADOWING FROM HYODO-KUN. COULDN'T DO COUPLES PRACTICE. GAJU CAME IN TO USE THE TOILET WHILE I WAS SHOWERING, WHICH WAS NOT PLEASANT.	SINCE A PASSIVE LEADER CAUSES PROBLEMS FOR THEIR PARTNER, I'LL TRY TO ACT STRONGER & MORE INDEPENDENT. I WANT TO BE FAITHFUL TO BASICS WHEN DANCING, BUT ALSO HAVE TO EXPRESS MYSELF, SO I'M CONFLICTED.	OUR MOVEMENTS AS A COUPLE HAVE BECOME EVEN MORE OUT OF SYNC THAN BEFORE. HYODO-KUN TOLD US THAT'S BECAUSE WE DON'T SHARE A COMMON VISION OF OUR DANCE.		

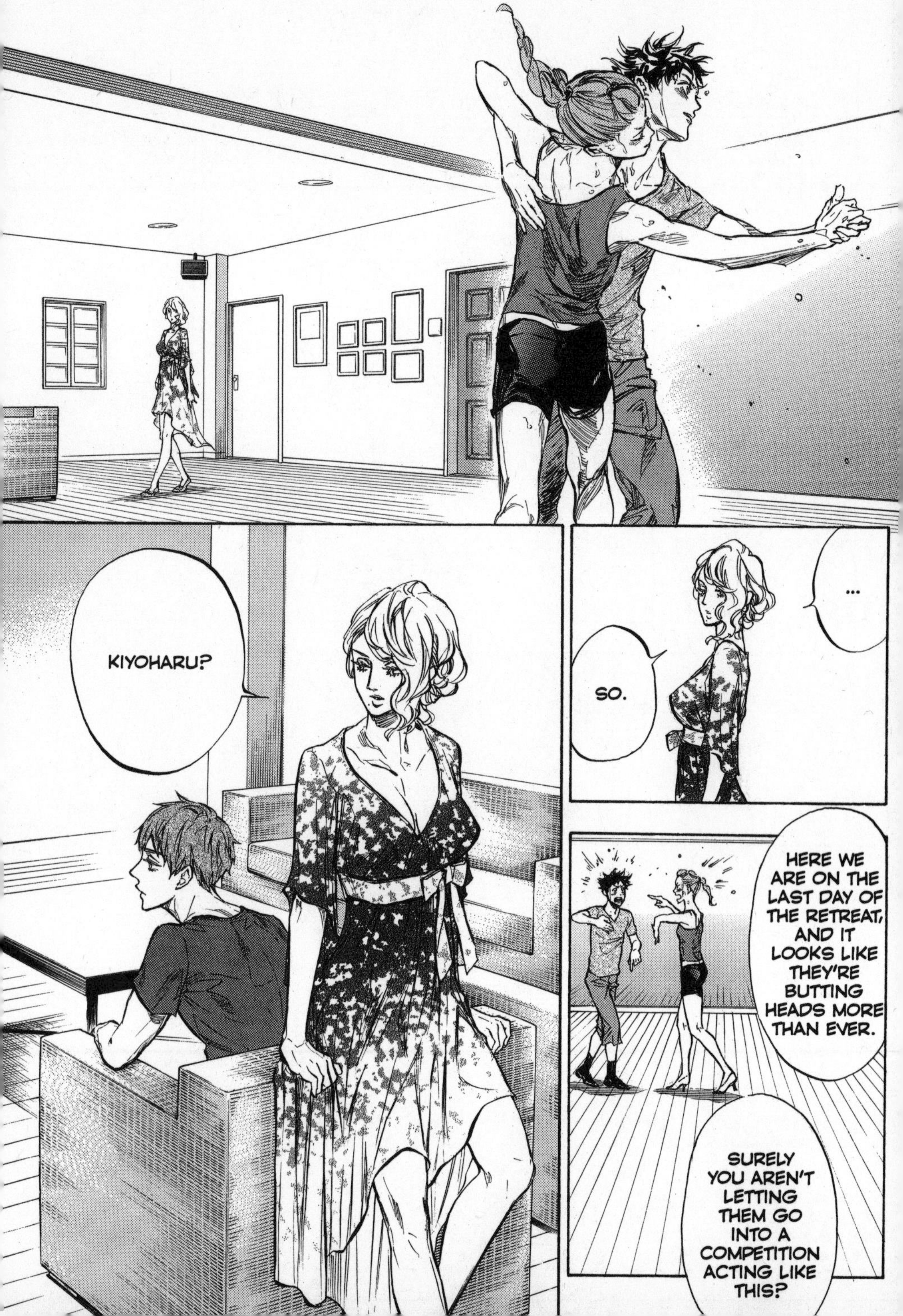
...
SO.
HERE WE ARE ON THE LAST DAY OF THE RETREAT, AND IT LOOKS LIKE THEY'RE BUTTING HEADS MORE THAN EVER.
SURELY YOU AREN'T LETTING THEM GO INTO A COMPETITION ACTING LIKE THIS?
KIYOHARU?

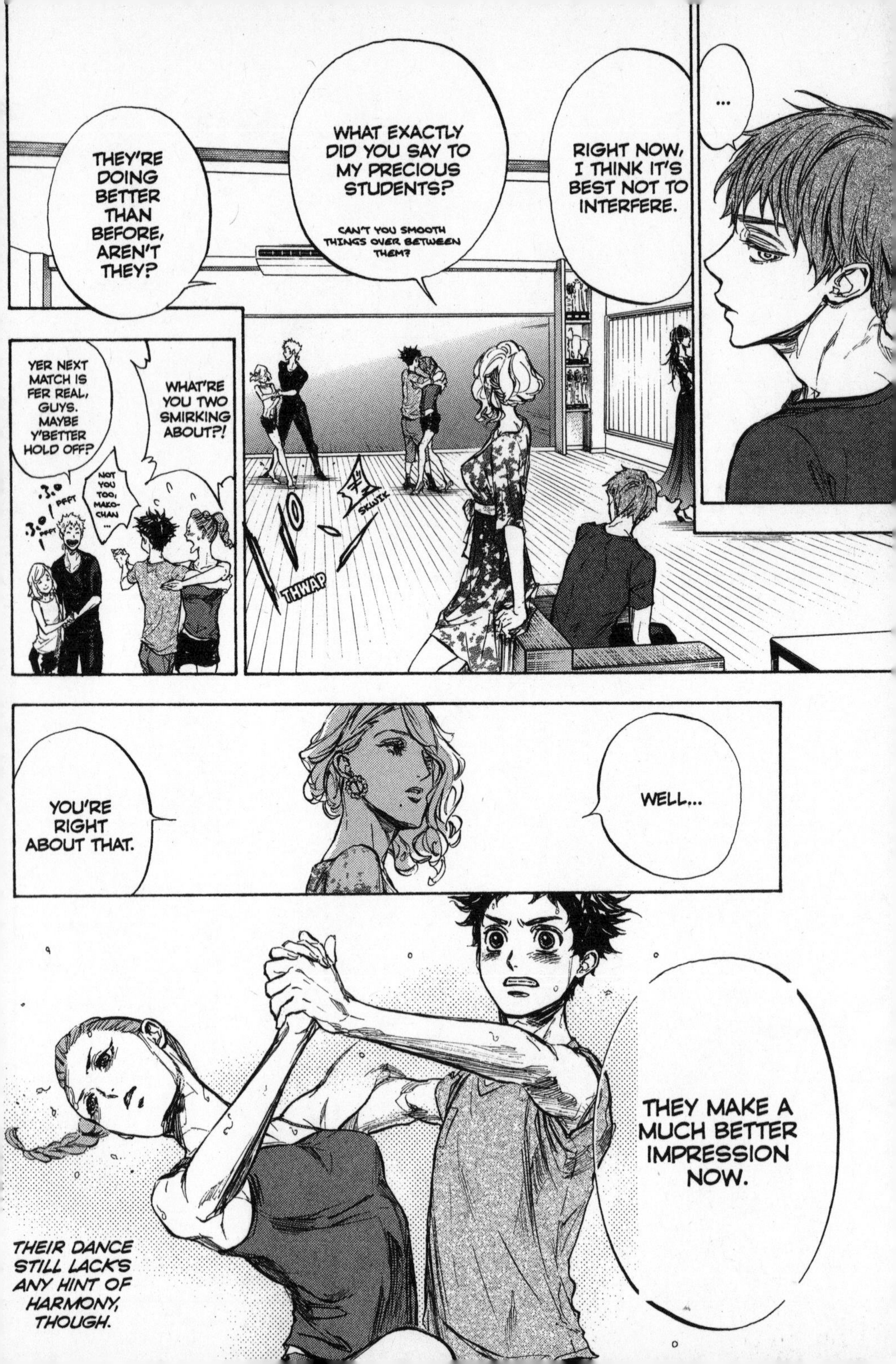
...
RIGHT NOW, I THINK IT'S BEST NOT TO INTERFERE.
WHAT EXACTLY DID YOU SAY TO MY PRECIOUS STUDENTS?
CAN'T YOU SMOOTH THINGS OVER BETWEEN THEM?
THEY'RE DOING BETTER THAN BEFORE, AREN'T THEY?
SKWIK
THWAP
WHAT'RE YOU TWO SMIRKING ABOUT?!
NOT YOU TOO, MAKO-CHAN...
YER NEXT MATCH IS FER REAL, GUYS. MAYBE Y'BETTER HOLD OFF?
PFFT
PFFT
WELL...
YOU'RE RIGHT ABOUT THAT.
THEY MAKE A MUCH BETTER IMPRESSION NOW.
THEIR DANCE STILL LACKS ANY HINT OF HARMONY, THOUGH.

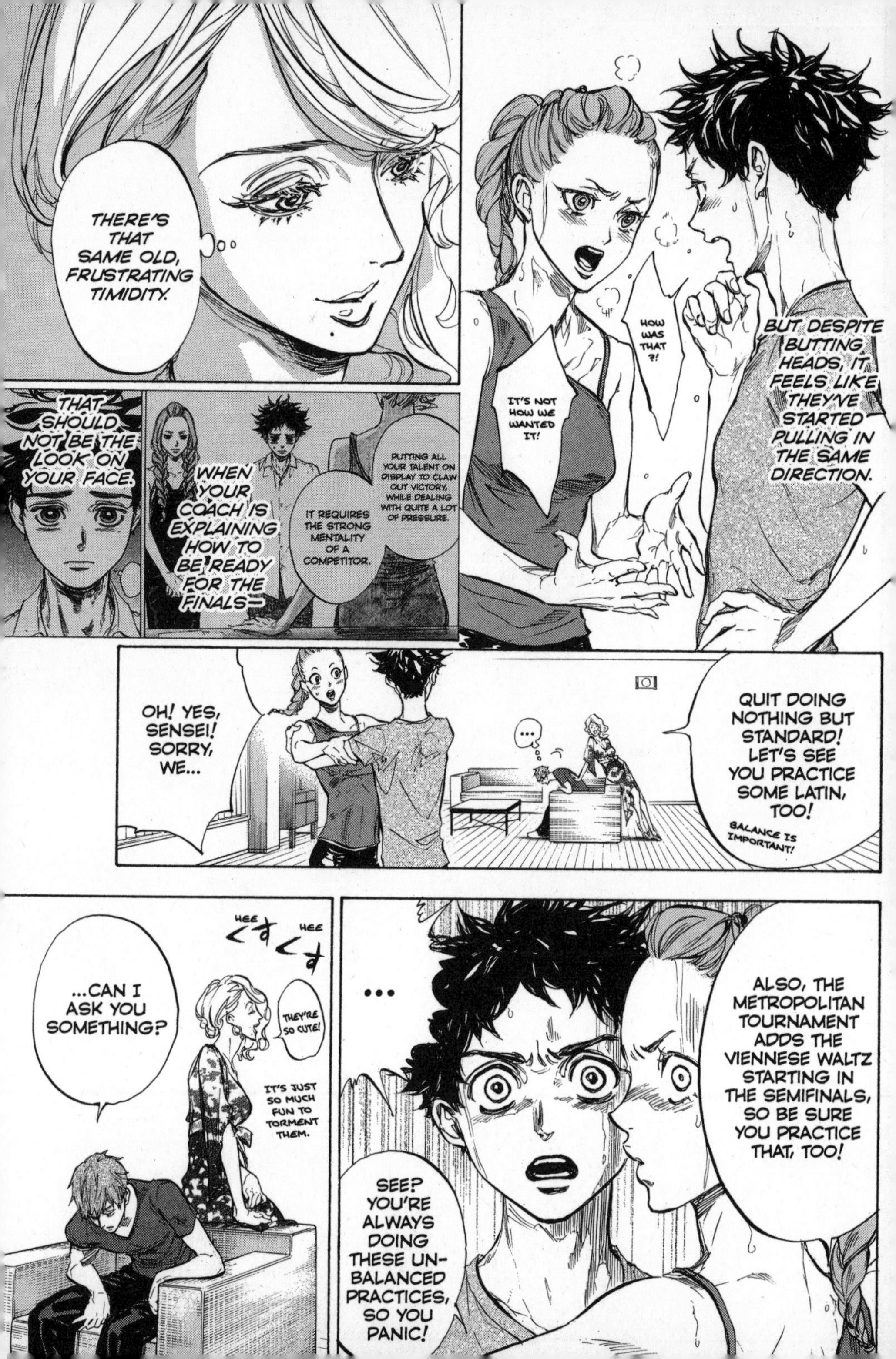
HOW WAS THAT?!
IT'S NOT HOW WE WANTED IT!
BUT DESPITE BUTTING HEADS, IT FEELS LIKE THEY'VE STARTED PULLING IN THE SAME DIRECTION.
THERE'S THAT SAME OLD, FRUSTRATING TIMIDITY.
PUTTING ALL YOUR TALENT ON DISPLAY TO CLAW OUT VICTORY, WHILE DEALING WITH QUITE A LOT OF PRESSURE.
IT REQUIRES THE STRONG MENTALITY OF A COMPETITOR.
WHEN YOUR COACH IS EXPLAINING HOW TO BE READY FOR THE FINALS—
THAT SHOULD NOT BE THE LOOK ON YOUR FACE.
QUIT DOING NOTHING BUT STANDARD! LET'S SEE YOU PRACTICE SOME LATIN, TOO!
BALANCE IS IMPORTANT!
...
OH! YES, SENSEI! SORRY, WE...
ALSO, THE METROPOLITAN TOURNAMENT ADDS THE VIENNESE WALTZ STARTING IN THE SEMIFINALS, SO BE SURE YOU PRACTICE THAT, TOO!
...
SEE? YOU'RE ALWAYS DOING THESE UN-BALANCED PRACTICES, SO YOU PANIC!
HEE くす HEE くす
THEY'RE SO CUTE!
IT'S JUST SO MUCH FUN TO TORMENT THEM.
...CAN I ASK YOU SOMETHING?

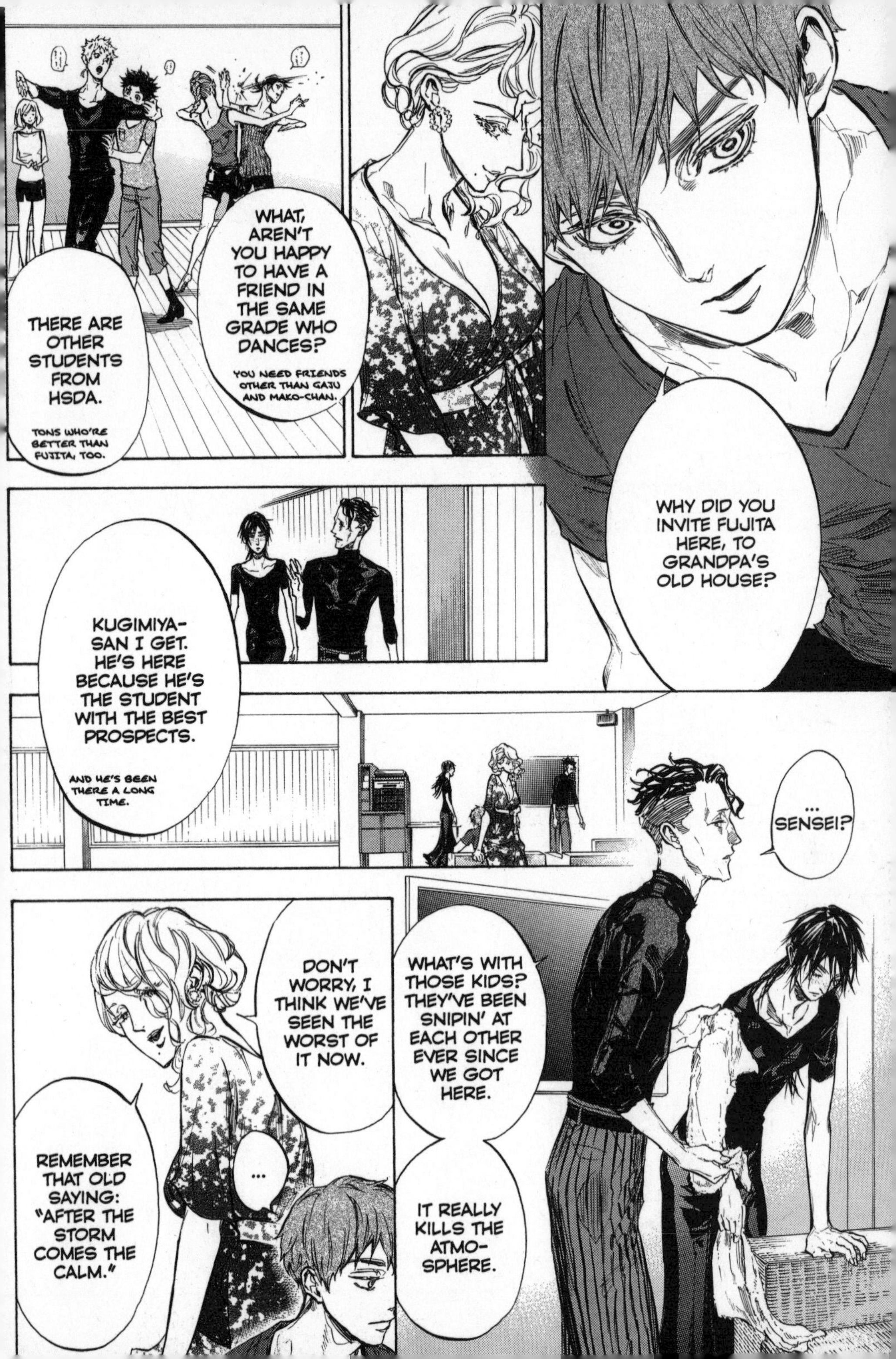
WHY DID YOU INVITE FUJITA HERE, TO GRANDPA'S OLD HOUSE?
WHAT, AREN'T YOU HAPPY TO HAVE A FRIEND IN THE SAME GRADE WHO DANCES?
YOU NEED FRIENDS OTHER THAN GAJU AND MAKO-CHAN.
THERE ARE OTHER STUDENTS FROM HSDA.
TONS WHO'RE BETTER THAN FUJITA, TOO.
KUGIMIYA-SAN I GET. HE'S HERE BECAUSE HE'S THE STUDENT WITH THE BEST PROSPECTS.
AND HE'S BEEN THERE A LONG TIME.
...SENSEI?
WHAT'S WITH THOSE KIDS? THEY'VE BEEN SNIPIN' AT EACH OTHER EVER SINCE WE GOT HERE.
IT REALLY KILLS THE ATMOSPHERE.
DON'T WORRY, I THINK WE'VE SEEN THE WORST OF IT NOW.
...
REMEMBER THAT OLD SAYING: "AFTER THE STORM COMES THE CALM."

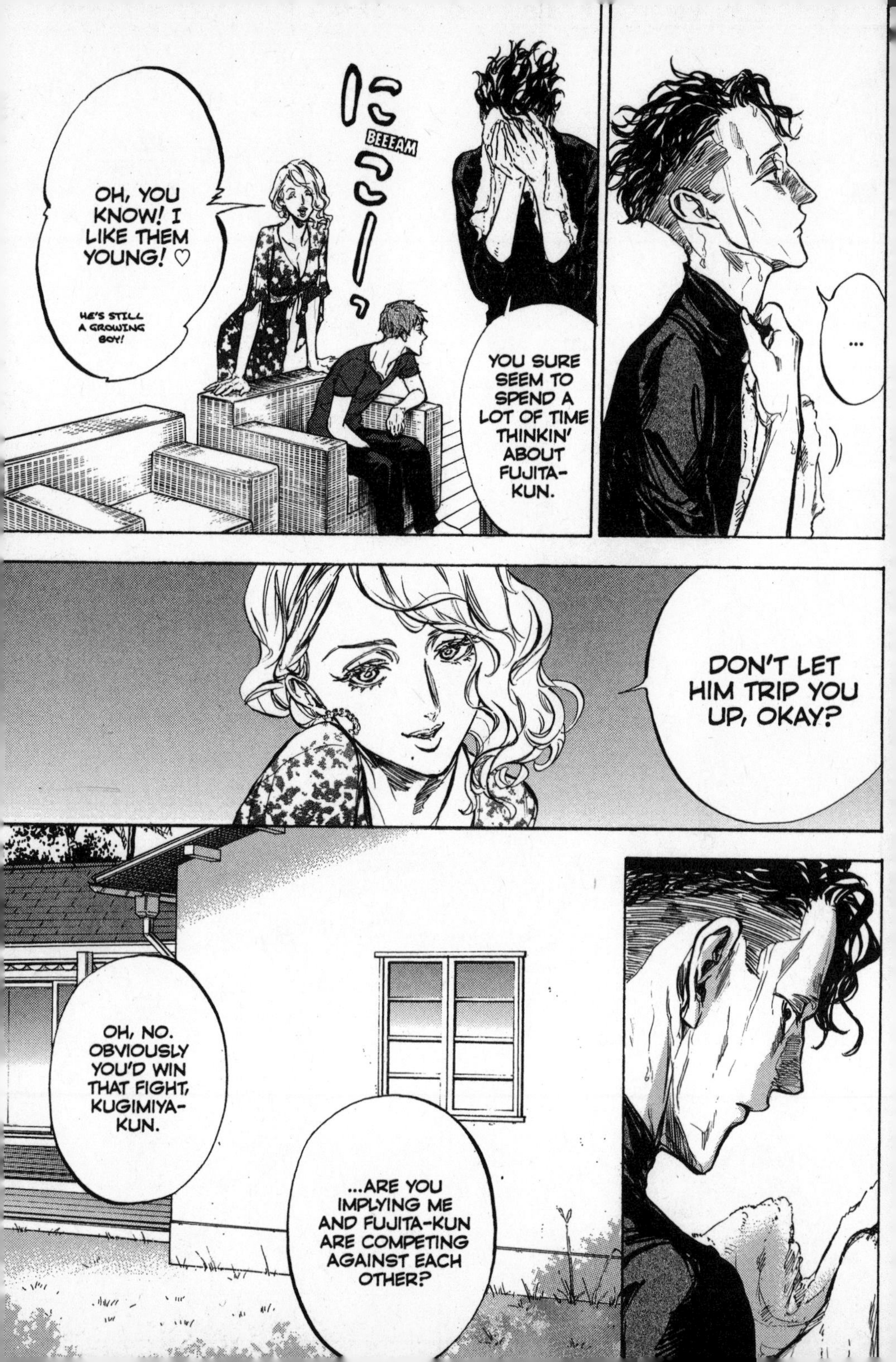
...
YOU SURE SEEM TO SPEND A LOT OF TIME THINKIN' ABOUT FUJITA-KUN.
にこーっ
BEEEAM
OH, YOU KNOW! I LIKE THEM YOUNG! ♡
HE'S STILL A GROWING BOY!
DON'T LET HIM TRIP YOU UP, OKAY?
...ARE YOU IMPLYING ME AND FUJITA-KUN ARE COMPETING AGAINST EACH OTHER?
OH, NO. OBVIOUSLY YOU'D WIN THAT FIGHT, KUGIMIYA-KUN.

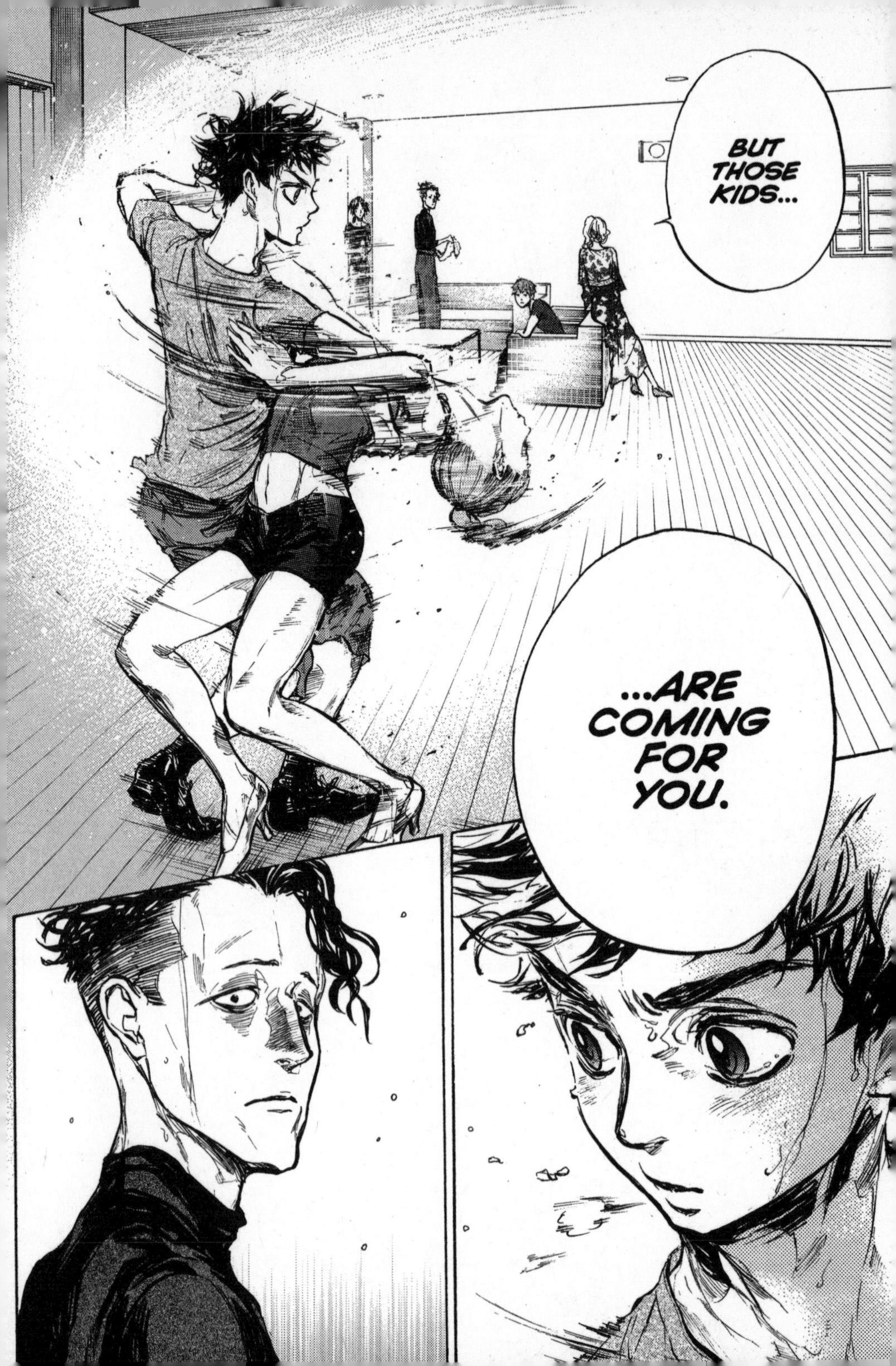
BUT THOSE KIDS...
...ARE COMING FOR YOU.

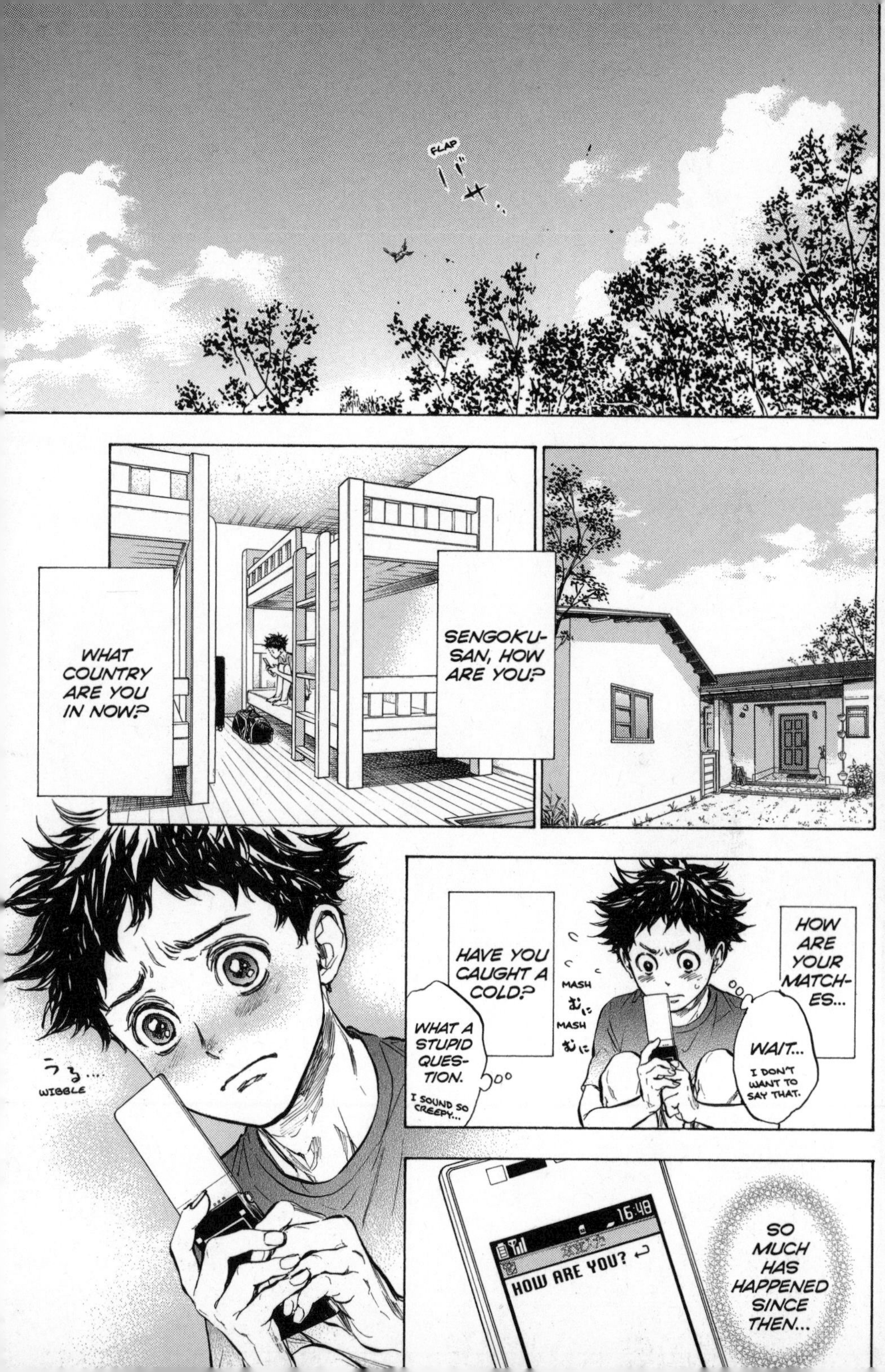
FLAP
SENGOKU-SAN, HOW ARE YOU?
WHAT COUNTRY ARE YOU IN NOW?
HOW ARE YOUR MATCHES...
WAIT...
I DON'T WANT TO SAY THAT.
MASH
MASH
HAVE YOU CAUGHT A COLD?
WHAT A STUPID QUESTION.
I SOUND SO CREEPY...
16:48
HOW ARE YOU?
SO MUCH HAS HAPPENED SINCE THEN...
WIBBLE

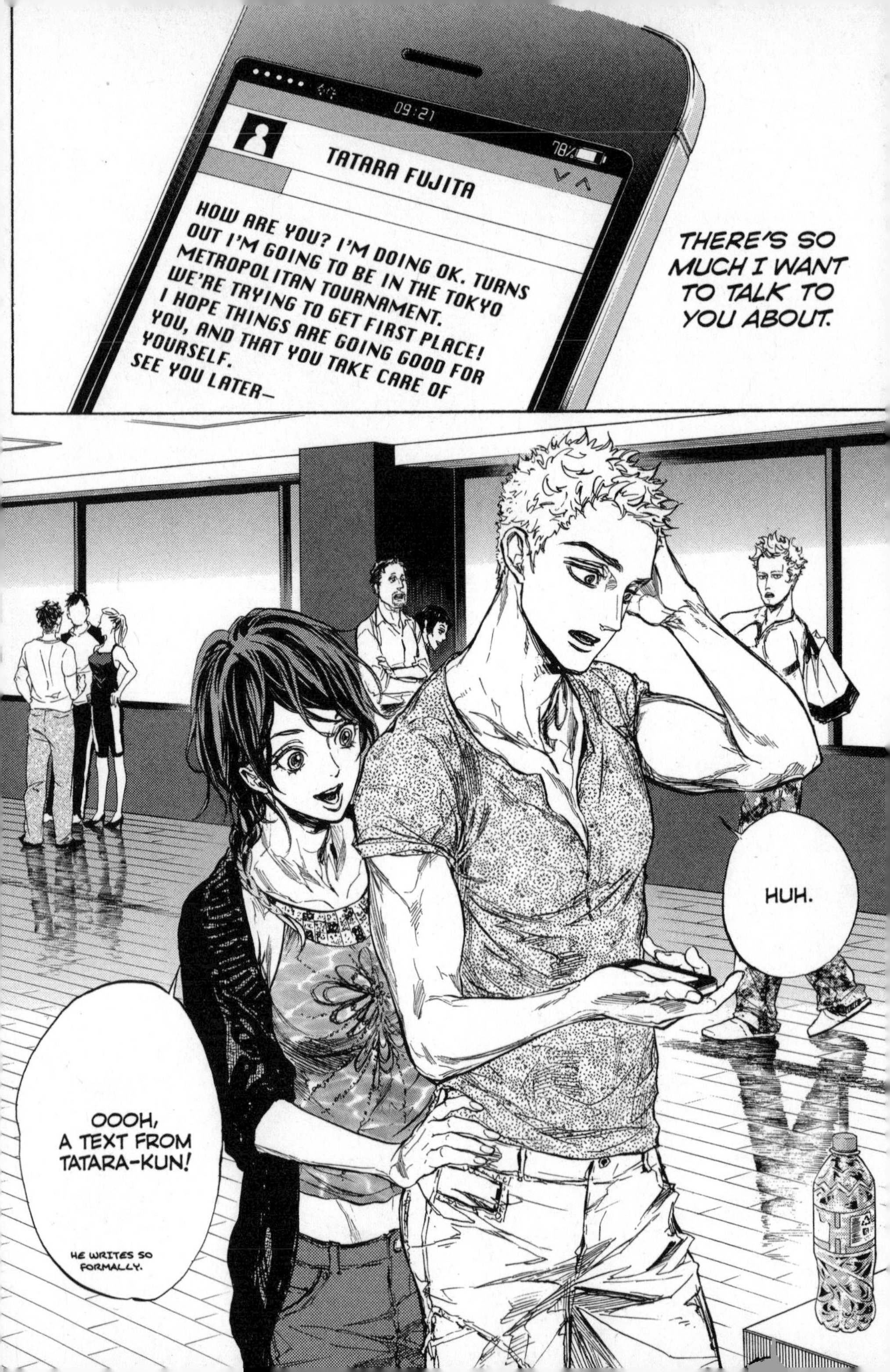
THERE'S SO MUCH I WANT TO TALK TO YOU ABOUT.
09:21
78%
TATARA FUJITA
HOW ARE YOU? I'M DOING OK. TURNS OUT I'M GOING TO BE IN THE TOKYO METROPOLITAN TOURNAMENT. WE'RE TRYING TO GET FIRST PLACE! I HOPE THINGS ARE GOING GOOD FOR YOU, AND THAT YOU TAKE CARE OF YOURSELF. SEE YOU LATER–
HUH.
OOOH, A TEXT FROM TATARA-KUN!
HE WRITES SO FORMALLY.

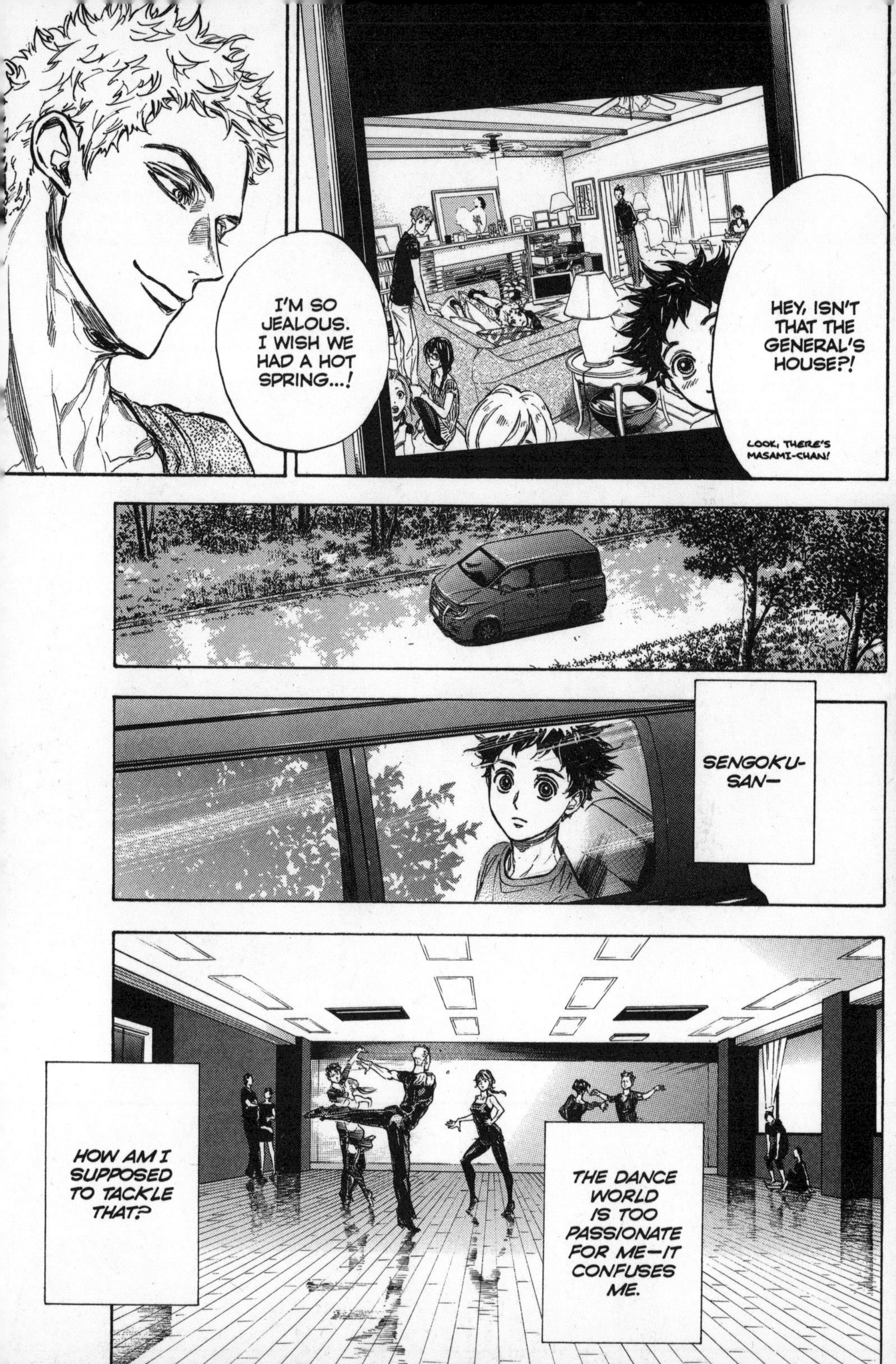
HEY, ISN'T THAT THE GENERAL'S HOUSE?!
LOOK, THERE'S MASAMI-CHAN!
I'M SO JEALOUS. I WISH WE HAD A HOT SPRING...!
SENGOKU-SAN—
THE DANCE WORLD IS TOO PASSIONATE FOR ME—IT CONFUSES ME.
HOW AM I SUPPOSED TO TACKLE THAT?

I'VE BEEN TAUGHT A LOT, BUT I DON'T KNOW HOW TO PROCESS IT.

AND I'M NOT SURE WHETHER I'VE DEVELOPED THE WAY I'VE BEEN TAUGHT.

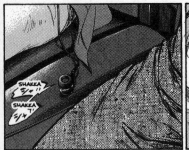

SHAKKA
SHAKKA

POP

I'VE LEARNED THAT I DON'T KNOW ENOUGH ABOUT DANCE TO BE ABLE TO CONVEY MY OWN DANCE.

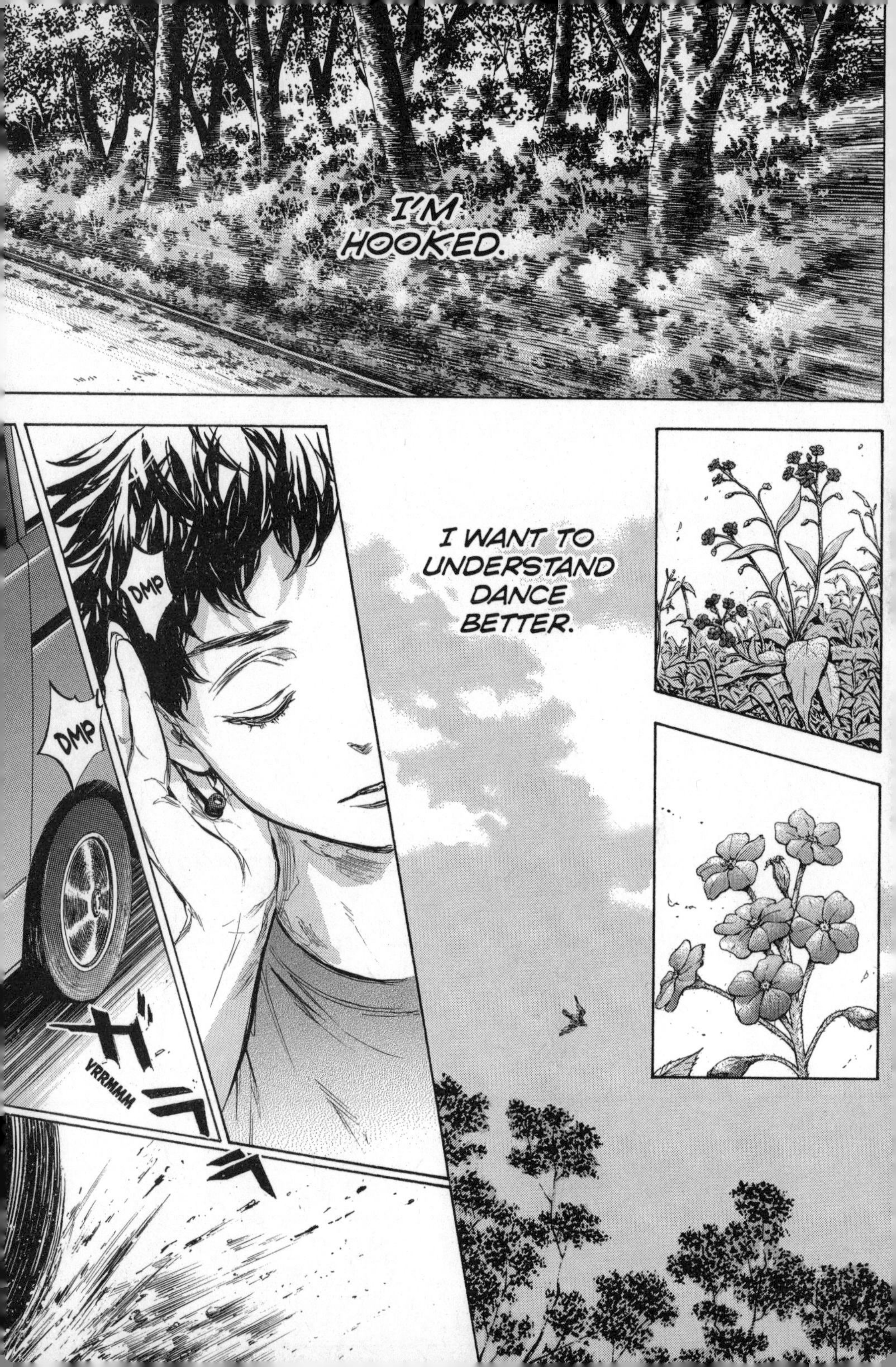
I'M HOOKED.
I WANT TO UNDERSTAND DANCE BETTER.
DMP
DMP
VRRMMM

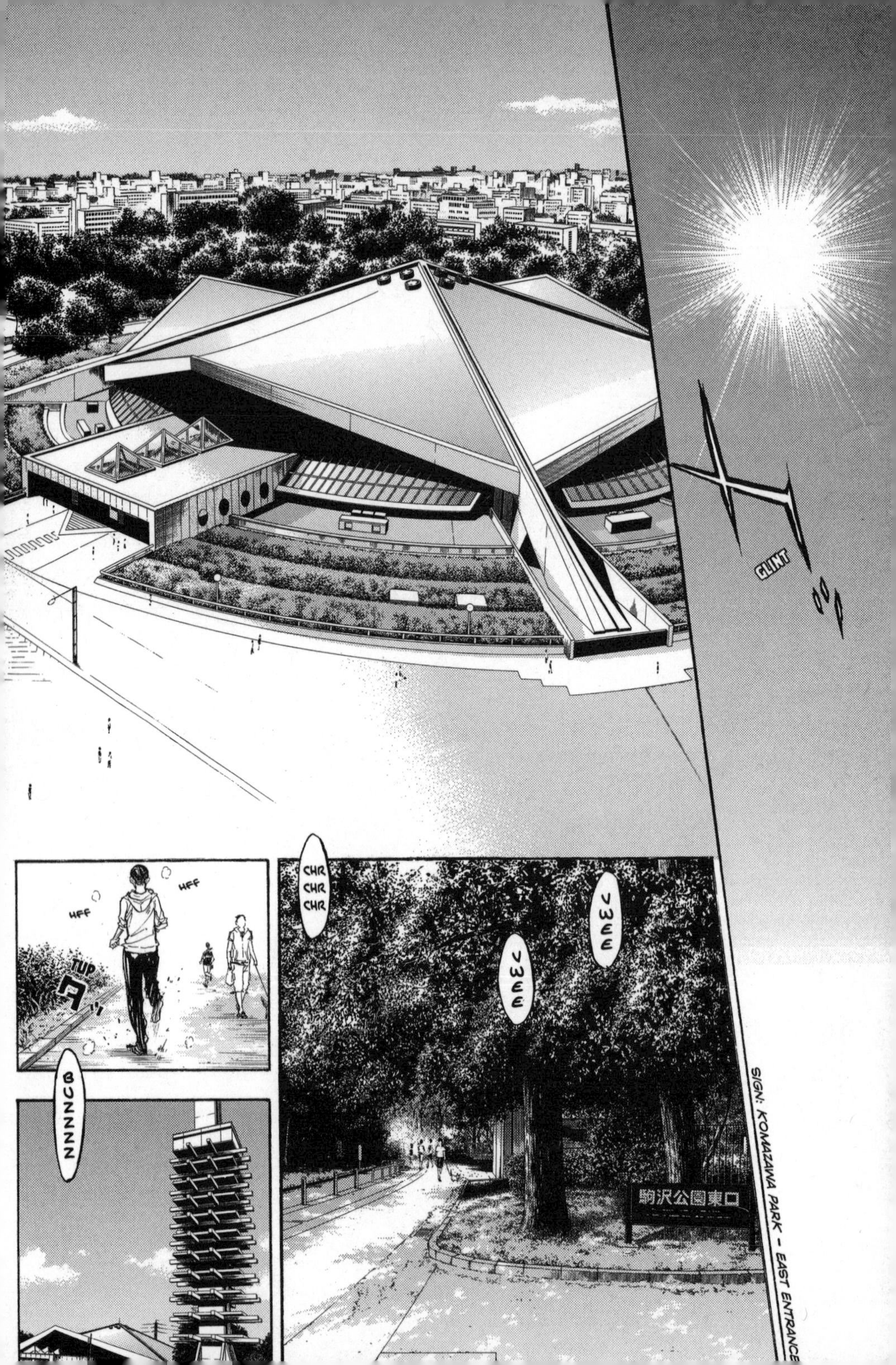
GLINT
CHR CHR CHR
VWEE
VWEE
駒沢公園東口
SIGN: KOMAZAWA PARK – EAST ENTRANCE
HFF
HFF
TUP
BUZZZZ

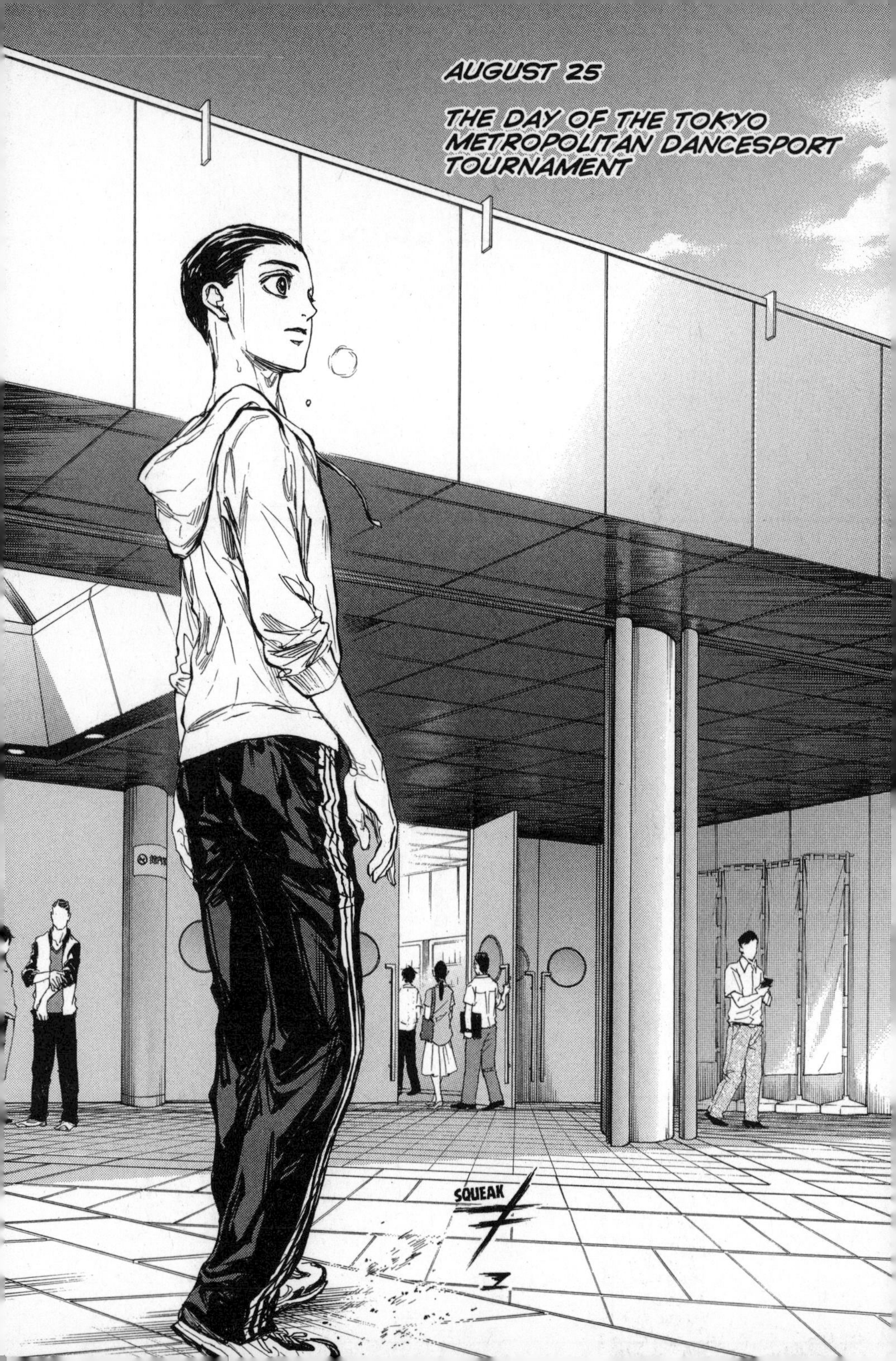
AUGUST 25
THE DAY OF THE TOKYO METROPOLITAN DANCESPORT TOURNAMENT
SQUEAK

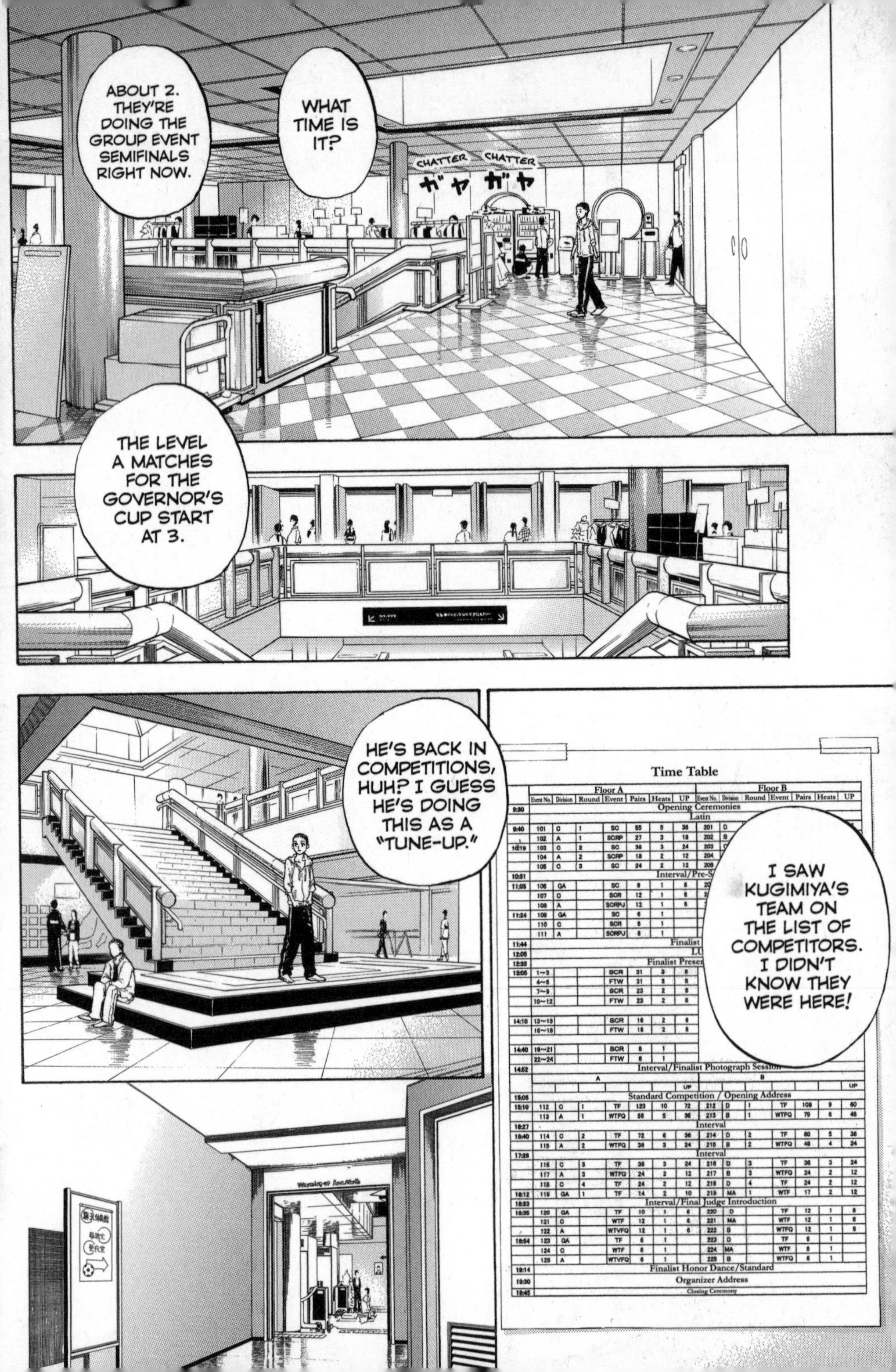
WHAT TIME IS IT?
ABOUT 2. THEY'RE DOING THE GROUP EVENT SEMIFINALS RIGHT NOW.
CHATTER CHATTER
ガヤガヤ
THE LEVEL A MATCHES FOR THE GOVERNOR'S CUP START AT 3.
Time Table
Floor A
Floor B
I SAW KUGIMIYA'S TEAM ON THE LIST OF COMPETITORS. I DIDN'T KNOW THEY WERE HERE!
HE'S BACK IN COMPETITIONS, HUH? I GUESS HE'S DOING THIS AS A "TUNE-UP."

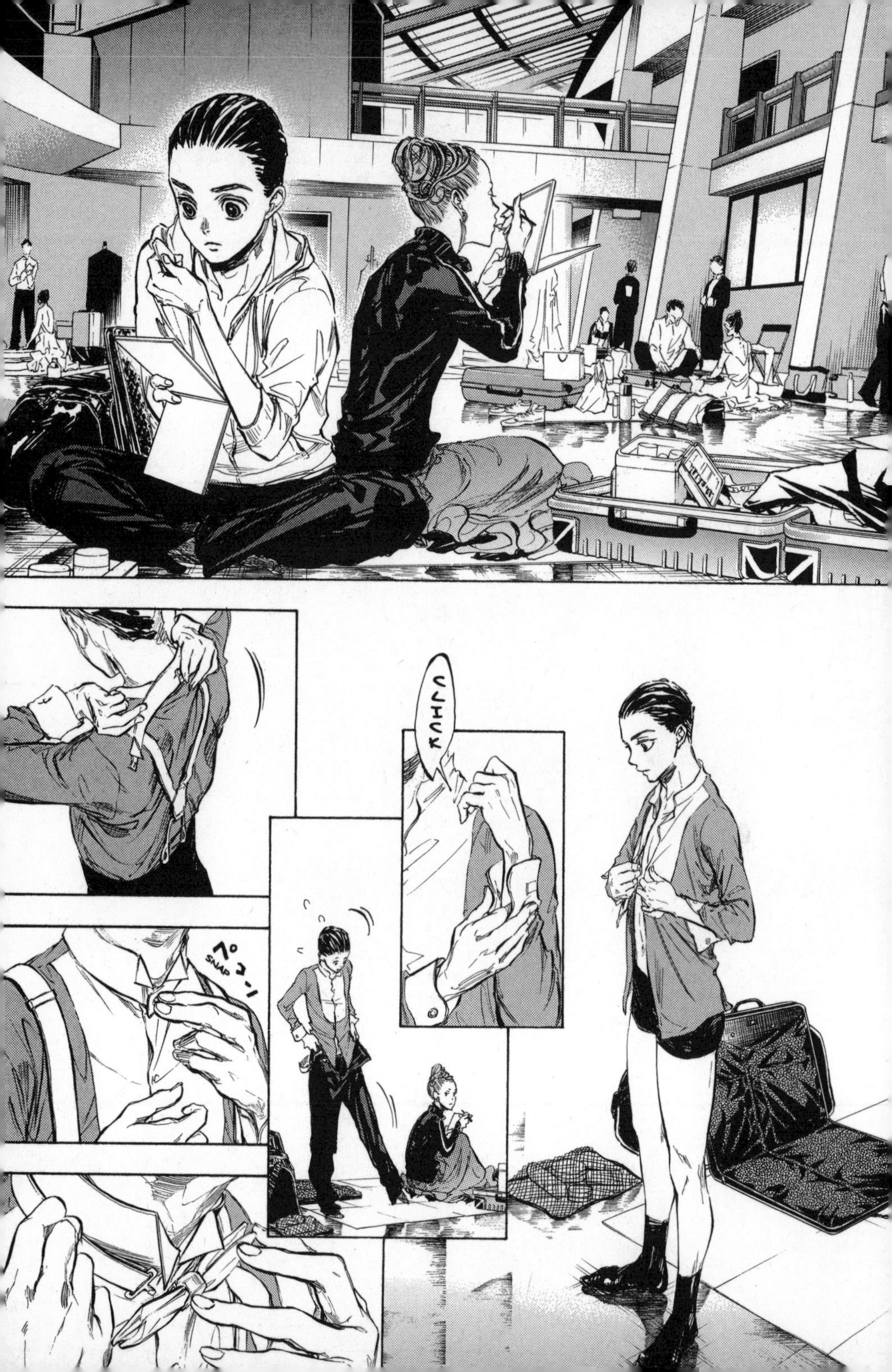
CLICK
ペコーン
SNAP

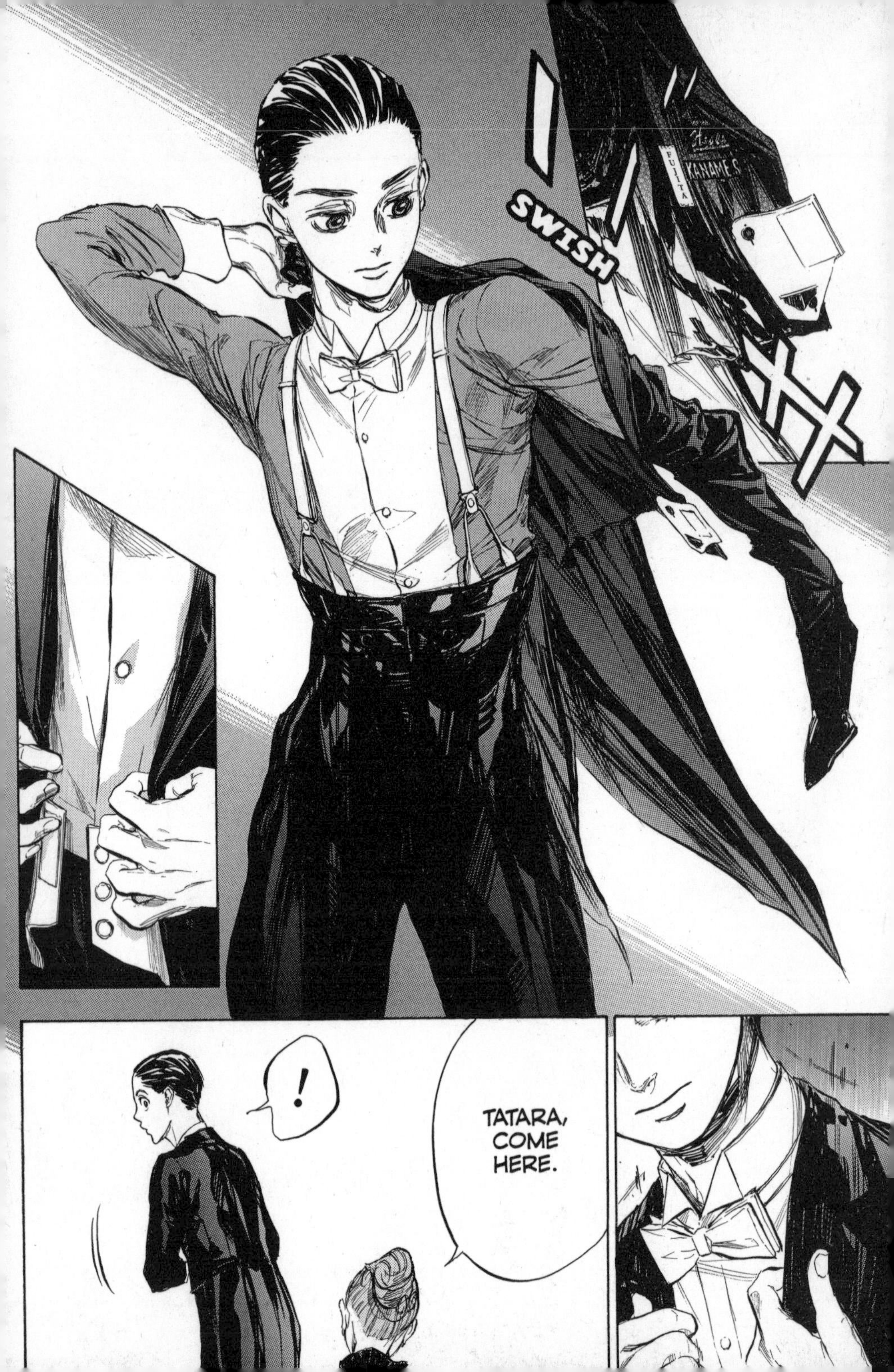
SWISH
KANAME S.
FUJITA
TATARA, COME HERE.
!

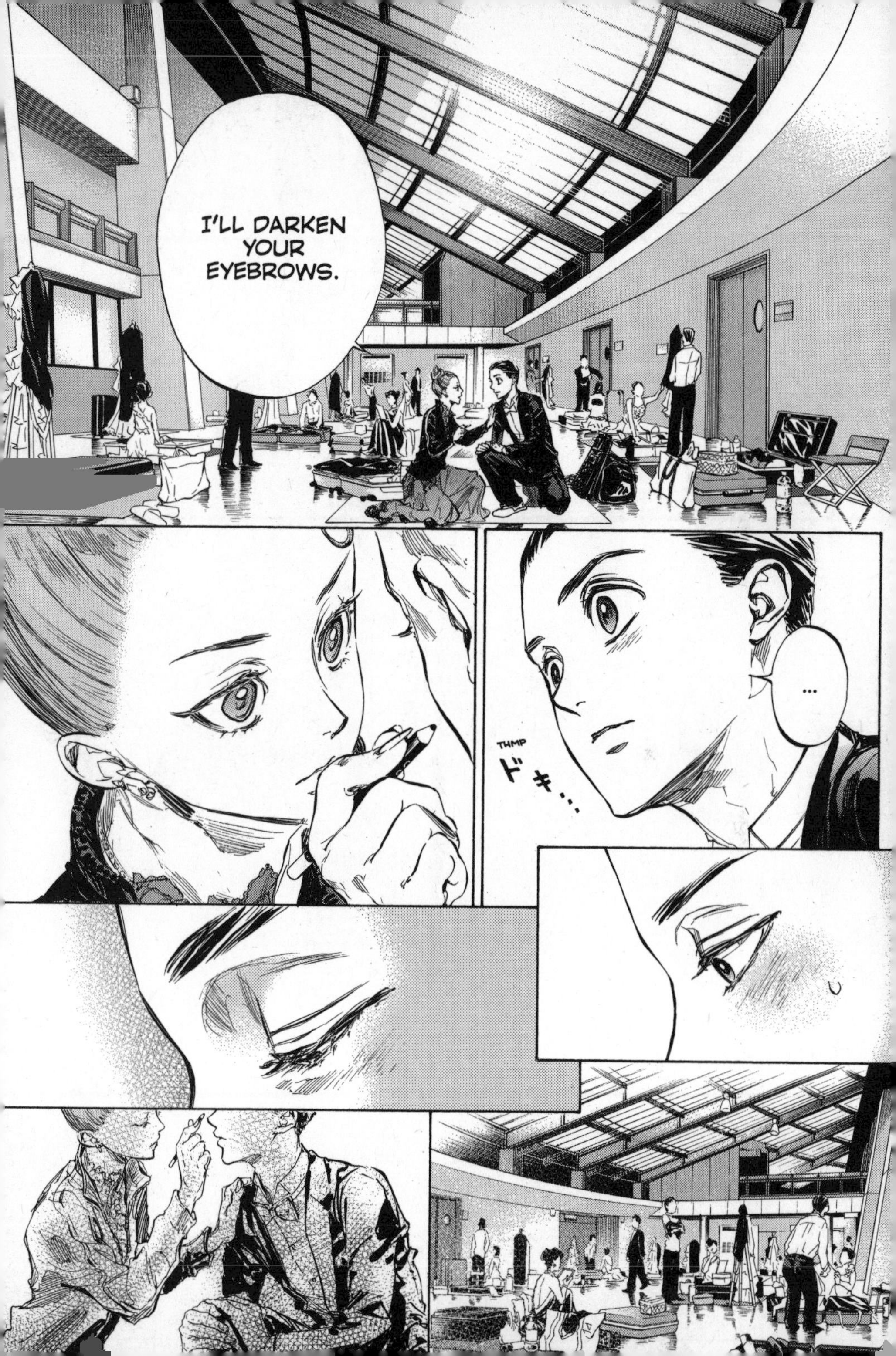
I'LL DARKEN YOUR EYEBROWS.
...
THMP
ドキ...

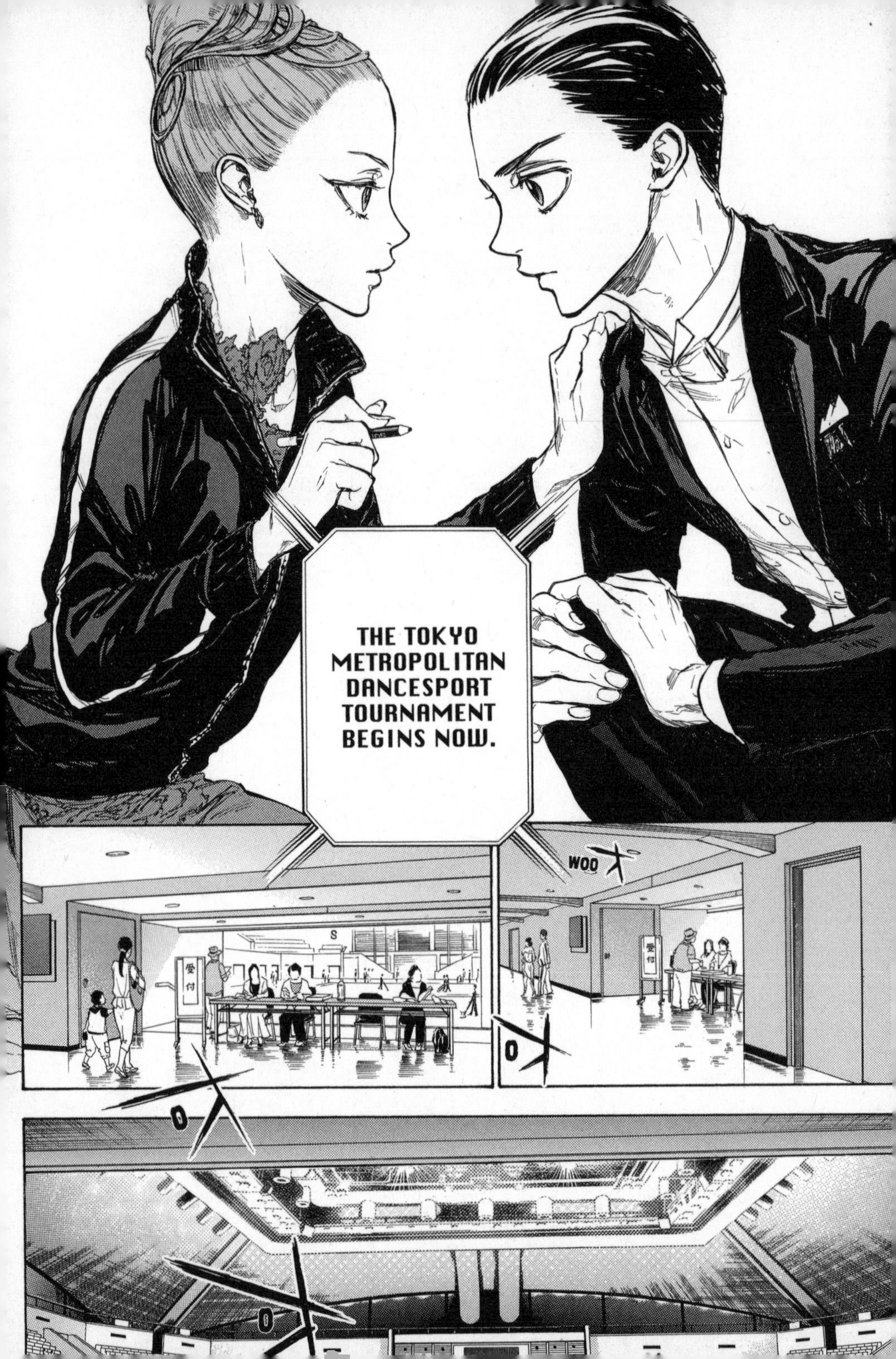
THE TOKYO METROPOLITAN DANCESPORT TOURNAMENT BEGINS NOW.
WOO
受付
O
受付
O
O

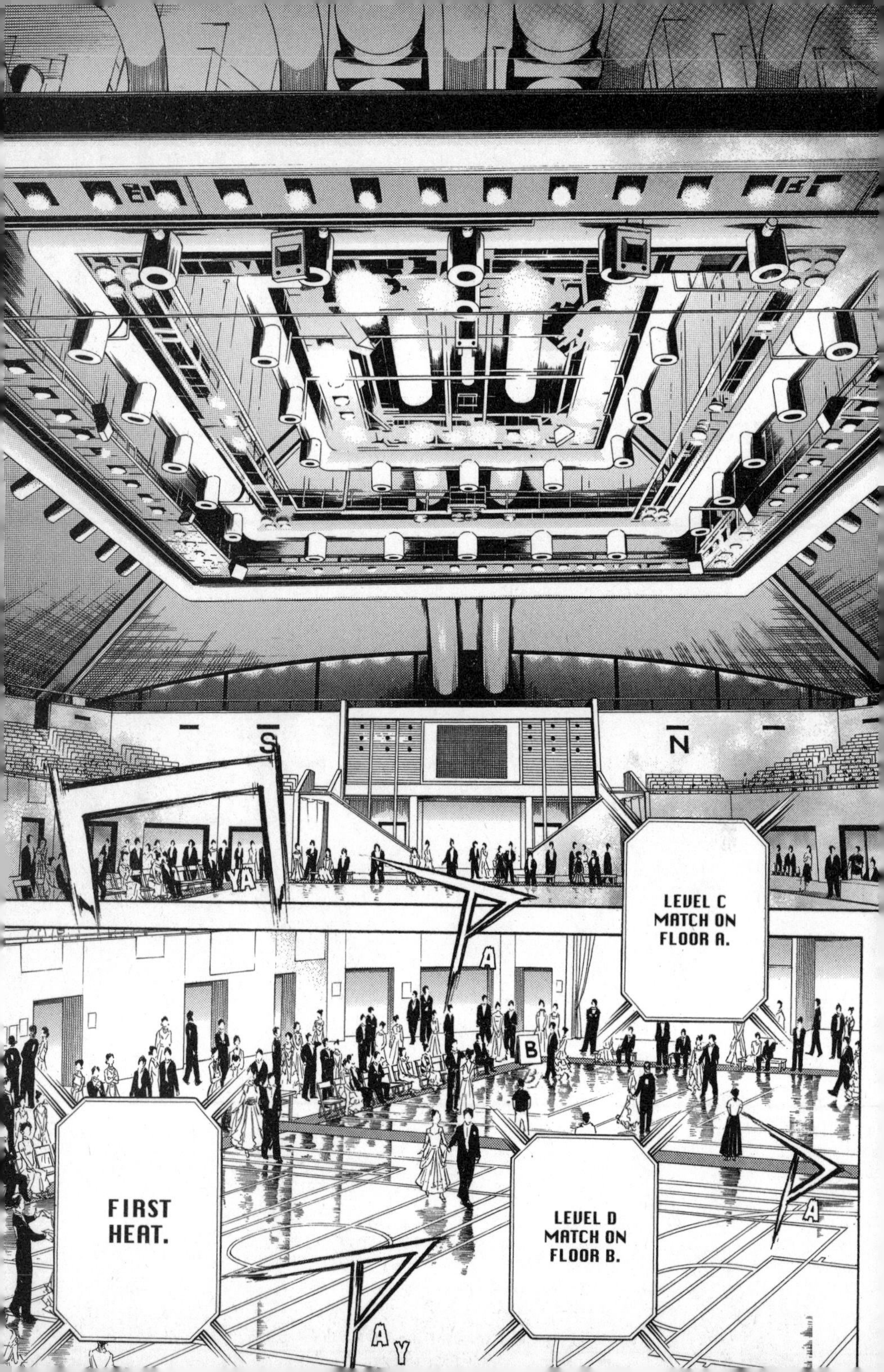
LEVEL C MATCH ON FLOOR A.
FIRST HEAT.
LEVEL D MATCH ON FLOOR B.

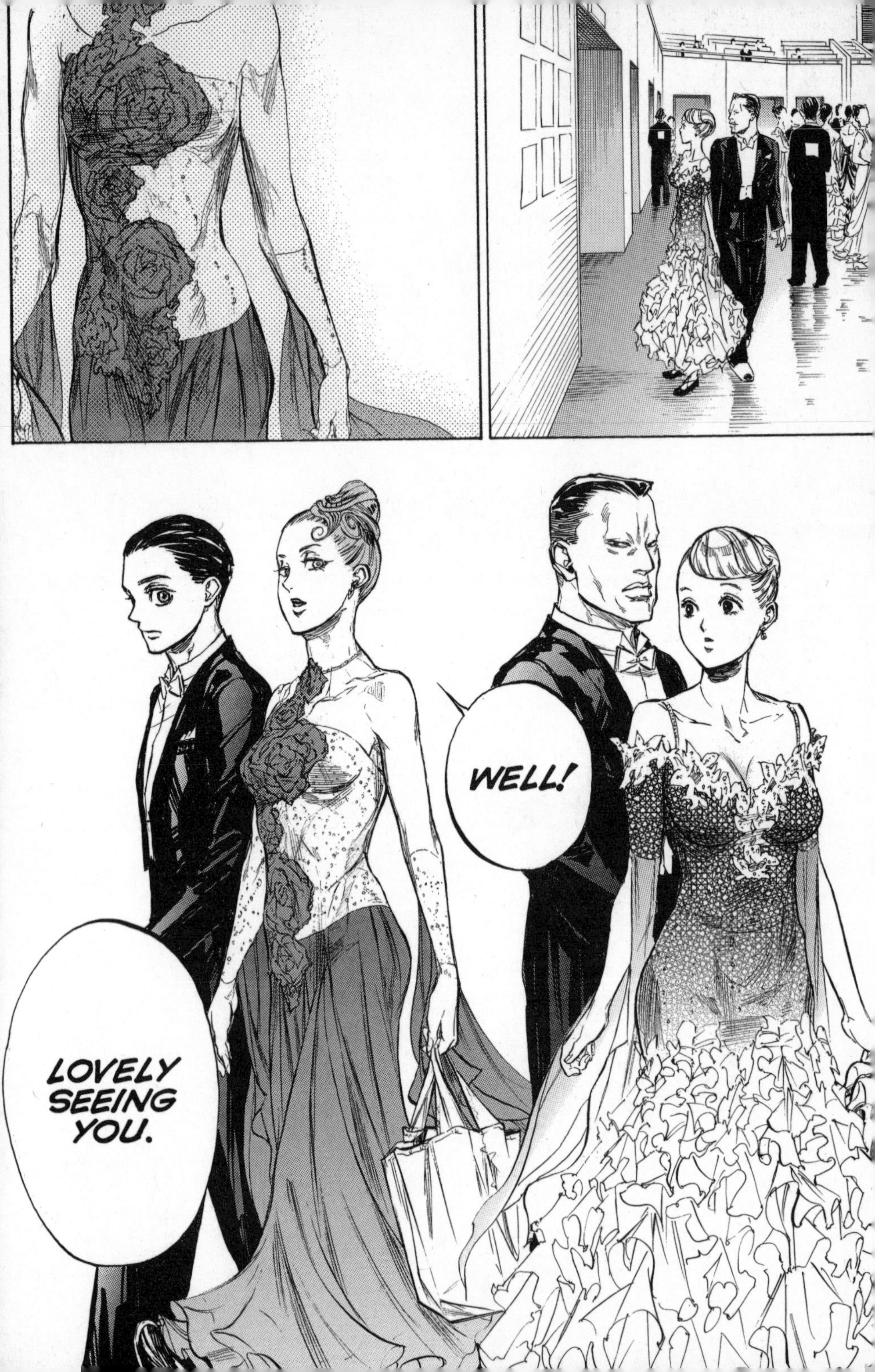
WELL!
LOVELY SEEING YOU.

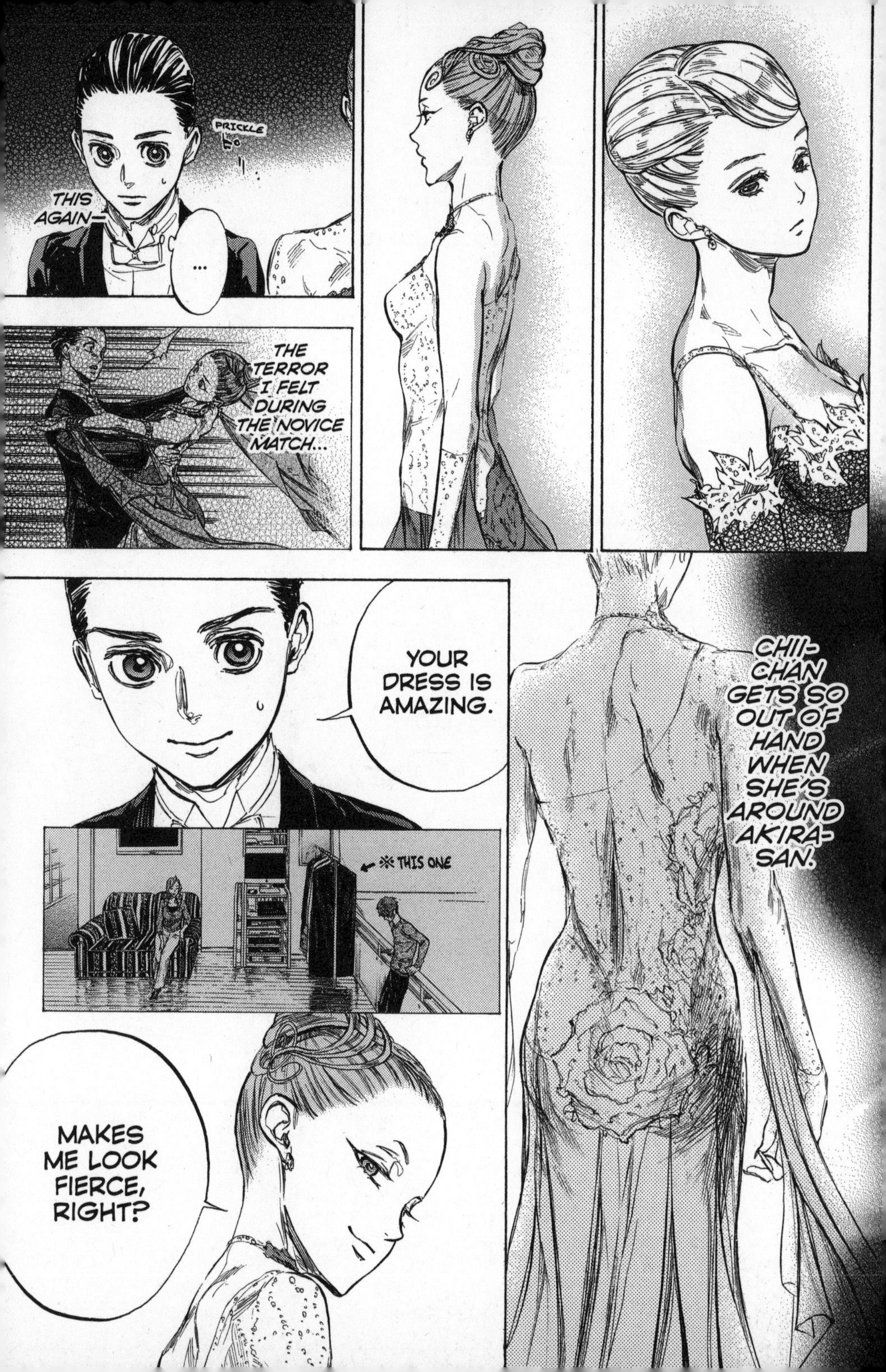
PRICKLE
THIS AGAIN—
...
THE TERROR I FELT DURING THE NOVICE MATCH...
CHII-CHAN GETS SO OUT OF HAND WHEN SHE'S AROUND AKIRA-SAN.
YOUR DRESS IS AMAZING.
※ THIS ONE
MAKES ME LOOK FIERCE, RIGHT?

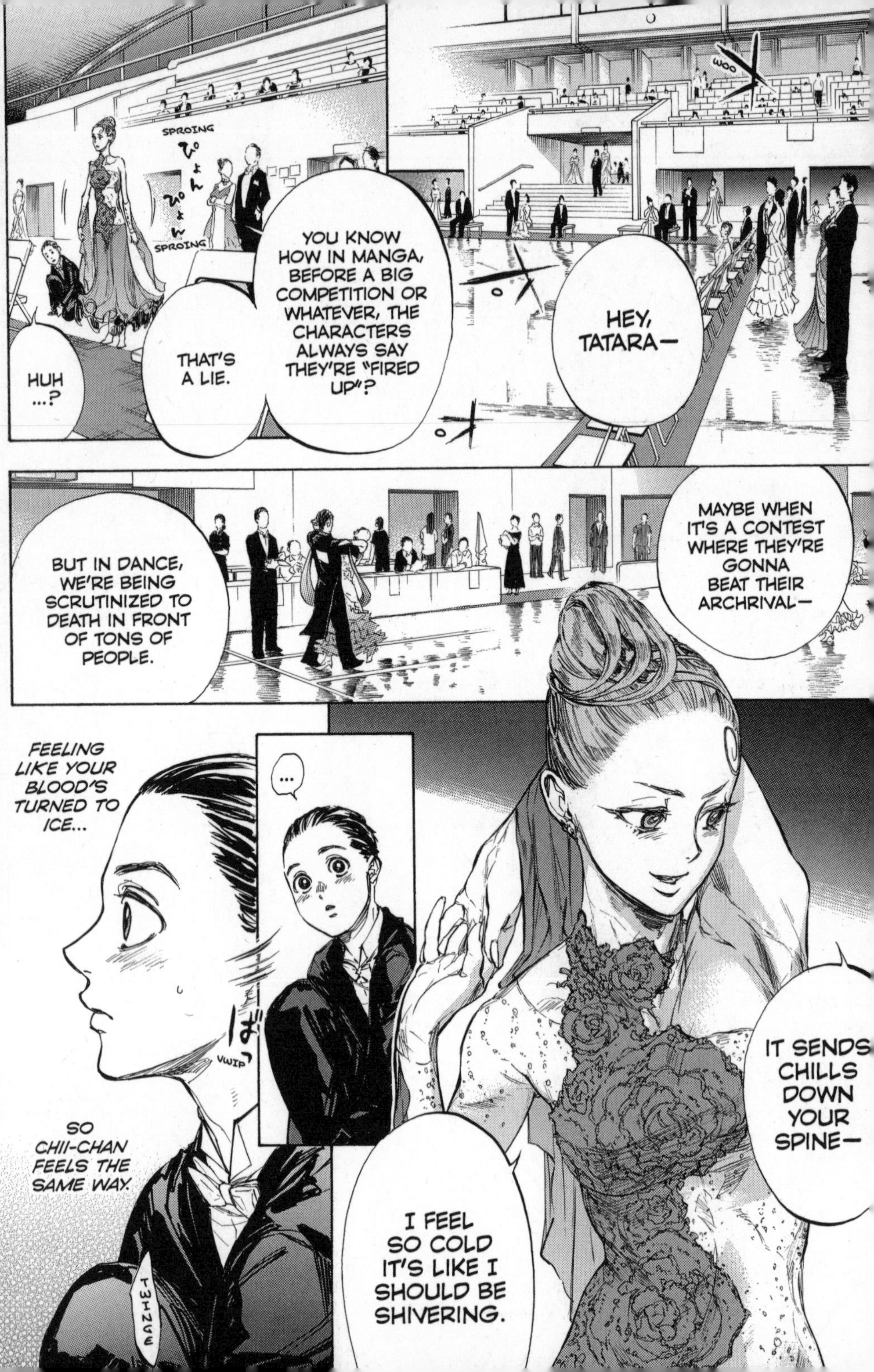
WOO
HEY, TATARA—
YOU KNOW HOW IN MANGA, BEFORE A BIG COMPETITION OR WHATEVER, THE CHARACTERS ALWAYS SAY THEY'RE "FIRED UP"?
SPROING
ぴょん
ぴょん
SPROING
THAT'S A LIE.
HUH ...?
MAYBE WHEN IT'S A CONTEST WHERE THEY'RE GONNA BEAT THEIR ARCHRIVAL—
BUT IN DANCE, WE'RE BEING SCRUTINIZED TO DEATH IN FRONT OF TONS OF PEOPLE.
IT SENDS CHILLS DOWN YOUR SPINE—
I FEEL SO COLD IT'S LIKE I SHOULD BE SHIVERING.
...
FEELING LIKE YOUR BLOOD'S TURNED TO ICE...
ば
VWIP
SO CHII-CHAN FEELS THE SAME WAY.
TWINGE

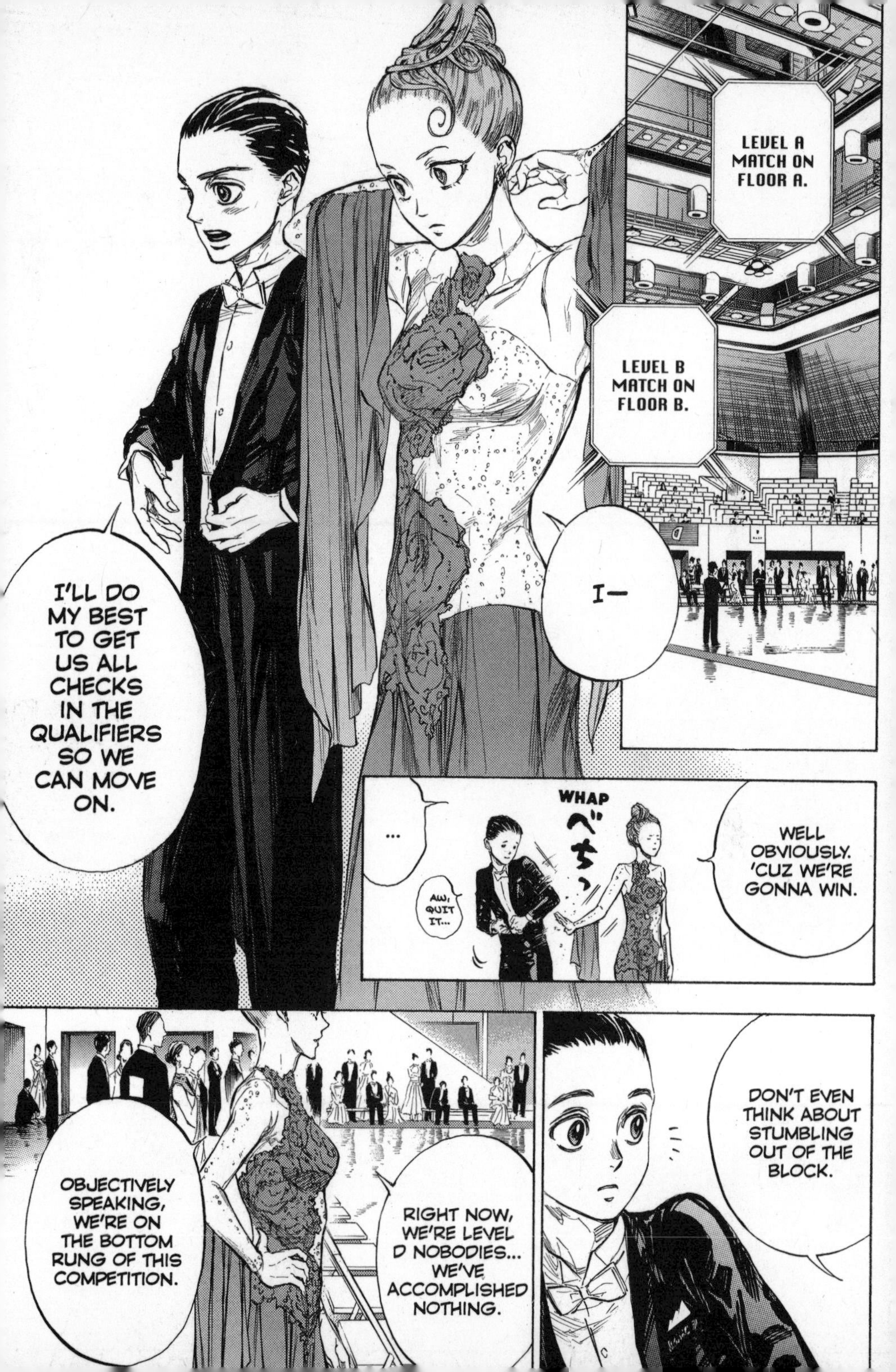
LEVEL A MATCH ON FLOOR A.
LEVEL B MATCH ON FLOOR B.
I—
WELL OBVIOUSLY. 'CUZ WE'RE GONNA WIN.
WHAP
べちっ
AW, QUIT IT...
...
I'LL DO MY BEST TO GET US ALL CHECKS IN THE QUALIFIERS SO WE CAN MOVE ON.
DON'T EVEN THINK ABOUT STUMBLING OUT OF THE BLOCK.
RIGHT NOW, WE'RE LEVEL D NOBODIES... WE'VE ACCOMPLISHED NOTHING.
OBJECTIVELY SPEAKING, WE'RE ON THE BOTTOM RUNG OF THIS COMPETITION.

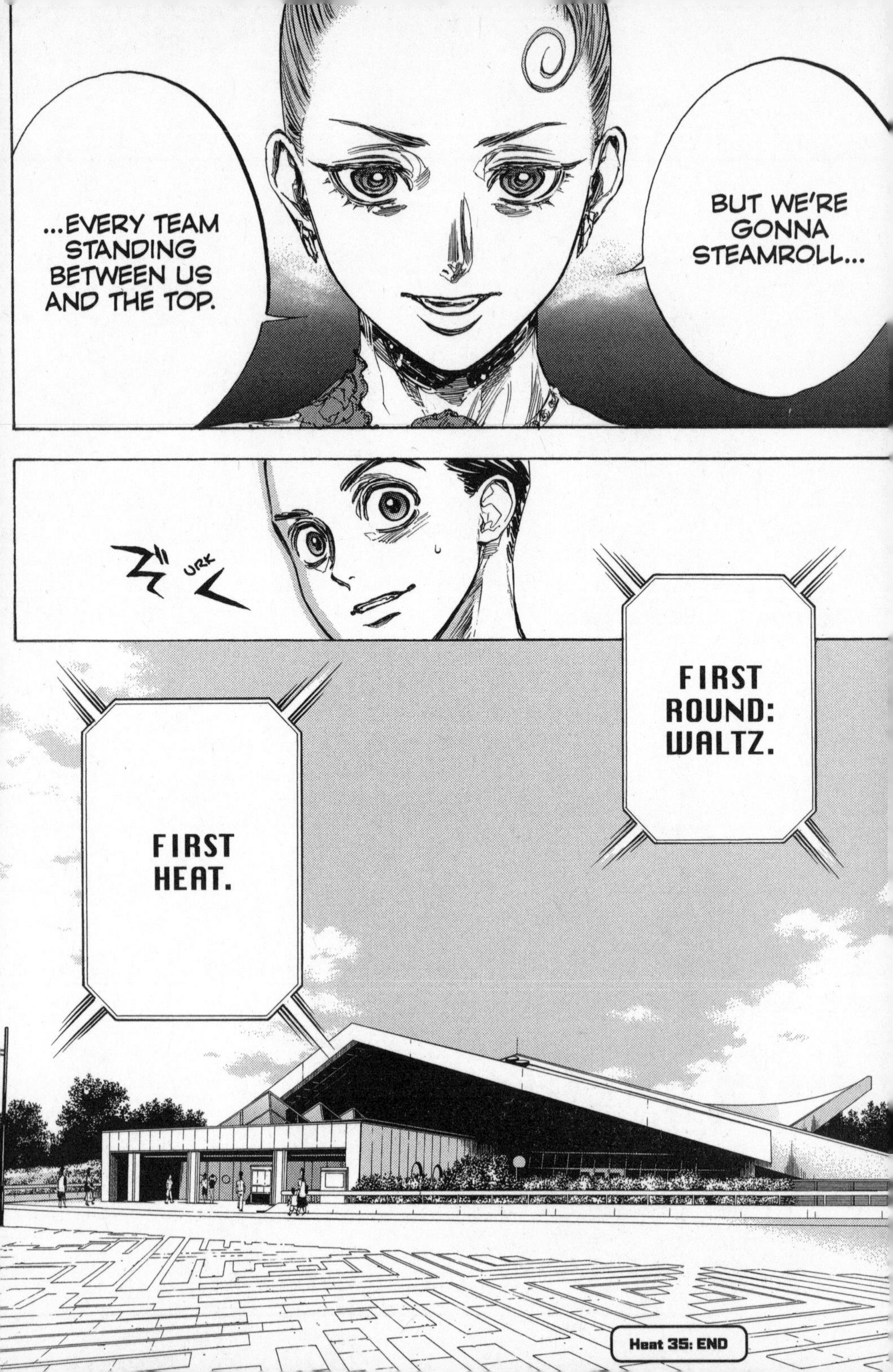
BUT WE'RE GONNA STEAMROLL...
...EVERY TEAM STANDING BETWEEN US AND THE TOP.
URK
FIRST ROUND: WALTZ.
FIRST HEAT.
Heat 35: END

RURISOU (TYPE OF FORGET-ME-NOT)
SYMBOLIZES "REMEMBRANCE."

CAMP LOG

	DAY 1	DAY 2	DAY 3	DAY 4	DAY 5	DAY 6
8AM	GET UP				RAIN	
	AM PRACTICE, JOGGING, STRETCHING	AM PRACTICE	AM PRACTICE	AM PRACTICE	AM PRACTICE, STRETCHING	AM PRACTICE, STRETCHING
					CLEANUP	BREAKFAST
	BREAKFAST	BREAKFAST	BREAKFAST	BREAKFAST	BREAKFAST	PHYSICAL & MUSCLE TRAINING
	CLEAN	WEEDING		WEEDING	PHYSICAL & MUSCLE TRAINING	LESSON W/ MARISA-SENSEI
10	WEEDING	SHADOW	WEEDING		EURHYTHMICS	
	LESSON W/ MARISA-SENSEI	HYODO-KUN		COUPLES PRACTICE	COUPLES PRACTICE	COUPLES PRACTICE
	COUPLES PRACTICE	SHADOW	SHADOW			
12PM			MUSCLE TRAINING			
		LUNCH	SHADOW	SHADOW	LUNCH	LUNCH
		JOGGING		LUNCH	VIDEO	EXCURSION
2	LESSON W/ TEAM HYODO	VIDEO		LESSON W/ MARISA-SENSEI	MENTAL TRAINING	
		PHYSICAL TRAINING	EXCURSION	COUPLES PRACTICE	ETIQUITTE PRACTICE	SHADOW
4				STRETCHING		LESSON W/ HYODO-KUN
		VIDEO (GRAND PRIX IN OSAKA)		PHYSICAL & MUSCLE TRAINING	COUPLES PRACTICE	
	SHADOW		LESSON W/ HANAOKA-SAN			COUPLES PRACTICE
6	PREP	SHOPPING (W/ IDOGAWA-SAN)		COUPLES PRACTICE	SHOPPING (WITH KUGIMIYA-SAN)	
	DINNER		COUPLES PRACTICE			PREP
	TIDY	PREP		PREP	PREP	DINNER
	BREAK	DINNER	DINNER	DINNER	DINNER	
8		TIDY		VIDEO		
	BATH	BREAK			PRACTICE	FIREWORKS
		SHADOW	COUPLES PRACTICE	SHADOW		
10	PM PRACTICE (SHADOW)	MUSCLE TRAINING		BATH		
		SHOWER			SHOWER	BATH
	STRETCH W/ MUSIC	STRETCHING	SHOWER	STRETCHING	STRETCHING	
12		ASLEEP	STRETCHING			VIDEO
	ASLEEP		ASLEEP	ASLEEP	ASLEEP	

| **IMPRESSIONS** | THE BARBEQUE I HAD FOR LUNCH WAS REALLY GOOD. CAN'T COMMUNICATE WITH MY PARTNER. HYODO-KUN & HANAOKA-SAN TAUGHT US LOTS OF VERY DIFFICULT THINGS. | GOT GUIDANCE ON SHADOWING FROM HYODO-KUN. COULDN'T DO COUPLES PRACTICE. GAJU CAME IN TO USE THE TOILET WHILE I WAS SHOWERING, WHICH WAS NOT PLEASANT. | SINCE A PASSIVE LEADER CAUSES PROBLEMS FOR THE PARTNER, I'LL TRY TO ACT STRONGER & MORE INDEPENDENT. I WANT TO BE FAITHFUL TO BASICS WHEN DANCING, BUT ALSO HAVE TO EXPRESS MYSELF, SO I'M CONFLICTED. | OUR MOVEMENTS AS A COUPLE HAVE BECOME EVEN MORE OUT OF SYNC THAN BEFORE. HYODO-KUN TOLD US THAT'S BECAUSE WE DON'T SHARE A COMMON VISION OF OUR DANCE. | TODAY WE PRACTICED DANCE ETIQUETTE AND HOW TO ENTER THE FLOOR. I LEARNED A LOT WATCHING COMPETITION VIDEOS. | THE DINNER PARTY AND FIREWORKS WERE A LOT OF FUN. THIS TRAINING CAMP'S BEEN REALLY IMPORTANT FOR ME. I'LL DO MY BEST IN THE COMPETITION. |

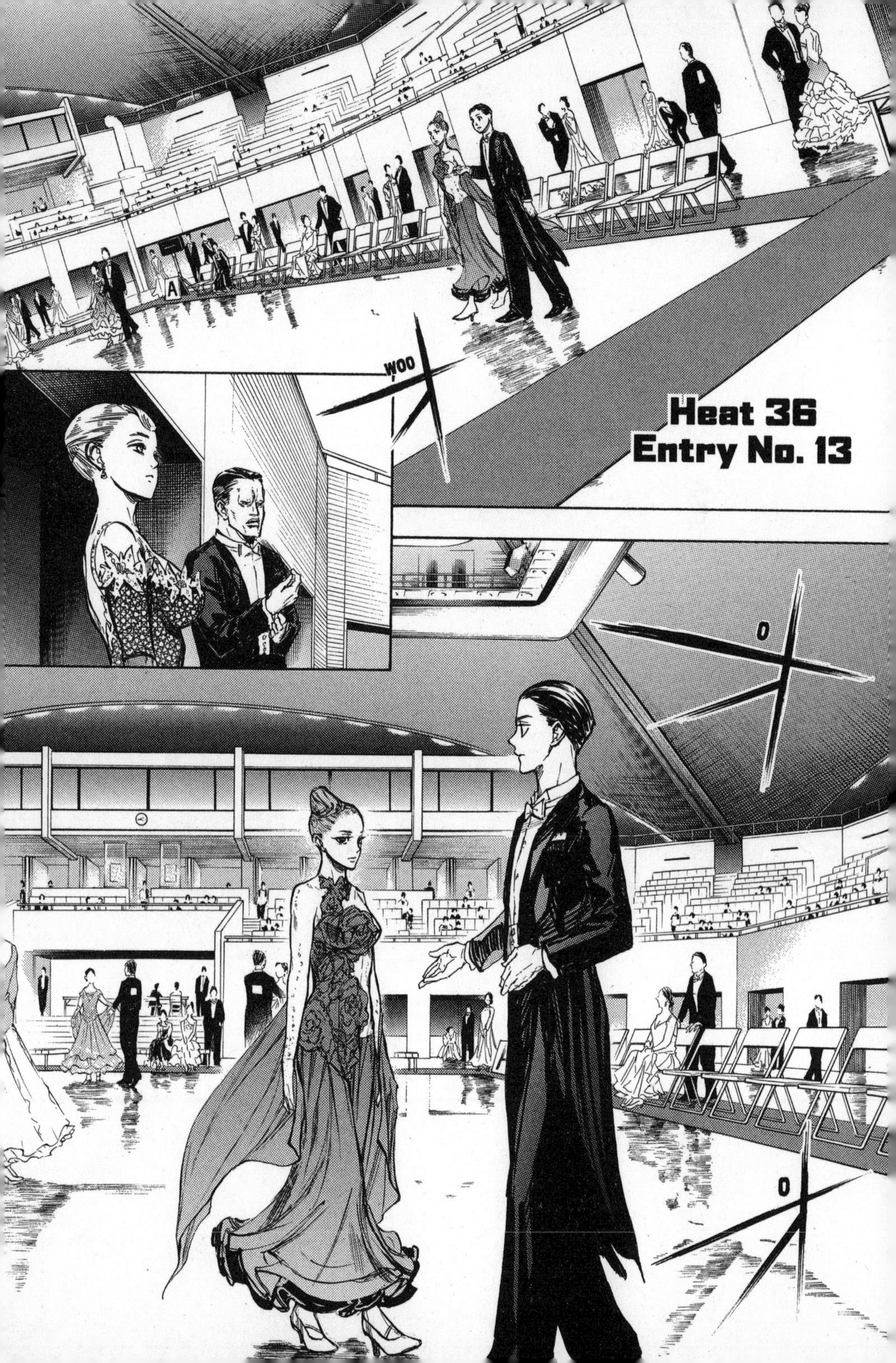
WOO
Heat 36
Entry No. 13
O
O

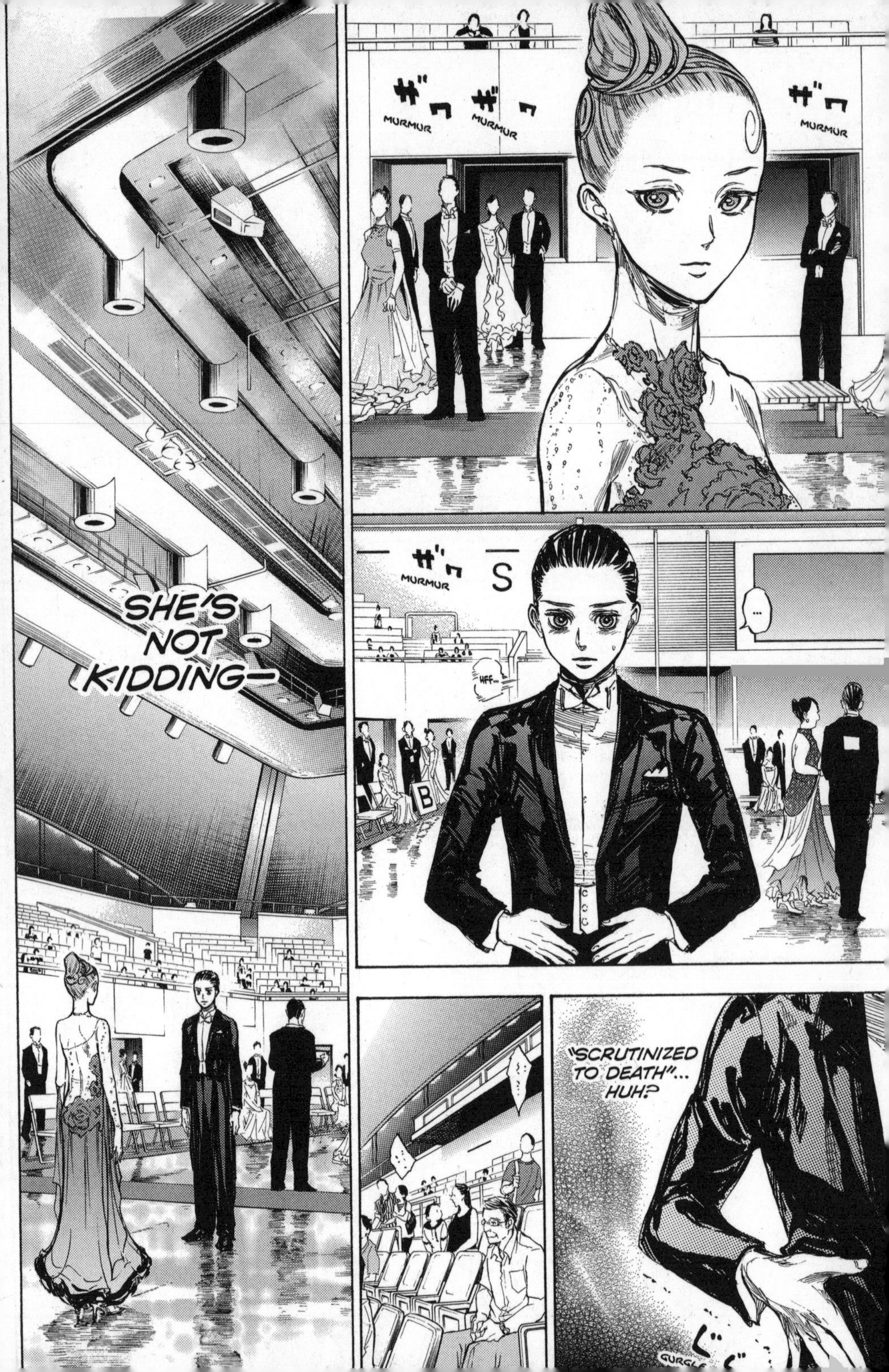
ザワ
MURMUR
ザワ
MURMUR
ザワ
MURMUR
ザワ
MURMUR
S
...
HFF...
B
"SCRUTINIZED TO DEATH"... HUH?
GURGLE
SHE'S NOT KIDDING—

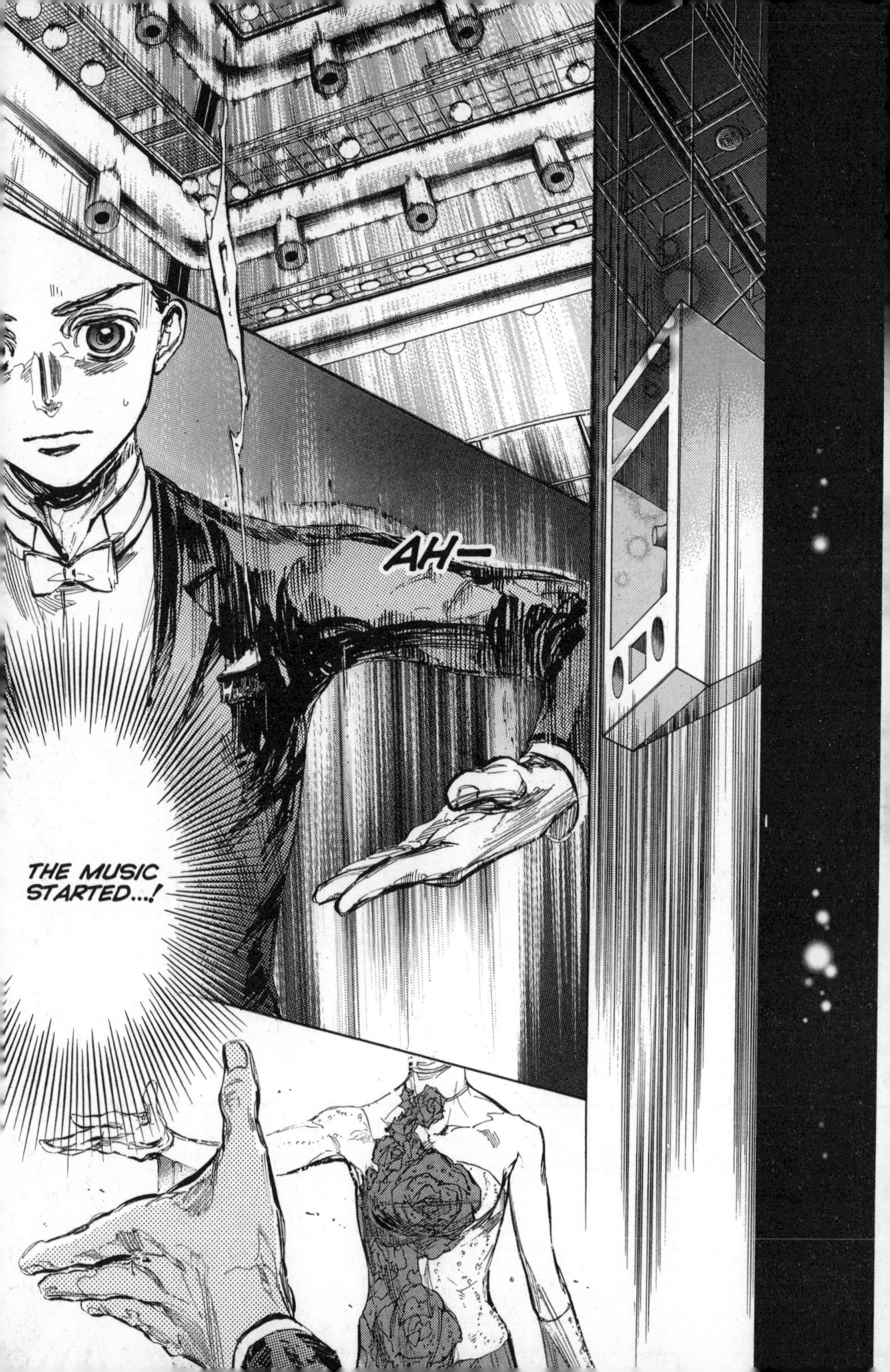
AH–
THE MUSIC STARTED...!

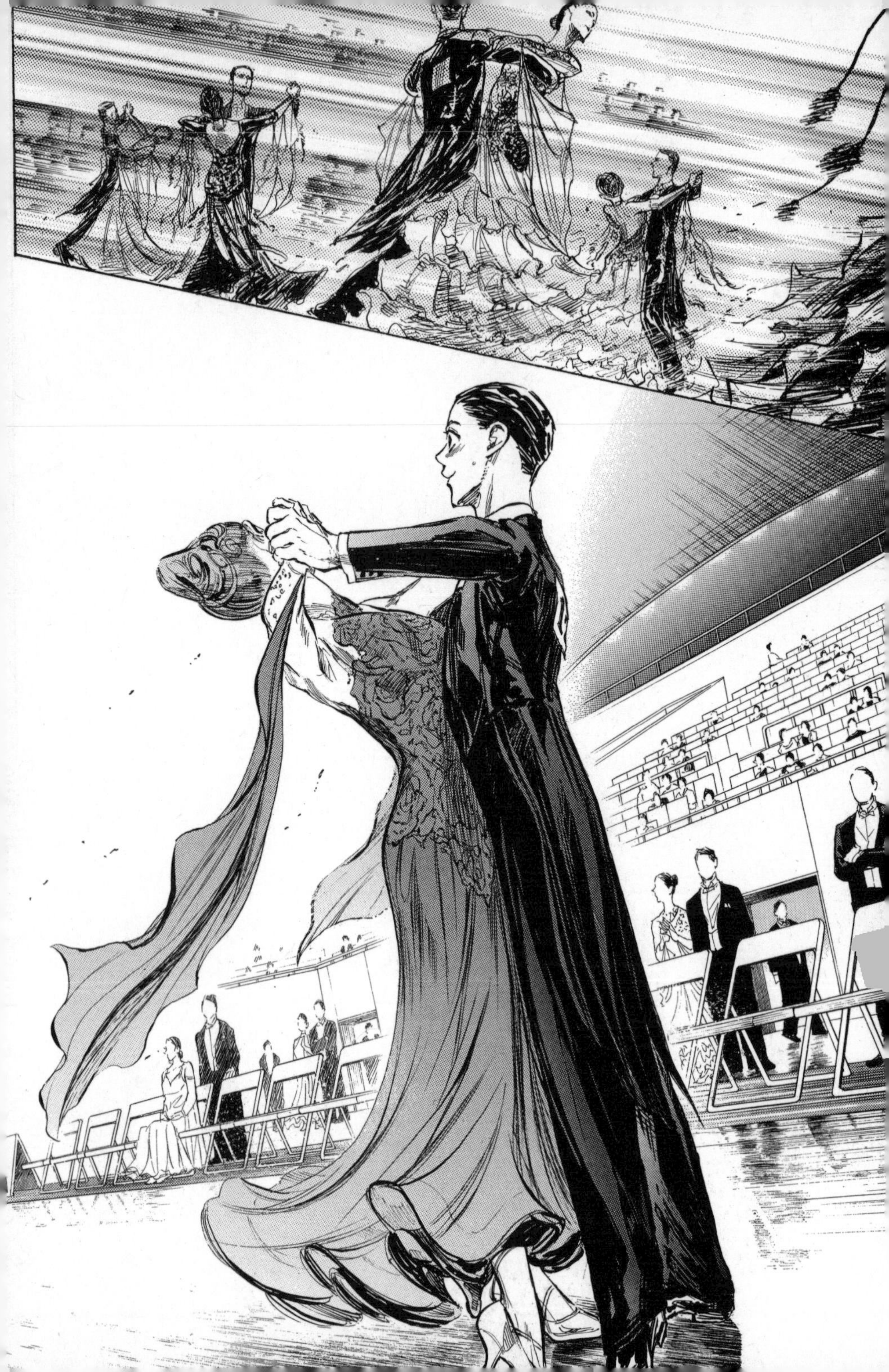

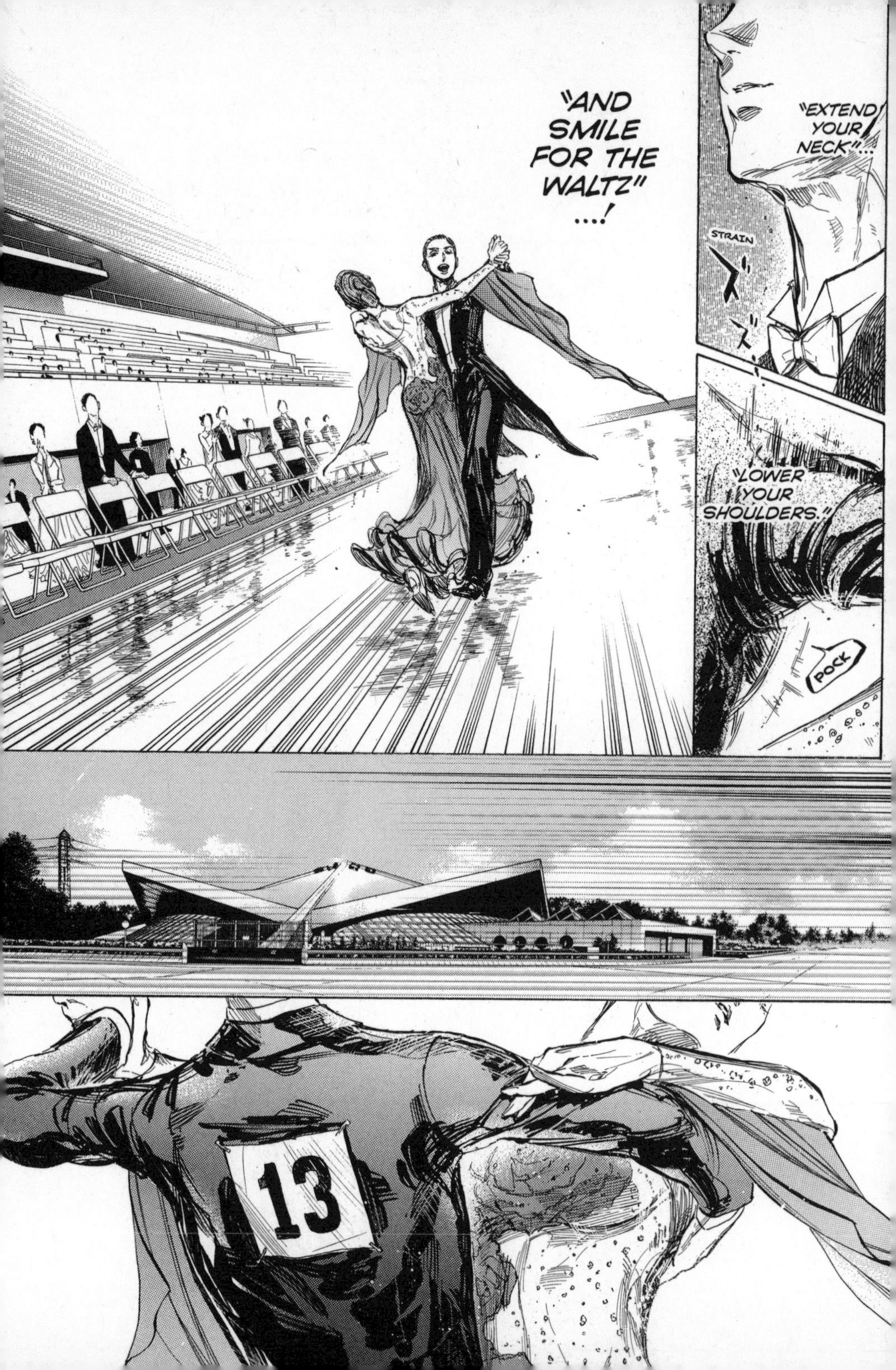
"EXTEND YOUR NECK"...
STRAIN
"LOWER YOUR SHOULDERS."
POCK
"AND SMILE FOR THE WALTZ" ...!
13

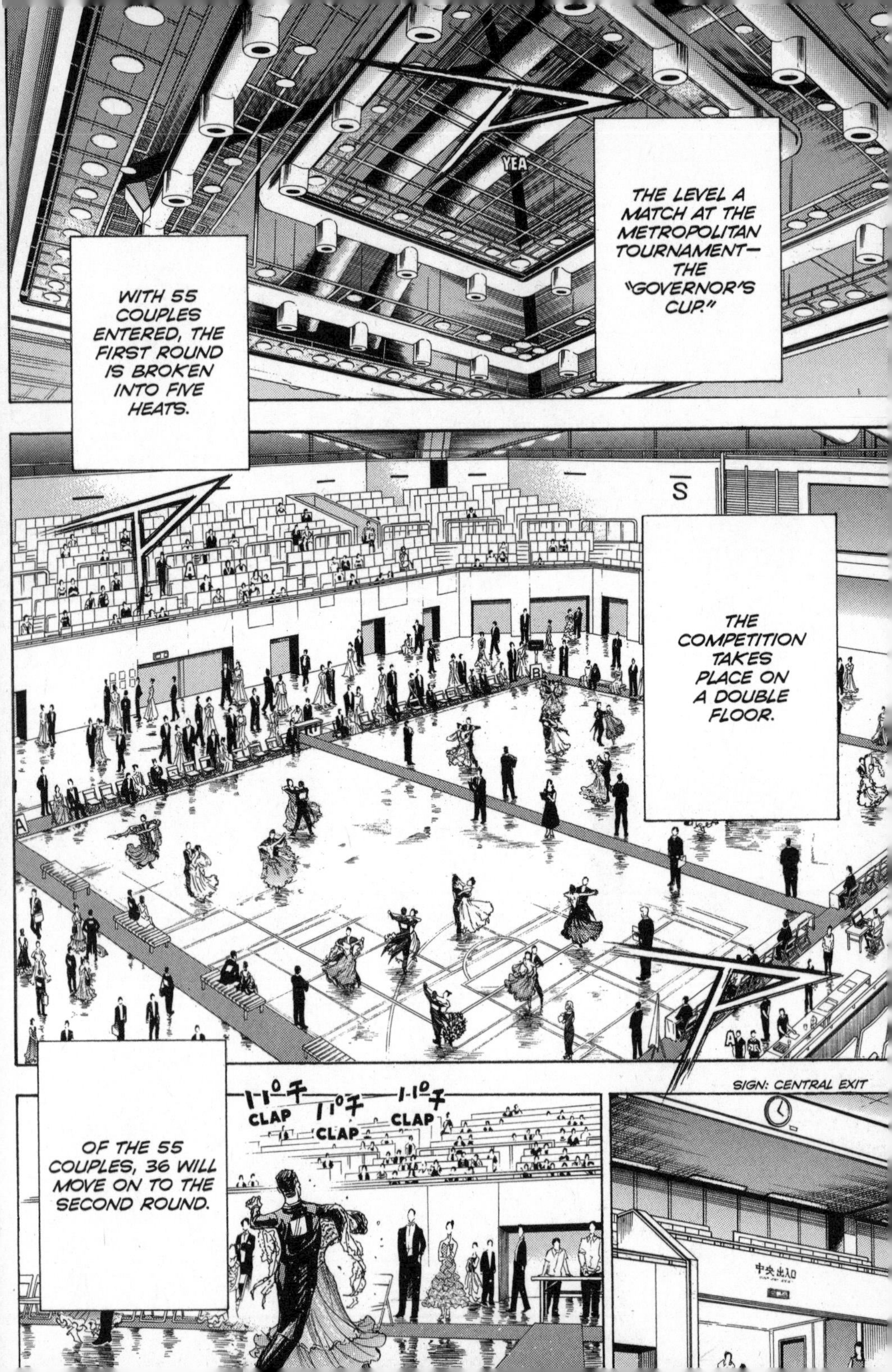
THE LEVEL A MATCH AT THE METROPOLITAN TOURNAMENT—THE "GOVERNOR'S CUP."
YEA
WITH 55 COUPLES ENTERED, THE FIRST ROUND IS BROKEN INTO FIVE HEATS.
THE COMPETITION TAKES PLACE ON A DOUBLE FLOOR.
SIGN: CENTRAL EXIT
中央出入口
CLAP
CLAP
CLAP
OF THE 55 COUPLES, 36 WILL MOVE ON TO THE SECOND ROUND.

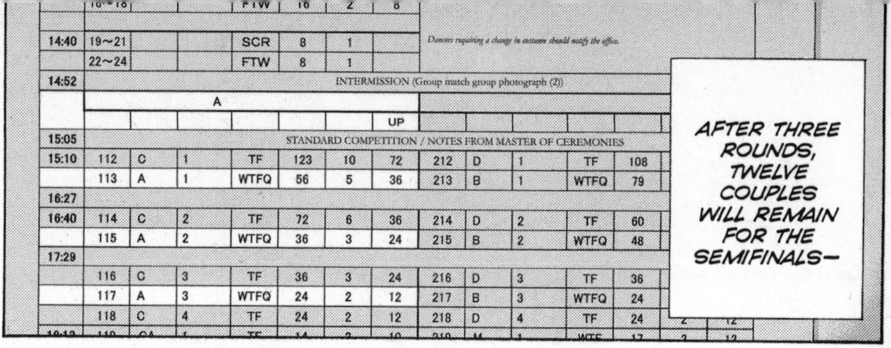
Dancers requiring a change in costume should notify the office.
INTERMISSION (Group match group photograph (2))
STANDARD COMPETITION / NOTES FROM MASTER OF CEREMONIES
AFTER THREE ROUNDS, TWELVE COUPLES WILL REMAIN FOR THE SEMIFINALS—

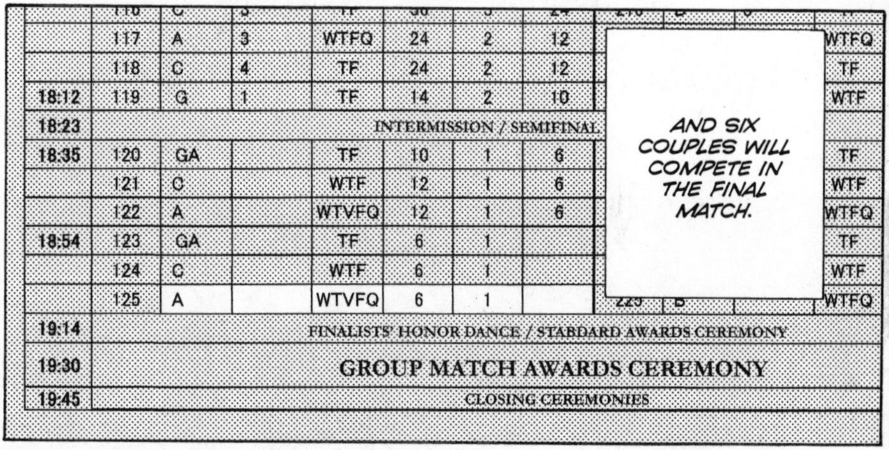
INTERMISSION / SEMIFINAL
AND SIX COUPLES WILL COMPETE IN THE FINAL MATCH.
FINALISTS' HONOR DANCE / STABDARD AWARDS CEREMONY
GROUP MATCH AWARDS CEREMONY
CLOSING CEREMONIES

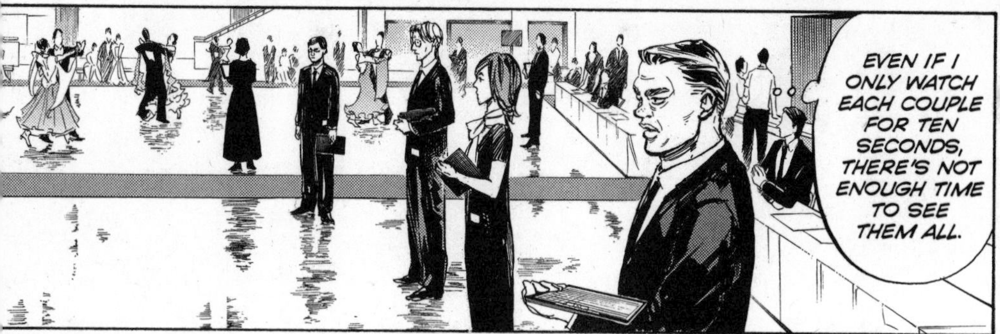
EVEN IF I ONLY WATCH EACH COUPLE FOR TEN SECONDS, THERE'S NOT ENOUGH TIME TO SEE THEM ALL.

*AT PUBLIC COMPETITIONS, A SONG'S RUNTIME IS REQUIRED TO BE AT LEAST 1:15 IN THE QUALIFYING AND SEMIFINAL ROUNDS, AND AT LEAST 1:30 IN THE FINAL.

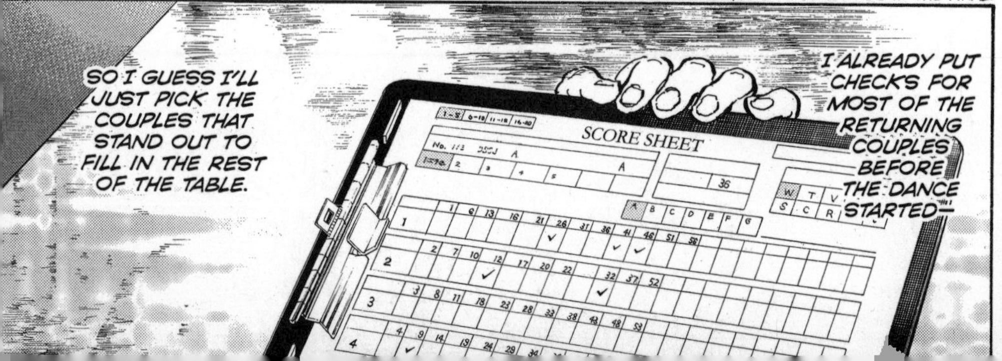
I ALREADY PUT CHECKS FOR MOST OF THE RETURNING COUPLES BEFORE THE DANCE STARTED—
SO I GUESS I'LL JUST PICK THE COUPLES THAT STAND OUT TO FILL IN THE REST OF THE TABLE.
SCORE SHEET

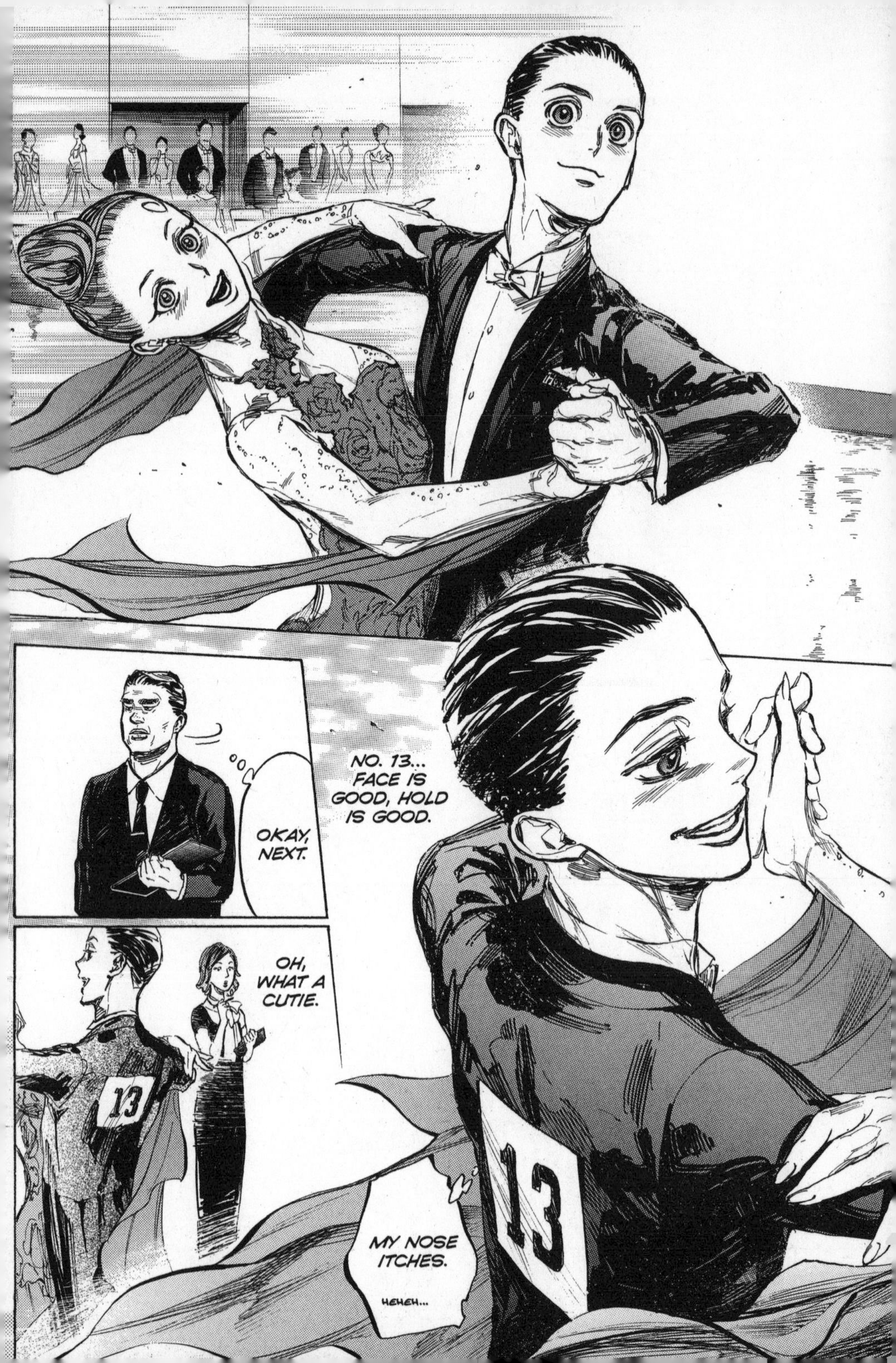
NO. 13... FACE IS GOOD, HOLD IS GOOD.
MY NOSE ITCHES.
HEHEH...
OKAY, NEXT.
OH, WHAT A CUTIE.

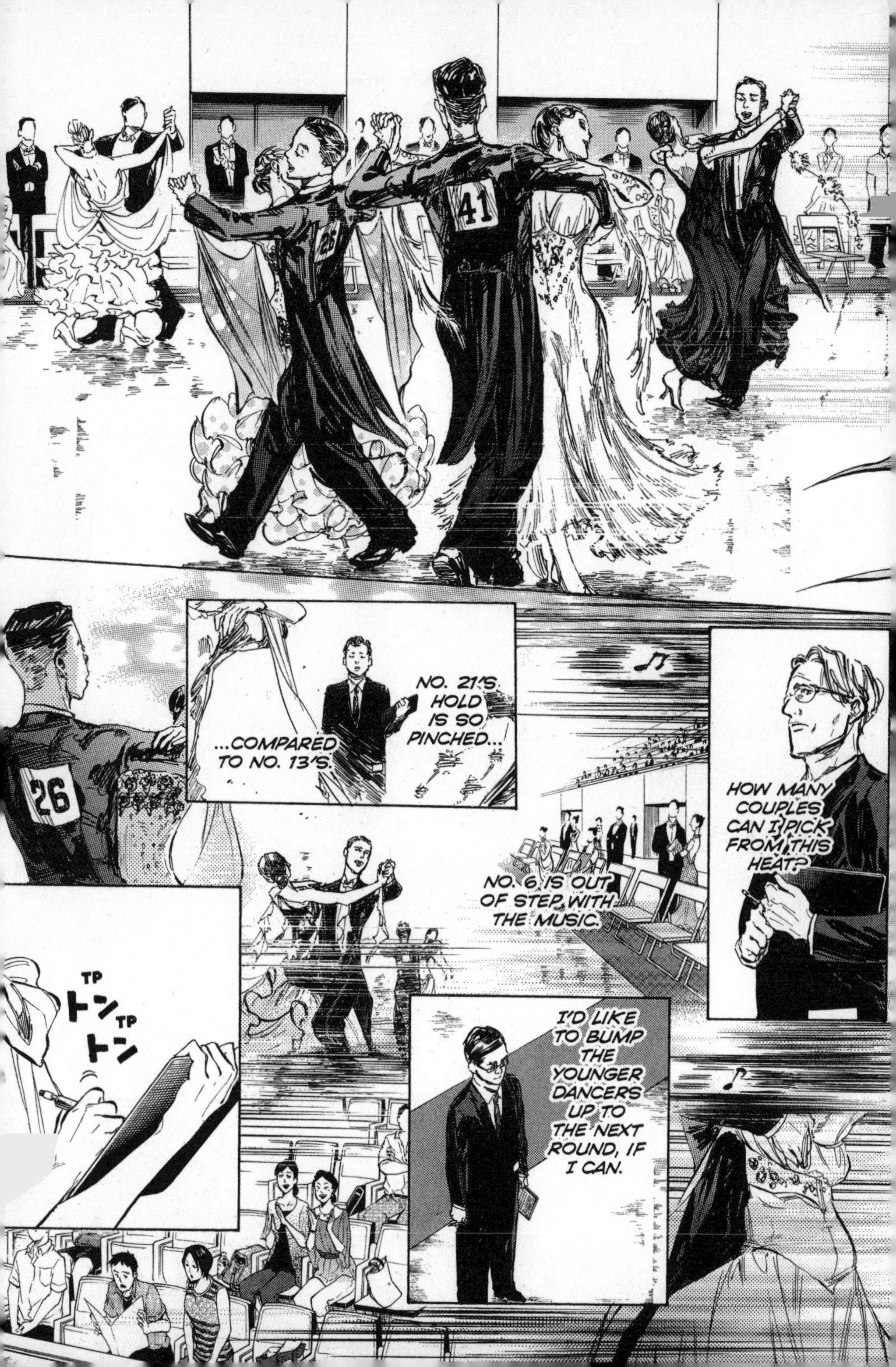

HOW MANY COUPLES CAN I PICK FROM THIS HEAT?
NO. 21'S HOLD IS SO PINCHED...
...COMPARED TO NO. 13'S.
NO. 6 IS OUT OF STEP WITH THE MUSIC.
I'D LIKE TO BUMP THE YOUNGER DANCERS UP TO THE NEXT ROUND, IF I CAN.
TP トン TP トン

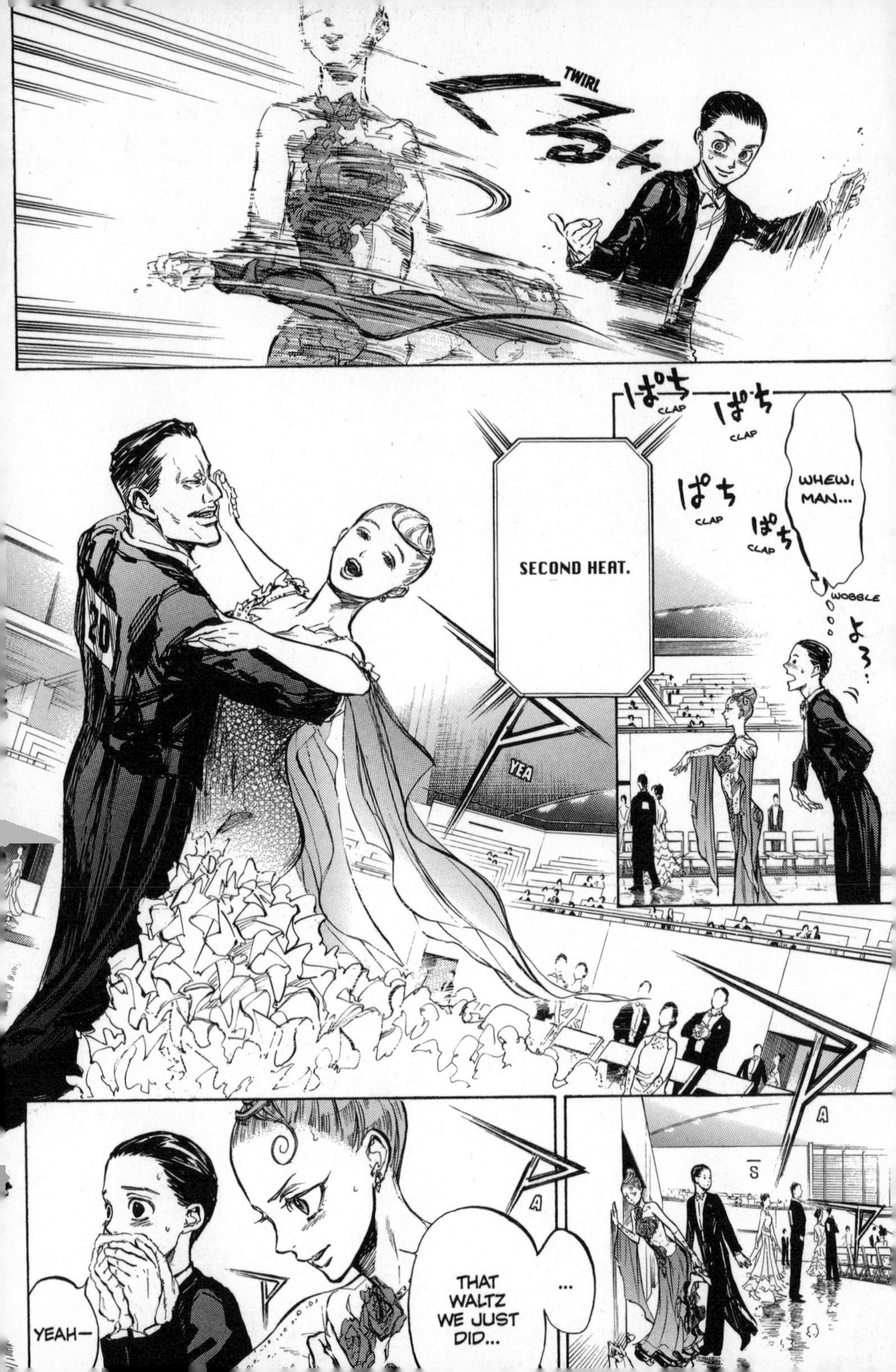

TWIRL
ぱち
CLAP
ぱち
CLAP
ぱち
CLAP
ぱち
CLAP
WHEW, MAN...
WOBBLE
SECOND HEAT.
YEA
A
S
A
THAT WALTZ WE JUST DID...
...
YEAH—

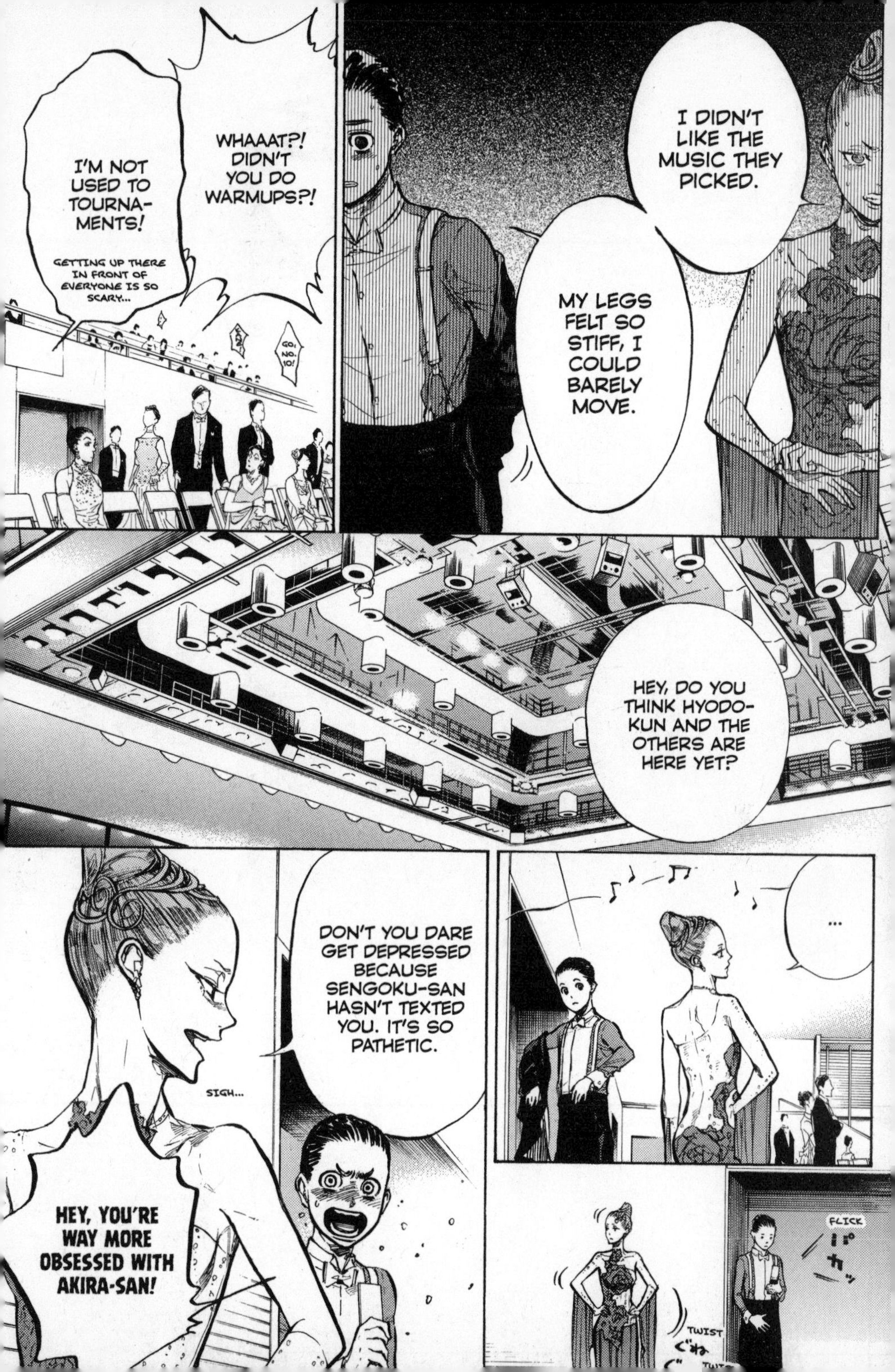
I DIDN'T LIKE THE MUSIC THEY PICKED.
MY LEGS FELT SO STIFF, I COULD BARELY MOVE.
WHAAAT?! DIDN'T YOU DO WARMUPS?!
I'M NOT USED TO TOURNA-MENTS!
GETTING UP THERE IN FRONT OF EVERYONE IS SO SCARY...
GO! NO. 10!
HEY, DO YOU THINK HYODO-KUN AND THE OTHERS ARE HERE YET?
...
FLICK
TWIST
DON'T YOU DARE GET DEPRESSED BECAUSE SENGOKU-SAN HASN'T TEXTED YOU. IT'S SO PATHETIC.
SIGH...
HEY, YOU'RE WAY MORE OBSESSED WITH AKIRA-SAN!

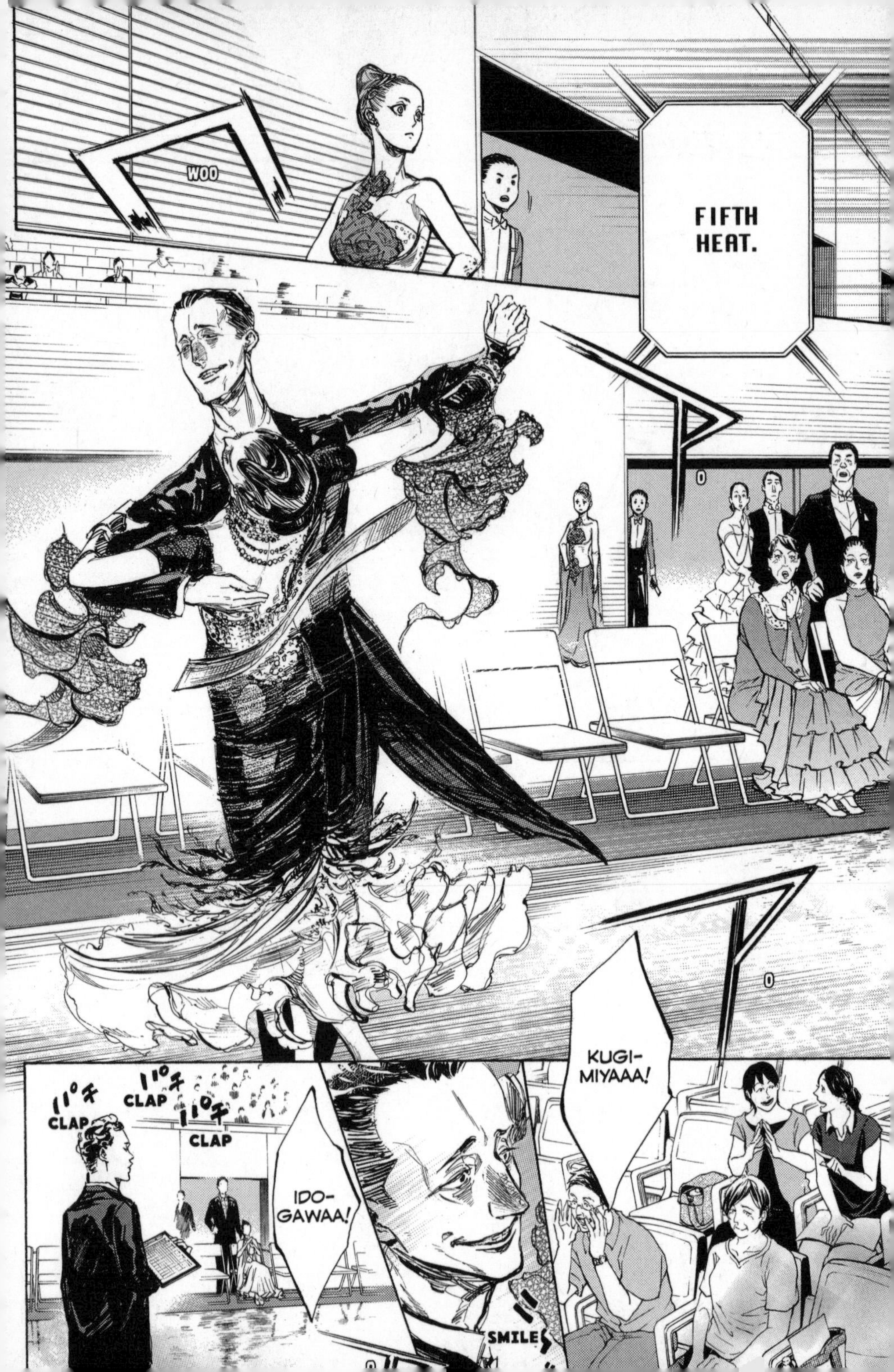

FIFTH HEAT.
WOO
KUGI-MIYAAA!
IDO-GAWAA!
SMILE
パチ CLAP
パチ CLAP
パチ CLAP

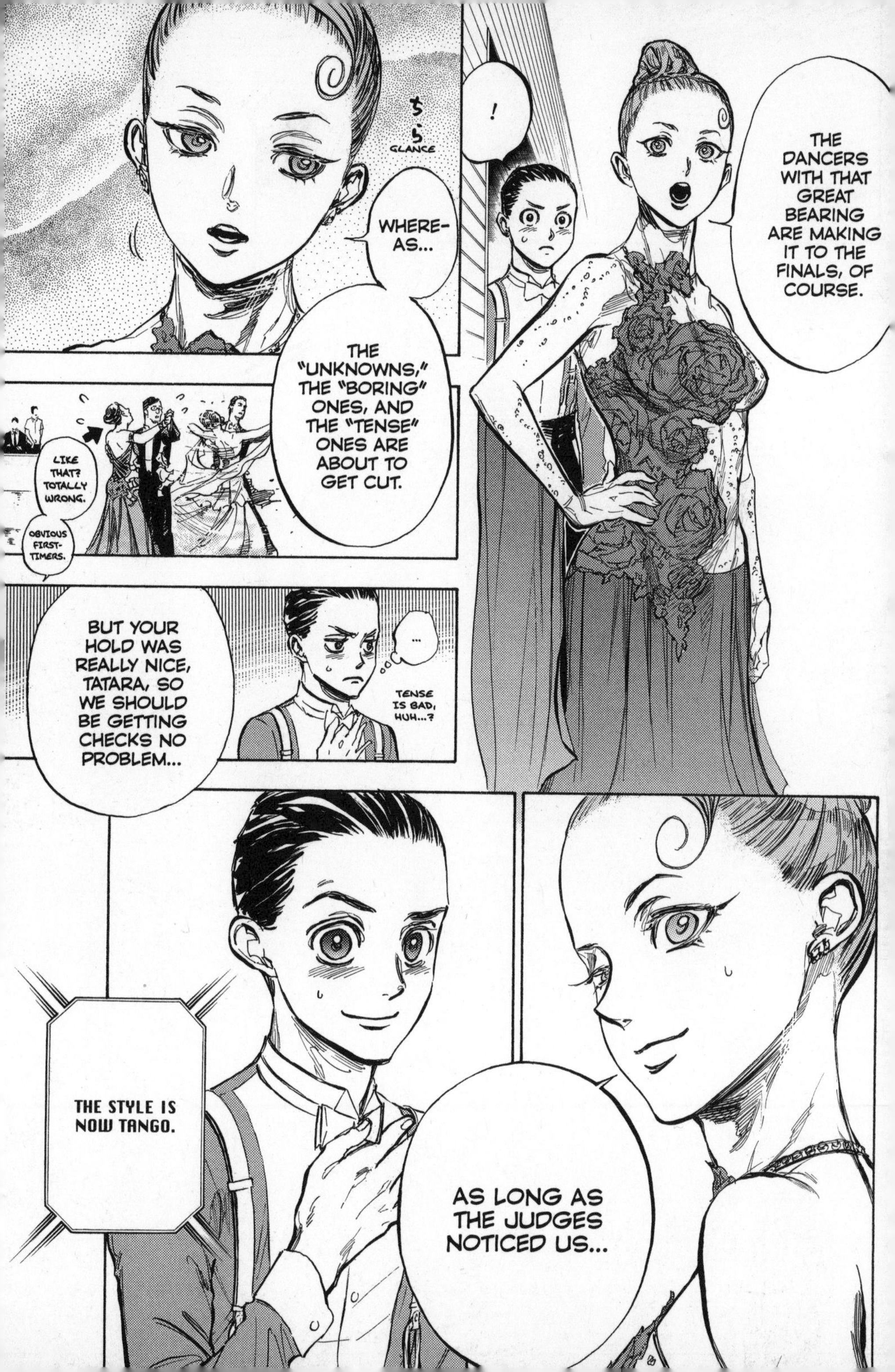

THE DANCERS WITH THAT GREAT BEARING ARE MAKING IT TO THE FINALS, OF COURSE.
!
ちら
GLANCE
WHERE-AS...
THE "UNKNOWNS," THE "BORING" ONES, AND THE "TENSE" ONES ARE ABOUT TO GET CUT.
LIKE THAT? TOTALLY WRONG.
OBVIOUS FIRST-TIMERS.
...
TENSE IS BAD, HUH...?
BUT YOUR HOLD WAS REALLY NICE, TATARA, SO WE SHOULD BE GETTING CHECKS NO PROBLEM...
AS LONG AS THE JUDGES NOTICED US...
THE STYLE IS NOW TANGO.

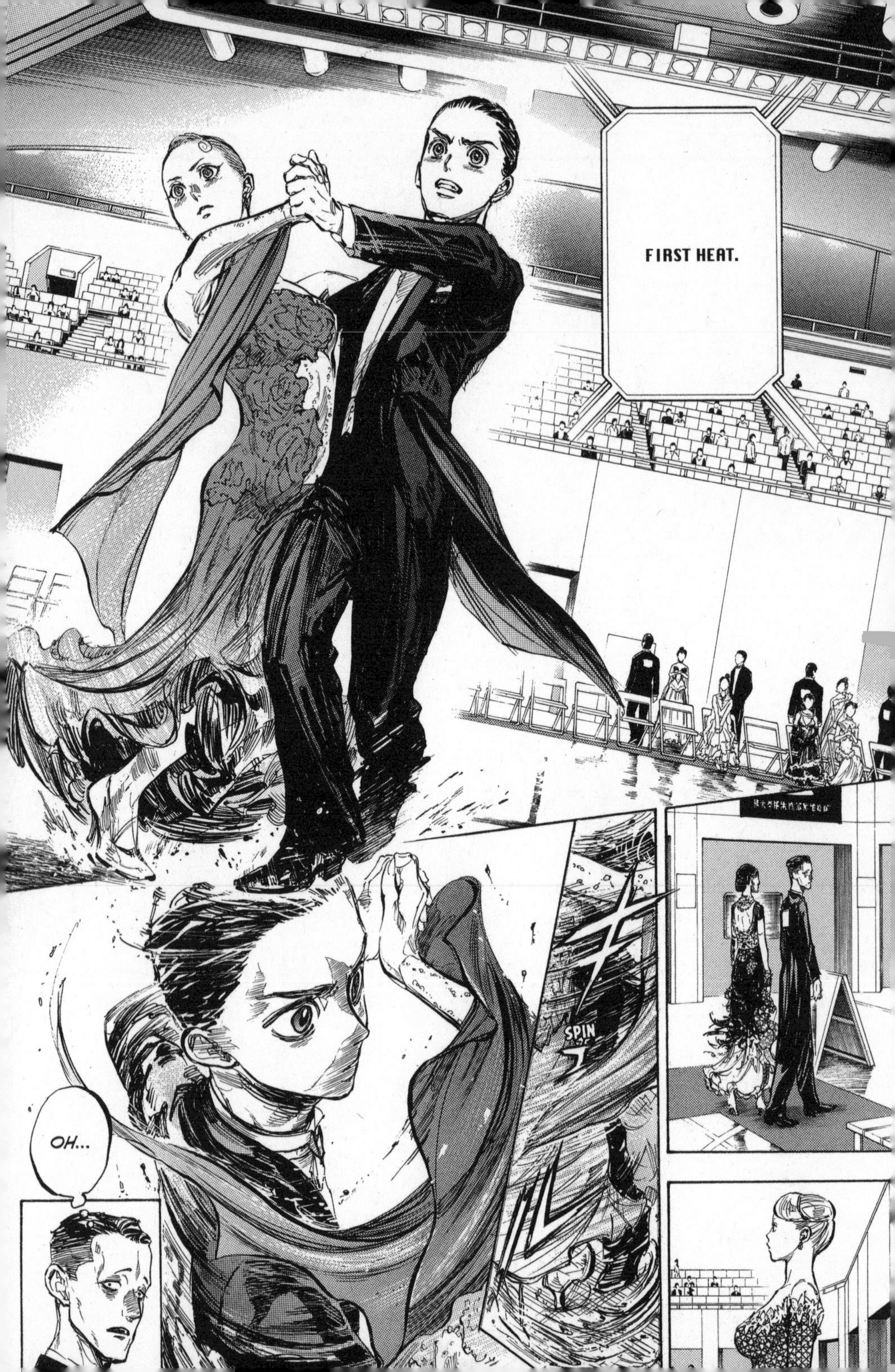
FIRST HEAT.
SPIN
OH...

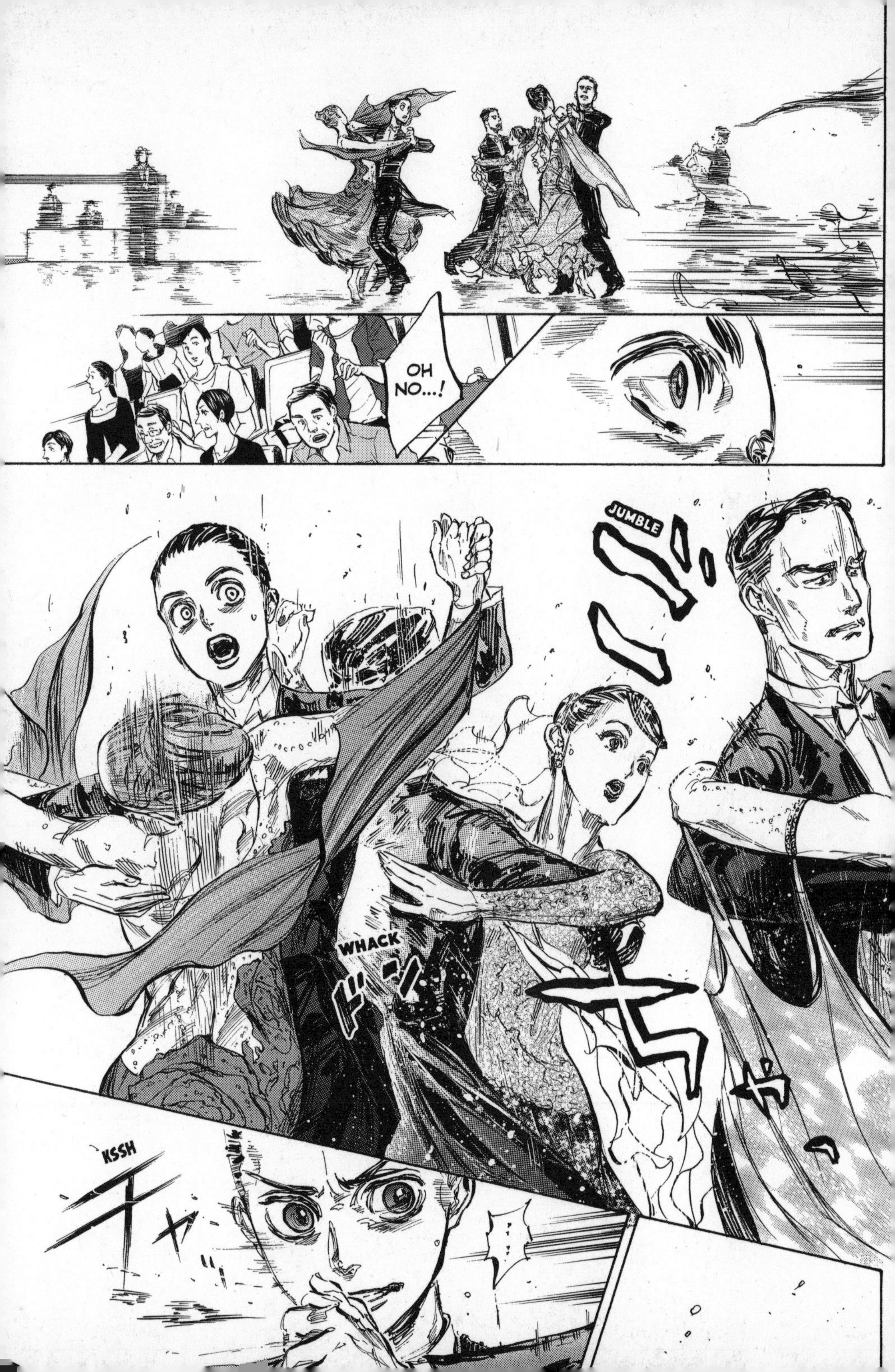
OH NO...!
JUMBLE
WHACK
KSSH

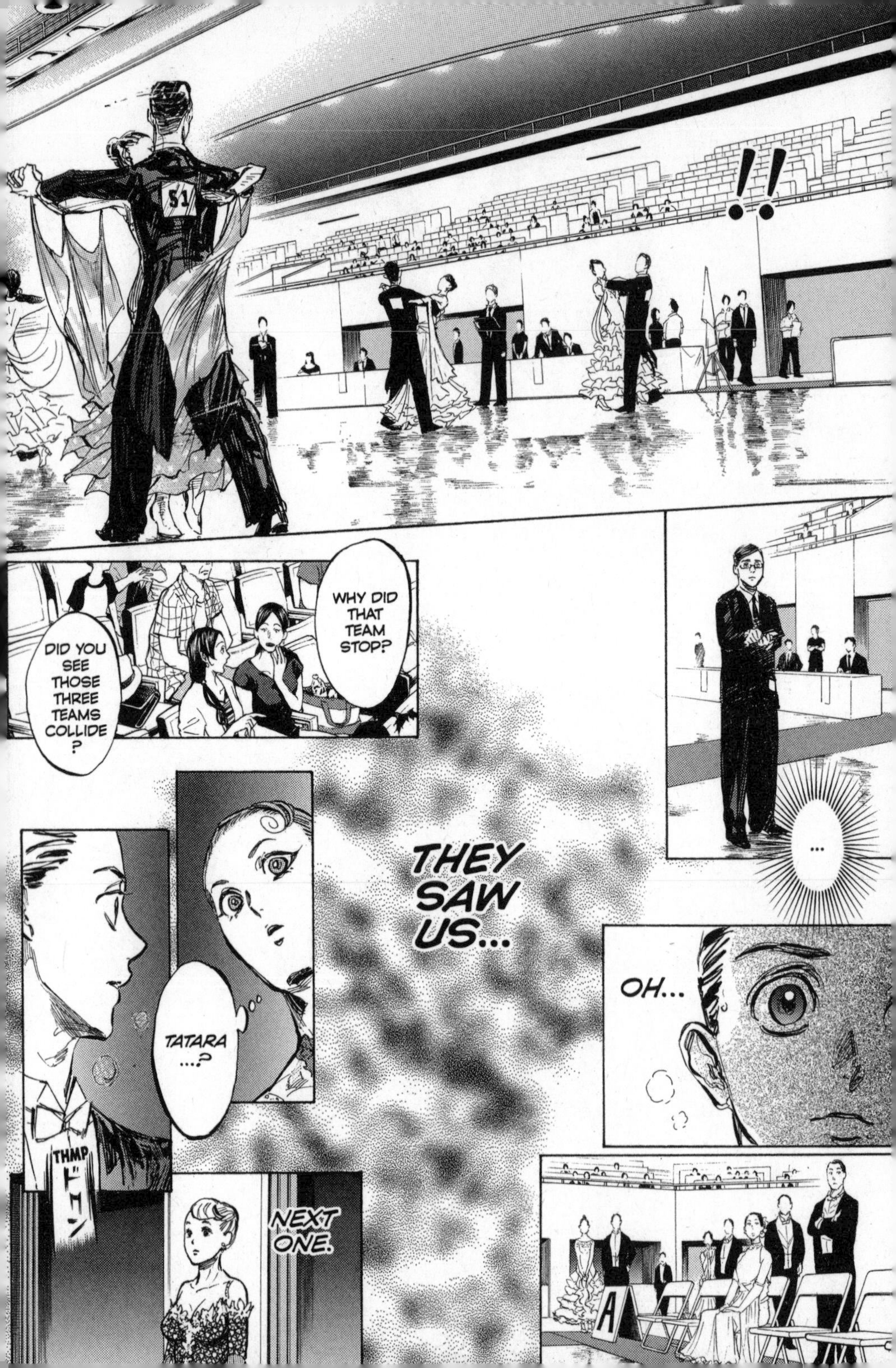

51
!!
...
WHY DID THAT TEAM STOP?
DID YOU SEE THOSE THREE TEAMS COLLIDE?
THEY SAW US...
OH...
TATARA ...?
THMP
ドゴン
A
NEXT ONE.

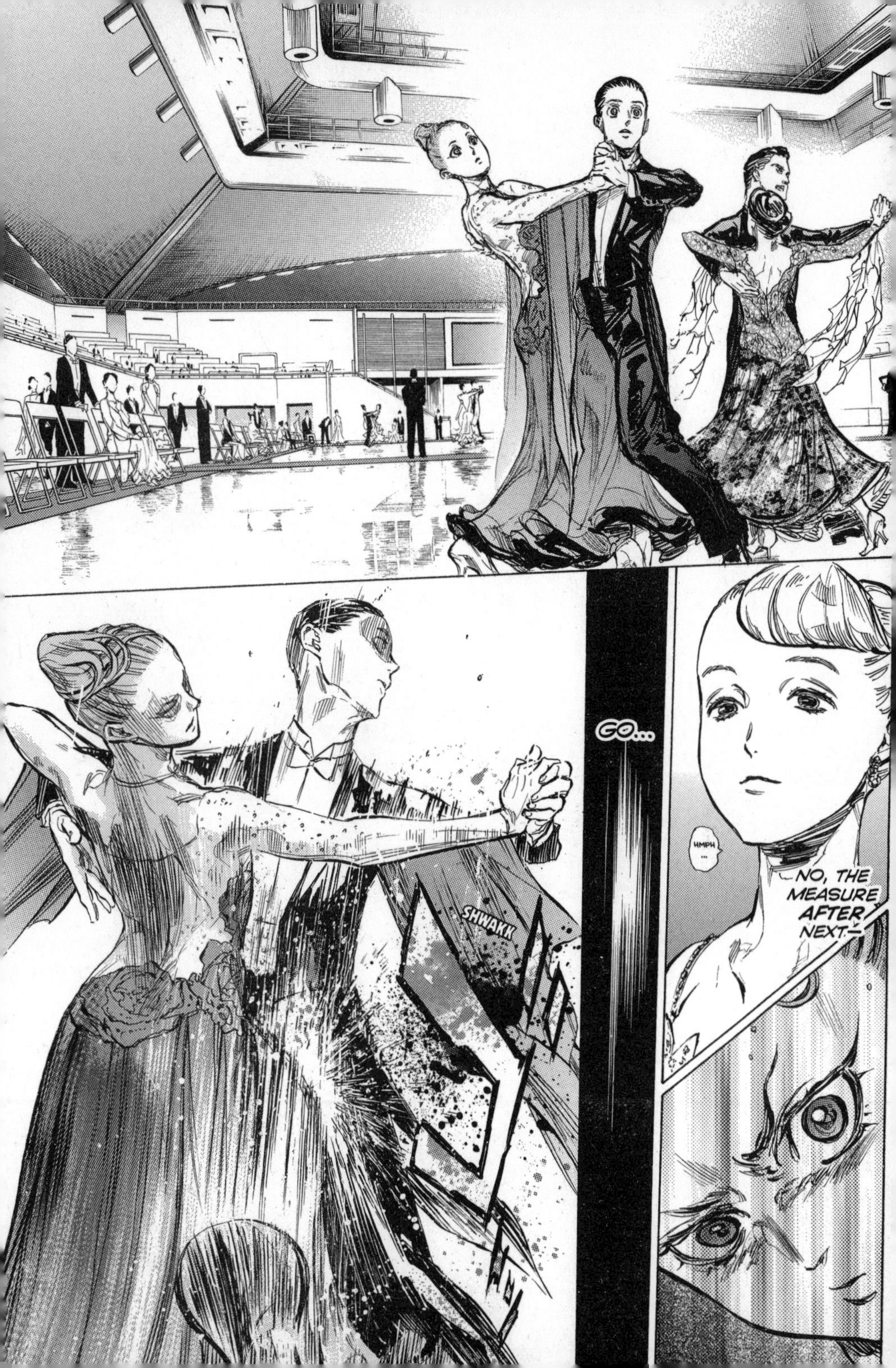
HMPH...
NO, THE MEASURE AFTER NEXT—
GO...
SHWAKK

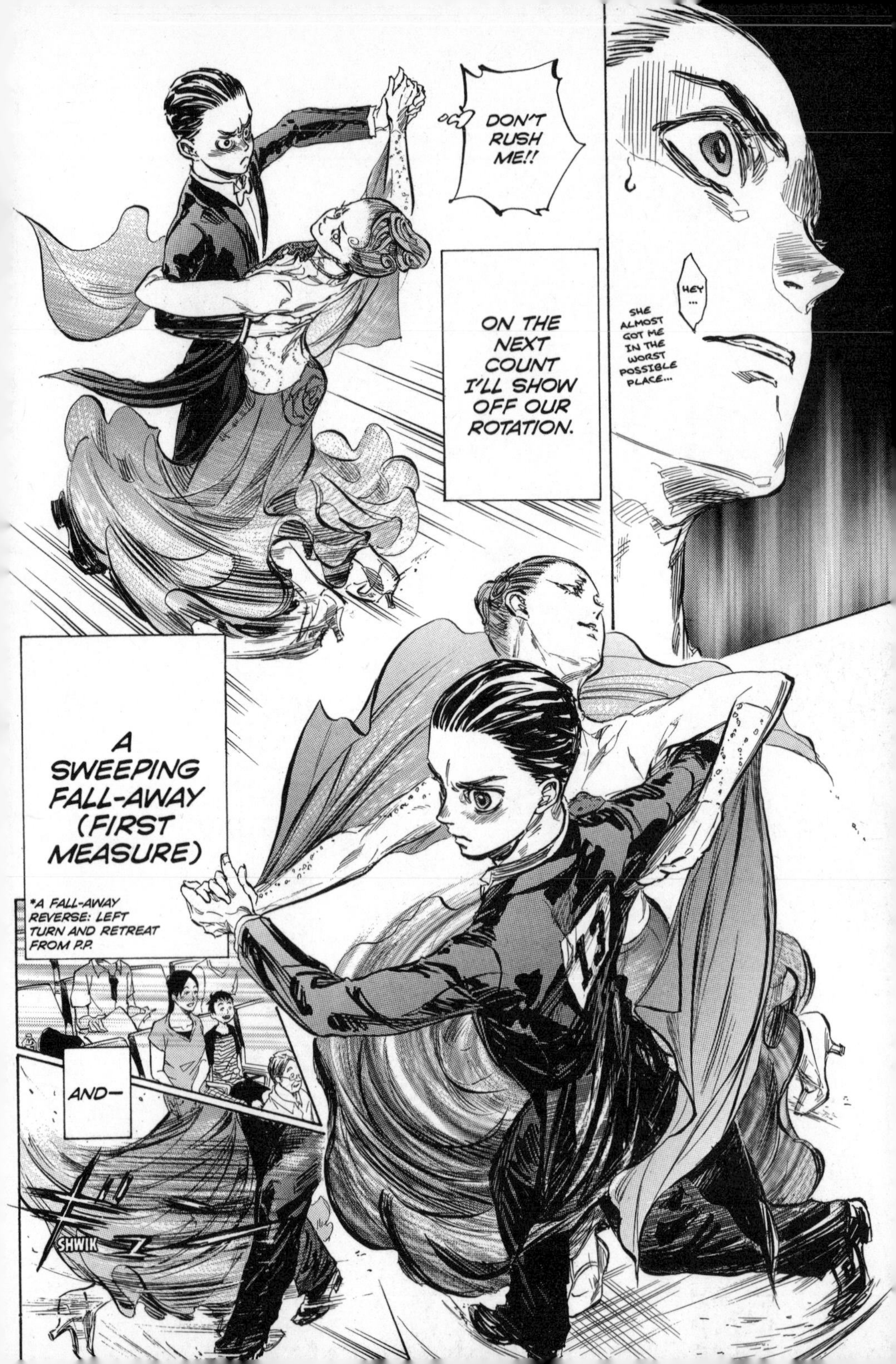
HEY...
SHE ALMOST GOT ME IN THE WORST POSSIBLE PLACE...
DON'T RUSH ME!!
ON THE NEXT COUNT I'LL SHOW OFF OUR ROTATION.
A SWEEPING FALL-AWAY (FIRST MEASURE)
*A FALL-AWAY REVERSE: LEFT TURN AND RETREAT FROM P.P.
AND—
SHWIK

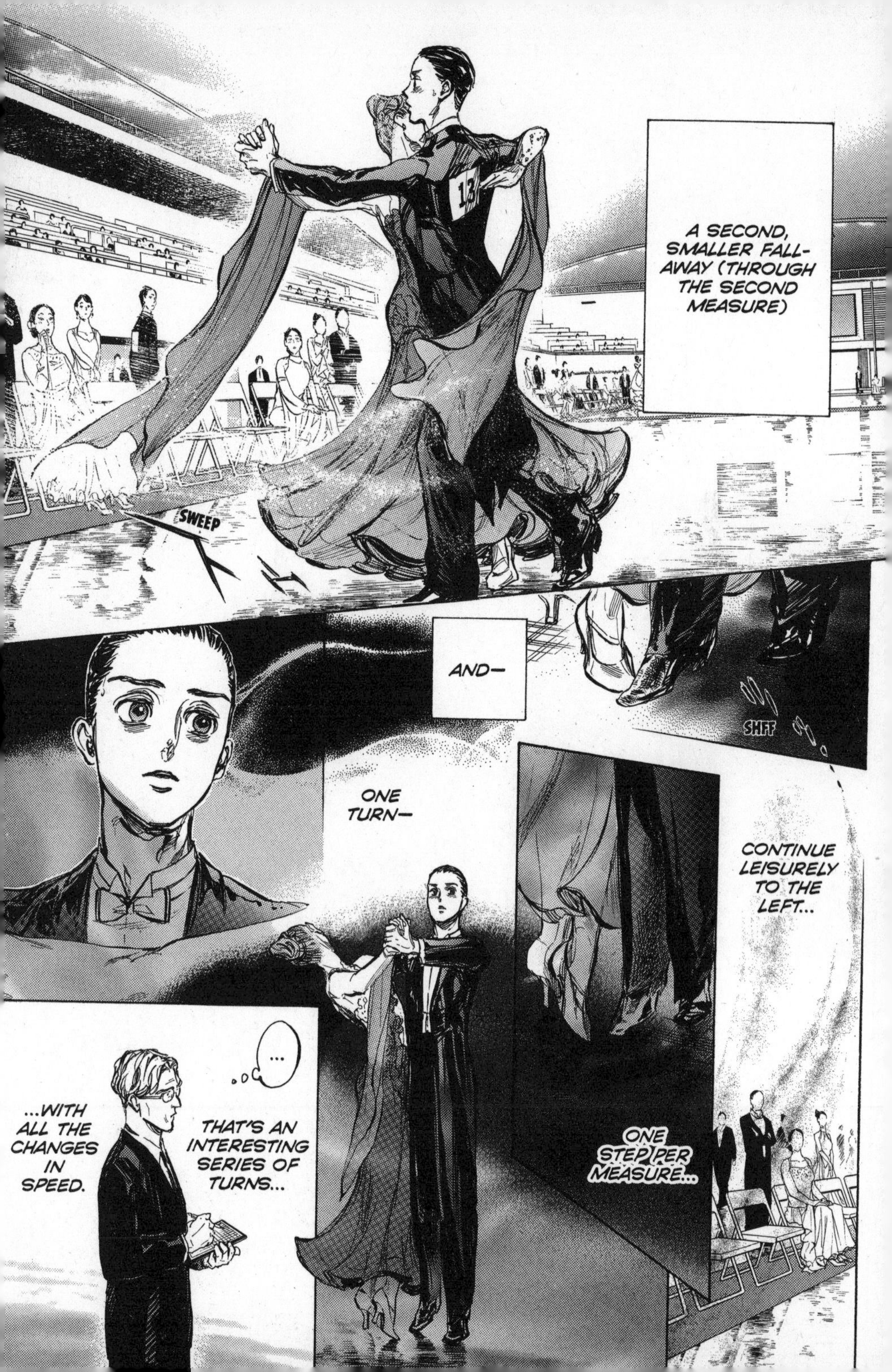
A SECOND, SMALLER FALL-AWAY (THROUGH THE SECOND MEASURE)
SWEEP
SHFF
AND—
CONTINUE LEISURELY TO THE LEFT...
ONE TURN—
ONE STEP PER MEASURE...
...
THAT'S AN INTERESTING SERIES OF TURNS...
...WITH ALL THE CHANGES IN SPEED.

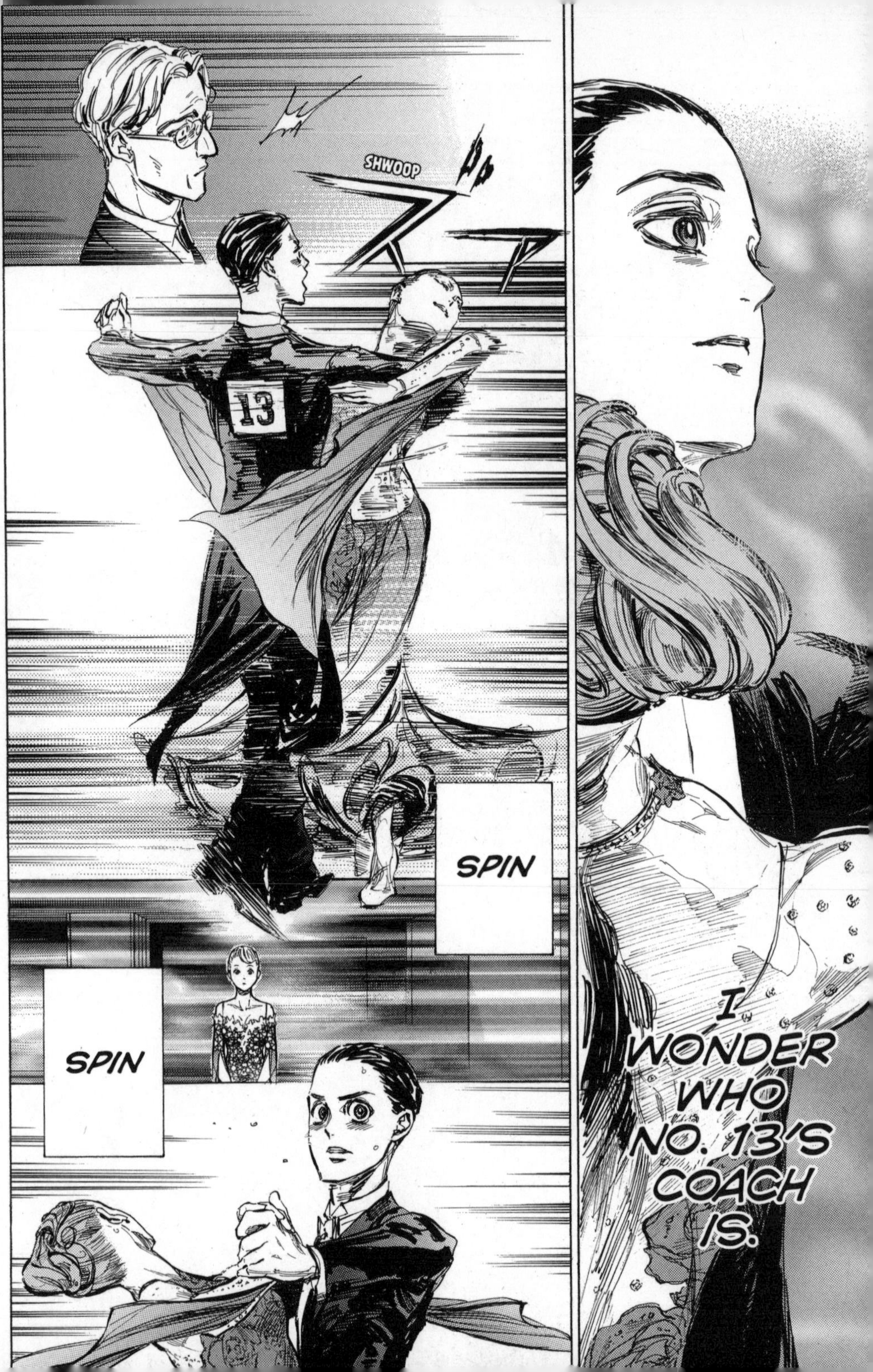
I WONDER WHO NO. 13'S COACH IS.
SHWOOP
13
SPIN
SPIN

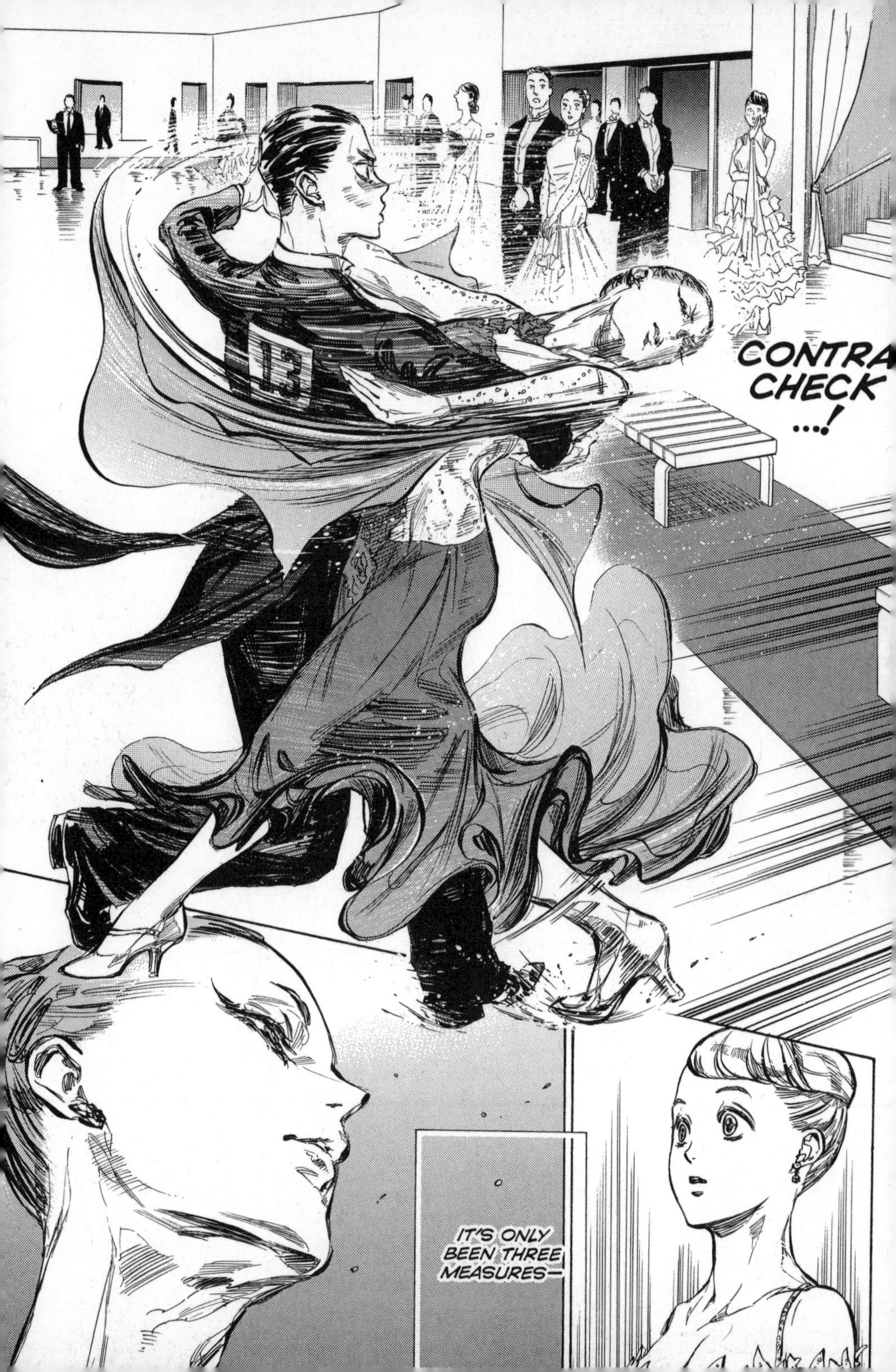
CONTRA CHECK ...!
IT'S ONLY BEEN THREE MEASURES—

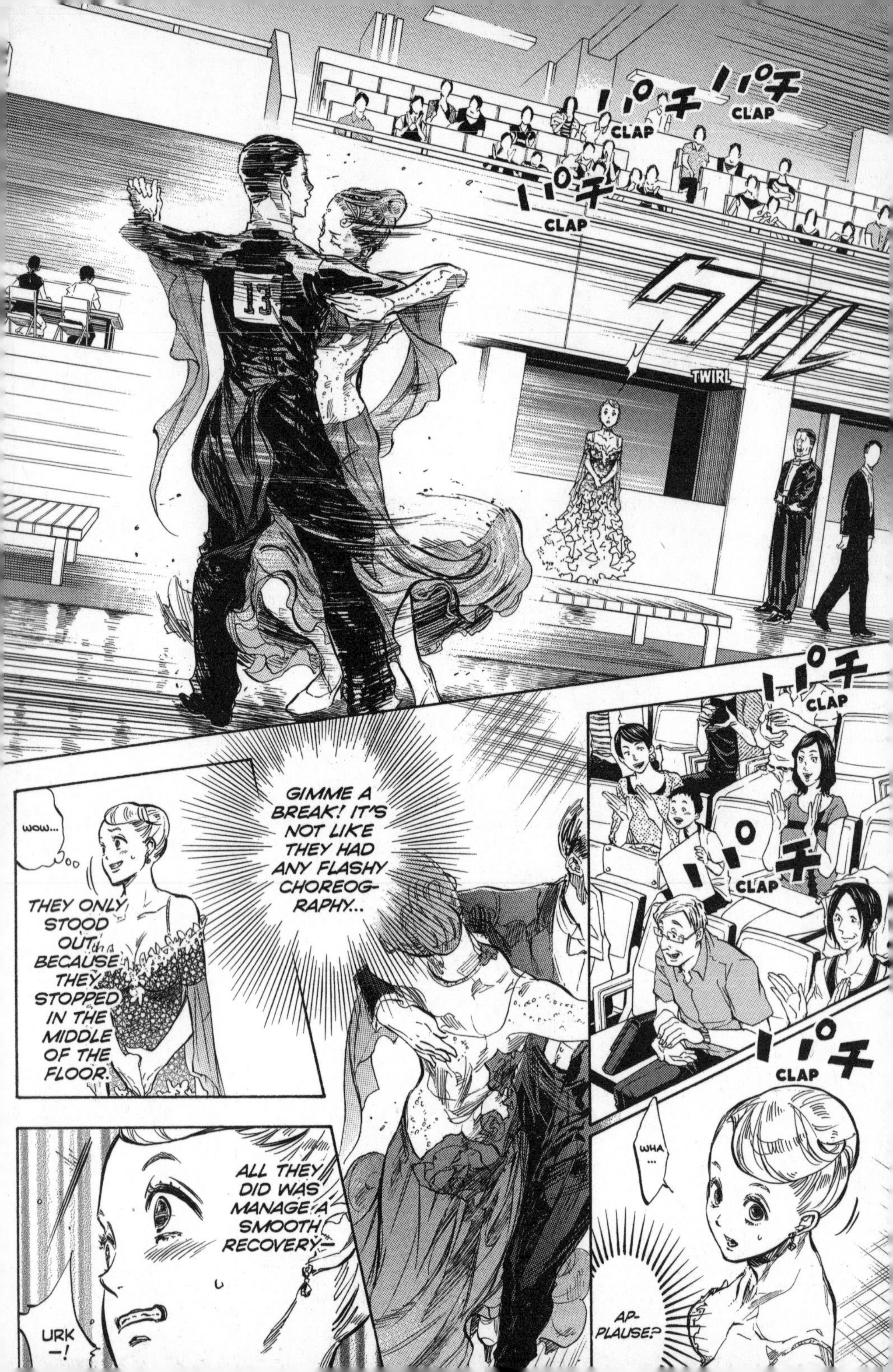
パチ
CLAP
パチ
CLAP
パチ
CLAP
クル
TWIRL
パチ
CLAP
パチ
CLAP
パチ
CLAP
WHA...
AP-PLAUSE?
GIMME A BREAK! IT'S NOT LIKE THEY HAD ANY FLASHY CHOREOG-RAPHY...
ALL THEY DID WAS MANAGE A SMOOTH RECOVERY—
WOW...
THEY ONLY STOOD OUT BECAUSE THEY STOPPED IN THE MIDDLE OF THE FLOOR.
URK—!

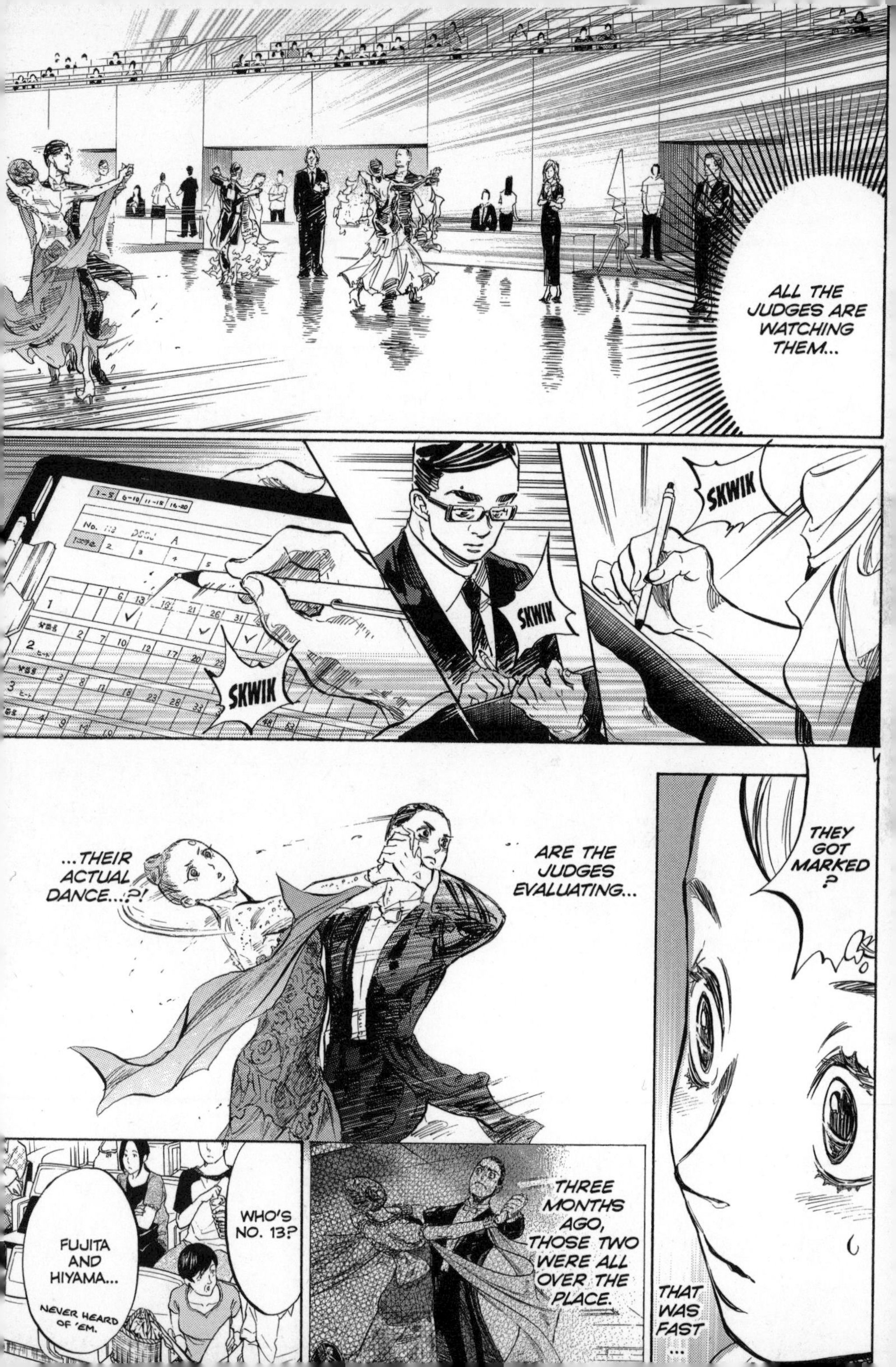
ALL THE JUDGES ARE WATCHING THEM...
SKWIK
SKWIK
SKWIK
THEY GOT MARKED?
THAT WAS FAST...
ARE THE JUDGES EVALUATING...
...THEIR ACTUAL DANCE...?!
THREE MONTHS AGO, THOSE TWO WERE ALL OVER THE PLACE.
WHO'S NO. 13?
FUJITA AND HIYAMA...
NEVER HEARD OF 'EM.

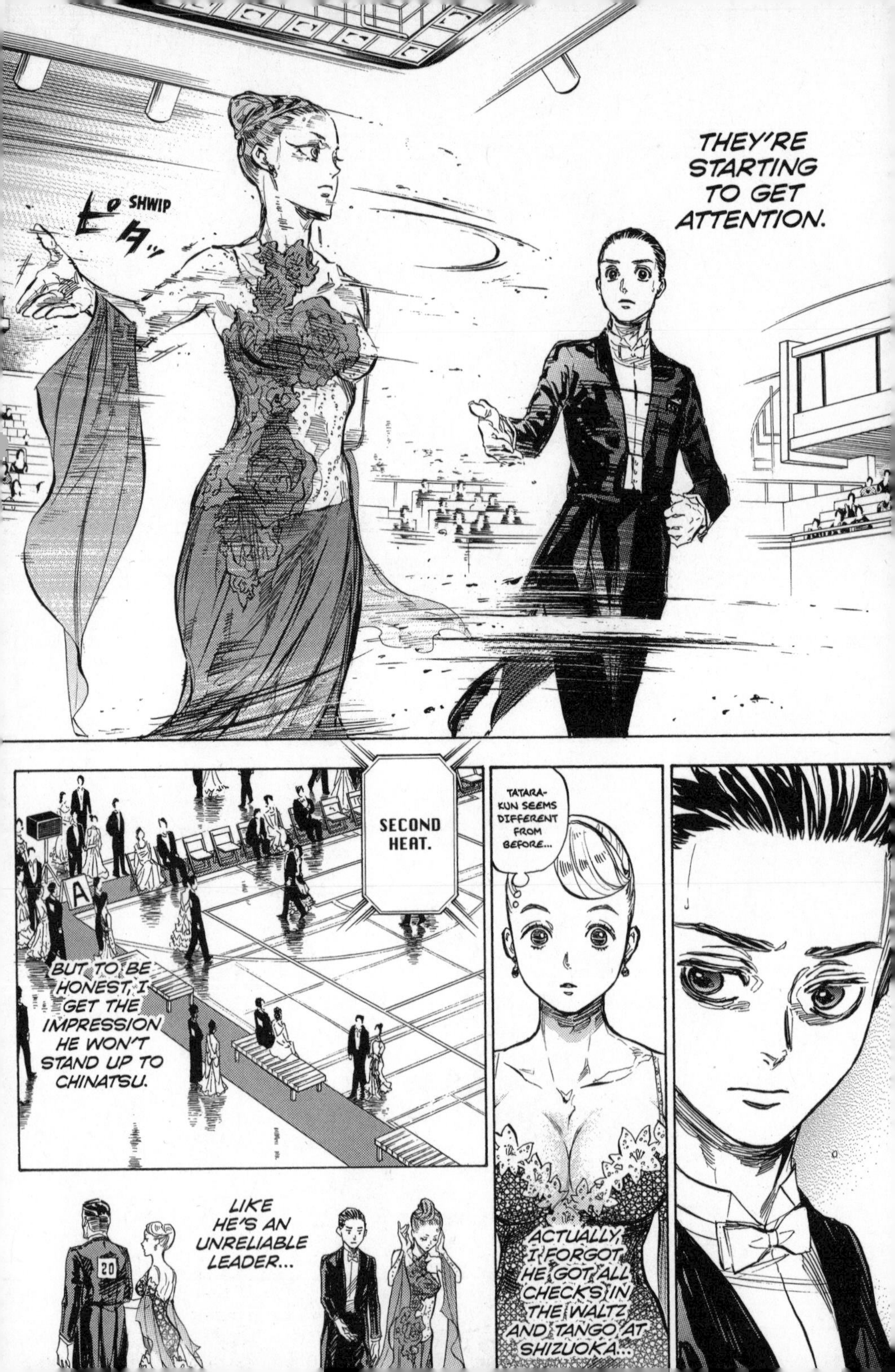

SHWIP
THEY'RE STARTING TO GET ATTENTION.
TATARA-KUN SEEMS DIFFERENT FROM BEFORE...
ACTUALLY, I FORGOT HE GOT ALL CHECKS IN THE WALTZ AND TANGO AT SHIZUOKA...
SECOND HEAT.
BUT TO BE HONEST, I GET THE IMPRESSION HE WON'T STAND UP TO CHINATSU.
LIKE HE'S AN UNRELIABLE LEADER...
20

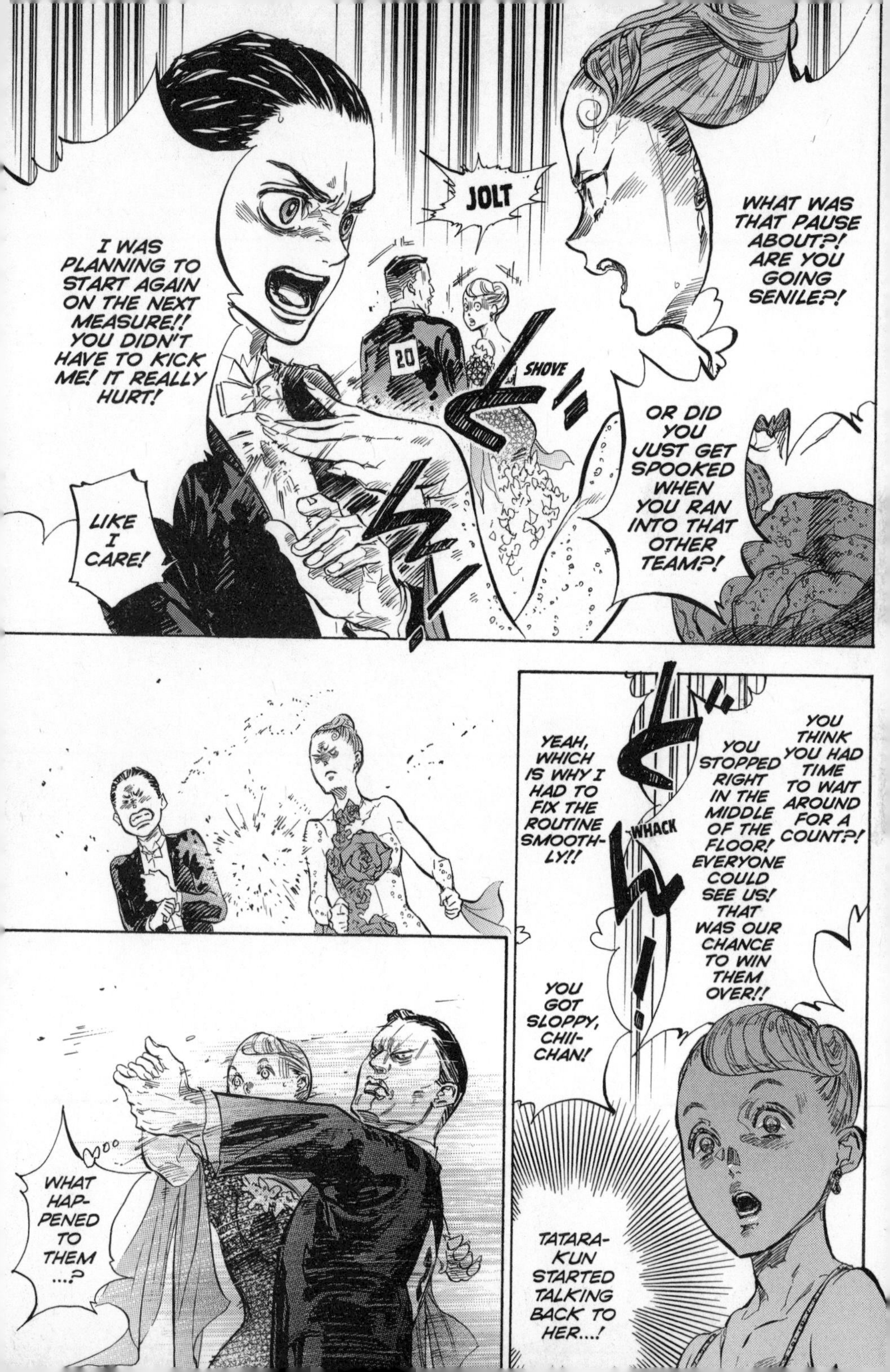
WHAT WAS THAT PAUSE ABOUT?! ARE YOU GOING SENILE?!
JOLT
I WAS PLANNING TO START AGAIN ON THE NEXT MEASURE!! YOU DIDN'T HAVE TO KICK ME! IT REALLY HURT!
SHOVE
OR DID YOU JUST GET SPOOKED WHEN YOU RAN INTO THAT OTHER TEAM?!
LIKE I CARE!
YOU THINK YOU HAD TIME TO WAIT AROUND FOR A COUNT?!
YOU STOPPED RIGHT IN THE MIDDLE OF THE FLOOR! EVERYONE COULD SEE US! THAT WAS OUR CHANCE TO WIN THEM OVER!!
YEAH, WHICH IS WHY I HAD TO FIX THE ROUTINE SMOOTH-LY!!
WHACK
YOU GOT SLOPPY, CHII-CHAN!
TATARA-KUN STARTED TALKING BACK TO HER...!
WHAT HAP-PENED TO THEM ...?

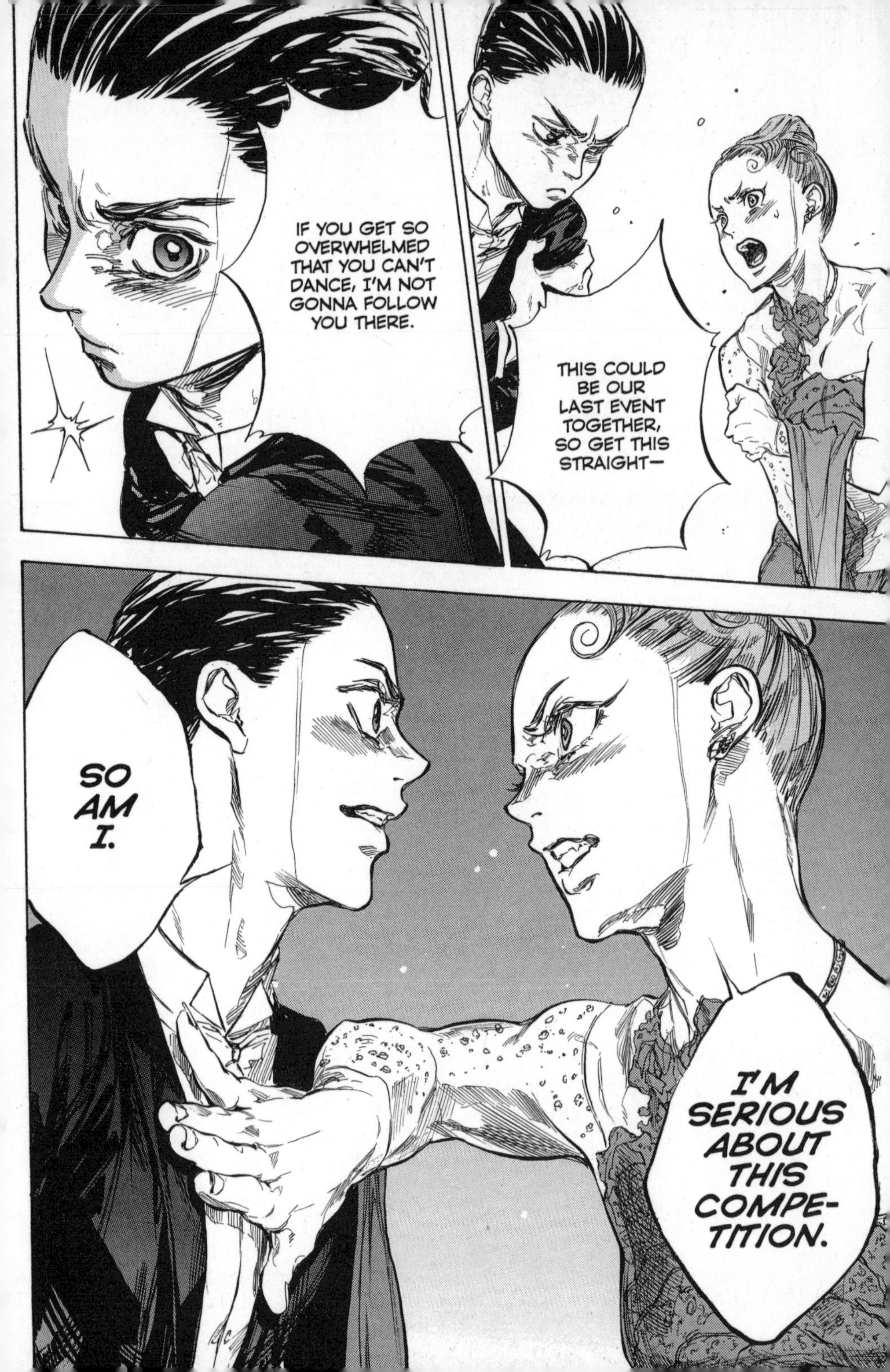
THIS COULD BE OUR LAST EVENT TOGETHER, SO GET THIS STRAIGHT—
IF YOU GET SO OVERWHELMED THAT YOU CAN'T DANCE, I'M NOT GONNA FOLLOW YOU THERE.
I'M SERIOUS ABOUT THIS COMPE-TITION.
SO AM I.

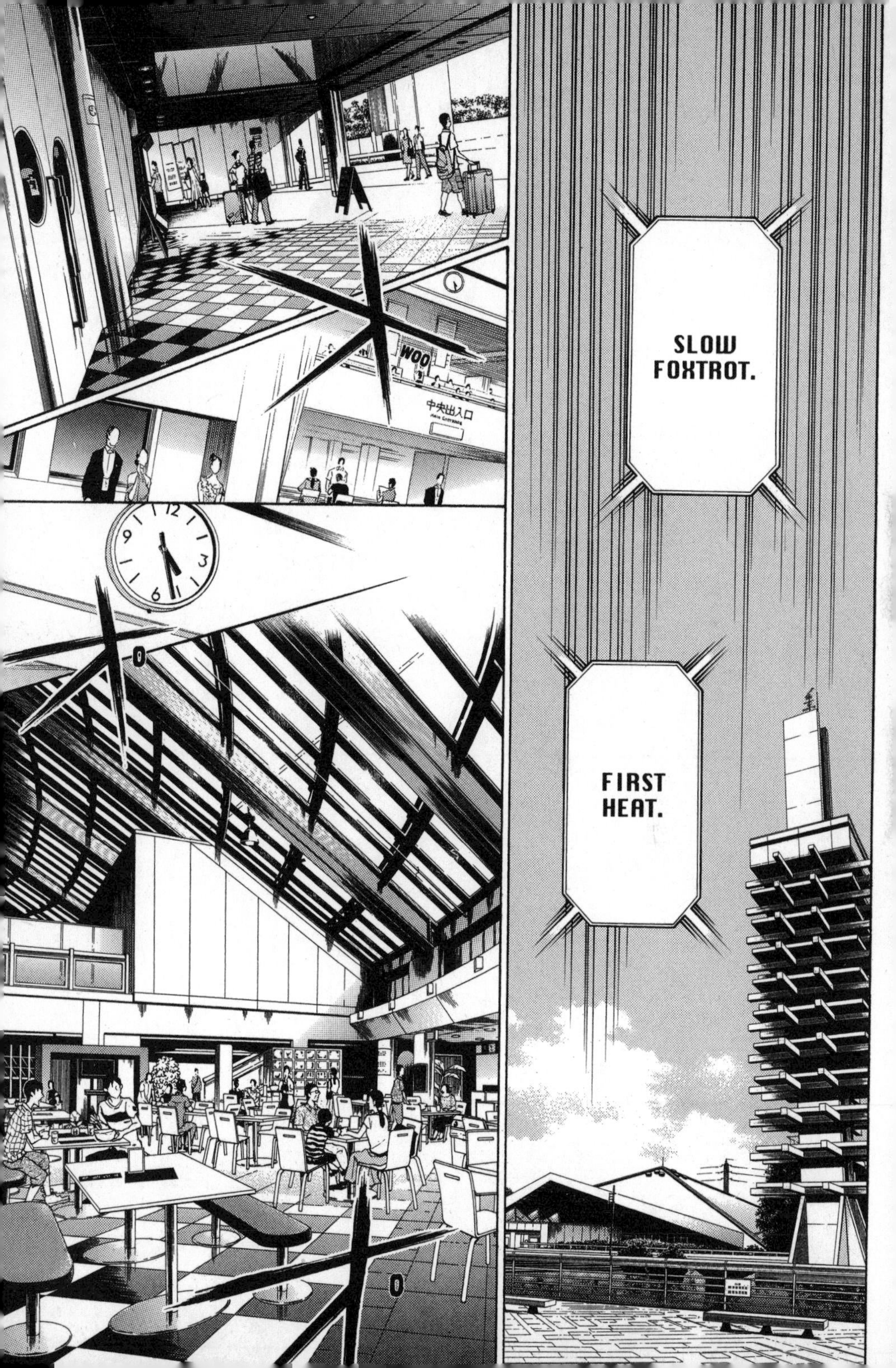
SLOW FOXTROT.
FIRST HEAT.
中央出入口

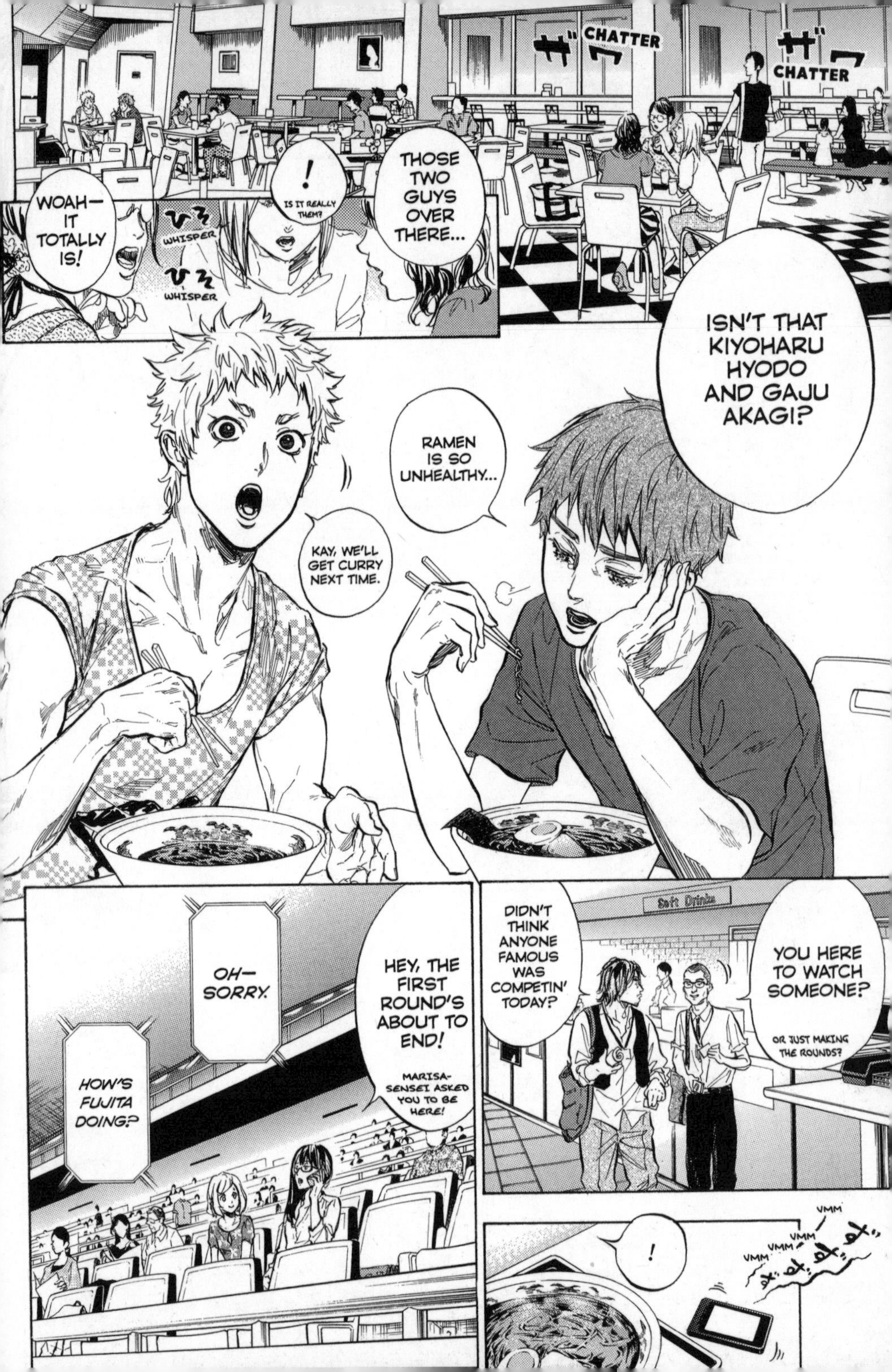
CHATTER
CHATTER
THOSE TWO GUYS OVER THERE...
!
IS IT REALLY THEM?
WHISPER
WHISPER
WOAH— IT TOTALLY IS!
ISN'T THAT KIYOHARU HYODO AND GAJU AKAGI?
RAMEN IS SO UNHEALTHY...
KAY, WE'LL GET CURRY NEXT TIME.
YOU HERE TO WATCH SOMEONE?
OR JUST MAKING THE ROUNDS?
DIDN'T THINK ANYONE FAMOUS WAS COMPETIN' TODAY?
VMM
VMM
VMM
VMM
!
HEY, THE FIRST ROUND'S ABOUT TO END!
MARISA-SENSEI ASKED YOU TO BE HERE!
OH— SORRY.
HOW'S FUJITA DOING?

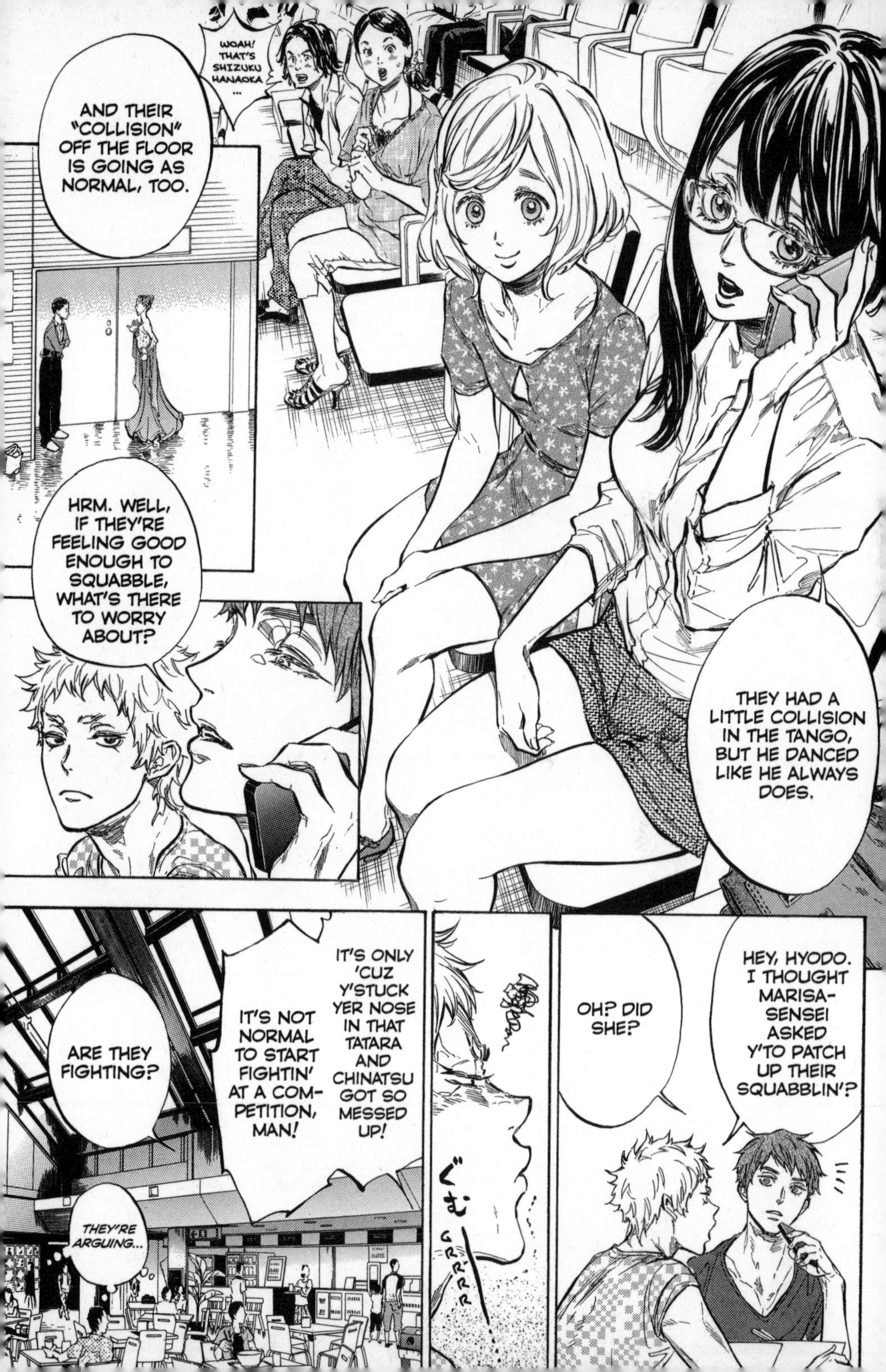
WOAH! THAT'S SHIZUKU HANAOKA ...
THEY HAD A LITTLE COLLISION IN THE TANGO, BUT HE DANCED LIKE HE ALWAYS DOES.
AND THEIR "COLLISION" OFF THE FLOOR IS GOING AS NORMAL, TOO.
HRM. WELL, IF THEY'RE FEELING GOOD ENOUGH TO SQUABBLE, WHAT'S THERE TO WORRY ABOUT?
HEY, HYODO. I THOUGHT MARISA-SENSEI ASKED Y'TO PATCH UP THEIR SQUABBLIN'?
OH? DID SHE?
ぐむ
GRRRR
IT'S ONLY 'CUZ Y'STUCK YER NOSE IN THAT TATARA AND CHINATSU GOT SO MESSED UP!
IT'S NOT NORMAL TO START FIGHTIN' AT A COMPETITION, MAN!
ARE THEY FIGHTING?
THEY'RE ARGUING...

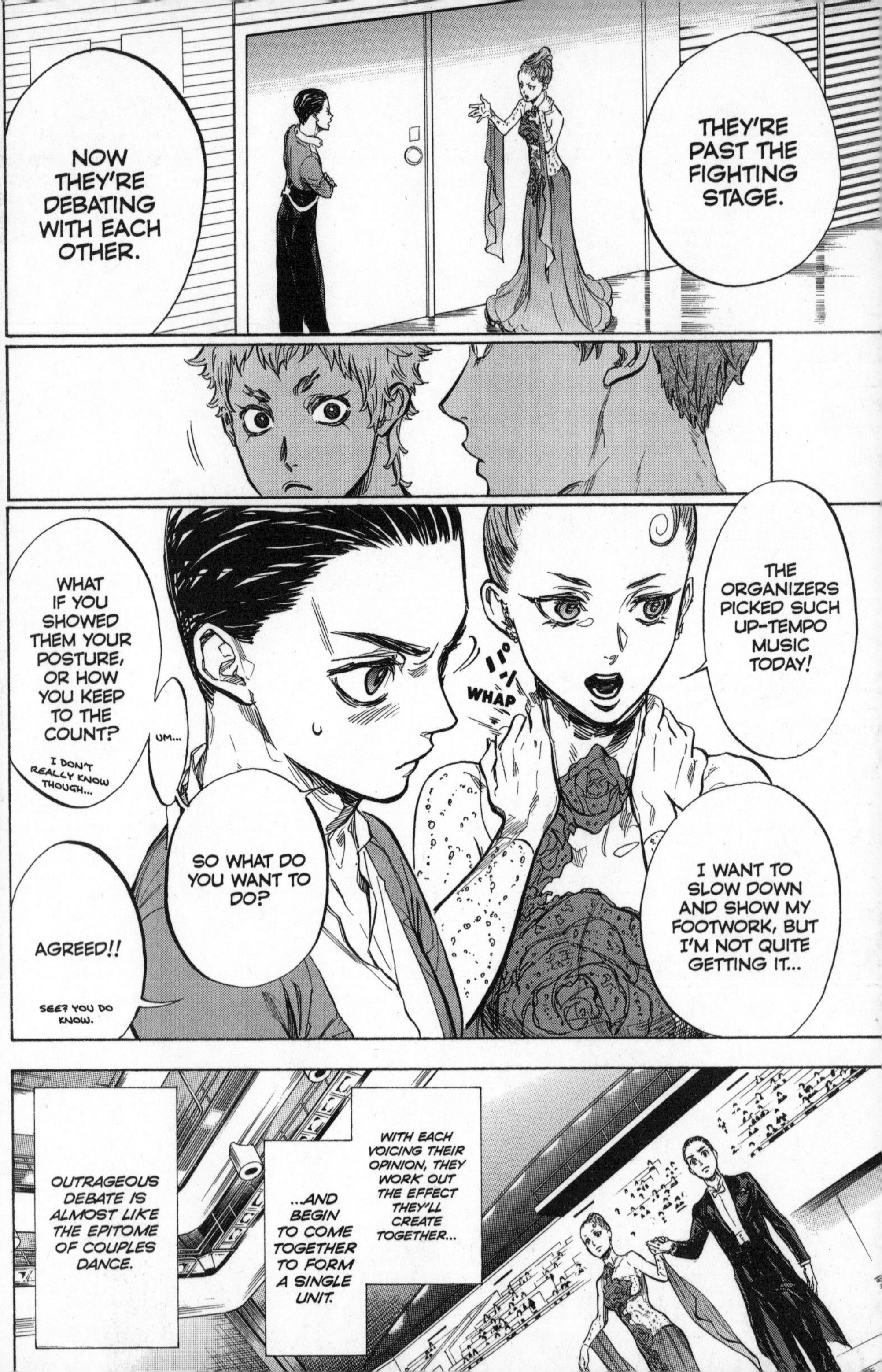
THEY'RE PAST THE FIGHTING STAGE.
NOW THEY'RE DEBATING WITH EACH OTHER.
THE ORGANIZERS PICKED SUCH UP-TEMPO MUSIC TODAY!
WHAP
WHAT IF YOU SHOWED THEM YOUR POSTURE, OR HOW YOU KEEP TO THE COUNT?
UM...
I DON'T REALLY KNOW THOUGH...
I WANT TO SLOW DOWN AND SHOW MY FOOTWORK, BUT I'M NOT QUITE GETTING IT...
SO WHAT DO YOU WANT TO DO?
AGREED!!
SEE? YOU DO KNOW.
WITH EACH VOICING THEIR OPINION, THEY WORK OUT THE EFFECT THEY'LL CREATE TOGETHER...
...AND BEGIN TO COME TOGETHER TO FORM A SINGLE UNIT.
OUTRAGEOUS DEBATE IS ALMOST LIKE THE EPITOME OF COUPLES DANCE.

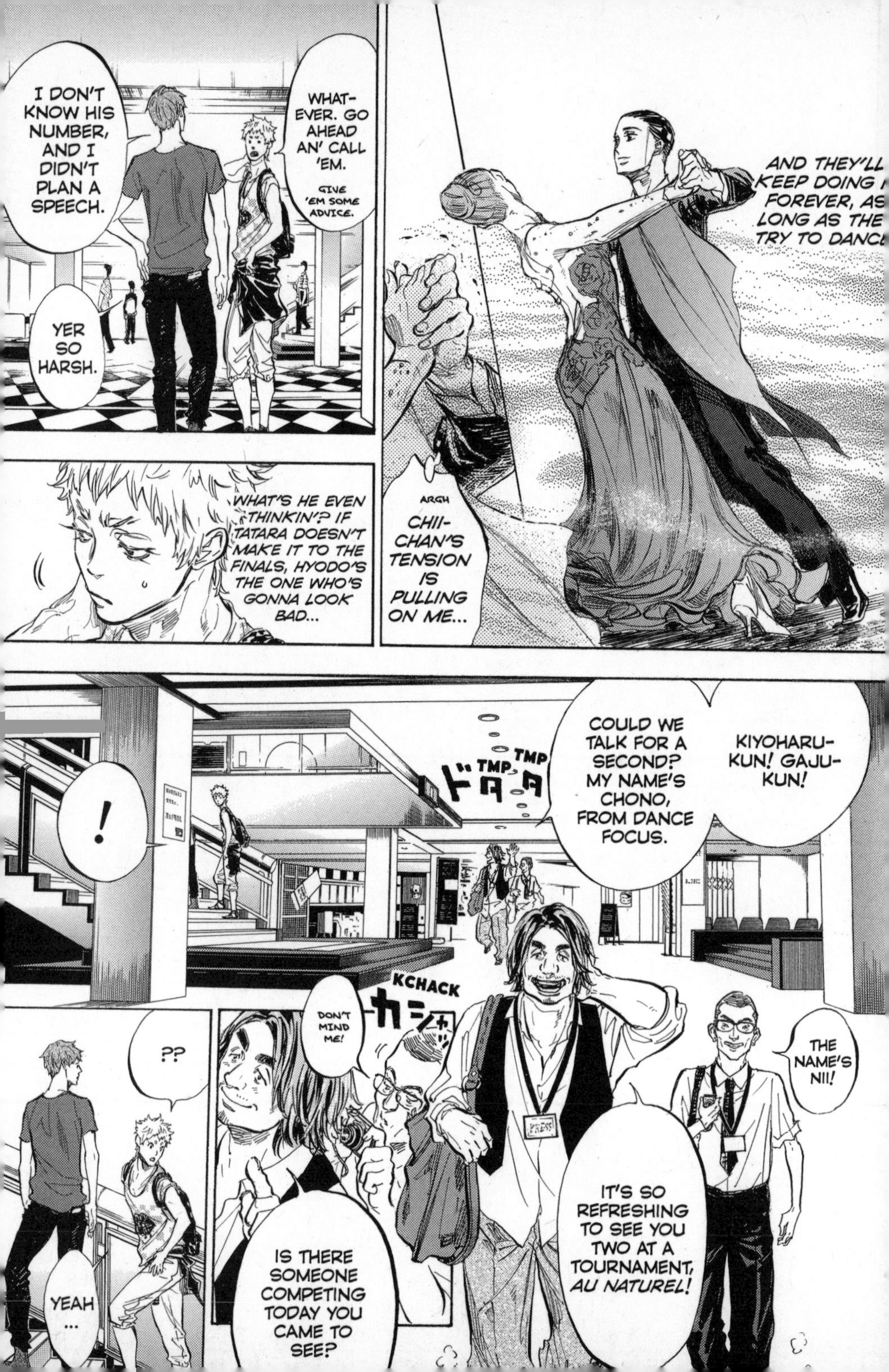
AND THEY'LL KEEP DOING FOREVER, AS LONG AS THE TRY TO DANC
ARGH
CHII-CHAN'S TENSION IS PULLING ON ME...
WHAT-EVER. GO AHEAD AN' CALL 'EM.
GIVE 'EM SOME ADVICE.
I DON'T KNOW HIS NUMBER, AND I DIDN'T PLAN A SPEECH.
YER SO HARSH.
WHAT'S HE EVEN THINKIN'? IF TATARA DOESN'T MAKE IT TO THE FINALS, HYODO'S THE ONE WHO'S GONNA LOOK BAD...
KIYOHARU-KUN! GAJU-KUN!
COULD WE TALK FOR A SECOND? MY NAME'S CHONO, FROM DANCE FOCUS.
TMP TMP TMP
!
THE NAME'S NII!
IT'S SO REFRESHING TO SEE YOU TWO AT A TOURNAMENT, AU NATUREL!
KCHACK
DON'T MIND ME!
IS THERE SOMEONE COMPETING TODAY YOU CAME TO SEE?
??
YEAH ...

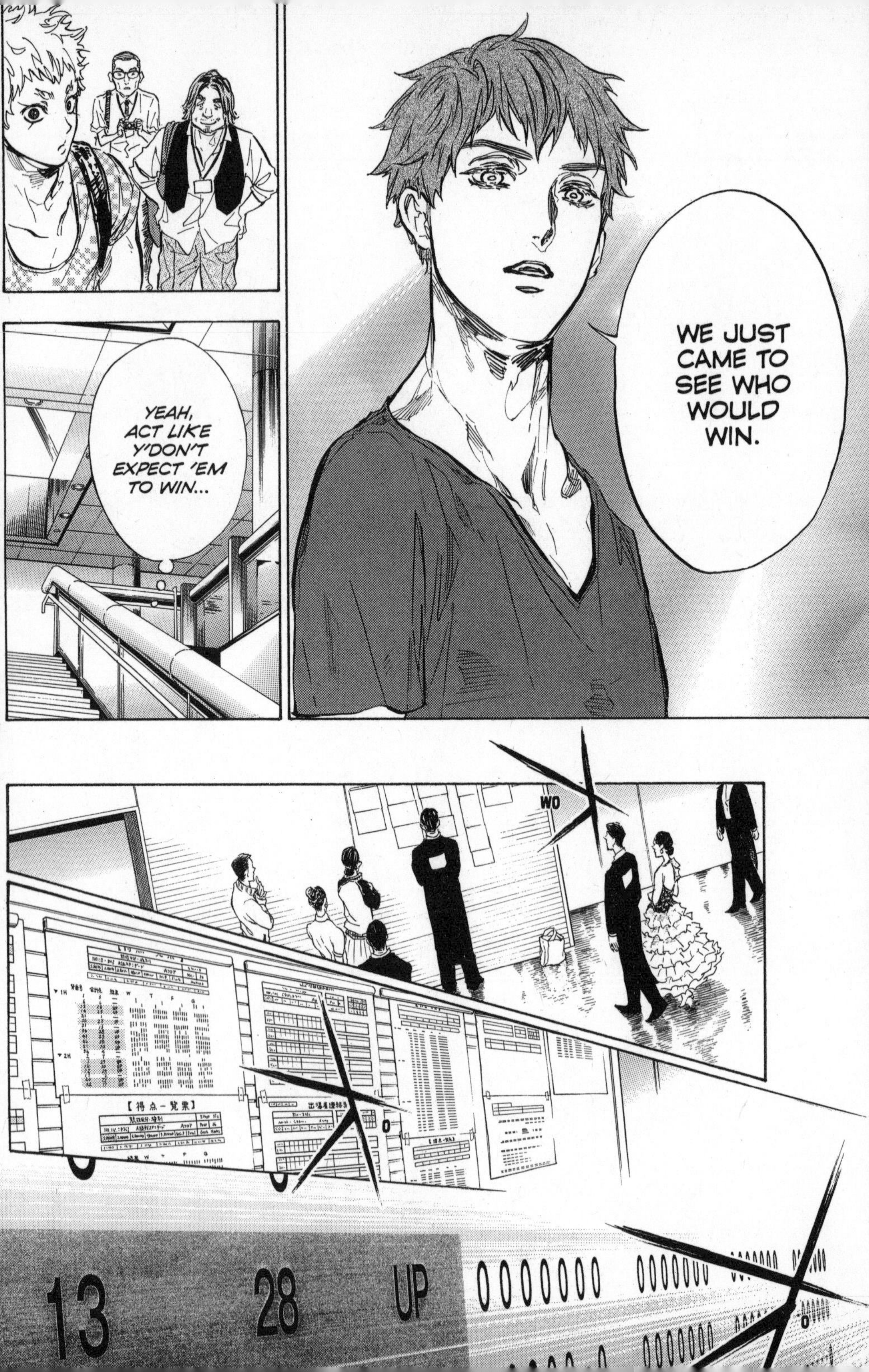
WE JUST CAME TO SEE WHO WOULD WIN.
YEAH, ACT LIKE Y'DON'T EXPECT 'EM TO WIN...
WO
O
【得点一覧票】
13
28
UP

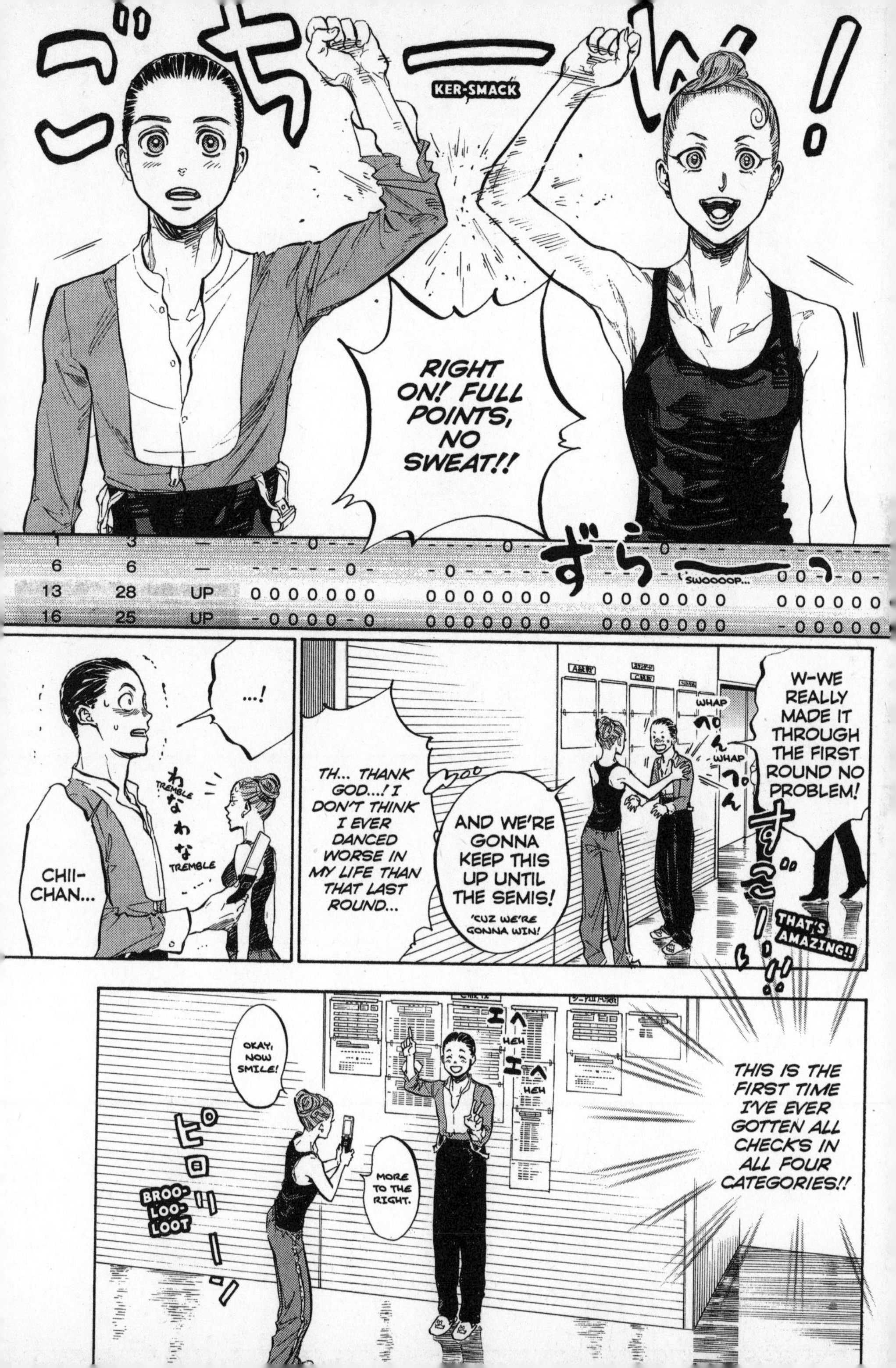
ごちーん!
KER-SMACK
RIGHT ON! FULL POINTS, NO SWEAT!!
1 3 —
6 6 —
13 28 UP 0000000 0000000 0000000 000000
16 25 UP -0000-0 0000000 0000000 -00000
ずらーっ
SWOOOOP...
W-WE REALLY MADE IT THROUGH THE FIRST ROUND NO PROBLEM!
WHAP
WHAP
THAT'S AMAZING!!
AND WE'RE GONNA KEEP THIS UP UNTIL THE SEMIS!
'CUZ WE'RE GONNA WIN!
TH... THANK GOD...! I DON'T THINK I EVER DANCED WORSE IN MY LIFE THAN THAT LAST ROUND...
...!
TREMBLE
TREMBLE
CHII-CHAN...
THIS IS THE FIRST TIME I'VE EVER GOTTEN ALL CHECKS IN ALL FOUR CATEGORIES!!
HEH
HEH
OKAY, NOW SMILE!
MORE TO THE RIGHT.
BROO-LOO-LOOT

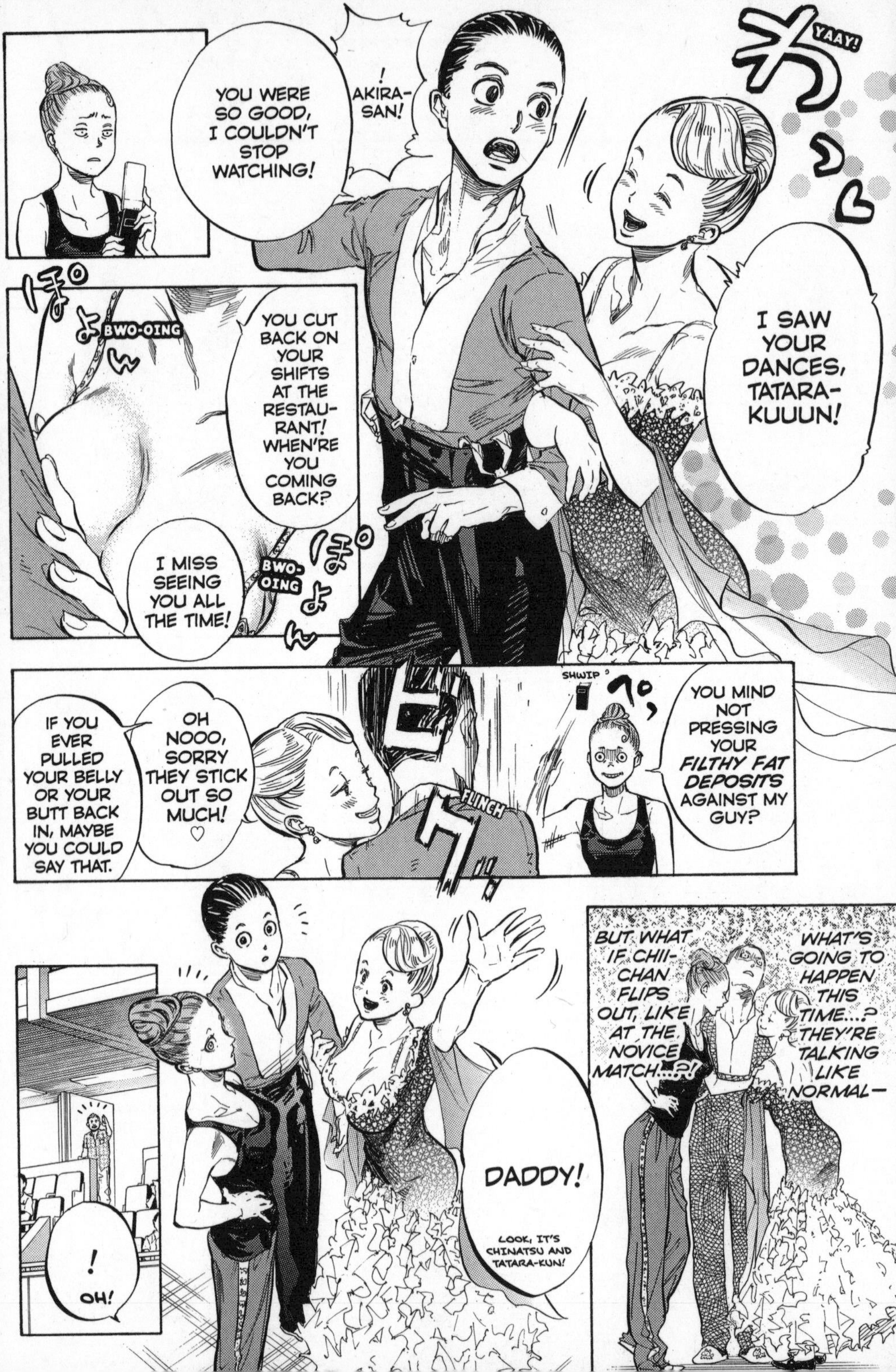
YAAY!
I SAW YOUR DANCES, TATARA-KUUUN!
! AKIRA-SAN!
YOU WERE SO GOOD, I COULDN'T STOP WATCHING!
BWO-OING
YOU CUT BACK ON YOUR SHIFTS AT THE RESTAU-RANT! WHEN'RE YOU COMING BACK?
BWO-OING
I MISS SEEING YOU ALL THE TIME!
SHWIP
YOU MIND NOT PRESSING YOUR FILTHY FAT DEPOSITS AGAINST MY GUY?
FLINCH
OH NOOO, SORRY THEY STICK OUT SO MUCH! ♡
IF YOU EVER PULLED YOUR BELLY OR YOUR BUTT BACK IN, MAYBE YOU COULD SAY THAT.
WHAT'S GOING TO HAPPEN THIS TIME...? THEY'RE TALKING LIKE NORMAL—
BUT WHAT IF CHII-CHAN FLIPS OUT, LIKE AT THE NOVICE MATCH...?!
DADDY!
LOOK, IT'S CHINATSU AND TATARA-KUN!
! OH!

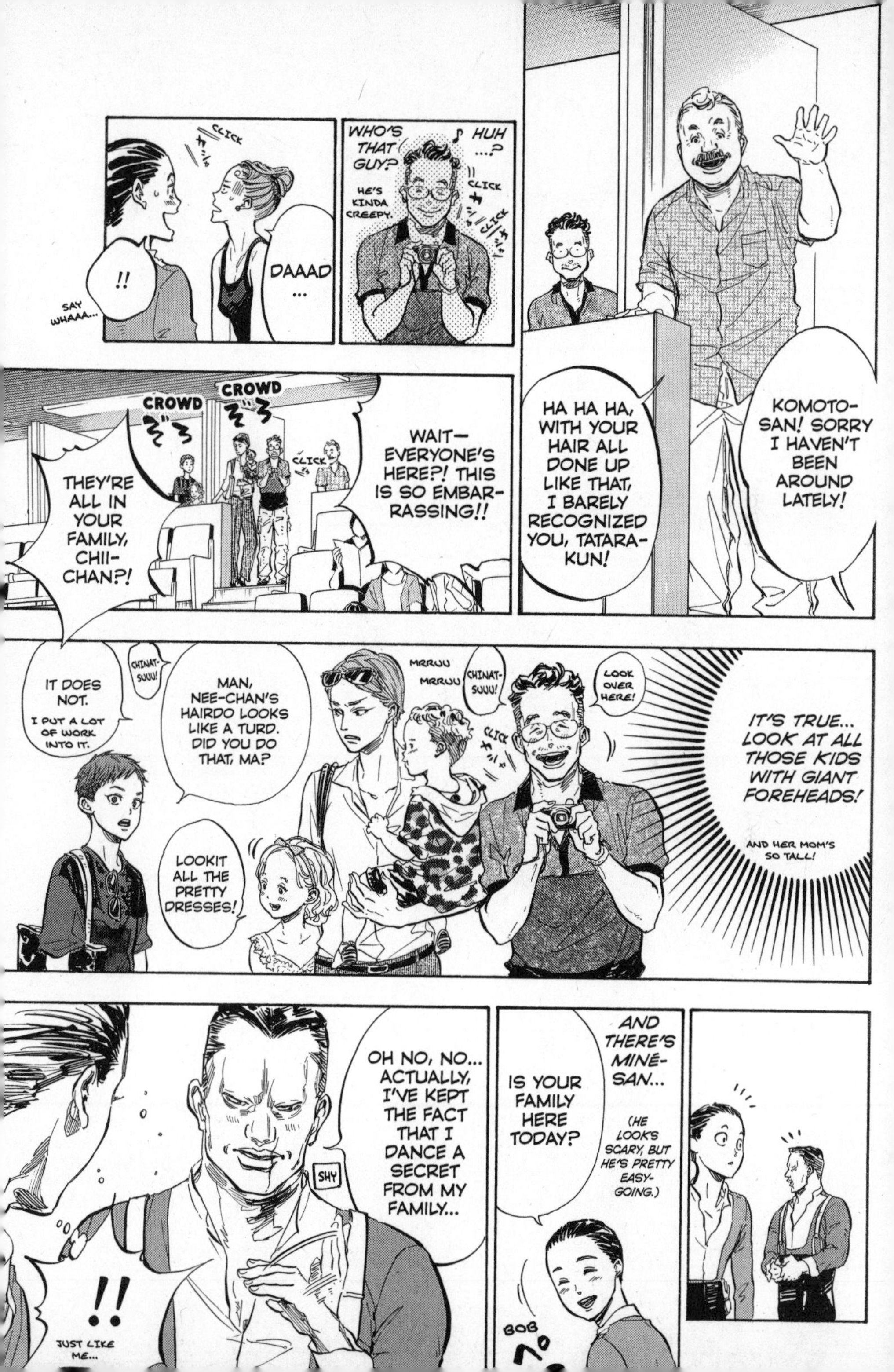
KOMOTO-SAN! SORRY I HAVEN'T BEEN AROUND LATELY!
HA HA HA, WITH YOUR HAIR ALL DONE UP LIKE THAT, I BARELY RECOGNIZED YOU, TATARA-KUN!
WHO'S THAT GUY?
HUH ...?
CLICK
CLICK
HE'S KINDA CREEPY.
CLICK
DAAAD ...
!!
SAY WHAAA...
WAIT— EVERYONE'S HERE?! THIS IS SO EMBARRASSING!!
CROWD
CROWD
CLICK
THEY'RE ALL IN YOUR FAMILY, CHII-CHAN?!
IT'S TRUE... LOOK AT ALL THOSE KIDS WITH GIANT FOREHEADS!
AND HER MOM'S SO TALL!
LOOK OVER HERE!
CLICK
CHINAT-SUUU!
MRRUU
MRRUU
MAN, NEE-CHAN'S HAIRDO LOOKS LIKE A TURD. DID YOU DO THAT, MA?
CHINAT-SUUU!
IT DOES NOT.
I PUT A LOT OF WORK INTO IT.
LOOKIT ALL THE PRETTY DRESSES!
AND THERE'S MINÉ-SAN...
(HE LOOKS SCARY, BUT HE'S PRETTY EASY-GOING.)
IS YOUR FAMILY HERE TODAY?
BOB
OH NO, NO... ACTUALLY, I'VE KEPT THE FACT THAT I DANCE A SECRET FROM MY FAMILY...
SHY
!!
JUST LIKE ME...

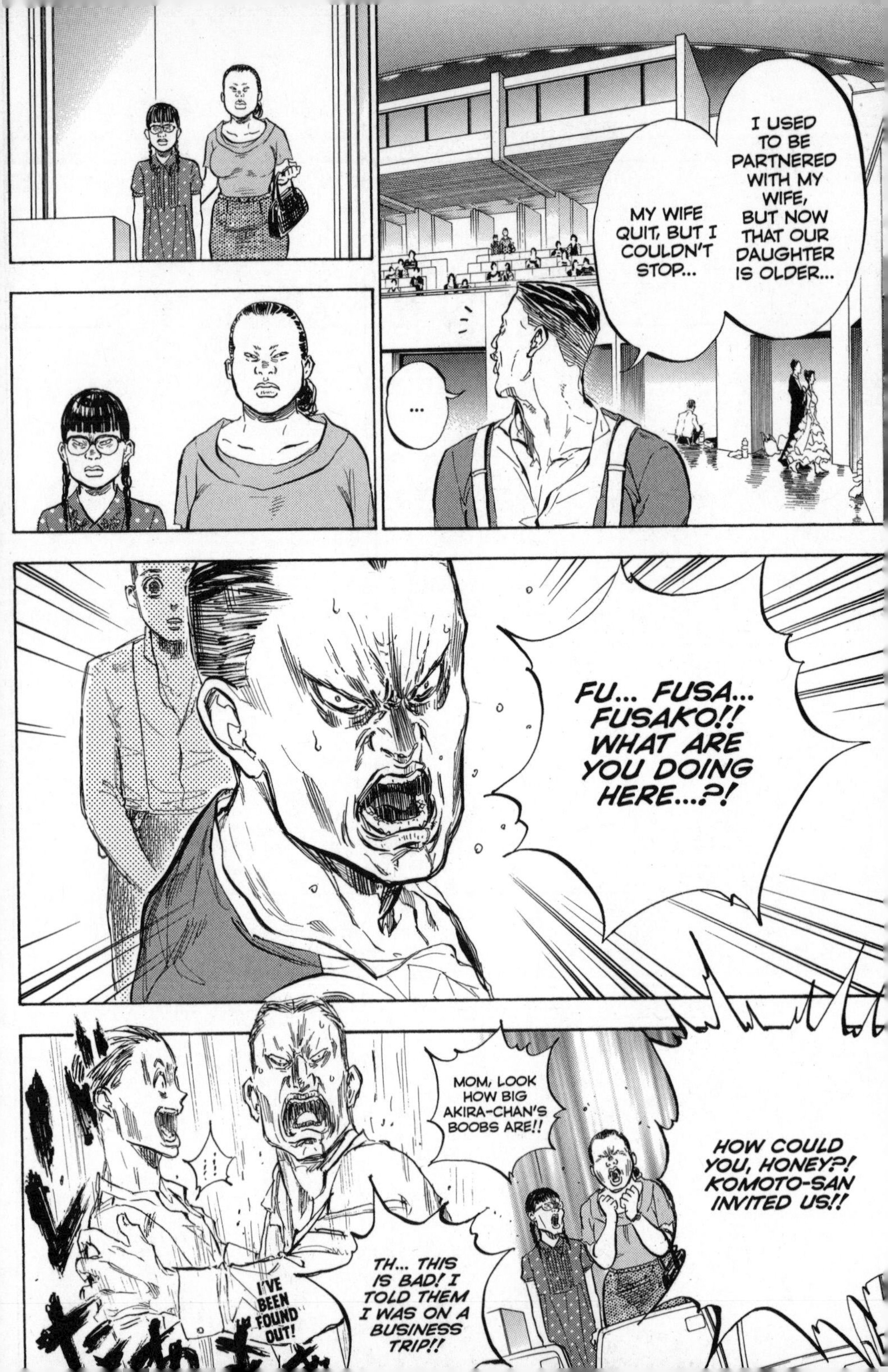
I USED TO BE PARTNERED WITH MY WIFE, BUT NOW THAT OUR DAUGHTER IS OLDER...
MY WIFE QUIT, BUT I COULDN'T STOP...
...
FU... FUSA... FUSAKO!! WHAT ARE YOU DOING HERE...?!
HOW COULD YOU, HONEY?! KOMOTO-SAN INVITED US!!
MOM, LOOK HOW BIG AKIRA-CHAN'S BOOBS ARE!!
TH... THIS IS BAD! I TOLD THEM I WAS ON A BUSINESS TRIP!!
!!
I'VE BEEN FOUND OUT!

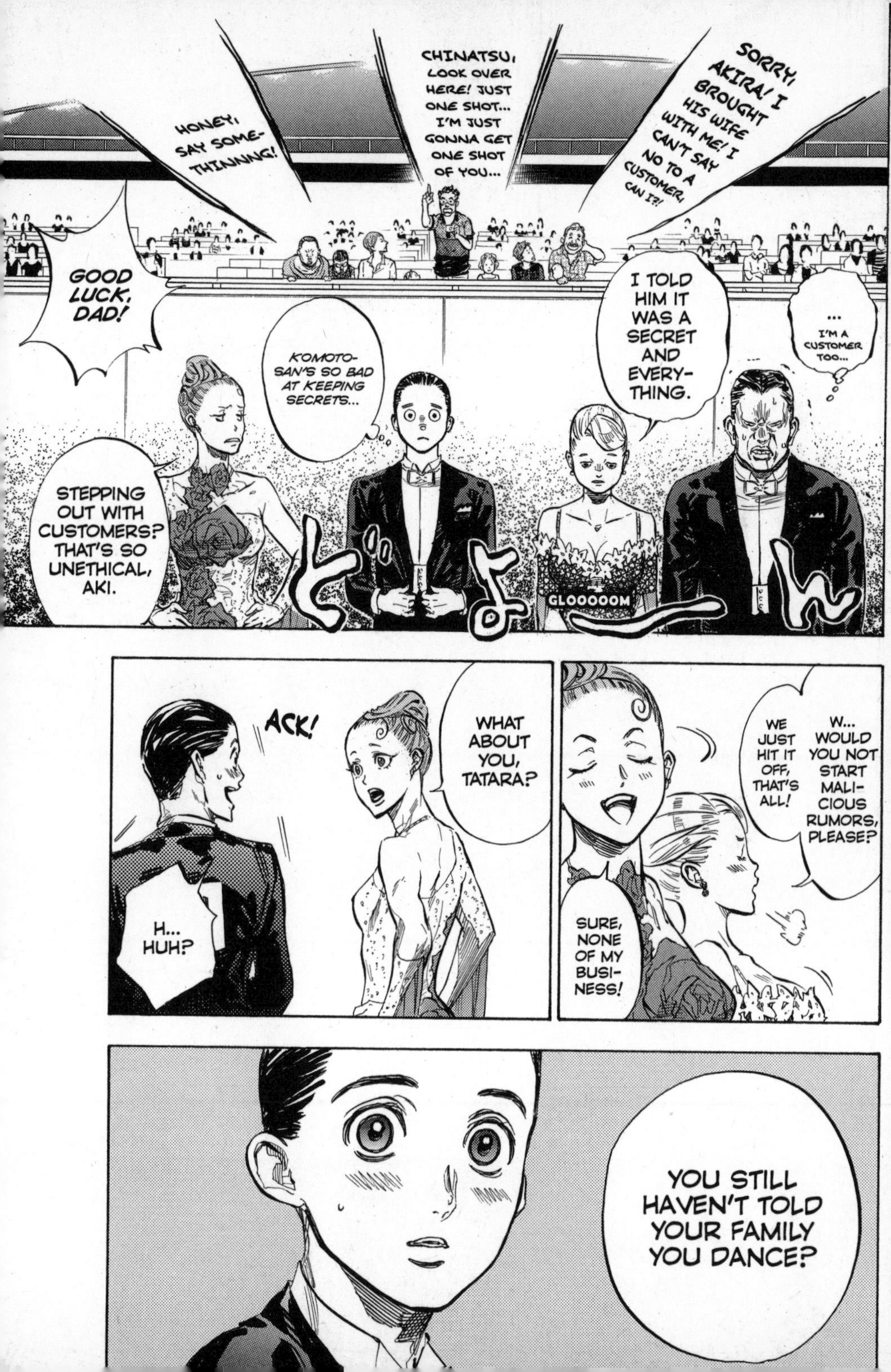
SORRY, AKIRA! I BROUGHT HIS WIFE WITH ME! I CAN'T SAY NO TO A CUSTOMER, CAN I?!
CHINATSU, LOOK OVER HERE! JUST ONE SHOT... I'M JUST GONNA GET ONE SHOT OF YOU...
HONEY, SAY SOME-THINNNG!
... I'M A CUSTOMER TOO...
I TOLD HIM IT WAS A SECRET AND EVERY-THING.
KOMOTO-SAN'S SO BAD AT KEEPING SECRETS...
GOOD LUCK, DAD!
STEPPING OUT WITH CUSTOMERS? THAT'S SO UNETHICAL, AKI.
どよーん
GLOOOOOM
W... WOULD YOU NOT START MALI-CIOUS RUMORS, PLEASE?
WE JUST HIT IT OFF, THAT'S ALL!
SURE, NONE OF MY BUSI-NESS!
WHAT ABOUT YOU, TATARA?
ACK!
H... HUH?
YOU STILL HAVEN'T TOLD YOUR FAMILY YOU DANCE?

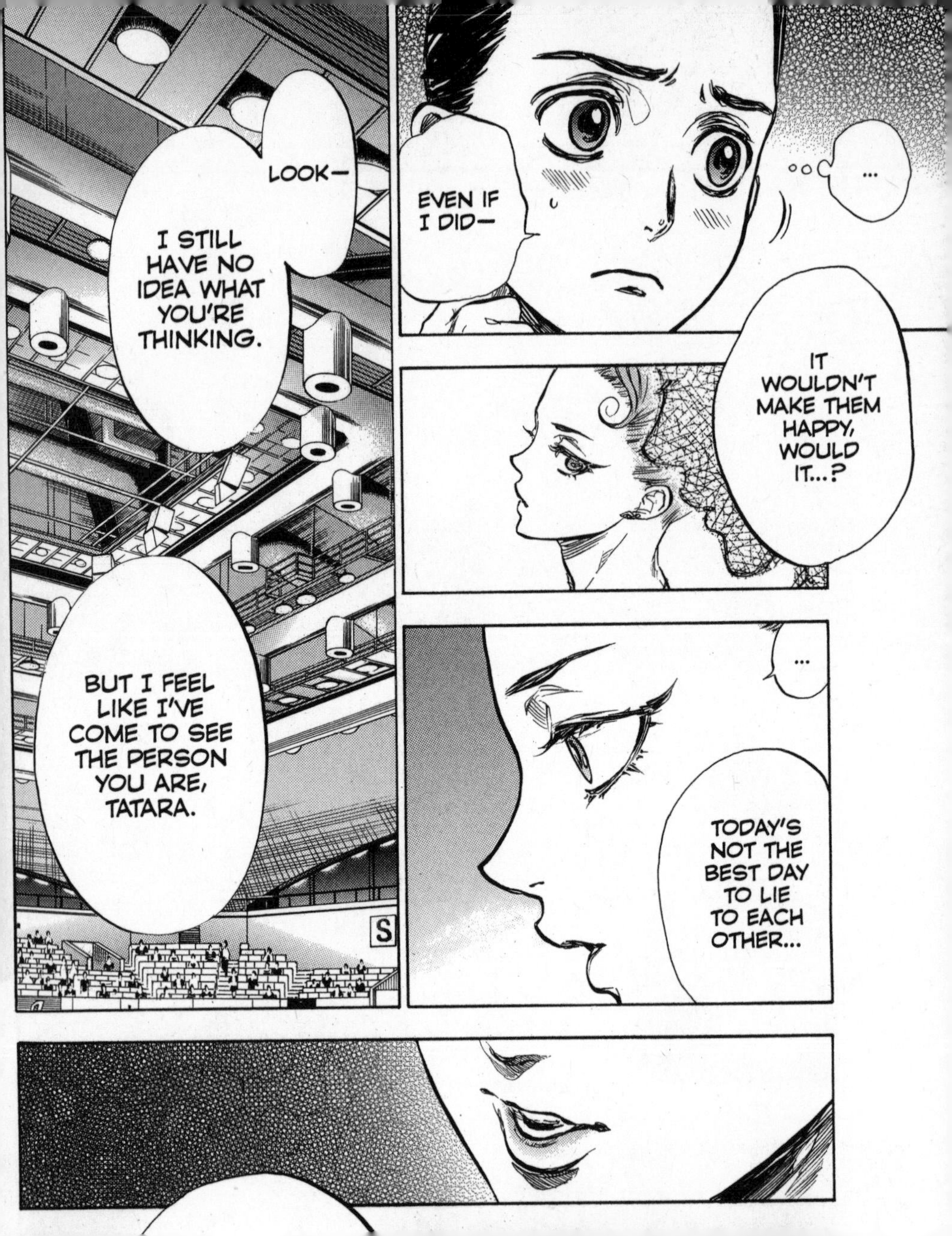
...
EVEN IF I DID—
IT WOULDN'T MAKE THEM HAPPY, WOULD IT...?
...
TODAY'S NOT THE BEST DAY TO LIE TO EACH OTHER...
LOOK—
I STILL HAVE NO IDEA WHAT YOU'RE THINKING.
BUT I FEEL LIKE I'VE COME TO SEE THE PERSON YOU ARE, TATARA.

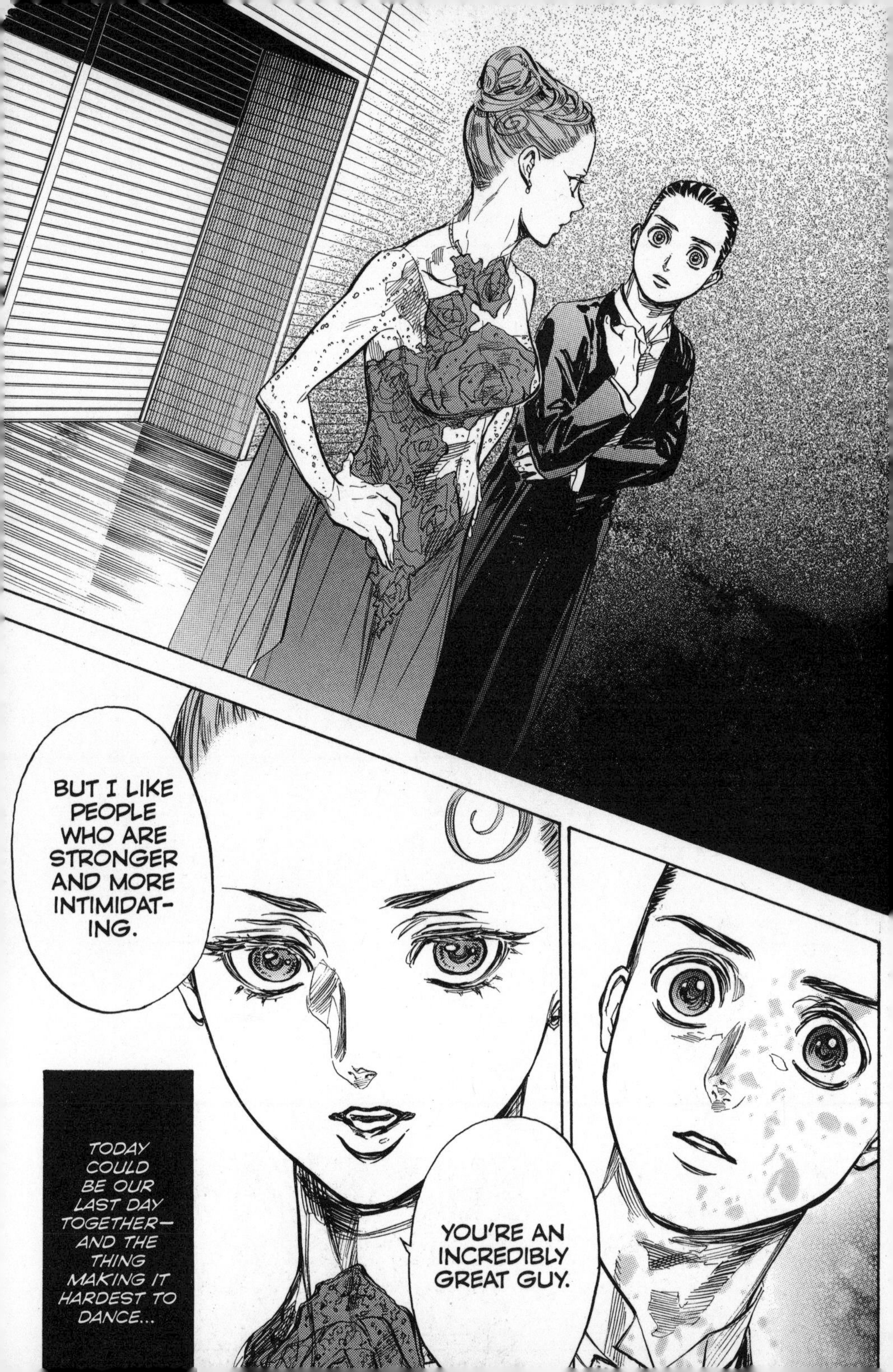

BUT I LIKE PEOPLE WHO ARE STRONGER AND MORE INTIMIDAT-ING.
YOU'RE AN INCREDIBLY GREAT GUY.
TODAY COULD BE OUR LAST DAY TOGETHER—AND THE THING MAKING IT HARDEST TO DANCE...

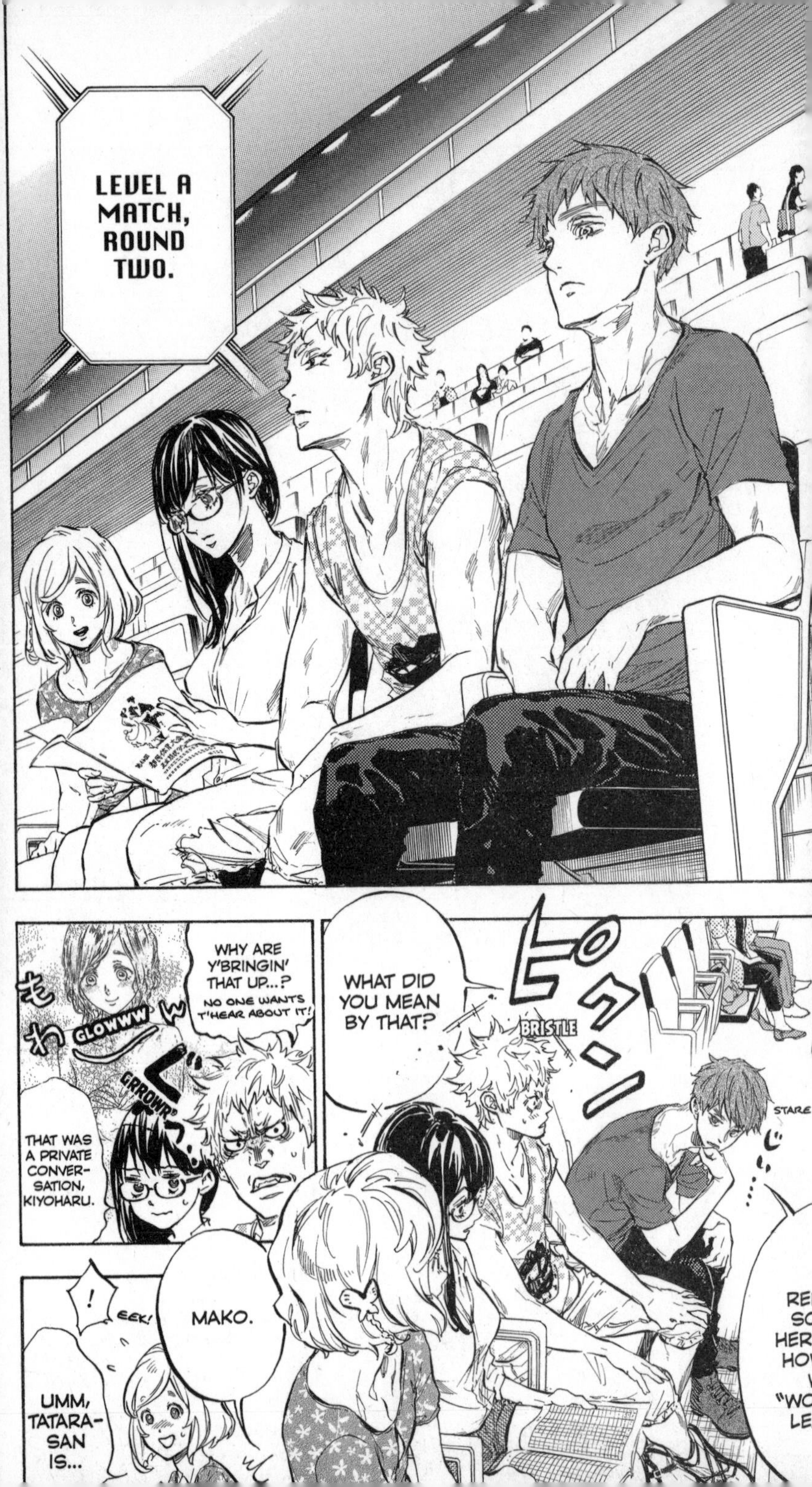
LEVEL A MATCH, ROUND TWO.
STARE
BRISTLE
WHAT DID YOU MEAN BY THAT?
WHY ARE Y'BRINGIN' THAT UP...?
NO ONE WANTS T'HEAR ABOUT IT!
GLOWWW
GRROWR
THAT WAS A PRIVATE CONVERSATION, KIYOHARU.
!
EEK!
MAKO.
UMM, TATARA-SAN IS...

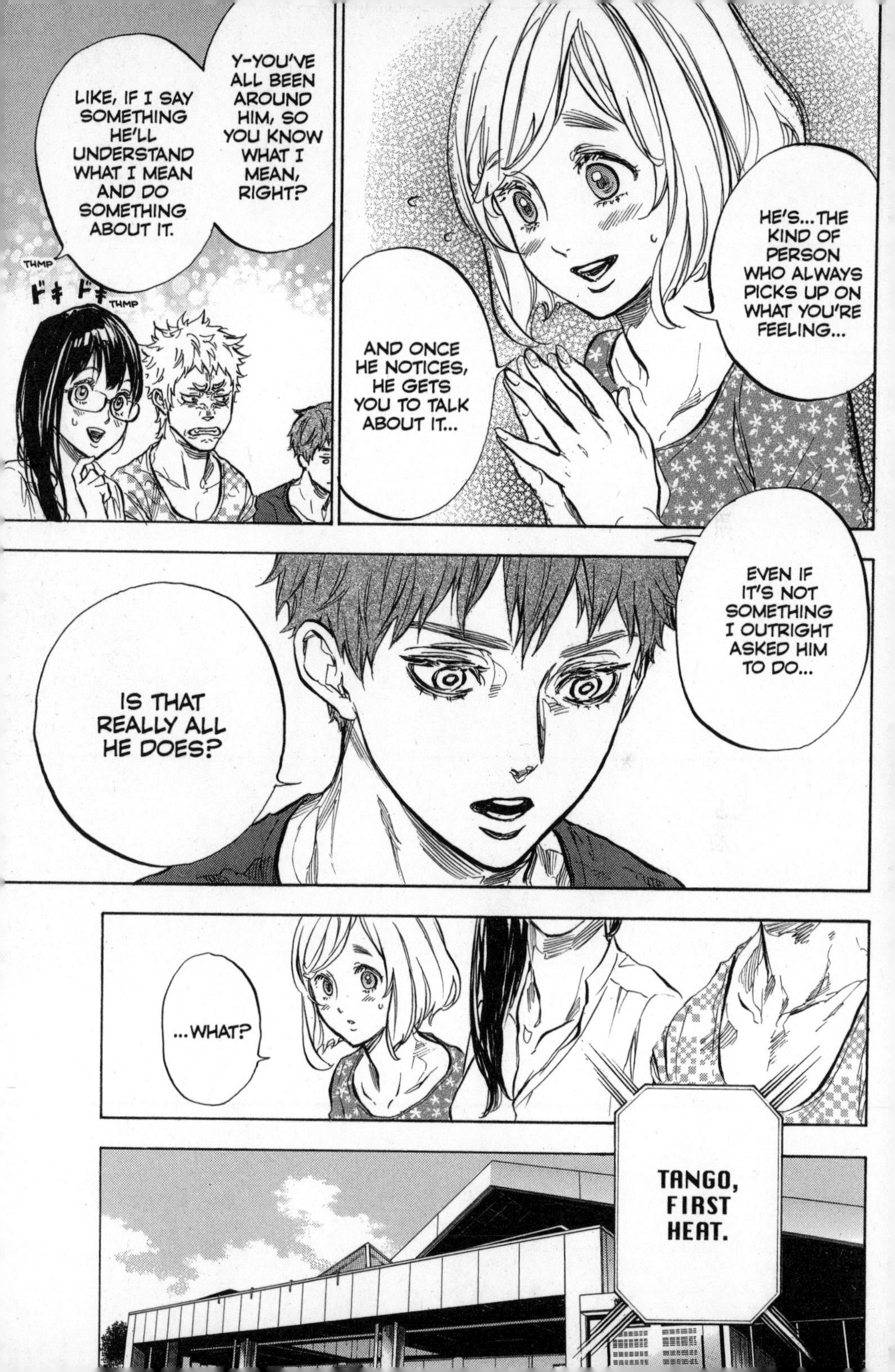
HE'S...THE KIND OF PERSON WHO ALWAYS PICKS UP ON WHAT YOU'RE FEELING...
AND ONCE HE NOTICES, HE GETS YOU TO TALK ABOUT IT...
Y-YOU'VE ALL BEEN AROUND HIM, SO YOU KNOW WHAT I MEAN, RIGHT?
LIKE, IF I SAY SOMETHING HE'LL UNDERSTAND WHAT I MEAN AND DO SOMETHING ABOUT IT.
THMP
ドキドキ
THMP
EVEN IF IT'S NOT SOMETHING I OUTRIGHT ASKED HIM TO DO...
IS THAT REALLY ALL HE DOES?
...WHAT?
TANGO, FIRST HEAT.

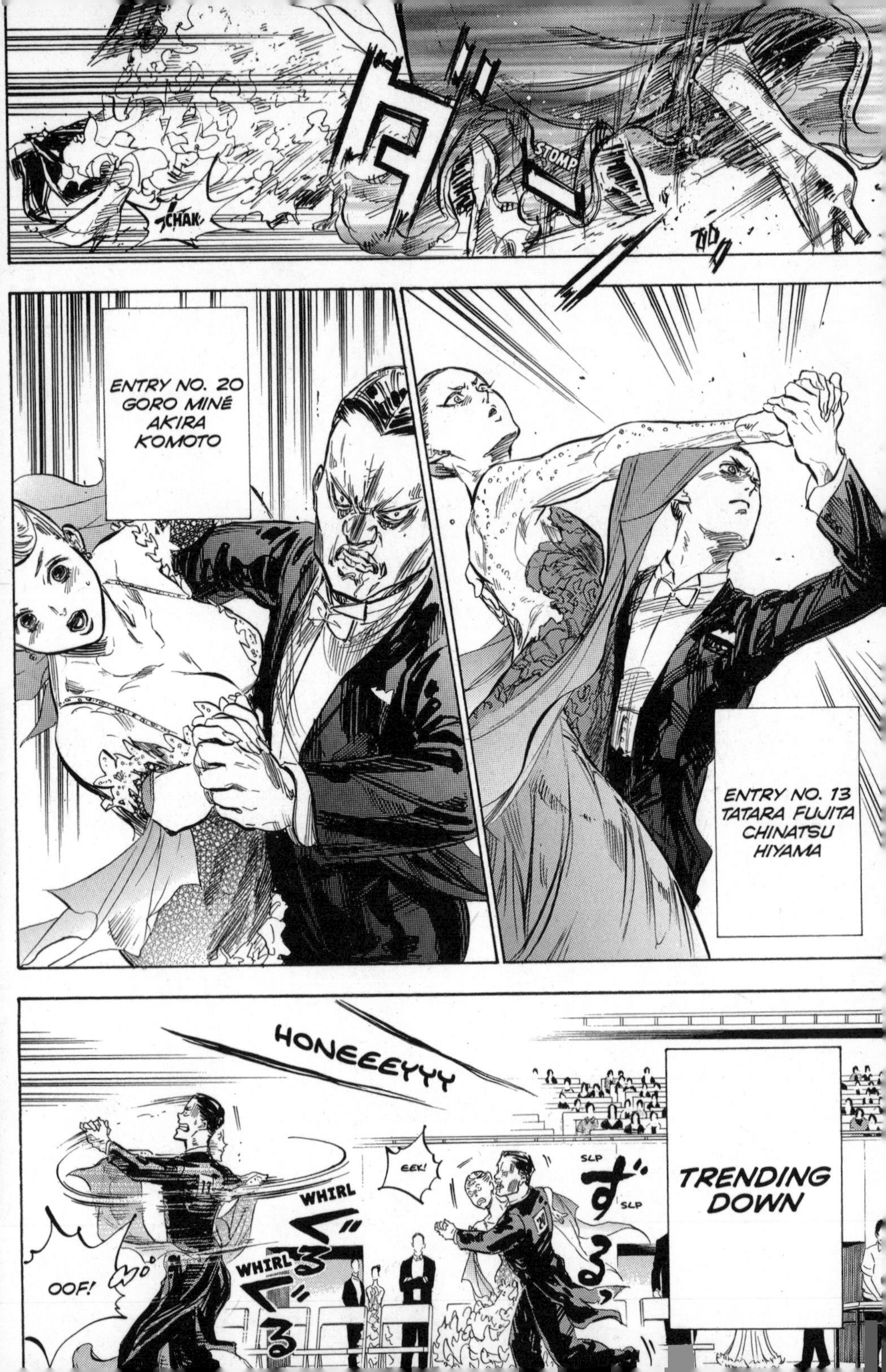
STOMP
CHAK
ENTRY NO. 13
TATARA FUJITA
CHINATSU
HIYAMA
ENTRY NO. 20
GORO MINÉ
AKIRA
KOMOTO
TRENDING
DOWN
SLP
SLP
EEK!
HONEEEYYY
WHIRL
WHIRL
OOF!

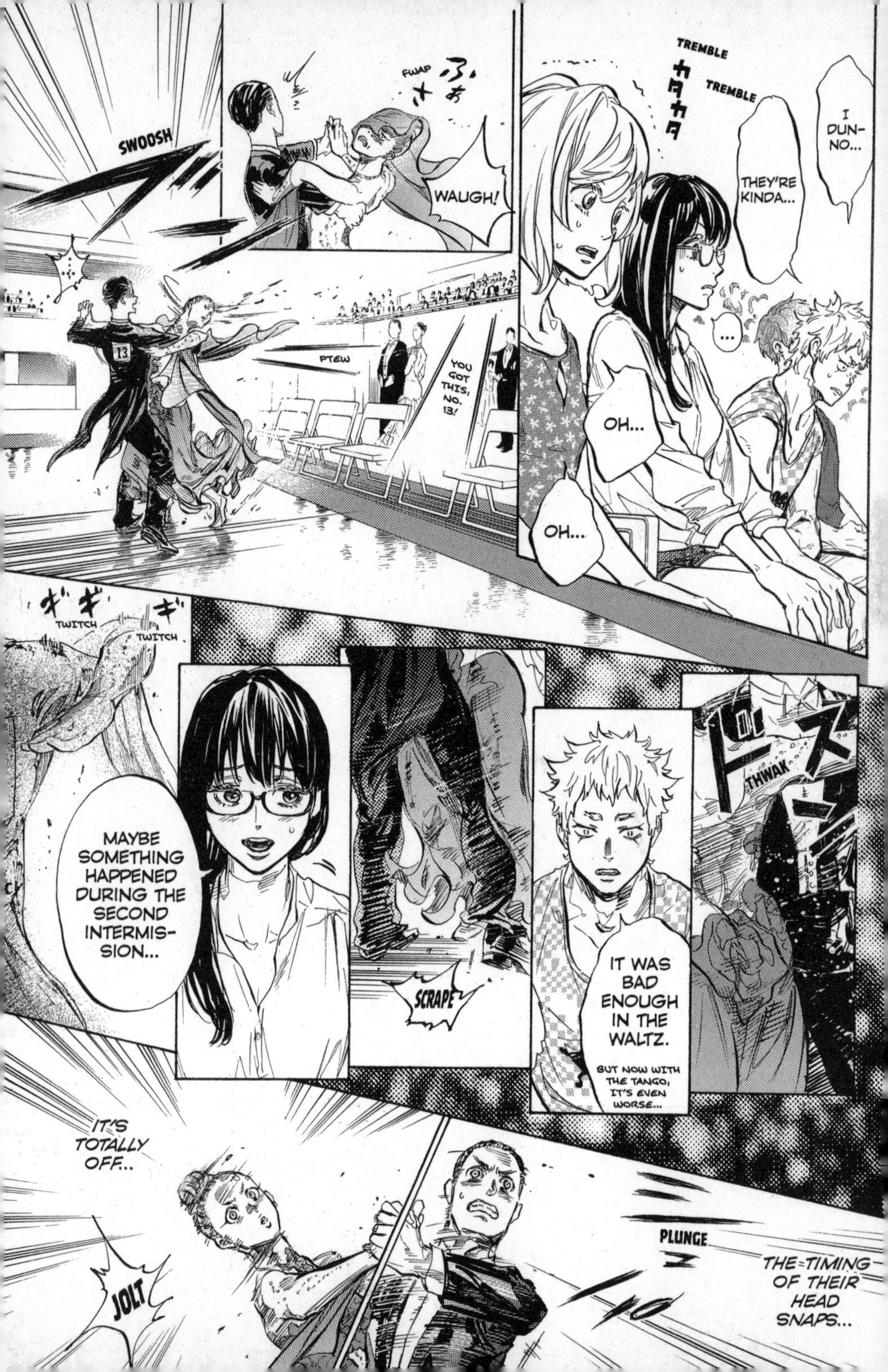

TREMBLE
カタカタ
TREMBLE
...~
I DUN-NO...
THEY'RE KINDA...
...
OH...
OH...
ふぁさ
FWAP
WAUGH!
SWOOSH
PTEW
YOU GOT THIS, NO. 13!
ドーン
THWAK
IT WAS BAD ENOUGH IN THE WALTZ.
BUT NOW WITH THE TANGO, IT'S EVEN WORSE...
SCRAPE
MAYBE SOMETHING HAPPENED DURING THE SECOND INTERMIS-SION...
ギギギ
TWITCH
TWITCH
THE TIMING OF THEIR HEAD SNAPS...
PLUNGE
IT'S TOTALLY OFF...
JOLT

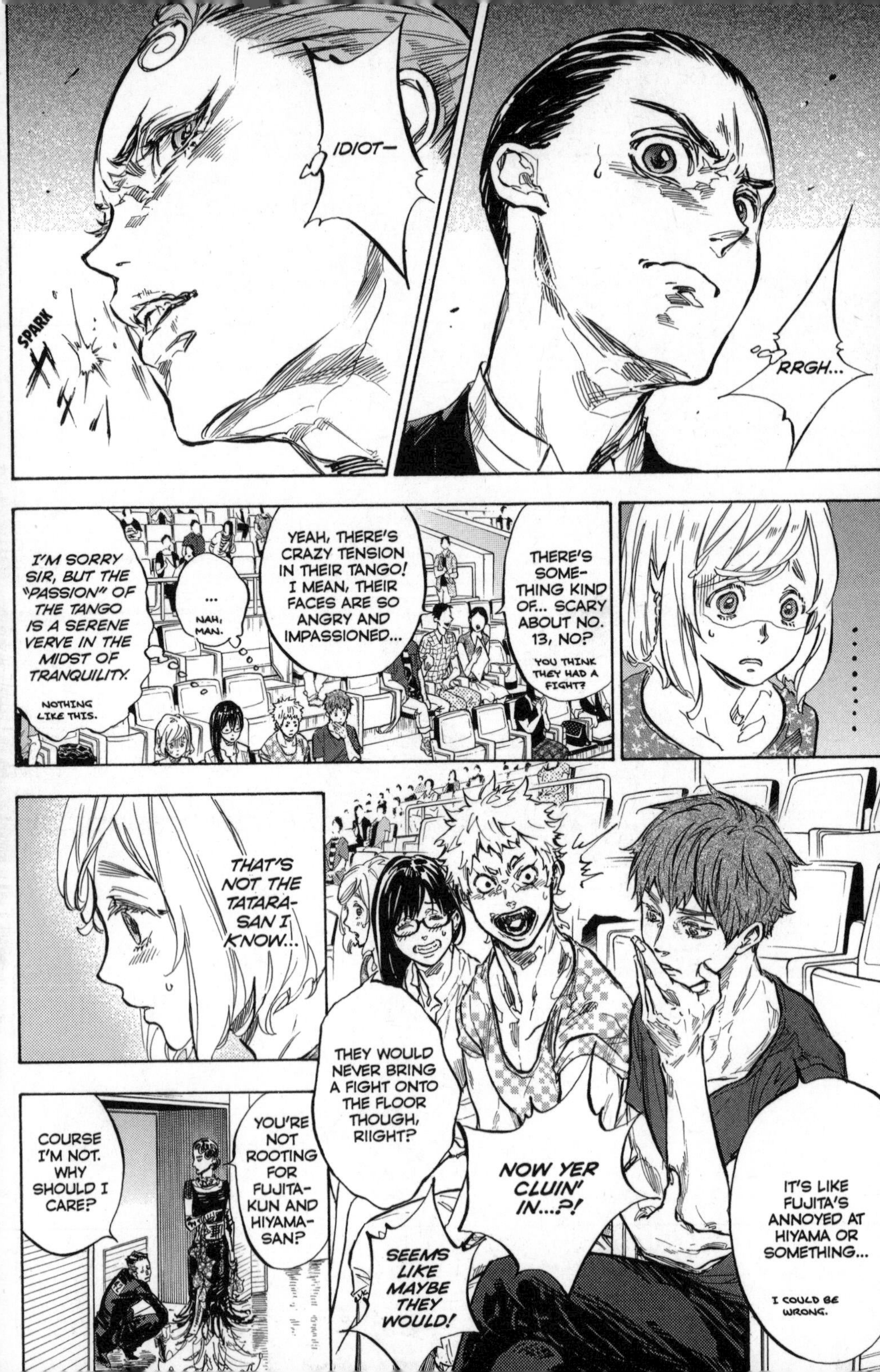
RRGH...
IDIOT—
SPARK
......
THERE'S SOME-THING KIND OF... SCARY ABOUT NO. 13, NO?
YOU THINK THEY HAD A FIGHT?
YEAH, THERE'S CRAZY TENSION IN THEIR TANGO! I MEAN, THEIR FACES ARE SO ANGRY AND IMPASSIONED...
... NAH, MAN.
I'M SORRY SIR, BUT THE "PASSION" OF THE TANGO IS A SERENE VERVE IN THE MIDST OF TRANQUILITY.
NOTHING LIKE THIS.
IT'S LIKE FUJITA'S ANNOYED AT HIYAMA OR SOMETHING...
I COULD BE WRONG.
THEY WOULD NEVER BRING A FIGHT ONTO THE FLOOR THOUGH, RIIGHT?
NOW YER CLUIN' IN...?!
SEEMS LIKE MAYBE THEY WOULD!
THAT'S NOT THE TATARA-SAN I KNOW...
YOU'RE NOT ROOTING FOR FUJITA-KUN AND HIYAMA-SAN?
COURSE I'M NOT. WHY SHOULD I CARE?

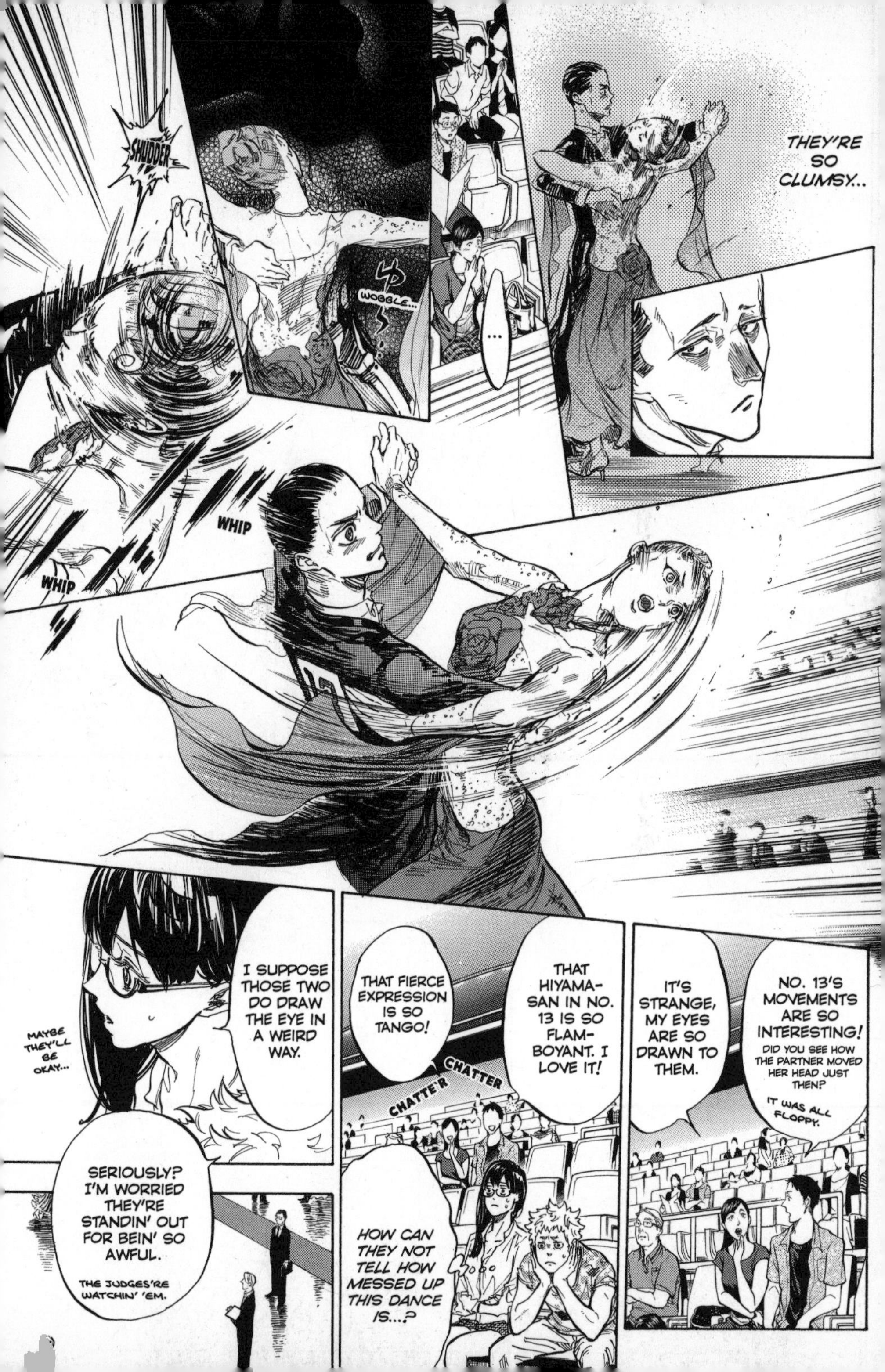
THEY'RE SO CLUMSY...
...
WOBBLE...
SHUDDER
WHIP
WHIP
NO. 13'S MOVEMENTS ARE SO INTERESTING!
DID YOU SEE HOW THE PARTNER MOVED HER HEAD JUST THEN?
IT WAS ALL FLOPPY.
IT'S STRANGE, MY EYES ARE SO DRAWN TO THEM.
THAT HIYAMA-SAN IN NO. 13 IS SO FLAM-BOYANT. I LOVE IT!
THAT FIERCE EXPRESSION IS SO TANGO!
CHATTER
CHATTER
HOW CAN THEY NOT TELL HOW MESSED UP THIS DANCE IS...?
I SUPPOSE THOSE TWO DO DRAW THE EYE IN A WEIRD WAY.
MAYBE THEY'LL BE OKAY...
SERIOUSLY? I'M WORRIED THEY'RE STANDIN' OUT FOR BEIN' SO AWFUL.
THE JUDGES'RE WATCHIN' 'EM.

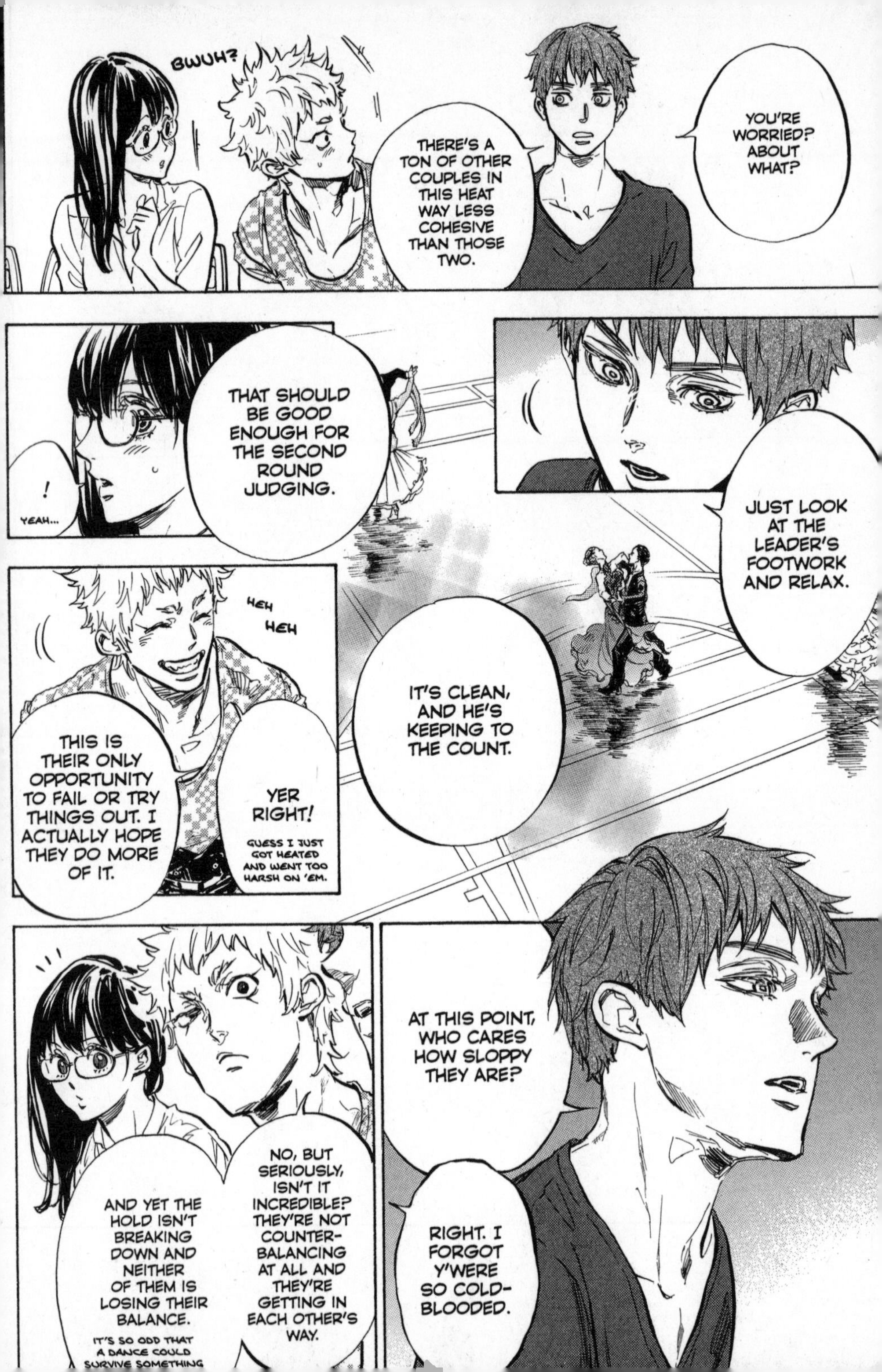
YOU'RE WORRIED? ABOUT WHAT?
THERE'S A TON OF OTHER COUPLES IN THIS HEAT WAY LESS COHESIVE THAN THOSE TWO.
BWUH?
JUST LOOK AT THE LEADER'S FOOTWORK AND RELAX.
THAT SHOULD BE GOOD ENOUGH FOR THE SECOND ROUND JUDGING.
!
YEAH...
IT'S CLEAN, AND HE'S KEEPING TO THE COUNT.
HEH HEH
YER RIGHT!
GUESS I JUST GOT HEATED AND WENT TOO HARSH ON 'EM.
THIS IS THEIR ONLY OPPORTUNITY TO FAIL OR TRY THINGS OUT. I ACTUALLY HOPE THEY DO MORE OF IT.
AT THIS POINT, WHO CARES HOW SLOPPY THEY ARE?
RIGHT. I FORGOT Y'WERE SO COLD-BLOODED.
NO, BUT SERIOUSLY, ISN'T IT INCREDIBLE? THEY'RE NOT COUNTER-BALANCING AT ALL AND THEY'RE GETTING IN EACH OTHER'S WAY.
AND YET THE HOLD ISN'T BREAKING DOWN AND NEITHER OF THEM IS LOSING THEIR BALANCE.
IT'S SO ODD THAT A DANCE COULD SURVIVE SOMETHING

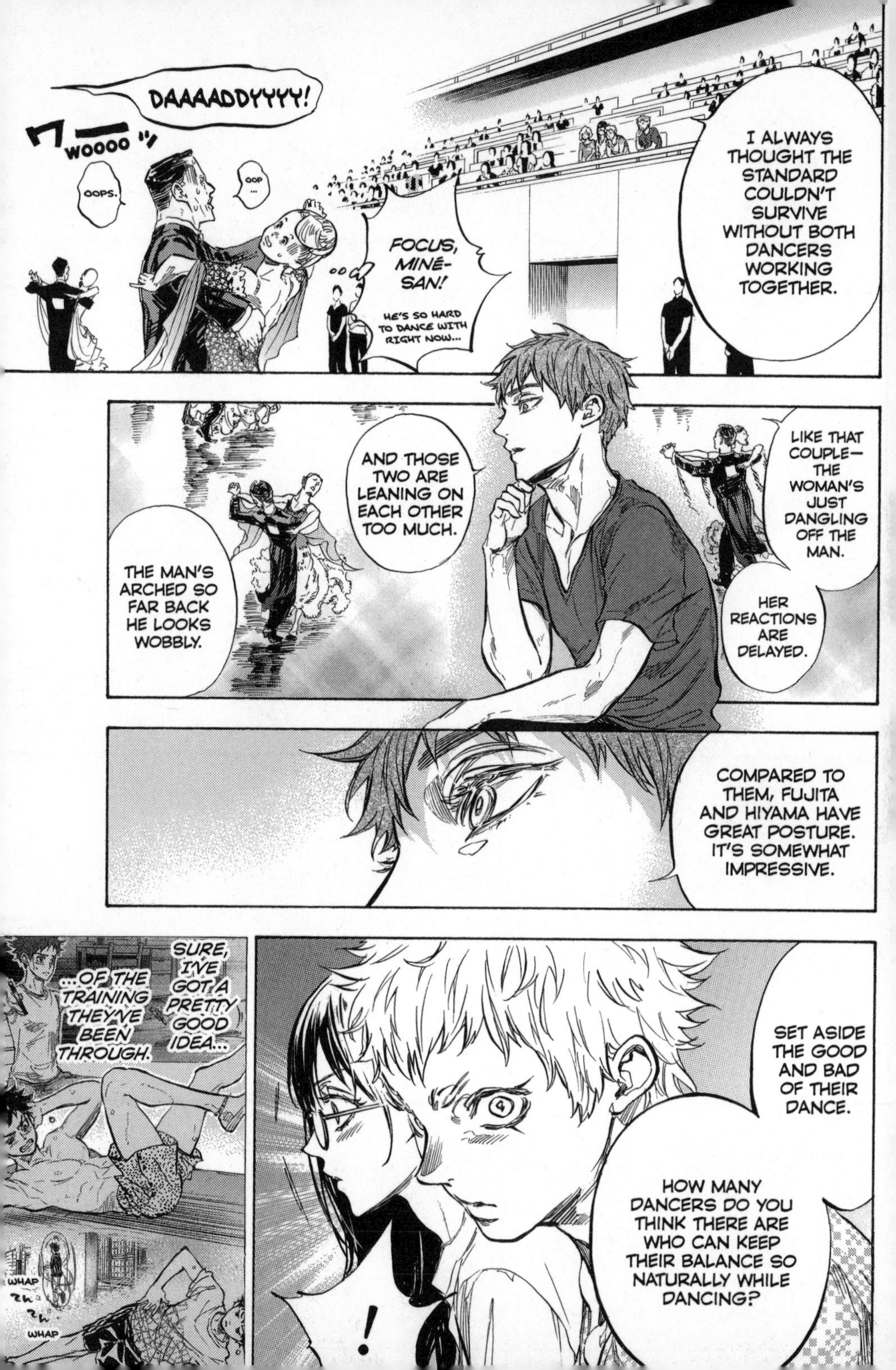
I ALWAYS THOUGHT THE STANDARD COULDN'T SURVIVE WITHOUT BOTH DANCERS WORKING TOGETHER.
FOCUS, MINÉ-SAN!
HE'S SO HARD TO DANCE WITH RIGHT NOW...
OOP...
OOPS.
DAAAADDYYYY!
WOOOO
LIKE THAT COUPLE— THE WOMAN'S JUST DANGLING OFF THE MAN.
HER REACTIONS ARE DELAYED.
AND THOSE TWO ARE LEANING ON EACH OTHER TOO MUCH.
THE MAN'S ARCHED SO FAR BACK HE LOOKS WOBBLY.
COMPARED TO THEM, FUJITA AND HIYAMA HAVE GREAT POSTURE. IT'S SOMEWHAT IMPRESSIVE.
SET ASIDE THE GOOD AND BAD OF THEIR DANCE.
HOW MANY DANCERS DO YOU THINK THERE ARE WHO CAN KEEP THEIR BALANCE SO NATURALLY WHILE DANCING?
!
SURE, I'VE GOT A PRETTY GOOD IDEA...
...OF THE TRAINING THEY'VE BEEN THROUGH.
WHAP
WHAP

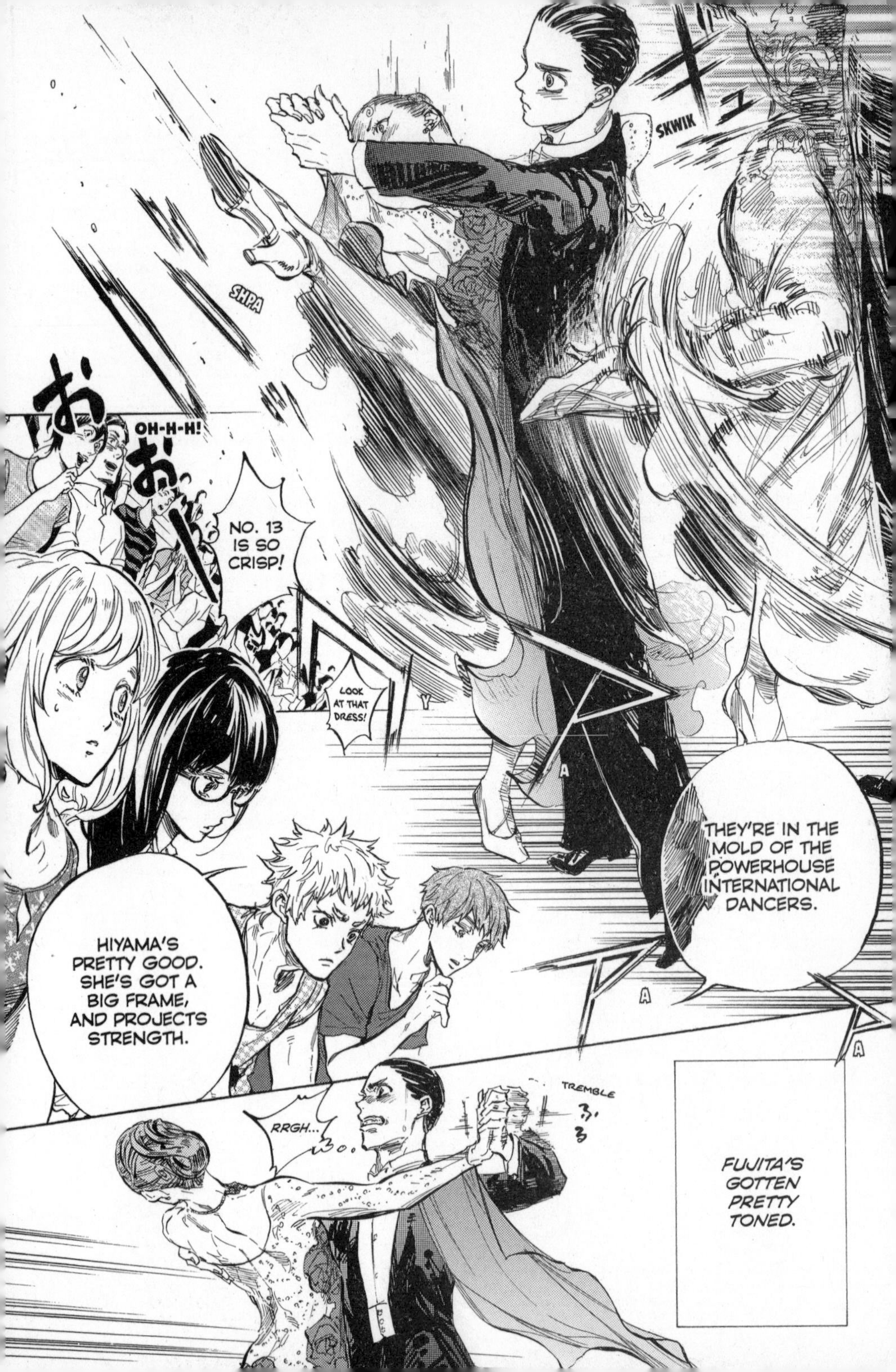
SKWIK
SHPA
OH-H-H!
NO. 13 IS SO CRISP!
LOOK AT THAT DRESS!
THEY'RE IN THE MOLD OF THE POWERHOUSE INTERNATIONAL DANCERS.
HIYAMA'S PRETTY GOOD. SHE'S GOT A BIG FRAME, AND PROJECTS STRENGTH.
FUJITA'S GOTTEN PRETTY TONED.
TREMBLE
RRGH...

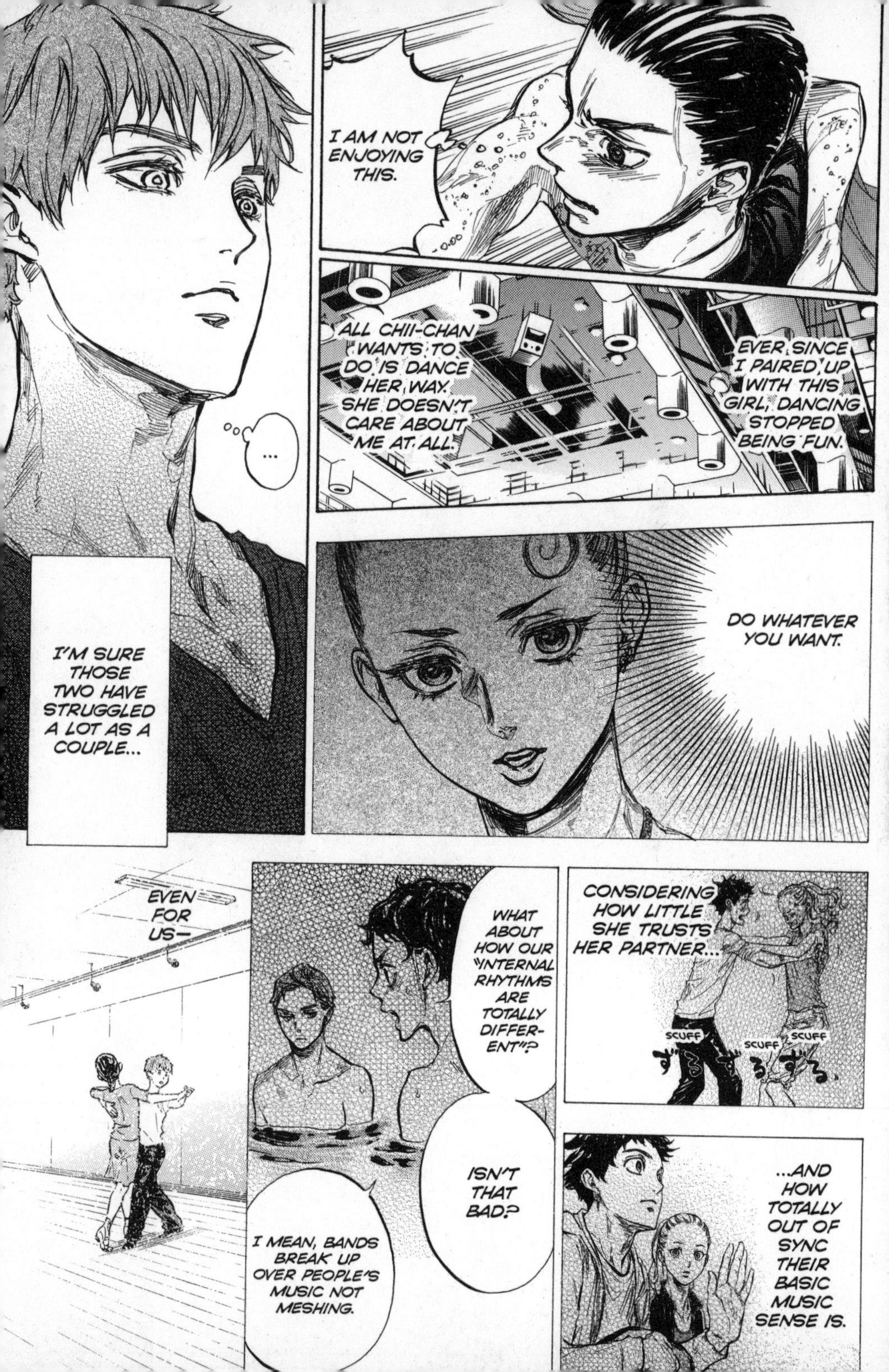
I AM NOT ENJOYING THIS.
EVER SINCE I PAIRED UP WITH THIS GIRL, DANCING STOPPED BEING FUN.
ALL CHII-CHAN WANTS TO DO IS DANCE HER WAY. SHE DOESN'T CARE ABOUT ME AT ALL.
DO WHATEVER YOU WANT.
...
I'M SURE THOSE TWO HAVE STRUGGLED A LOT AS A COUPLE...
CONSIDERING HOW LITTLE SHE TRUSTS HER PARTNER...
SCUFF SCUFF SCUFF
ずるずるずる
...AND HOW TOTALLY OUT OF SYNC THEIR BASIC MUSIC SENSE IS.
WHAT ABOUT HOW OUR "INTERNAL RHYTHMS ARE TOTALLY DIFFERENT"?
ISN'T THAT BAD?
I MEAN, BANDS BREAK UP OVER PEOPLE'S MUSIC NOT MESHING.
EVEN FOR US—

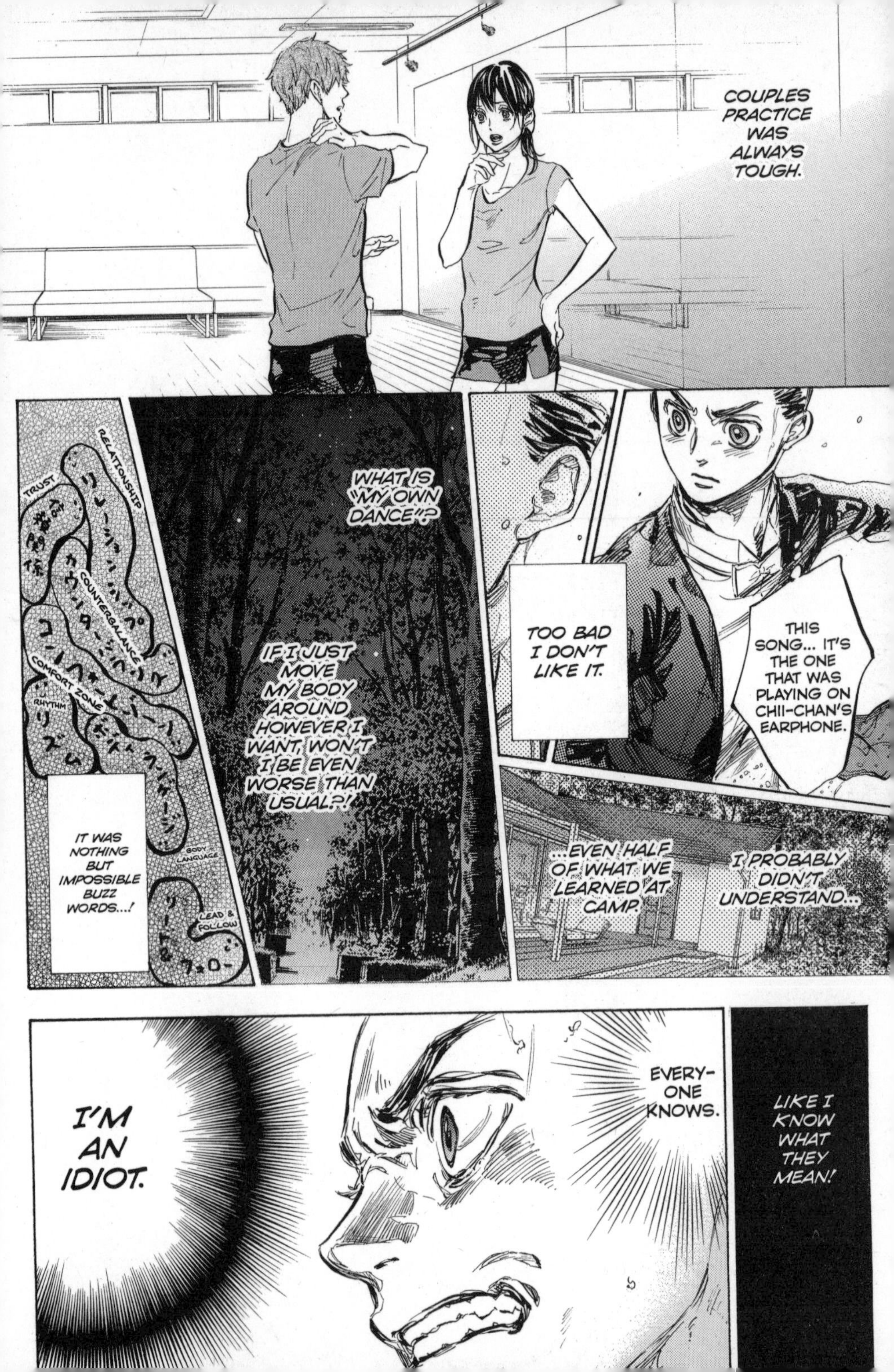
COUPLES PRACTICE WAS ALWAYS TOUGH.
THIS SONG... IT'S THE ONE THAT WAS PLAYING ON CHII-CHAN'S EARPHONE.
TOO BAD I DON'T LIKE IT.
I PROBABLY DIDN'T UNDERSTAND...
...EVEN HALF OF WHAT WE LEARNED AT CAMP.
WHAT IS "MY OWN DANCE"?
IF I JUST MOVE MY BODY AROUND HOWEVER I WANT, WON'T I BE EVEN WORSE THAN USUAL?!
RELATIONSHIP
TRUST
COUNTERBALANCE
COMFORT ZONE
RHYTHM
BODY LANGUAGE
LEAD & FOLLOW
IT WAS NOTHING BUT IMPOSSIBLE BUZZ WORDS...!
LIKE I KNOW WHAT THEY MEAN!
EVERY-ONE KNOWS.
I'M AN IDIOT.

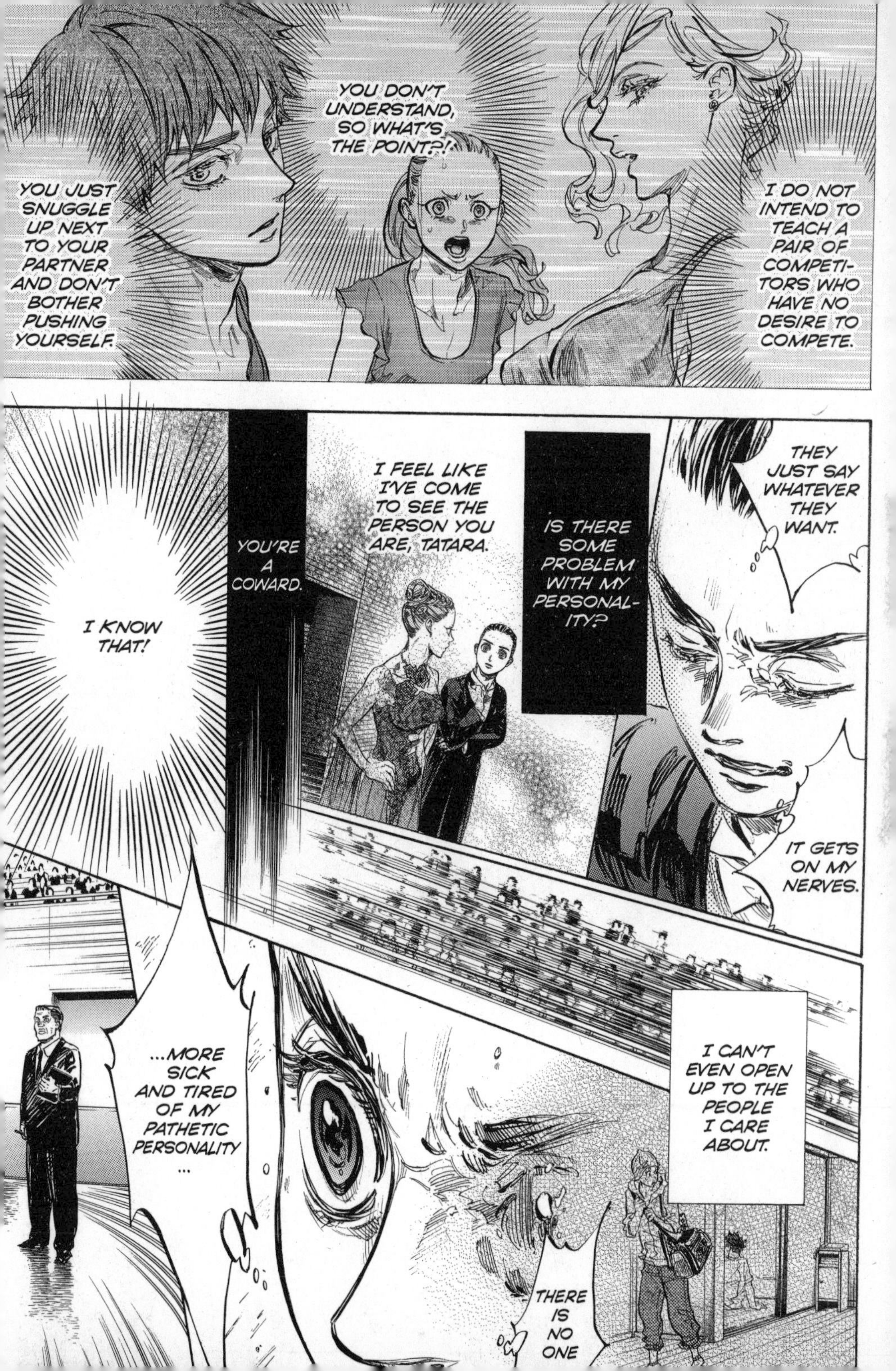
I DO NOT INTEND TO TEACH A PAIR OF COMPETITORS WHO HAVE NO DESIRE TO COMPETE.
YOU DON'T UNDERSTAND, SO WHAT'S THE POINT?!
YOU JUST SNUGGLE UP NEXT TO YOUR PARTNER AND DON'T BOTHER PUSHING YOURSELF.
THEY JUST SAY WHATEVER THEY WANT.
IT GETS ON MY NERVES.
IS THERE SOME PROBLEM WITH MY PERSONALITY?
I FEEL LIKE I'VE COME TO SEE THE PERSON YOU ARE, TATARA.
YOU'RE A COWARD.
I KNOW THAT!
I CAN'T EVEN OPEN UP TO THE PEOPLE I CARE ABOUT.
THERE IS NO ONE
...MORE SICK AND TIRED OF MY PATHETIC PERSONALITY ...

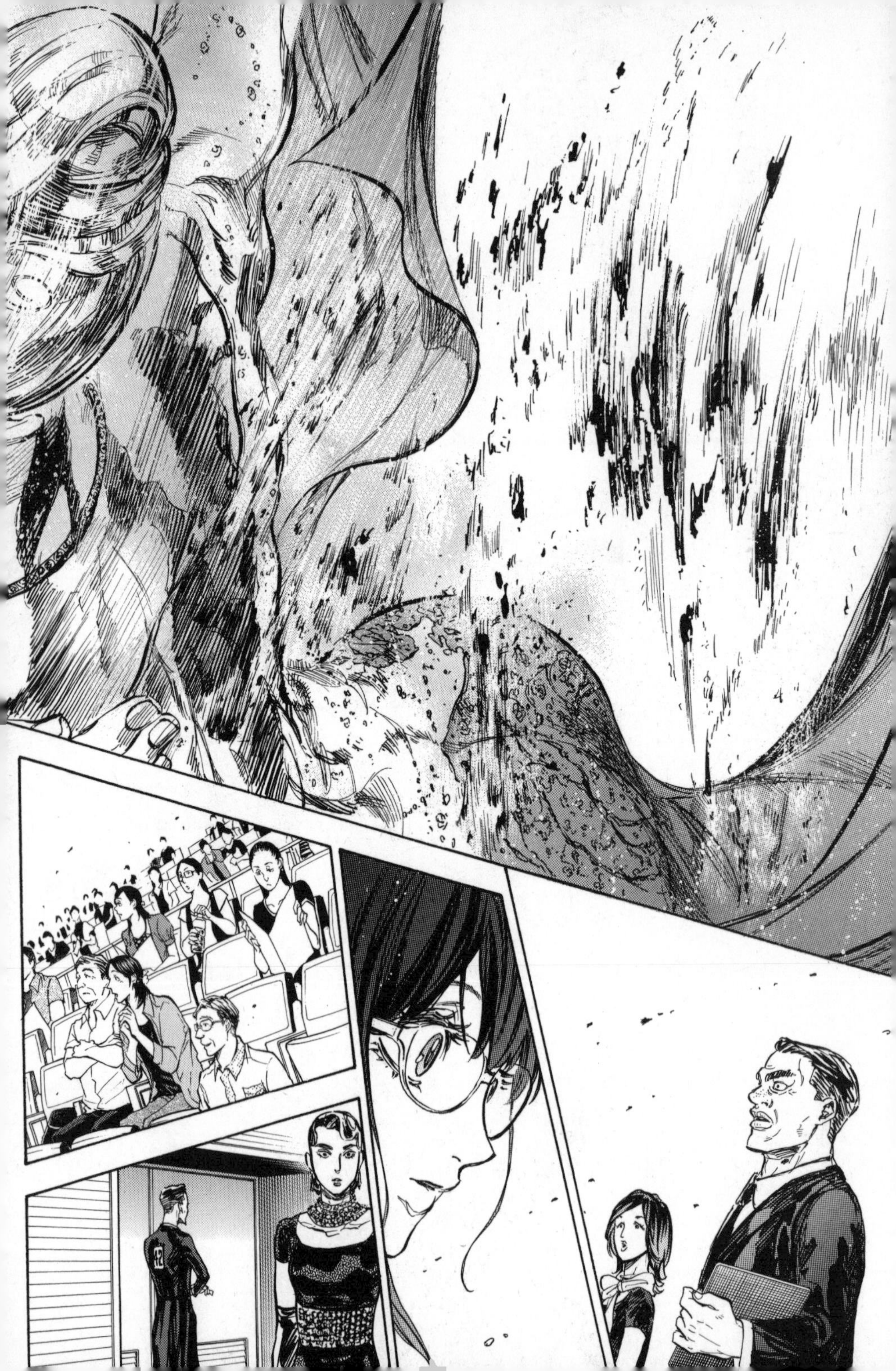
42

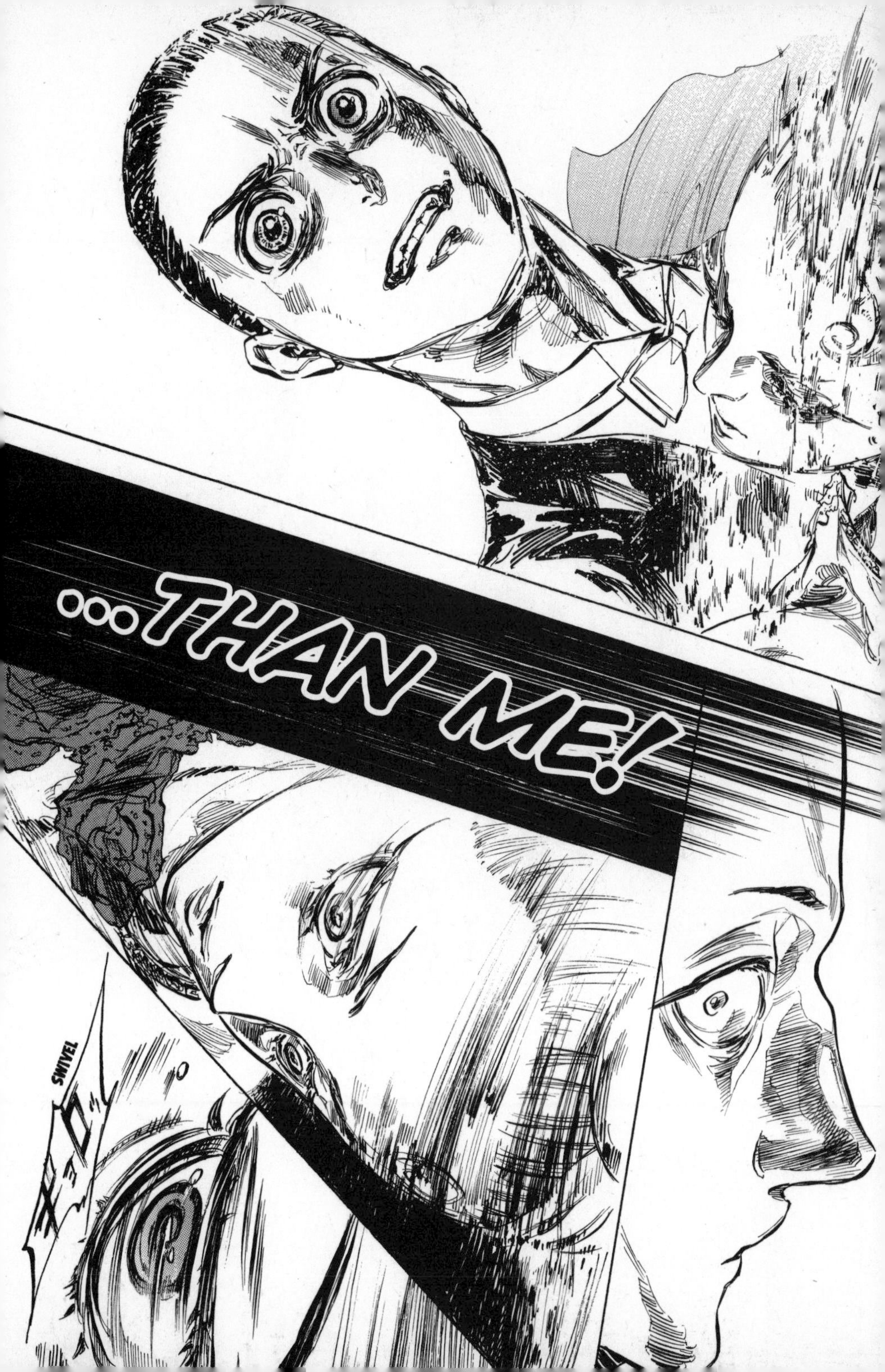
...THAN ME!
SWIVEL

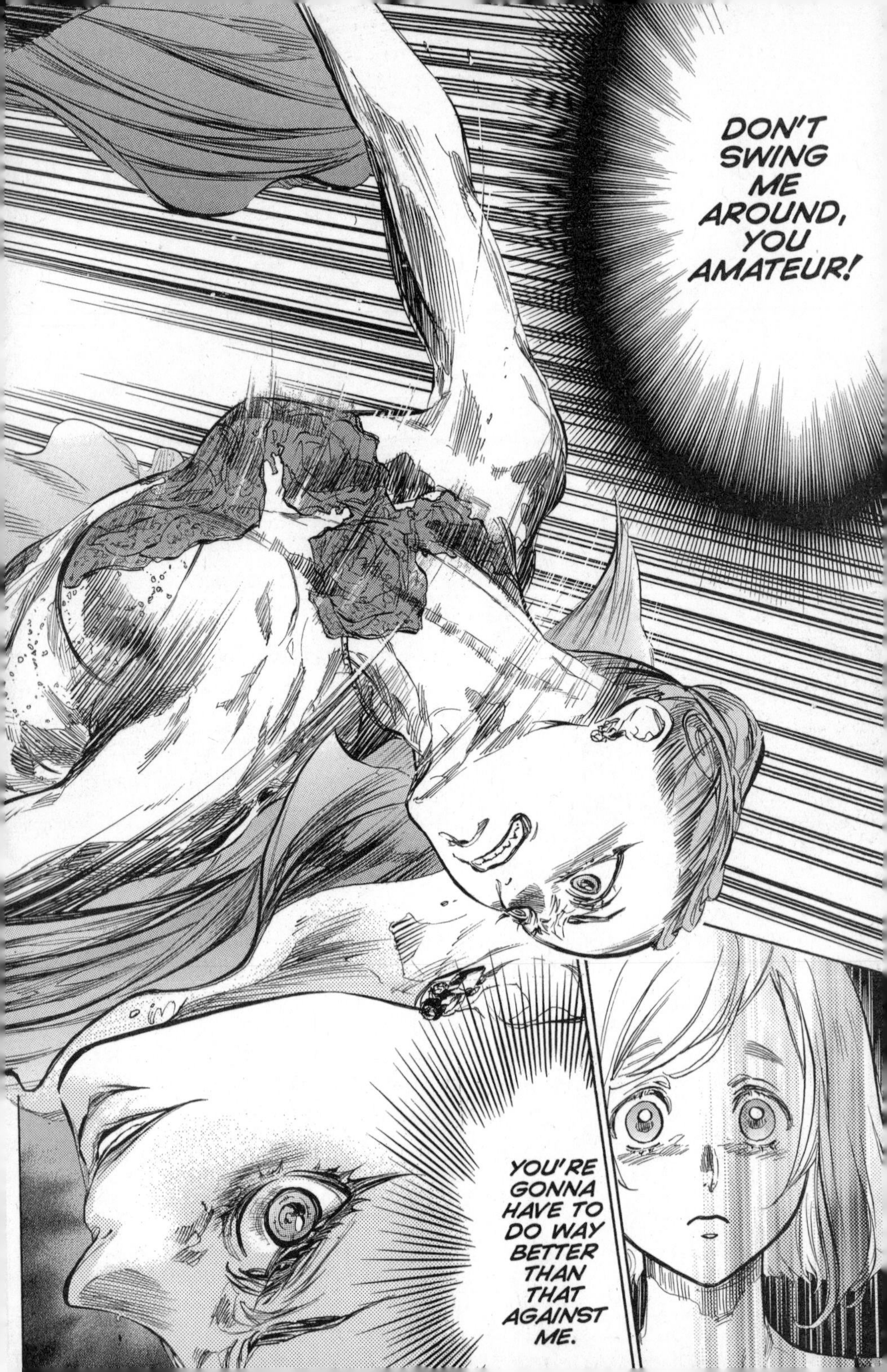
DON'T SWING ME AROUND, YOU AMATEUR!
YOU'RE GONNA HAVE TO DO WAY BETTER THAN THAT AGAINST ME.

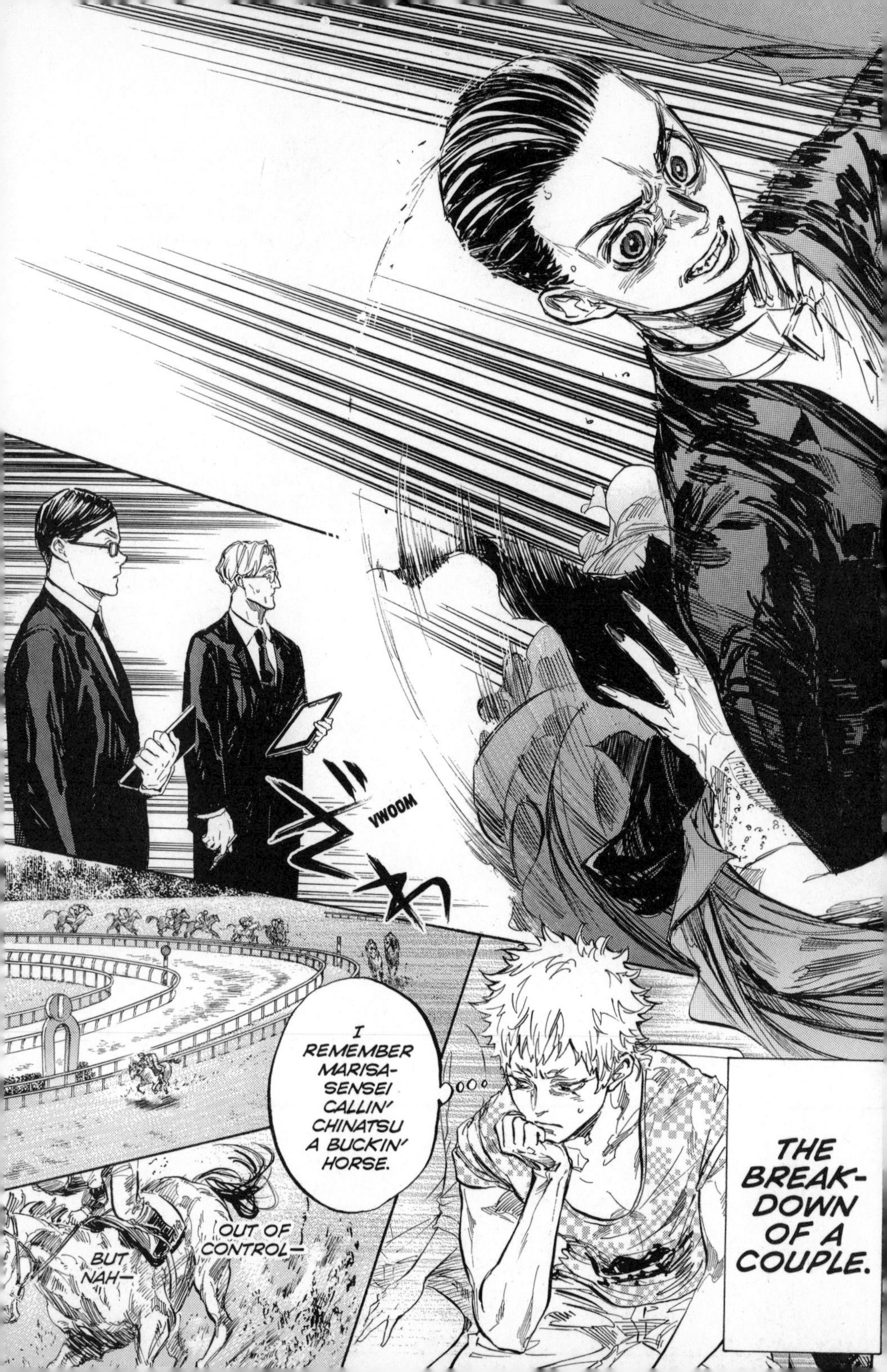
VWOOM
THE BREAK-DOWN OF A COUPLE.
I REMEMBER MARISA-SENSEI CALLIN' CHINATSU A BUCKIN' HORSE.
OUT OF CONTROL—
BUT NAH—

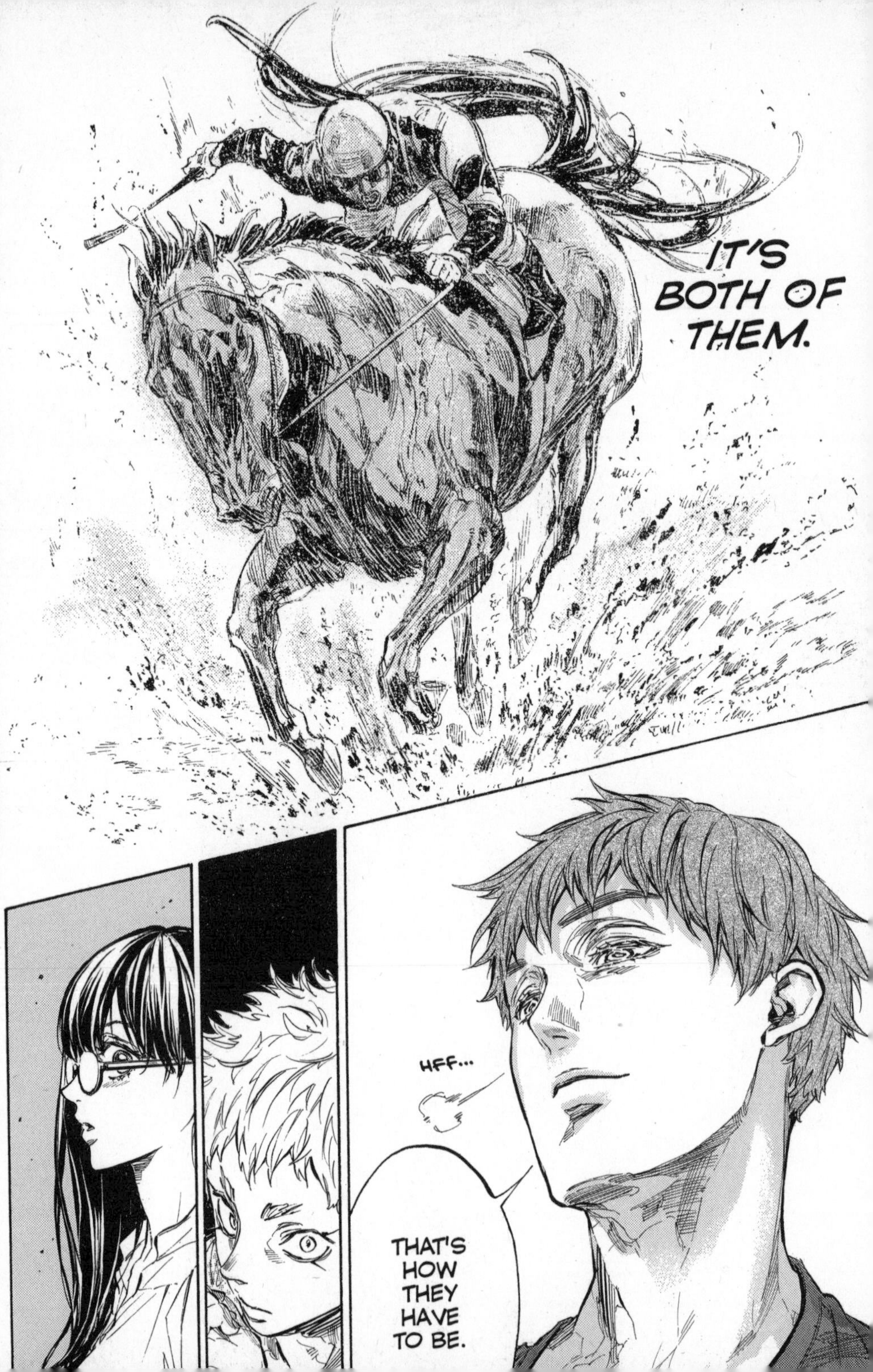
IT'S BOTH OF THEM.
HFF...
THAT'S HOW THEY HAVE TO BE.

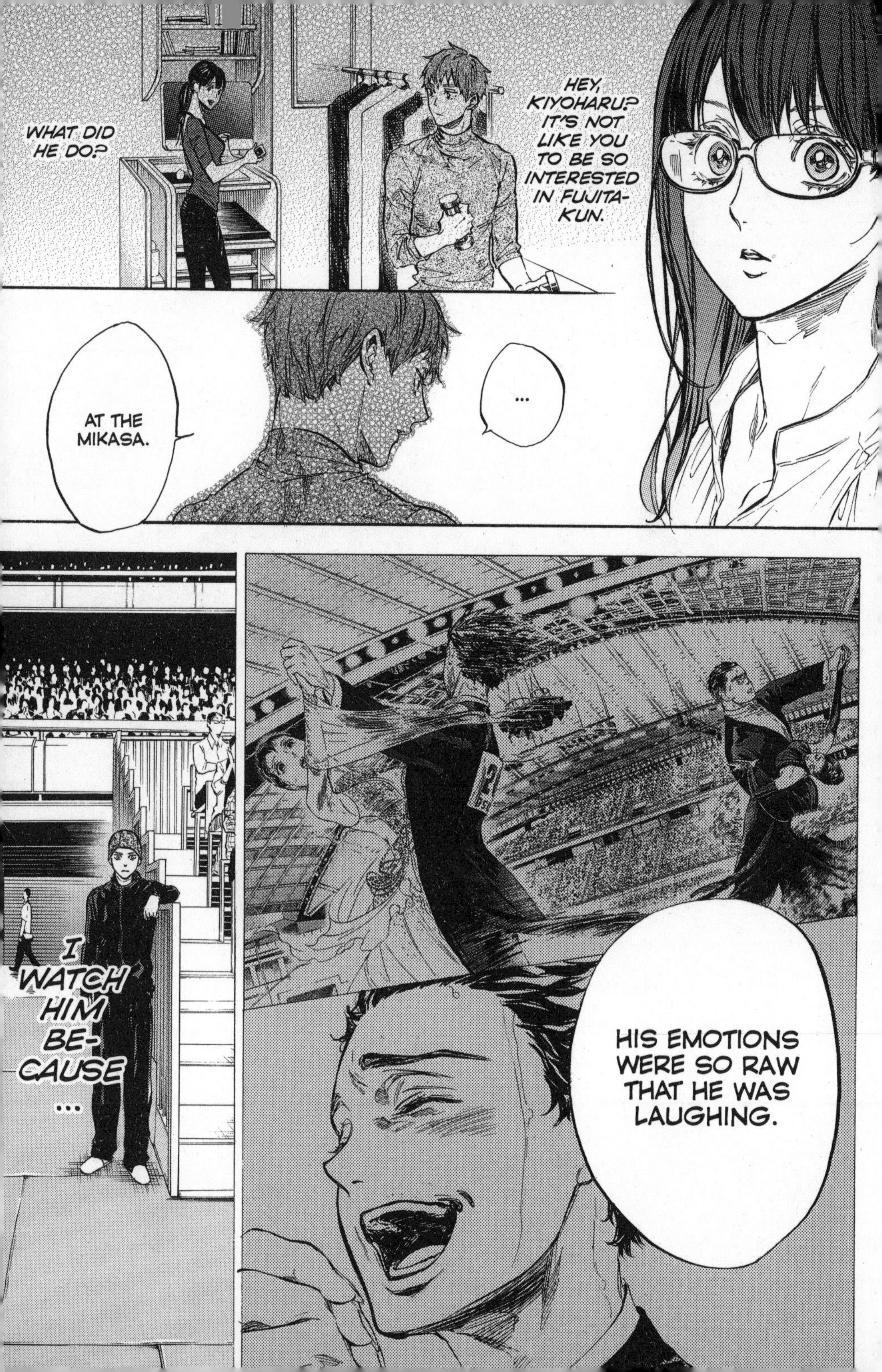
HEY, KIYOHARU? IT'S NOT LIKE YOU TO BE SO INTERESTED IN FUJITA-KUN.
WHAT DID HE DO?
...
AT THE MIKASA.
HIS EMOTIONS WERE SO RAW THAT HE WAS LAUGHING.
I WATCH HIM BE-CAUSE ...

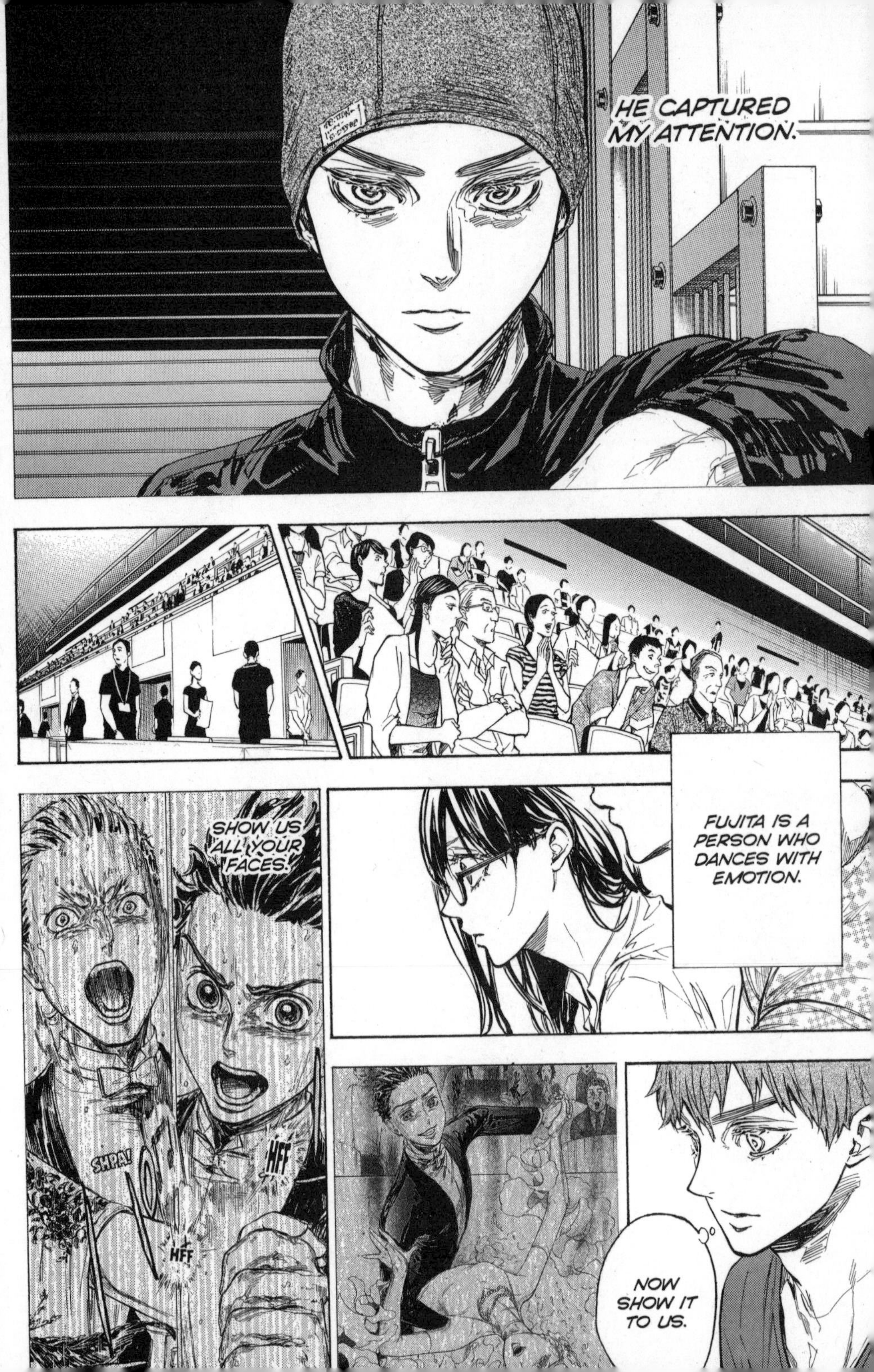
HE CAPTURED MY ATTENTION.
FUJITA IS A PERSON WHO DANCES WITH EMOTION.
NOW SHOW IT TO US.
SHOW US ALL YOUR FACES!
HFF
SHPA!
HFF

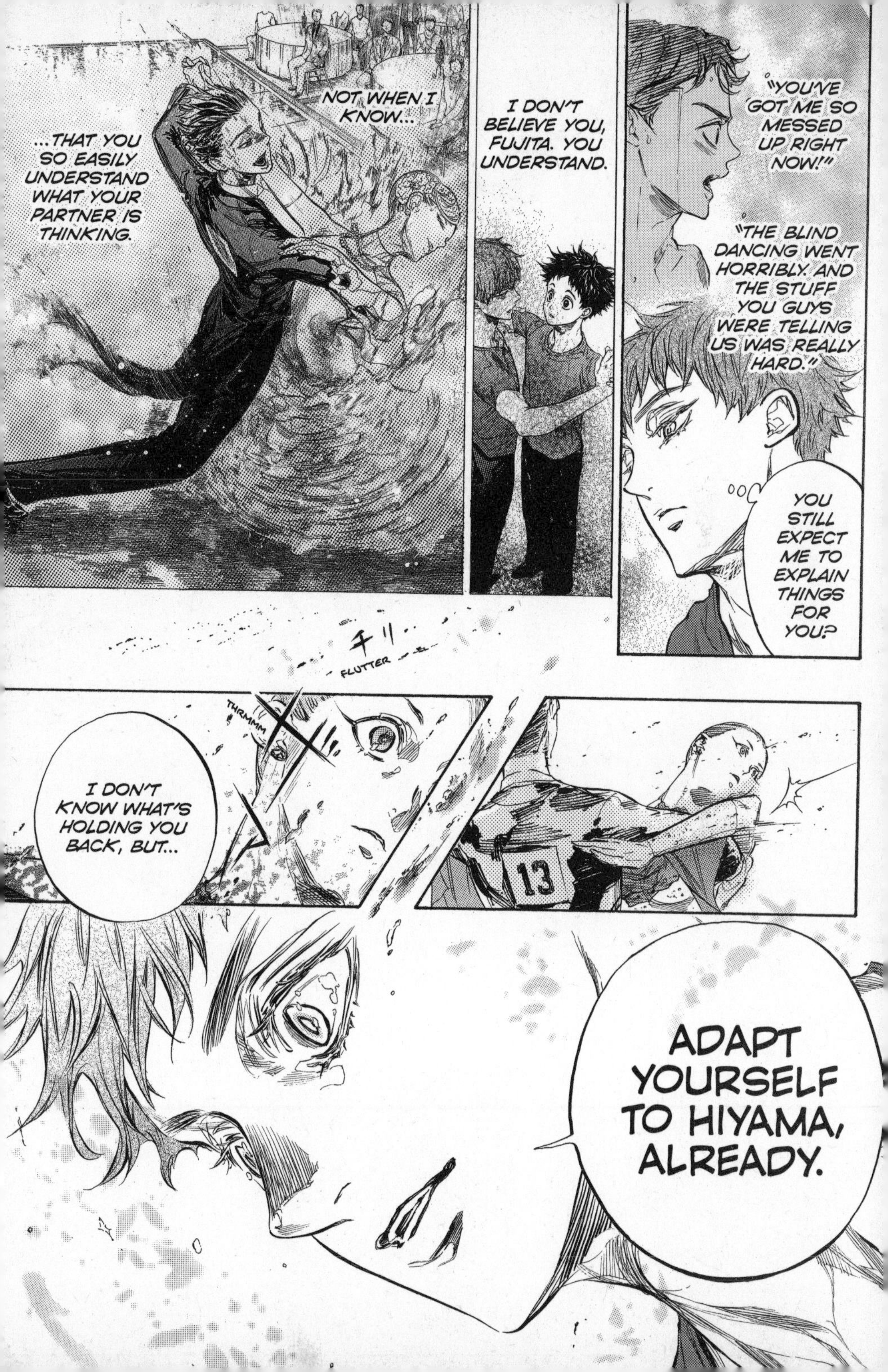
"YOU'VE GOT ME SO MESSED UP RIGHT NOW!"
"THE BLIND DANCING WENT HORRIBLY. AND THE STUFF YOU GUYS WERE TELLING US WAS REALLY HARD."
YOU STILL EXPECT ME TO EXPLAIN THINGS FOR YOU?
I DON'T BELIEVE YOU, FUJITA. YOU UNDERSTAND.
NOT WHEN I KNOW...
...THAT YOU SO EASILY UNDERSTAND WHAT YOUR PARTNER IS THINKING.
チリ
FLUTTER
13
THRMMM
I DON'T KNOW WHAT'S HOLDING YOU BACK, BUT...
ADAPT YOURSELF TO HIYAMA, ALREADY.

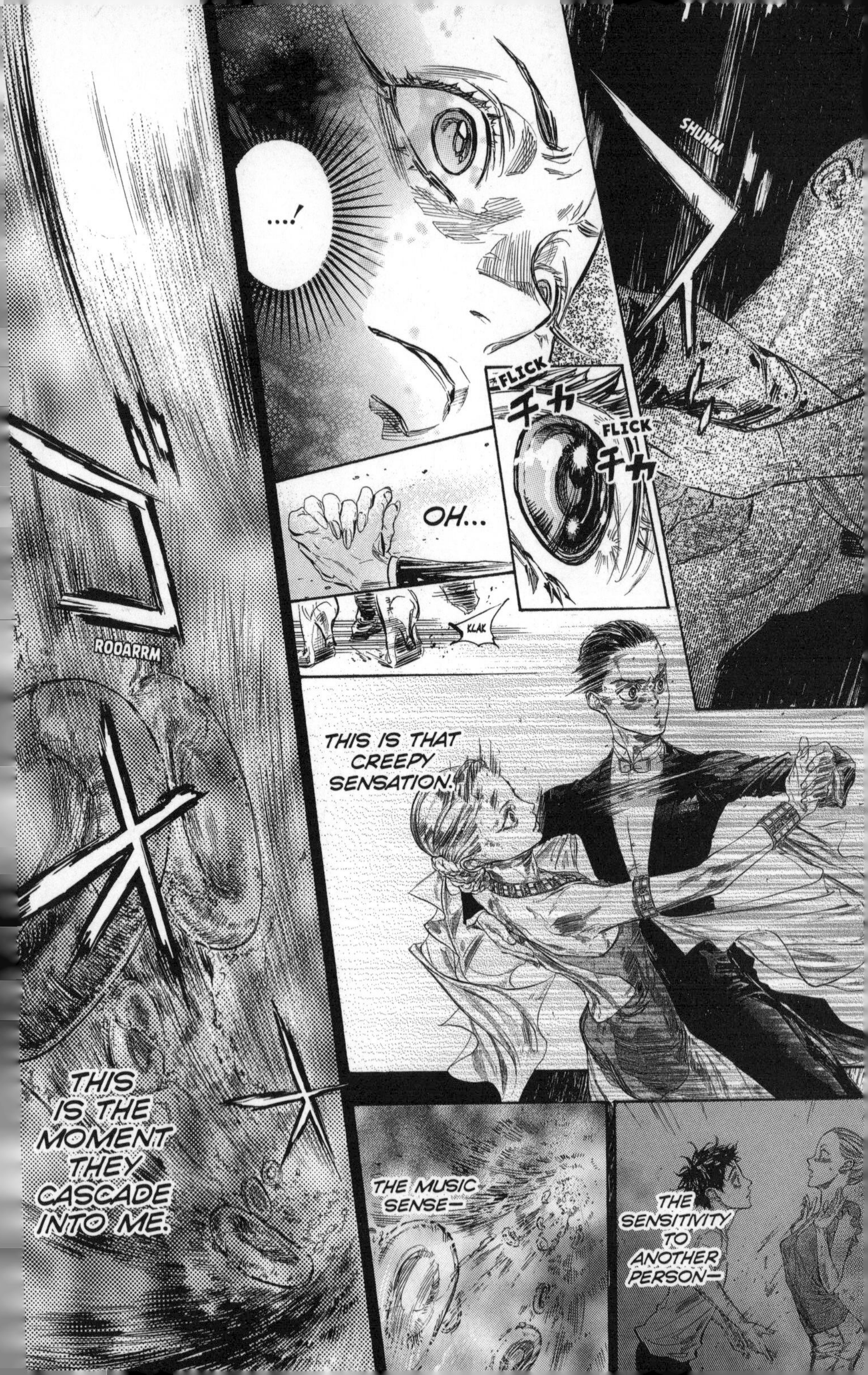

SHUMM
...!
FLICK
チカ
FLICK
チカ
OH...
KLAK
THIS IS THAT CREEPY SENSATION.
THE SENSITIVITY TO ANOTHER PERSON—
THE MUSIC SENSE—
ROOARRM
THIS IS THE MOMENT THEY CASCADE INTO ME.

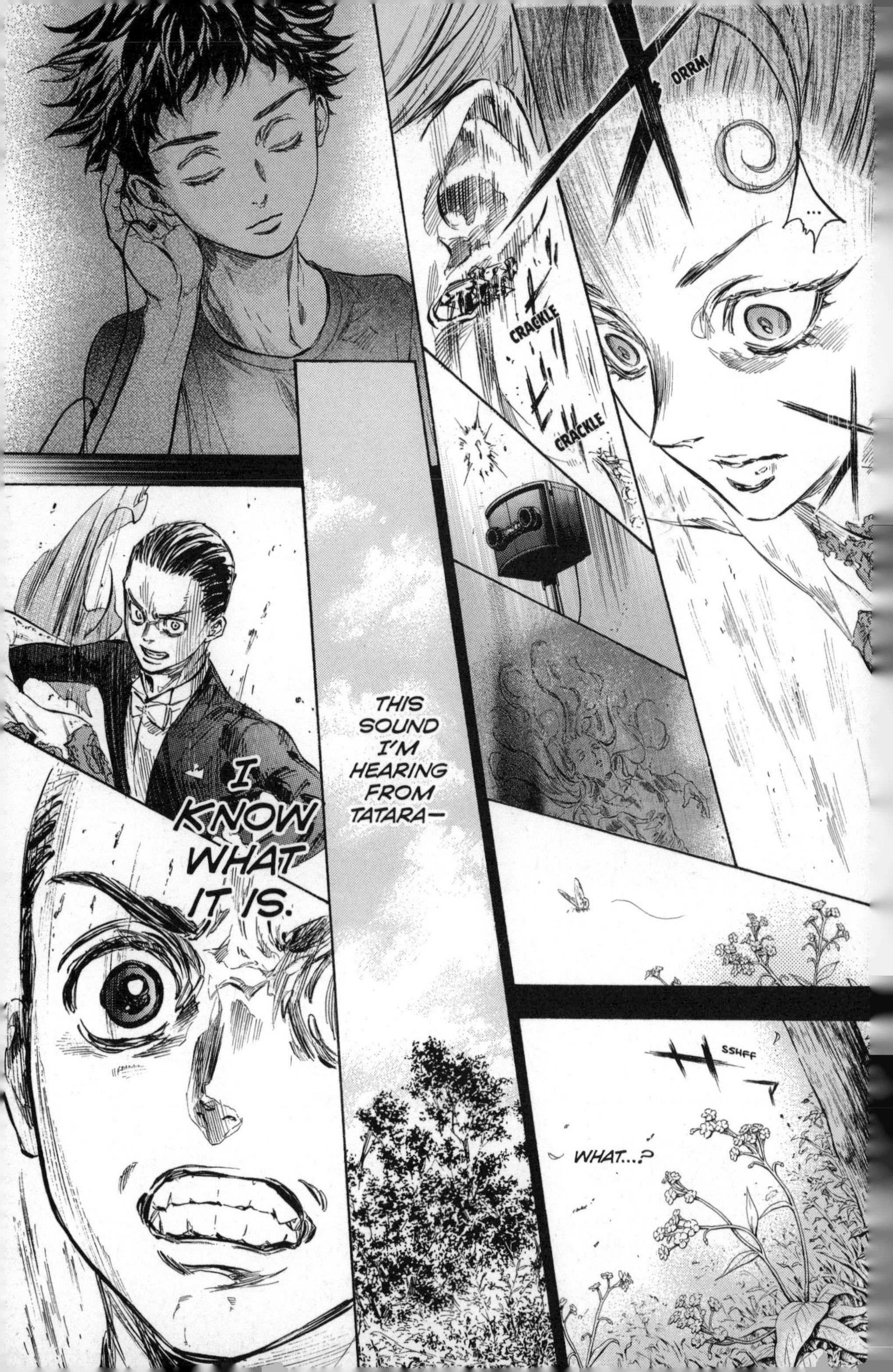
ORRM
...
CRACKLE
CRACKLE
SSHFF
WHAT...?
THIS SOUND I'M HEARING FROM TATARA—
I KNOW WHAT IT IS.

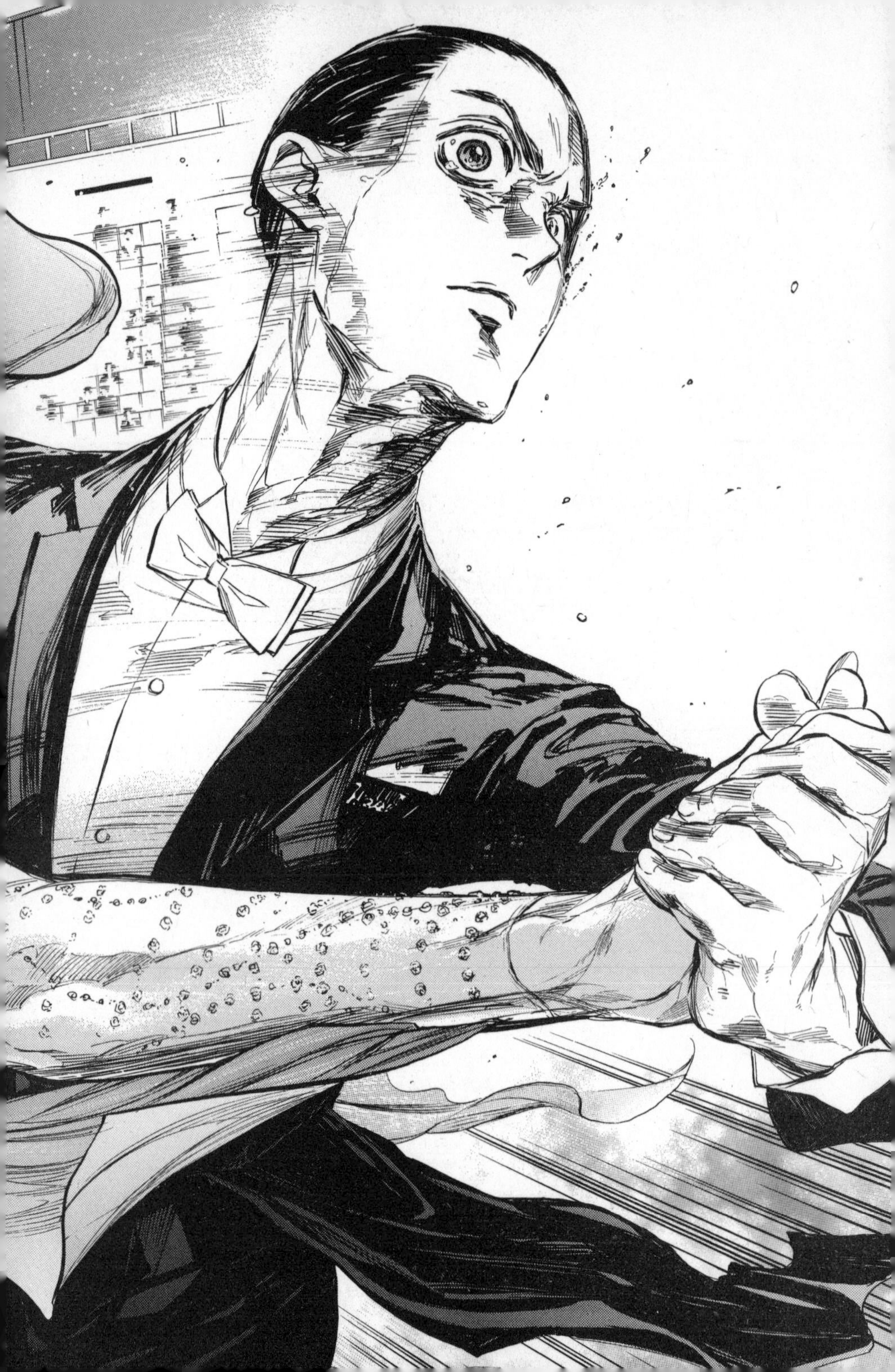

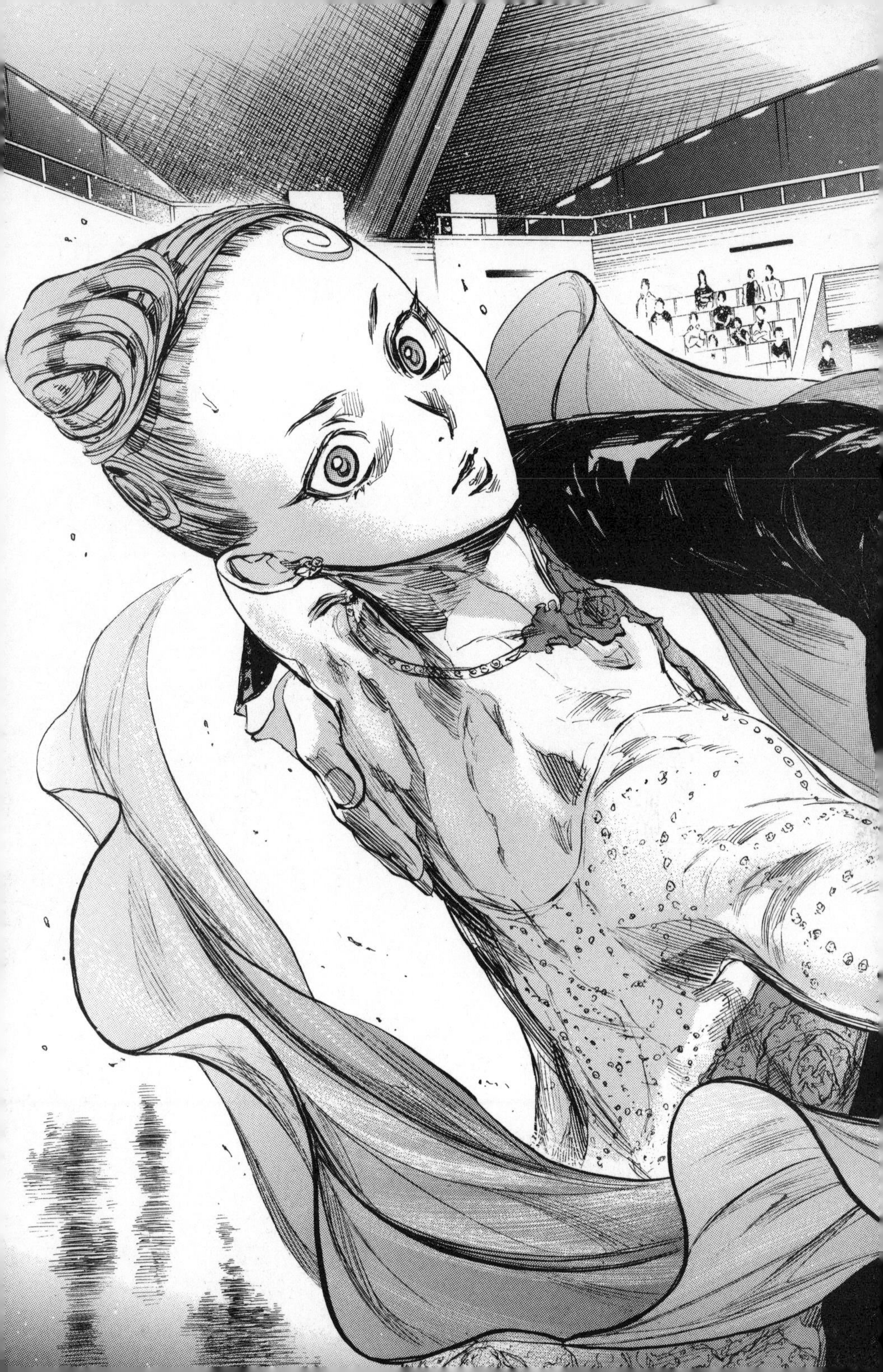

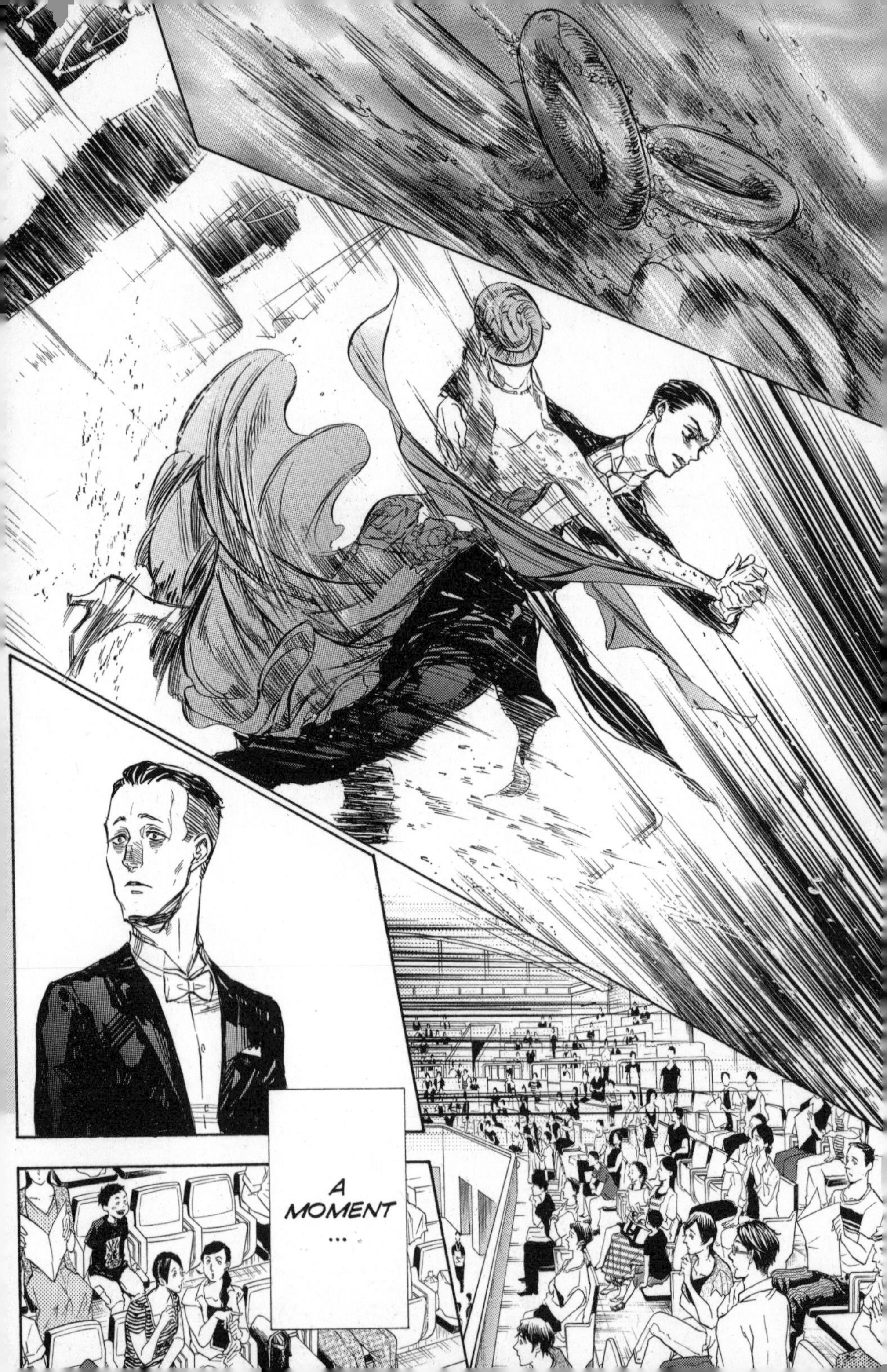
A MOMENT ...

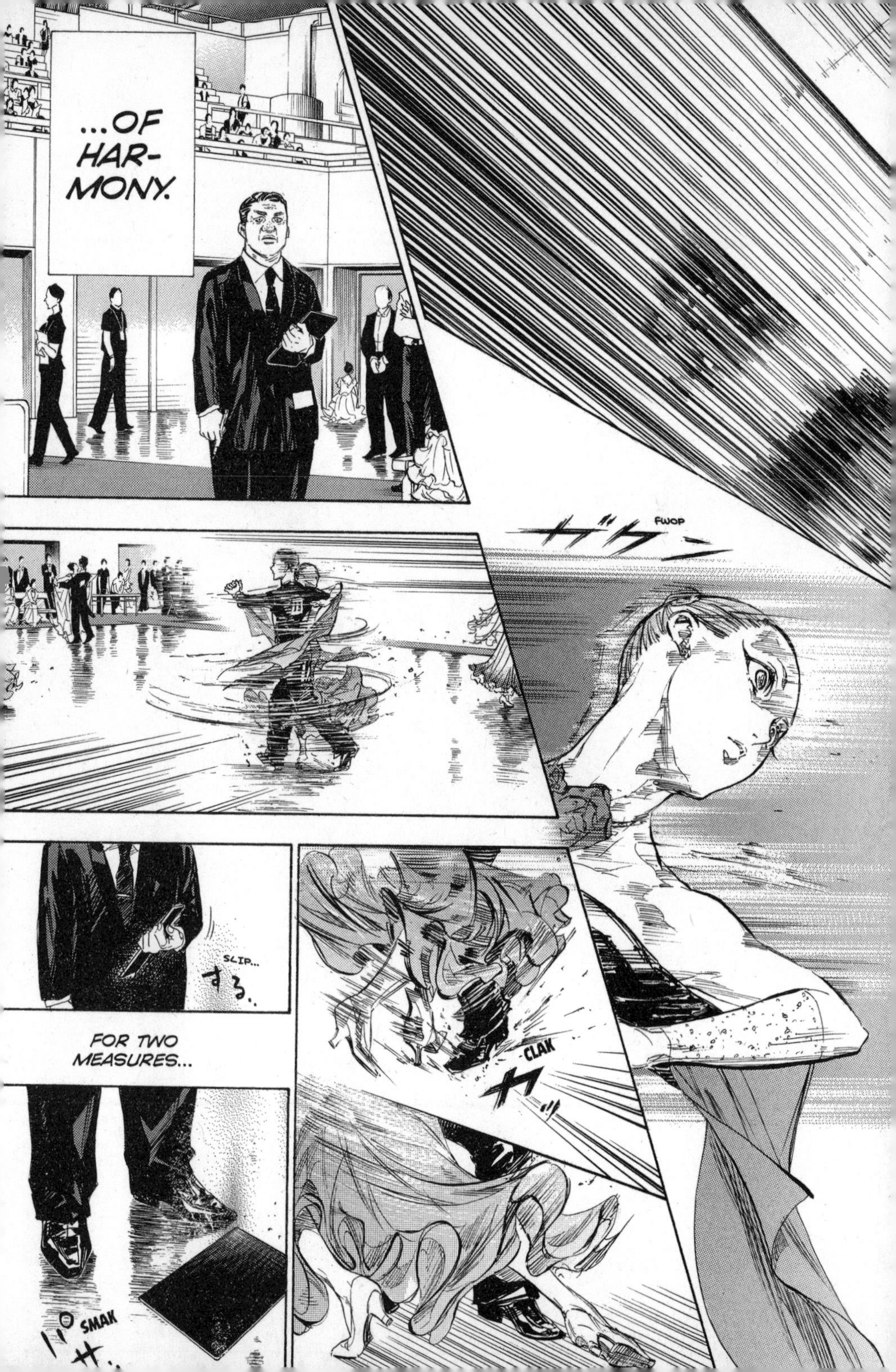

...OF HARMONY.
FWOP
CLAK
SLIP...
する..
FOR TWO MEASURES...
SMAK

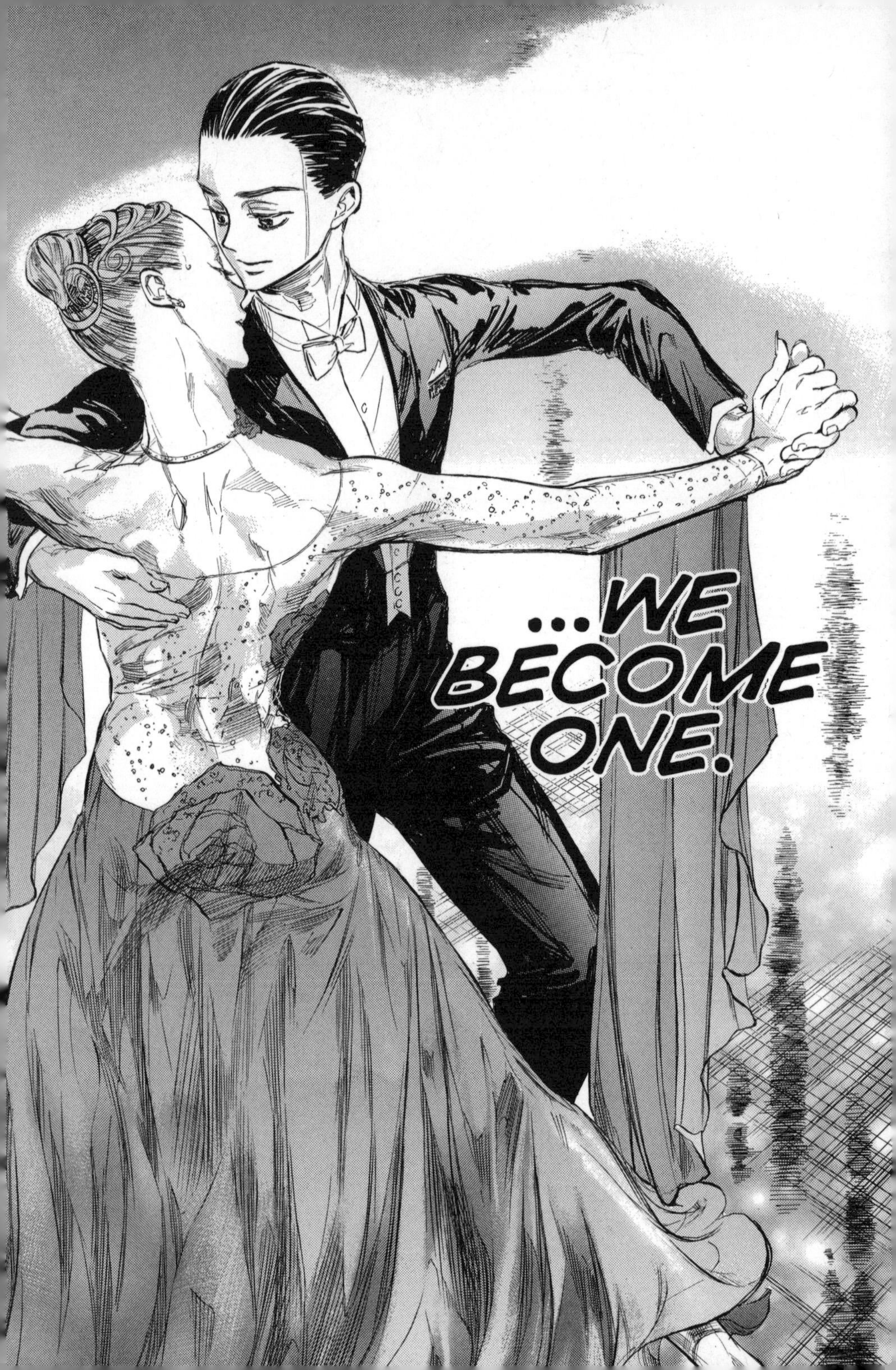
...WE BECOME ONE.

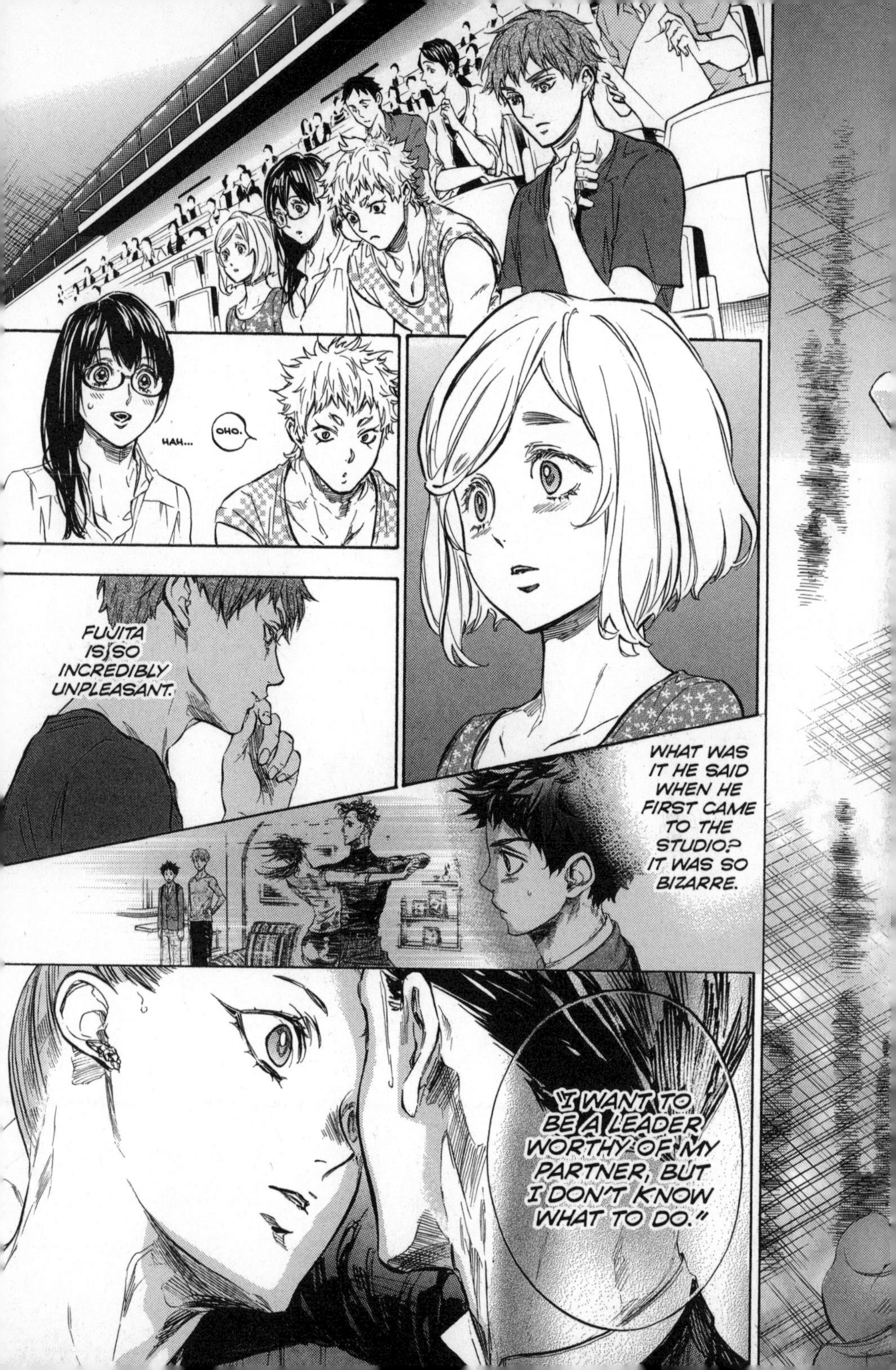
OHO.
HAH...
FUJITA IS SO INCREDIBLY UNPLEASANT.
WHAT WAS IT HE SAID WHEN HE FIRST CAME TO THE STUDIO? IT WAS SO BIZARRE.
"I WANT TO BE A LEADER WORTHY OF MY PARTNER, BUT I DON'T KNOW WHAT TO DO."

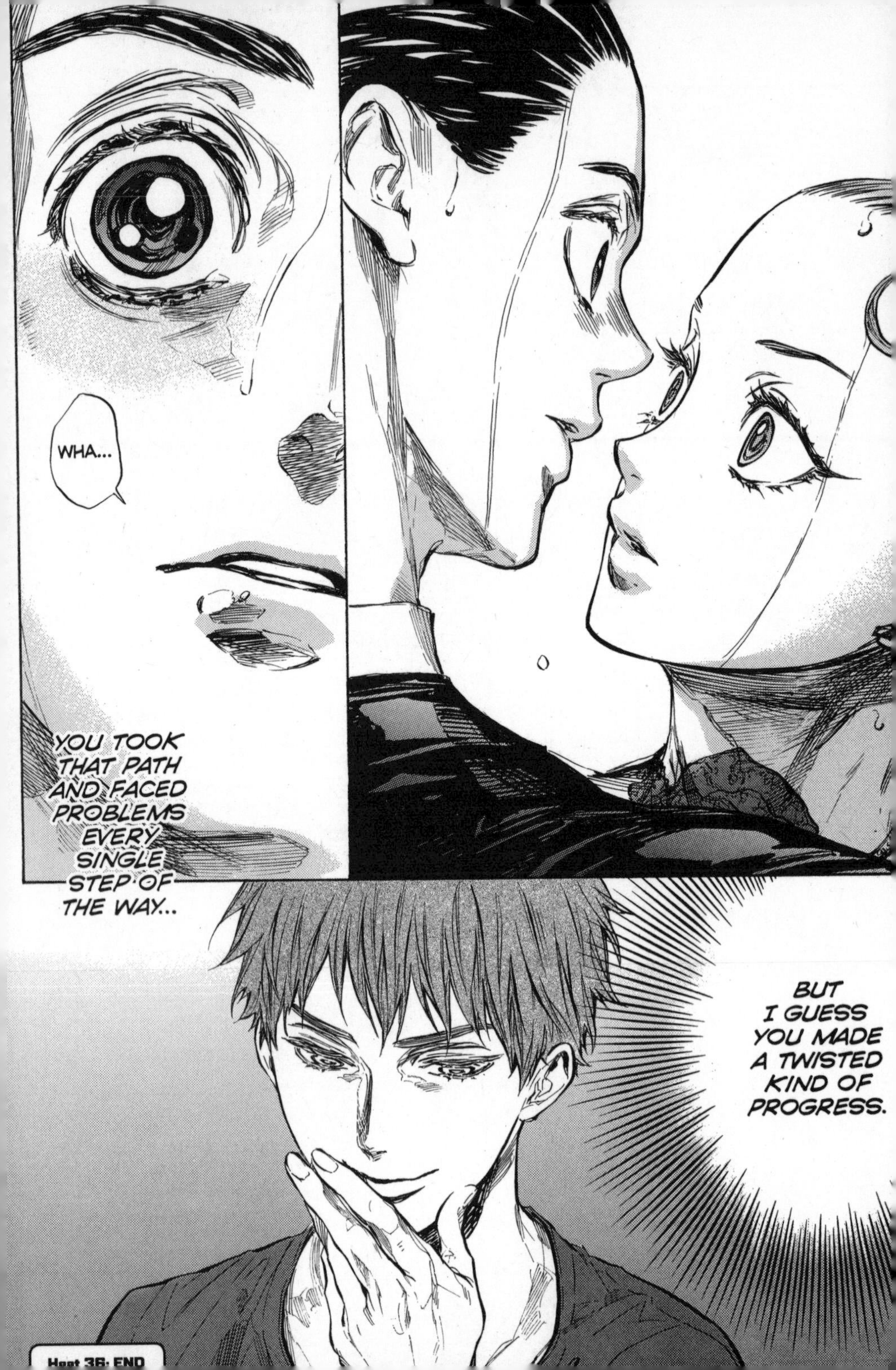
WHA...
YOU TOOK THAT PATH AND FACED PROBLEMS EVERY SINGLE STEP OF THE WAY...
BUT I GUESS YOU MADE A TWISTED KIND OF PROGRESS.
Heat 36: END

Special Thanks!

For help with tango variations

Mr. Minato Kojima & Ms. Megumi Morita

For help with research

Hasebe Dance Costumes

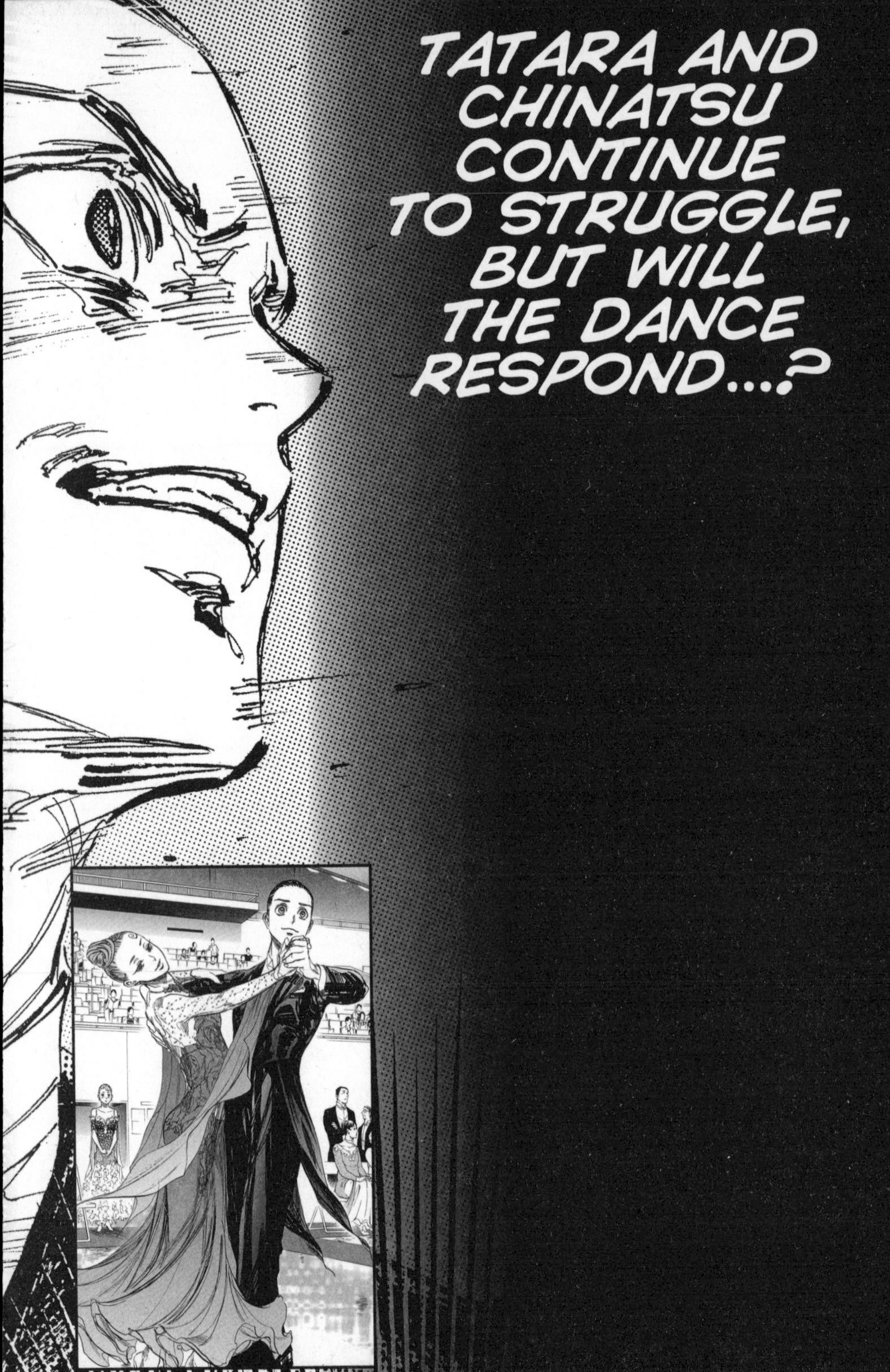
TATARA AND CHINATSU CONTINUE TO STRUGGLE, BUT WILL THE DANCE RESPOND...?

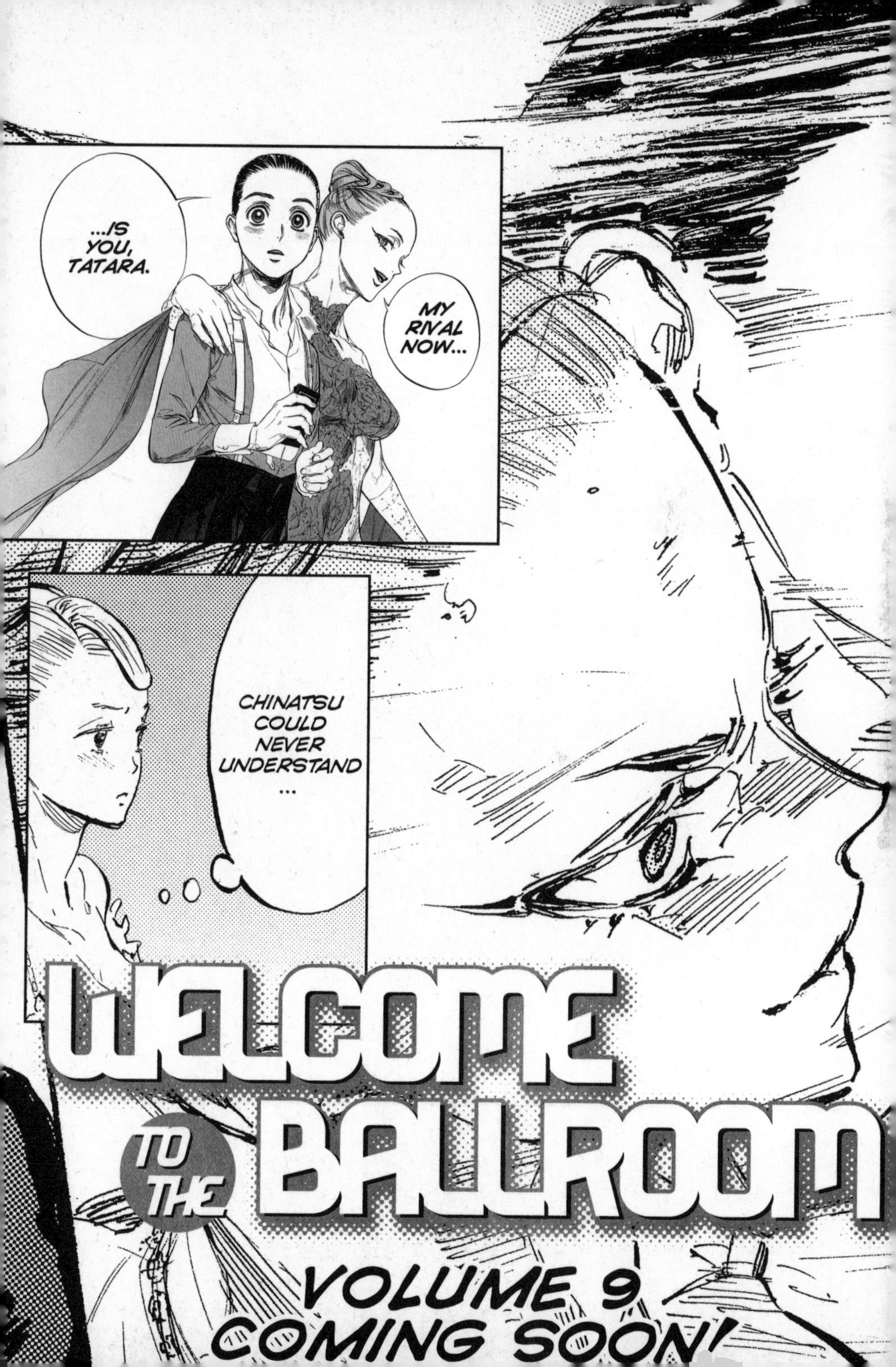
MY RIVAL NOW...
...IS YOU, TATARA.
CHINATSU COULD NEVER UNDERSTAND ...
WELCOME TO THE BALLROOM
VOLUME 9 COMING SOON!

"I'm pleasantly surprised to find modern shojo using cross-dressing as a dramatic device to deliver social commentary... Recommended."

-Otaku USA Magazine

The prince in his dark days

By Hico Yamanaka

A drunkard for a father, a household of poverty... For 17-year-old Atsuko, misfortune is all she knows and believes in. Until one day, a chance encounter with Itaru—the wealthy heir of a huge corporation—changes everything. The two look identical, uncannily so. When Itaru curiously goes missing, Atsuko is roped into being his stand-in. There, in his shoes, Atsuko must parade like a prince in a palace. She encounters many new experiences, but at what cost…?

Based on the critically acclaimed classic horror manga

The first new *Parasyte* manga in over 20 years!

NEO
Parasyte f

BY ASUMIKO NAKAMURA, EMA TOYAMA, MIKI RINNO, LALAKO KOJIMA, KAORI YUKI, BANKO KUZE, YUUKI OBATA, KASHIO, YUI KUROE, ASIA WATANABE, MIKIMAKI, HIKARU SURUGA, HAJIME SHINJO, RENJURO KINDAICHI, AND YURI NARUSHIMA

A collection of chilling new *Parasyte* stories from Japan's top shojo artists!

Parasites: shape-shifting aliens whose only purpose is to assimilate with and consume the human race... but do these monsters have a different side? A parasite becomes a prince to save his romance-obsessed female host from a dangerous stalker. Another hosts a cooking show, in which the real monsters are revealed. These and 13 more stories, from some of the greatest shojo manga artists alive today, together make up a chilling, funny, and entertaining tribute to one of manga's horror classics!

**KC
KODANSHA
COMICS**

KC
KODANSHA
COMICS

New action series from Hiroyuki Takei, creator of the classic shonen franchise Shaman King!

In medieval Japan, a bell hanging on the collar is a sign that a cat has a master. Norachiyo's bell hangs from his katana sheath, but he is nonetheless a stray — a ronin. This one-eyed cat samurai travels across a dishonest world, cutting through pretense and deception with his blade.

Nekogahara

STRAY CAT SAMURAI

By

Hiroyuki Takei

Japan's most powerful spirit medium delves into the ghost world's greatest mysteries!

Story by Kyo Shirodaira, famed author of mystery fiction and creator of *Spiral*, *Blast of Tempest*, and *The Record of a Fallen Vampire*.

Both touched by spirits called yôkai, Kotoko and Kurô have gained unique superhuman powers. But to gain her powers Kotoko has given up an eye and a leg, and Kurô's personal life is in shambles. So when Kotoko suggests they team up to deal with renegades from the spirit world, Kurô doesn't have many other choices, but Kotoko might just have a few ulterior motives...

IN/SPECTRE

STORY BY KYO SHIRODAIRA
ART BY CHASHIBA KATASE

HAPPINESS

——ハピネス——

By Shuzo Oshimi

From the creator of *The Flowers of Evil*

Nothing interesting is happening in Makoto Ozaki's first year of high school. His life is a series of quiet humiliations: low-grade bullies, unreliable friends, and the constant frustration of his adolescent lust. But one night, a pale, thin girl knocks him to the ground in an alley and offers him a choice. Now everything is different. Daylight is searingly bright. Food tastes awful. And worse than anything is the terrible, consuming thirst...

Praise for Shuzo Oshimi's *The Flowers of Evil*

"A shockingly readable story that vividly—one might even say queasily—evokes the fear and confusion of discovering one's own sexuality. Recommended." —The Manga Critic

"A page-turning tale of sordid middle school blackmail." —Otaku USA Magazine

"A stunning new horror manga." —Third Eye Comics

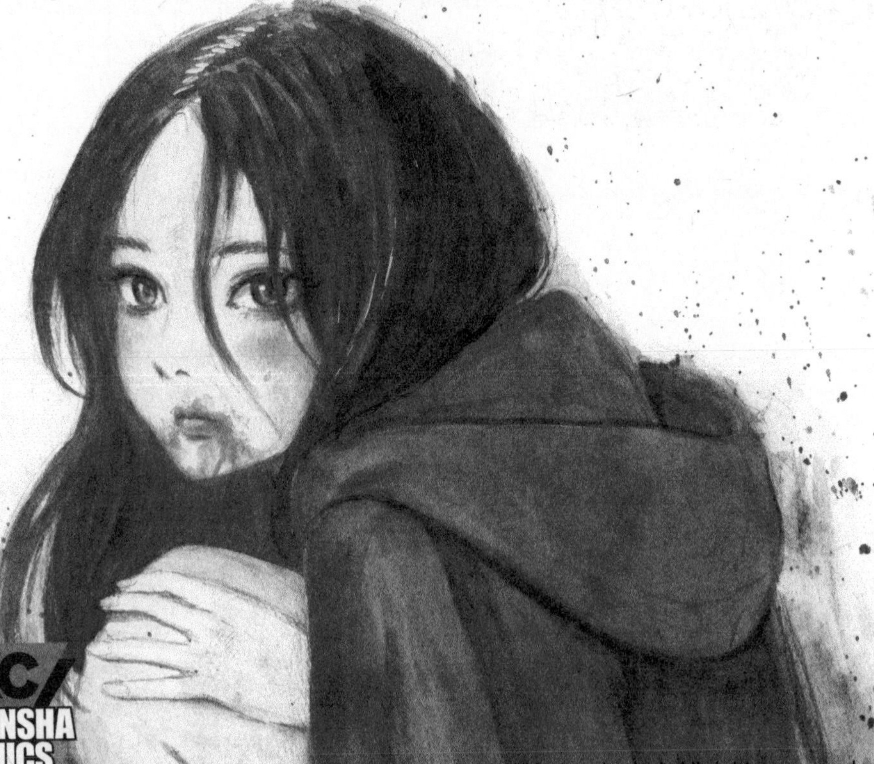

KC KODANSHA COMICS

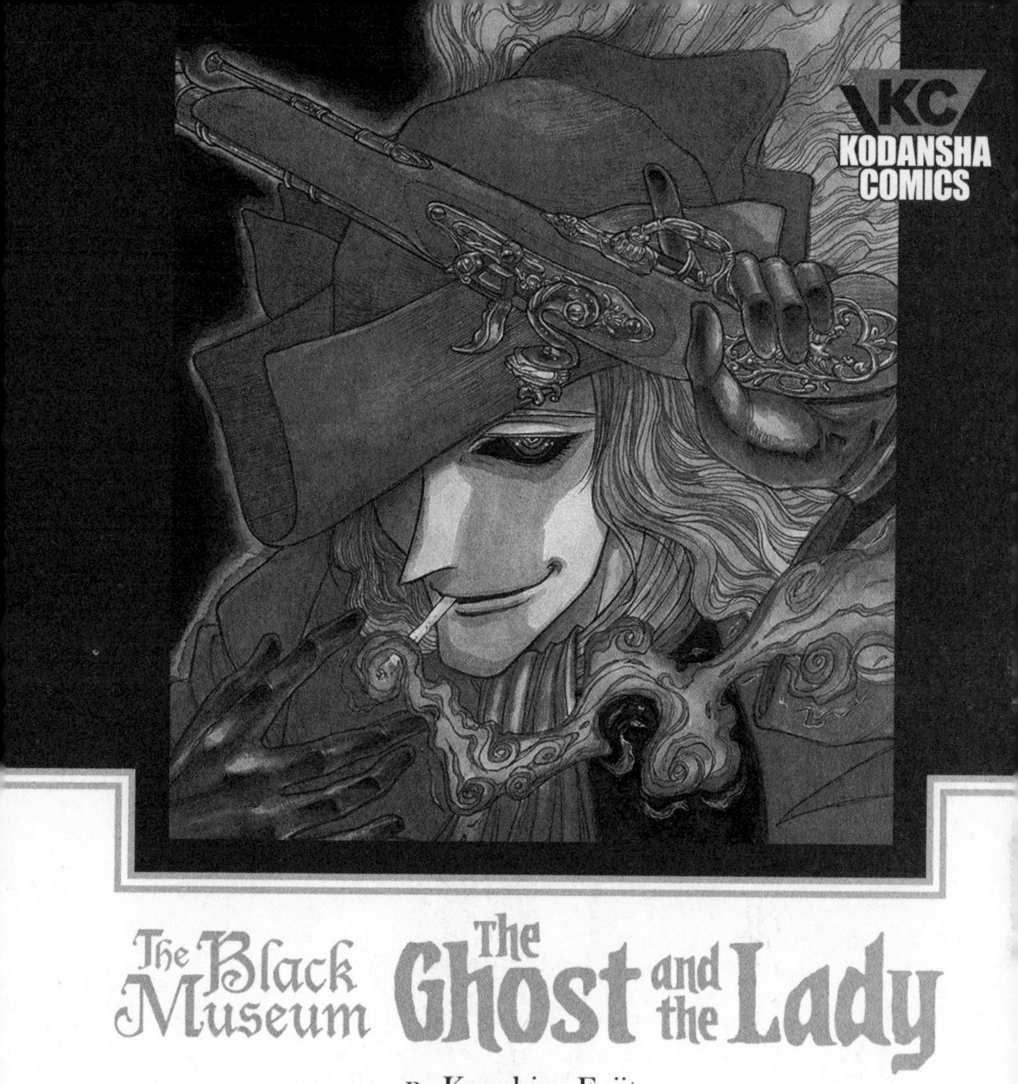
KC
KODANSHA
COMICS

The Black Museum: The Ghost and the Lady

By Kazuhiro Fujita

Deep in Scotland Yard in London sits an evidence room dedicated to the greatest mysteries of British history. In this "Black Museum" sits a misshapen hunk of lead—two bullets fused together—the key to a wartime encounter between Florence Nightingale, the mother of modern nursing, and a supernatural Man in Grey. This story is unknown to most scholars of history, but a special guest of the museum will tell the tale of The Ghost and the Lady...

Praise for Kazuhiro Fujita's *Ushio and Tora*

"A charming revival that combines a classic look with modern depth and pacing... **Essential viewing both for curmudgeons and new fans alike.**" — Anime News Network

"**GREAT!** The first episode of Ushio and Tora captures the essence of '90s anime." — IGN

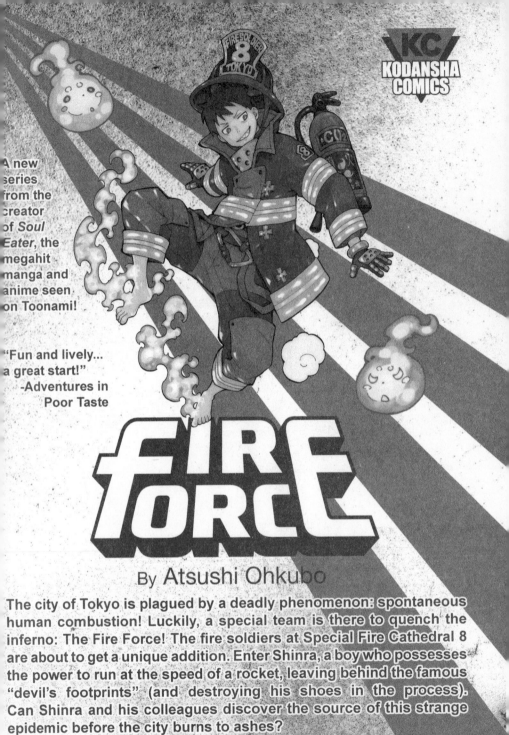

A new series from the creator of *Soul Eater*, the megahit manga and anime seen on Toonami!

"Fun and lively... a great start!"
-Adventures in Poor Taste

FIRE FORCE

By Atsushi Ohkubo

The city of Tokyo is plagued by a deadly phenomenon: spontaneous human combustion! Luckily, a special team is there to quench the inferno: The Fire Force! The fire soldiers at Special Fire Cathedral 8 are about to get a unique addition. Enter Shinra, a boy who possesses the power to run at the speed of a rocket, leaving behind the famous "devil's footprints" (and destroying his shoes in the process). Can Shinra and his colleagues discover the source of this strange epidemic before the city burns to ashes?

The award-winning manga about what happens inside you!

"Far more entertaining than it ought to be... what kid doesn't want to think that every time they sneeze a torpedo shoots out their nose?"
—Anime News Network

Strep throat! Hay fever! Influenza! The world is a dangerous place for a red blood cell just trying to get her deliveries finished. Fortunately, she's not alone...she's got a whole human body's worth of cells ready to help out! The mysterious white blood cells, the buff and brash killer T cells, even the cute little platelets— everyone's got to come together if they want to keep you healthy!

Cells at Work!

はたらく細胞

By Akane Shimizu

A Kodansha Comics Trade Paperback Original.

Published in the United States by Kodansha Comics, an imprint of Kodansha USA Publishing, LLC, New York.

Publication rights for this English edition arranged through Kodansha Ltd., Tokyo.

First published in Japan in 2015 by Kodansha Ltd., Tokyo, as *Booruruumu e Youkoso* volume 8.

ISBN 978-1-63236-521-7

Printed in the United States of America.

www.kodanshacomics.com

9 8 7 6 5 4 3 2 1

Translator: Karen McGillicuddy
Lettering: Brndn Blakeslee
Editing: Paul Starr
Kodansha Comics edition cover design by Phil Balsman